D1562782

STRIKING WITH THE BALLOT

STRIKING
WITH THE BALLOT

Ohio Labor and the Populist Party

MICHAEL PIERCE

Northern Illinois University Press

DeKalb

© 2010 by Northern Illinois University Press

Published by the Northern Illinois University Press, DeKalb, Illinois 60115

Manufactured in the United States using postconsumer-recycled, acid-free paper.

All Rights Reserved

Design by Shaun Allshouse

Library of Congress Cataloging-in-Publication Data

Pierce, Michael C. (Michael Cain)

Striking with the ballot: Ohio labor and the populist party / Michael Pierce.

    p.   cm.

  Includes bibliographical references and index

  ISBN 978-0-87580-418-7 (clothbound: alk. paper)

1. Labor movement—Ohio—History. 2. Labor unions—Ohio—History. 3. Populism—Ohio—History. 4. Progressivism (United States politics). I. Title.

HD8083.O3P54   2010

324.2732—dc22

2010001708

Contents

Illustrations and Tables

Acknowledgments

Growing up in Columbus, Ohio, I had no idea that the field abutting my family's backyard—the playing fields of St. Charles High School—had been the site of the 1894 Ohio Populist convention. There John McBride, who a short time later would be elected president of the American Federation of Labor, and his old friend Jacob Coxey forged the political alliance that figures so prominently in this book. As I have been finishing the book up, my thoughts have returned to that field and my family—for both their importance in this research and their significance to my life. My parents, Don and Pat Pierce, have helped me in so many ways that I cannot begin to thank them properly. My brother, Pete, my sister, Ann, and her family have provided support of all kinds, making it possible for me to finish.

This project began when I was in graduate school at Ohio State. I worked under the direction of Warren Van Tine, a man whose rare combination of intelligence and humanity should serve as a model to all scholars. Michael Les Benedict gave generously of his time and expertise, offering the right amount of criticism and encouragement. David Stebenne brought his broad knowledge of everything to the dissertation committee.

Others at Ohio State who helped this project along include Professors William Childs, K. Austin Kerr, Margaret Newell, and David Steigerwald and fellow graduate students Russ Coil, Phil Payne, and Barb Terzian. While I was in graduate school, fellowships from the Ohio Bicentennial Commission and the university's William Green Fund helped sustain me and my research. Special thanks for their support and friendship go to Sandy Jordan and the late C. J. Slanika of the university's now defunct Center for Labor Research.

At conferences a number of scholars—Leon Fink, Ken Fones-Wolf, Shelton Stromquist, Richard Schneirov—have been generous in offering suggestions and pushing me to expand my thinking. Portions of this book have already been published elsewhere. "The Populist President of the American Federation of Labor: The Career of John McBride, 1880–1895" appeared in *Labor History* 41 (Winter 2000): 5–24, and much of Chapter 2 was published in *Agricultural History* 74 (Winter 2000): 58–85. The editors of these journals—Craig Phelan and Claire Storm—have kindly given me permission to draw on these essays for this book. Writing "Organized Labor and the Law in Ohio" for Michael Les Benedict and John Winkler's *The History of Ohio Law* (Athens: Ohio University Press, 2004) transformed my thinking on the Ohio Constitutional Convention of 1912.

Much of the research for this book was done at the main branch of the Columbus Metropolitan Library, a place that *Library Journal* has rightfully called the top library in the nation. The entire staff, but especially those in the Ohio History and Biography section, has my everlasting appreciation. Lisa Leibfacher of the Ohio Historical Society also provided invaluable assistance as did the librarians and archivists at Bowling Green State University's Center for Archival Collections, the Cincinnati Historical Society, the Mahn Collection at Ohio University, the Western Reserve Historical Society, and the University of Cincinnati's Archives and Special Collections.

At my new home, the University of Arkansas, I am fortunate to be surrounded by friends and colleagues—Liang Cai, Linda Coon, Robert Finlay, Bob McMath, Charles Robinson, Beth Barton Schweiger, David Sloan, Kathryn Sloan, Rick Sonn, Tricia Starks, Dan Sutherland, Elliott West, Patrick Williams, Randall Woods—who have, often without even realizing it, made me a better historian. David Chappell would have been included in the above group had he not decamped from Fayetteville. Working with Patrick Williams on the *Arkansas Historical Quarterly* has improved my understanding of history in ways too numerous to mention. Larry Malley of the University of Arkansas Press has helped me navigate the publishing world. All of these folks have my gratitude.

At Northern Illinois University Press, Sara Hoerdeman has been a pleasure to work with. The suggestions and criticisms of the referees she found and the efforts of her colleagues—Alex Schwartz, Susan Bean, Julia Fauci, and Pippa Letsky—have made this a much better book.

This book would not have been possible without Tricia Starks. I dedicate it to her and our two sons, Ben and Sam.

STRIKING WITH THE BALLOT

Introduction

DISTURBED BY GOVERNMENTAL RESPONSES to the waves of labor and working-class unrest in the spring and summer of 1894, including the arrest of his old friend Jacob Coxey for demanding federal relief for the unemployed, the use of state militias during the nationwide coal strike, the mobilization of federal troops to defeat the Pullman strike, the increasing use of injunctions, and the imprisonment of Eugene Debs, John McBride, the president of the United Mine Workers of America (UMWA) and one of the founders of the American Federation of Labor (AFL), declared that conditions "will allow only one kind of strike on the part of labor, and that strike must be with the ballot." A longtime Democrat, McBride had always seen political action as an integral part of any solution to the labor problem, mixing his work on behalf of miners' unions with partisan activity. But now he urged trade unionists to leave the two major parties: "It is evident that labor cannot hope for relief at the hands of either the Republican or Democratic party." The Republicans, he insisted, were "responsible for the great power exercised by concentrated and corporate wealth" and the Democrats had recently been doing the bidding of "monopolies and the money power."[1]

The only solution, according to McBride, was for organized labor to form its own political party and merge it with the People's (or Populist) party. Thus, he called for Ohio's trade unionists to assemble in Columbus on August 15, 1894, to form a party with a platform designed to address the concerns of all of the state's producers. He also expected that the state's Populist party, which was already led by trade unionists and scheduled to meet in Columbus at the same time, would eagerly adopt labor's platform as its own, creating a labor–Populist alliance. Such an alliance, he insisted, would be the first step toward the "expiration of the evils which oppress labor."[2]

The response to McBride's call was tremendous. More than 110 Ohio trade union locals and central labor bodies sent over 250 delegates, including nearly every prominent labor leader in the state, to the convention in Columbus. Delegates came from every section of the state and represented nearly every craft. The largest numbers came from the UMWA, the Knights of Labor, and the American Railway Union, but urban labor federations and craft workers were also well represented. Toledo Central Labor Union president George Braunschweiger served as convention chairman, and the Columbus Trades and Labor Assembly, many of whose leaders had been active in the People's party since its inception in 1891, hosted the proceedings. The central labor bodies of Cleveland and Cincinnati, both of which had already forged alliances with the People's party, were also well represented. The *Cleveland Citizen*, published by that city's Central Labor Union (CLU), declared the convention to be "the largest, most enthusiastic, and harmonious gathering of the forces of labor" in the state's history.[3]

McBride and the new labor party had no problem convincing those assembled for the Populist convention to accept the labor platform. As E. J. Bracken, the Columbus Trades and Labor Assembly official who had been the People's party's gubernatorial nominee the year before, noted on the eve of the convention, most of those planning on attending the labor convention were already Populists and most of the delegates to the Populist convention were trade unionists. The People's party's resolutions committee, led by Jacob Coxey, readily accepted the labor platform with a few minor additions, and the two conventions assembled as one the next day in a grove east of Columbus to nominate a slate of candidates for Ohio's off-year election. Those assembled had no illusions about the party's chances in the fall. The *Cleveland Citizen* acknowledged that the results of the movement "may not be perceptible" in the coming election, but the movement would grow, and nothing "could prevent the ultimate triumph of this new alliance."[4]

Similar labor–Populist alliances were being forged in the summer of 1894 throughout the nation, but especially in the Industrial Midwest—that region bordered on the north by the Great Lakes and to the south by the Ohio River. The most important of these were in Illinois, where journalist Henry Demarest Lloyd and Chicago machinist Thomas Morgan led the labor forces, and Wisconsin, where Victor Berger and Robert Schilling transformed that state's People's party into a labor party. There was also tremendous labor support for the Populists in Indiana, Michigan, and Western Pennsylvania, especially among members of the UMWA and the American Railway Union.[5]

At the end of 1894, John McBride rode a wave of enthusiasm among trade unionists for the People's party and "independent political action" to the presidency of the American Federation of Labor, defeating longtime incumbent Samuel Gompers. Although the AFL represented only a small minority of the nation's workers, by the mid 1890s it had become the most prominent voice of the nation's working class. Upon taking office, McBride announced his intention to steer the federation along a different political course. Instead of following the example of his predecessor, Samuel Gompers, and avoiding partisan entanglements, he insisted that the federation should help create a "union of labor men" that would "place a presidential candidate in the field" in 1896. McBride's language echoed the words of the People's party's Omaha platform, which called the party a "union of labor forces," and his intent was unmistakable—he wanted the AFL to align itself with the People's party. According to the *Cleveland Citizen*, McBride would spend a good part of 1895 advocating "in favor of independent political action along the lines of Populism." That fall he told Pittsburgh-area trade unionists, "If I had my way there would be a labor party that would sweep all evils from the land."[6]

McBride never achieved his goal of aligning the AFL with the Populists, and the movement to transform the AFL into a partisan organization died with the collapse of the People's party following the fusion of 1896. But this study of the efforts of Ohio trade unionists to mobilize politically through the People's party challenges historians' understandings of the relationship between the labor movement and Populism, the political transformation of the AFL in the mid 1890s and its adoption of an anti-statist ideology, and the origins of the Progressive movement. The focus is on the labor movements in the state's three largest cities—Cleveland, Cincinnati, and Columbus—as well as the effort of McBride and the UMWA to build a statewide and national labor–Populist alliance. The three cities were chosen not only for their size and the availability of primary sources but because they represent three different types of urban development. Cincinnati emerged as an industrial giant at the beginning of the nineteenth century, attracting large immigrant communities from Ireland and Germany. Cleveland's period of rapid growth came much later, after the Civil War, and its large steel and chemical concerns attracted immigrants from all over

John McBride, president of the American Federation of Labor. From *Harper's Weekly*, January 5, 1895.

Europe. Columbus never industrialized to the degree of the other two cities; its economy remained rooted in government, banking, transportation, and merchandizing. Yet despite representing different types of industrial workers and working-class communities, the labor federations in each city responded to the crisis of the 1890s in the same way—joining with the Populists.[7]

The Ohio trade unionists who joined the Populist party were a diverse lot—veteran Greenbackers and Union Labor party activists, single taxers, Bellamyite nationalists, avowed Socialists, disgruntled Democrats, and even a few former Republicans. But they were united by a broad set of political ideals—labor republicanism—and its economic cousin—producerism. At the core of labor republicanism was the idea that citizens, especially workers, were responsible for the maintenance of the nation's republican system of government and needed to protect it from those who sought to pervert it. Ideally, the needs of the republic, the commonwealth, were more important than the interests of any single citizen or group. Since the main threat to republican government came from those seeking to use it for selfish ends (those who put their own interests before the needs of the commonwealth), labor republicans were especially vigilant about misuses of government power, insisting that large, swollen fortunes were both evidence of corruption and sources of future corruption. To purify republican government, labor-Populists argued that an even distribution of wealth was essential.[8] As John McBride, quoting Noah Webster, wrote in the AFL's monthly magazine, *American Federationist*, "An equal distribution of property is the foundation of the Republic."[9]

Producerism—rooted in the labor theory of value—posits that wealth is created only through labor and that labor is the only legitimate way to acquire wealth. Ohio's trade unionists heartily endorsed the People's party's 1892 Omaha platform insistence that "Wealth belongs to him who creates it, and every dollar taken from industry without an equivalent is robbery." For them, the nation was divided between two classes—those who toiled and produced (a group that could include factory owners and shopkeepers) and those parasites who lived off the wealth produced by others (stockholders, bankers, speculators, and many politicians). According to Ohio trade unionists, between the end of the Civil War and the 1890s, the power of the non-producers to extract wealth from those who had created it had grown, creating "a despotism that enthrals labor, prostitutes government, corrupts laws, defies justice and robs the people."[10]

The decisions of Ohio's trade unionists to cut their ties to the traditional parties and to join with the Populists did not come easy. Trade unionists needed allies at all levels on the federal system—attorney generals who did not call out federal troops during labor disputes, governors who controlled state militias, congressmen and state legislators who wrote labor laws, and mayors and municipal officials who appointed police officers, factory inspectors, and contracting officials. The People's party, with few elected officials in Ohio, offered no such friends, making it a poor ally for trade unionists. But local events and the governmental responses to the wave of labor unrest following the Panic of 1893 convinced Ohio labor leaders that both major parties had become so corrupted by corporate money they had to be abandoned and that the People's party offered the only salvation for the nation's producers and the survival of the republic.

Ohio trade unionists differed from traditional labor republicans and producerists not in their diagnoses of the problems confronting the nation's workers but in the solutions they offered. Unlike the Greenbackers who thought that a few changes to the nation's monetary system would bring prosperity, or single taxers who called for simplifying the ways that taxes were accessed, Ohio's trade union Populists called for a dramatic expansion of the role of government in protecting the rights of American workers, ensuring an equitable distribution of wealth, and curbing the abuses of the corporations. Ohio's labor-Populists did not want to go back to the small-scale economic life of the early nineteenth century; they appreciated the benefits of industrialization and mass production too much to do that. But they wanted to ensure that industrialization worked to their benefit rather than their detriment and thought that only an enlargement of government could do that.[11]

The labor-led Ohio People's party issued a platform demanding that governments at all levels of the federal system assume more active roles in protecting workers and all citizens from the depredations of the corporations. The state's public school system, that "potent agency for the advancement of civilization," should be enlarged, with every child required to attend and furnished with books. The delegates demanded that the state constitution be amended to allow municipal governments to take ownership of public utilities—street railways, gas and water companies, and electric power plants. Not only were these utilities sources of municipal corruption, they also took advantage of their monopoly positions to charge consumers high rates and to oppress workers. The state government should also require an eight-hour day for all workers, abolish child labor, inspect the sanitary and safety conditions in workshops and mines, end the contract system of public work, and make employers liable for the injuries workers suffered while on the job.

Those monopolies that posed the gravest threat to the welfare of the nation should be taken over by the federal government: "We demand the immediate nationalization of the telegraph and telephone, to be followed by government ownership of the railroads and mines." The platform also demanded the abolition of the system that allowed "private corporations" to control the nation's money supply. Instead, the delegates wanted greenbacks—"a national currency, safe, sound, and flexible, issued by the government . . . without the use of banking corporations." The federal government should also coin silver at a ratio of sixteen to one, end the "alien ownership of large tracts of land," redistribute that land to people who would put it to use, limit the immigration of "paupers and the criminal classes," and beef up laws prohibiting the importation of contract labor. The federal government should issue bonds to states and municipalities—on the same terms that it gave them to national banks—to be used to build roads and public works. Not only would these projects put people back to work; the bonds would function much like greenbacks, injecting needed currency into the economy.

Most controversially, the platform demanded that "the power of the government should be expanded as rapidly and as far as the good sense of an intelligent people and the teachings of experience should justify, along the lines of collective ownership by the people of all such means of production and distribution as the people may elect to operate."[12] The *Cleveland Citizen* insisted that this demand contained the "kernel" of what the trade unionists were trying to accomplish, explaining that the people should have the power to take over abusive corporations to ensure that wealth did not accumulate in the hands of a few and that workers were not pauperized. The paper assured readers that the property of those who set a just price and offered a fair wage would not be threatened. Only parasites who exploited their monopoly position to "despoil" their workers and "fleece the public" had anything to fear.[13]

As the Ohio labor-Populist platform was demanding an expansion of government control over the state and the nation's economic life, it was also insisting that the political system needed to be purified. Increasing government authority would do little good if public officials continued to "cater to monopolistic greed and corporate wealth." Ohio labor leaders thought that simply breaking the bonds between workers and the major parties would go a long way toward cleansing the nation's political system. The *Cleveland Citizen* argued that loyalty to the Republicans and Democrats had distracted workers from the real political issues: "for thirty years the workers have blindly fought each other with ballots, allowing party prejudices to overcome sound reason. . . . [But they are now] discovering that a revolution has taken place which has impoverished millions and built up colossal fortunes for a few drones."[14] But Ohio's Populist platform also demanded structural reforms. Most important, the trade unionists demanded "the Initiative and Referendum system of legislation." Long a part of the trade union agenda, direct legislation held the promise of ending corruption in the general assembly. The initiative would allow citizens to bypass a corrupt legislature to enact laws to their liking, and the referendum would allow the people to overturn those measures not in their interest. Additionally, the labor platform called for the enfranchisement of women. Not only was the "right to vote inherent in citizenship regardless of sex" but the votes of women would help cleanse the body politic.

Historians have wrongly portrayed trade unionists, especially those associated with the AFL, as being indifferent to Populist attempts to unite the producers of wealth into a political alliance to challenge the emergence of a capitalist system dominated by large corporations. These studies usually note that the People's party did best in regions such as the cotton South and the grain-producing Plains, which were heavily populated by farmers, and that the Populists did relatively poorly in the Industrial Midwest and the Northeast, areas with large urban centers and greater numbers of industrial and unionized workers. The blame for much of this disparity was laid on the labor movement. John Hicks, the most important early scholar of the People's party and the Alliance movement from which it sprang, declared, "The American Federation of Labor, whose cooperation would also have been gladly received, refused to have anything to do with the Alliances." Historians have been following his lead ever since, usually citing Samuel Gompers as though he was the only voice of the labor movement. Gompers publicly derided the notion that the farmer-led party was "one in which the wage-workers will find their haven," explaining, "Composed, as the People's Party is, mainly of *employing* farmers without any regard to the interests of the *employed* farmers of the country districts or the mechanics and laborers of the industrial centres, there must be a divergence of purposes, methods, and interests."[15]

Some historians find the AFL's apparent reluctance to work with the People's party understandable. Lawrence Goodwyn, whose interpretation of Populism centers on the sub-treasury plan and agricultural cooperatives, basically agrees with Gompers, arguing that the People's party's Omaha platform included little of interest to urban workers. But other historians fault the trade unionists and the AFL for ignoring the Populists' supposed pleas. For instance, Norman Pollack goes so far as to insist that the AFL's indifference to the People's party "guaranteed the ultimate downfall of Populism." But both Goodwyn and Pollack essentially agree with Hicks—in their view there was very little trade union support for the People's party.[16]

But when scholars compare the voting behavior of farmers on the Plains or in the South to that of urban workers in the Industrial Midwest, they are comparing apples to oranges. Farmers on the Great Plains or in the South voted in one-party systems, with Republicans dominating in the grain-producing areas and Democrats in the land of cotton. Industrial workers such as those in Ohio tended to vote in states with vigorous two-party systems. As Jeffrey Ostler's study of the People's party and farmers in Nebraska, Kansas, and Iowa makes clear, state political environments were crucial in determining the success of the Populist movement. In Iowa, a state marked by two-party competition, the Populist movement never gained much traction even though the farmers there faced many of the same economic hardships as their counterparts in nearby Kansas and Nebraska. Iowa Democrats appropriated several of the Populist demands, and many of the state's voters who were sympathetic to the aims of the People's party were reluctant to cast their ballots for a party that had little chance of winning, preferring instead to vote for the lesser of two evils. In two-party systems, election returns might not be the best gauge of the popularity or impact of a third-party movement.[17]

Those wanting to understand the relative contributions of farmers and industrial workers to the People's party should compare the two groups within the same political environment. When this is done, a different picture emerges. In Ohio, a state with large industrial centers and the nation's second-largest number of farms, farmers and their organizations would have little to do with the People's party. Instead, the UMWA and the urban labor federations of Cleveland, Cincinnati, and Columbus sustained Ohio's Populist movement, providing leadership, newspapers, organizers, and stability. Ohio was not alone in this. Throughout the Industrial Midwest, the region with the nation's greatest number of farms, agriculturalists remained committed to the two major parties, while trade unionists led the People's party.[18]

This study argues that, rather than welcoming trade unionists into the party, People's party leaders—both those such as James Weaver and Herman Taubeneck, who wanted the party to concentrate its platform on the silver issue, and middle-of-the-roaders like Tom Watson—took steps after the elections of 1894 to discourage midwestern trade unionists and their allies like Coxey and Lloyd from continuing to support the People's party. The party's agrarian leaders feared the trade unionists would taint the party with radicalism and that their demands—especially the qualified endorsement of the collective ownership of the means of production—would move the party further from mainstream American voters. In their efforts to alienate trade unionists, the leaders of both factions abandoned the Omaha platform and its call to unite all of the producers of wealth—with Weaver and Taubeneck justifying an emphasis on the free coinage of silver on the grounds that it would anger trade unionists and Watson calling for the party to embrace the Southern Alliance's Ocala platform.

Much like those who have studied the People's party, historians of the nation's labor movement have until recently largely ignored the efforts of Populists within the AFL and McBride's 1894 defeat of Gompers. In Philip Taft's classic *The American Federation of Labor in the Time of Gompers*, the People's party rates only a single mention, one that concerns the Knights of Labor's attitude toward the third party. One of the problems these historians have faced is that within the labor and Populist movements those advocating an AFL–People's party alliance were called "Socialists." As the *Chicago Tribune* noted in an account of the "Populist craze" within the AFL, "For want of a better name the new faction was called the 'Socialists,' while the men belonging to the conservative element, wishing their organizations to have nothing to do with politics, called themselves 'strict trade unionists.'"[19] Historians have been confused as to who these "Socialists" were, assuming that Gompers's railings against the "Socialists" were directed at those belonging to the Daniel DeLeon–led Socialist Labor party (SLP) rather than labor-Populists. Since McBride challenged Gompers but was not a member of the SLP, historians have not known how to interpret his election and the movement he led. For example, the editors of *The Samuel Gompers Papers* note that "John McBride described himself as a socialist and speculated that the labor movement might field a presidential candidate. . . . The SLP, however, dismissed McBride as a 'pure and simpler.'"[20] It never occurs to these historians that a significant number of trade unionists considered Populism to have been a viable alternative to both the pure and simple unionism of Gompers and the dogmatic socialism of DeLeon—or that those united behind the Populist banner offered the most serious challenge to Gompers and his allies for control of the federation between 1886 and 1923.

The lack of attention to the efforts of Populists within the AFL is surprising considering that historians have long identified the 1890s as a critical period in the transformation of the AFL. From the federation's inception in 1886 until the mid 1890s, trade unionists bitterly contested the organization's political orientation. Just as the *Chicago Tribune* noted, there were two main factions. One faction wanted the labor movement to confine the struggle between labor and capital to the shop floor and steer the federation away from political action, especially if it entailed partisan entanglements. These trade unionists, led by Gompers and called "pure and simple unionists" or "business unionists," insisted that the labor problem was essentially an economic conflict between workers and capital and to use anything other than economic weapons—strikes, boycotts, worker education, and organization, collective bargaining— missed the target. Besides, governments were too beholden to the capitalist class to give labor a fair shake, and workers were too divided when it came to party politics to form an effective political force. Not challenging the legitimacy of corporations or the concentration of wealth, Gompers and his allies wanted workers to have "more"—"more leisure, more rest, more opportunity . . . for going to parks, of having better homes, of reading more books, of creating more desires"—rather than seeking to transform the nation's economic system.[21]

Other trade unionists remained rooted in the republican and producerist traditions, insisting that workers had obligations to mobilize politically and looking to governments to help solve labor conflict. These trade unionists wanted to use governments to check the power of corporations, ensure an even distribution of wealth, and allow workers to profit from the wealth they had produced. Some of these politically oriented trade unionists believed in the collective ownership of the means of production, but others simply wanted an activist government willing to use its power on behalf of those who produced the nation's wealth. By the late 1890s, though, Gompers and his allies had triumphed, and he would steer the AFL through the Great War.[22]

Scholars have been trying to understand the triumph of Gompers and his brand of unionism in the late 1890s in part to understand the peculiar nature of the nation's labor movement. Just as American trade unionists embraced business unionism, trade unionists in the two other leading industrialized nations, Germany and the United Kingdom, were forming political parties to contest the emergence of corporate capitalism. Scholars (none of whom recognize the efforts of the labor-Populists in the mid 1890s) have attributed the triumph of Gompers to a change in philosophy among the nation's trade unionists, that is, the emergence of business unionism as the defining philosophy of the American labor movement reflected a shift in the thinking of a substantial number of the nation's workers. For instance, Victoria Hattam suggests that the triumph of business unionism represented a strategic response to the structure of the American state, most specifically the influence of the judiciary and the use of the conspiracy doctrine to undermine broader based unionism. William Forbath also emphasizes the role of the judiciary in the ultimate triumph of Gompers, but he attributes the change to the use of the labor injunction and decisions striking down laws passed at the behest of labor. According to Forbath, trade unionists concluded that governments were more likely to intervene in labor relations on the behalf of capital and thus developed an anti-statist orientation. Kim Voss attributes the triumph of business unionism to the growth of big business and powerful corporations that "were able to crush broad-based unionism before class-patterned ways of acting and thinking had established deep roots." Despite attributing the changes to different causes, these scholars agree that the business unionism of the American labor movement after the mid 1890s reflected the attitudes of the federation's membership.[23]

This study argues that the collapse of Populism played a critical role in the triumph of Gompers and pure and simple unionism within the AFL. After the fusion of 1896, the fragile coalition of trade unionists that had supported the People's party fragmented. Some followed McBride into the Bryan wing of the Democratic party. Others, most notably Clevelanders Max Hayes and Robert Bandlow, joined Daniel DeLeon's Socialist Labor party. But ill at ease with DeLeon and his dogmatism, they quickly left, helping other former Populists from the Industrial Midwest—Eugene Debs, Victor Berger, Thomas Morgan—form the Socialist party. Still other Ohio trade unionists remained faithful to the remnants of the People's party, and a few probably joined with the Republicans. The fusion of 1896 destroyed the political unity of those opposed to pure and simple unionism, making it difficult, if not impossible, for them to mount an effective challenge to Gompers. Nobody realized this better than John McBride. After Gompers's name was placed in nomination for the presidency at the AFL's December 1896 convention, McBride, who had run against Gompers every year since 1893, moved that the convention suspend its rules and elect Gompers by acclamation. McBride's motion passed, and never again would Gompers face a serious challenge to his control of the federation.[24]

The studies by Voss, Forbath, and Hattam seeking to understand the rise of business unionism are part of a historiography that sees the 1890s as something of a watershed. The demise of producerism and labor republicanism and the emergence of liberalism with its emphasis on the sanctity of private property foreclosed the possibility of a more democratic and egalitarian nation in the twentieth century. Building on Leon Fink's study of the Knights of Labor, Lawrence Goodwyn's treatment of the

Populist movement, and a number of works detailing corporate or elite attempts to co-opt Progressive era reforms, these studies assume that the nation's producers in general and the AFL in particular stood idly by while elites remade the nation in the first two decades of the twentieth century.[25]

In the last decade, though, historians of both Populism's legacy and the labor movement have questioned this historiography, advancing new interpretations of Progressivism that present the movement and its reforms as more egalitarian and democratic. In the ground-breaking *Roots of Reform: Farmers, Workers, and the American State*, Elizabeth Sanders argues that agrarian Democrats representing former Populist strongholds in the West and the South were the main architects of the Progressive reforms that made it through Congress. Robert Johnston maintains that a radical petit bourgeoisie, motivated by Populist ideas of democracy and a sense that unregulated capitalism threatened to tear communities apart, formed the heart of Portland's Progressive movement. Both Sanders and Johnston, though, leave little room for organized labor in the Progressive coalition, never realizing the scope of labor's involvement in the People's party.[26]

Labor historians have put the AFL and its state and local affiliates at the center of the Progressive movement. Julie Greene documents how the federation maintained an official policy of nonpartisanship while forging a de facto alliance with the Democratic party that paid off during the Wilson administration. Richard Schneirov argues that the defeat of labor Populism after the Pullman strike fostered the emergence by 1897 of a new urban reform liberalism in Chicago, which sought to moderate class conflict, recognized the need for intervention in the marketplace, and accepted the legitimacy of corporations. This liberalism, Schneirov argues, was not incompatible with many of the ideas of labor republicanism and found its fullest expression during the Progressive era with labor's participation in the National Civic Federation (NCF), the organization of business and labor leaders founded in 1900 that pushed through a number of moderate reform measures. Although Greene and Schneirov are among the few historians to recognize that those seeking a labor–Populist alliance were a significant force in the 1890s labor movement, neither scholar connects the efforts of the labor-Populists to the reforms of the Progressive era.[27]

This examination of labor Populism in Ohio joins these two strands of Progressive era historiography, linking labor's embrace of the People's party to the state's Progressive movement. In Ohio, the end of labor Populism played out differently than it did in Schneirov's Chicago. The state's labor movement—except for the UMWA—never embraced the type of liberalism associated with the NCF. In fact, after the turn of the twentieth century

NCF's organizer and first president, Mark Hanna, denounced Ohio's labor movement and its allies for promoting a "Populistic, Socialistic, and Anarchistic" platform.[28] Following the fragmentation of Ohio's labor movement in the wake of the fusion of 1896, the state's trade unionists came back together to push for the initiative, referendum, and recall. Direct legislation promised to provide the means through which labor could enact an agenda that was largely unchanged from the Populist era, fight the corruption that was threatening the health of the republic, and allow the labor movement to overcome its partisan divisions and to unite with farmers or other allies. The fight for direct legislation formed the core of the state's Progressive movement, pushing the Ohio State Federation of Labor (OSFL), led by Populists-turned-Socialists, into an alliance with the Bryan wing of the Democratic party, led by Cleveland mayor Tom L. Johnson, a former monopolist who had come to embrace the single tax and other anti-monopoly measures. The labor-Bryanite coalition pushed through a series of state constitutional amendments in 1912 that enacted much of the Populist agenda as it pertained to state issues. As one observer noted, these reforms gave Ohio "a taste of that which populism, in its wildest vagaries, never dared to dream."[29]

1 Organized Labor in Ohio Politics, 1877–1890

ON SUNDAY AFTERNOON, JULY 22, 1877, the great railroad strike, which had begun in Martinsburg, West Virginia, five days earlier, reached Columbus, Ohio. Some three or four hundred firemen and brakemen of the Pittsburgh, Cincinnati & St. Louis Railroad (better known as the Pan Handle Road) gathered at Goodale Park, insisting that recent wage cuts had made it impossible "to provide the necessaries of life for ourselves and our families." After hearing speakers tell them that united action was the only way to protect honest labor from the onslaught of capital, the men resolved not to allow freight trains to roll out of the city until the line, controlled by the massive Pennsylvania Railroad, restored wages to their January 1874 level. Later that evening, workers on several of the other rail lines with yards or shops in the city—the Cleveland, Columbus, Cincinnati & Indianapolis; the Scioto Valley; the Piqua Line—joined the strike. These actions and similar ones throughout the region shut down rail traffic moving into and out of this major rail hub. Like most of those around the nation who would participate in the strike, the Columbus railroaders were not members of one of the railroad brotherhoods or any other branch of organized labor. Their decision to strike was largely the spontaneous result of deteriorating working conditions and the example being set in Martinsburg and elsewhere.[1]

At the outset, leaders advised the Columbus strikers to be "sober and law abiding" and asked "all men who are in sympathy with us" to be the same.

Despite these requests, chaos and lawlessness reigned the next day. A crowd of three hundred formed in the early morning and began demanding that the city's large factories close. According to newspaper accounts, the crowd was composed largely of "tramps" and the city's chronically unemployed—men who had not been able to find steady work since the beginning of hard times in 1873. Moving from the Wassall Fire Clay Works, Patton's Pot Works, Adams' Planing Mill, and Franklin Machine Company to Peters' Dash Company, Columbus Buggy Company, and Columbus Rolling Mill, the crowd targeted only the largest of the city's industrial concerns, leaving smaller shops, merchants, banks, professional offices, and public institutions unmolested. The protestors threatened to burn any large factory that remained in operation, telling managers and owners to either "shut up or burn up." Fearing the wrath of the crowd, which was fueled by the summer heat and had grown to two thousand by midday, the factories complied, banking their furnaces, and sending their workers home without pay.[2]

Among those forced to stop working were the iron rollers, hookers, roughers, catchers, and puddlers at the Columbus Rolling Mill, men whom historian David Montgomery uses as archetypes of highly skilled trade unionists in Gilded Age America.[3] The ironworkers belonged to one of the few local unions that had not collapsed following the onset of hard times in 1873. Led by William Martin and David A. Plant, whom the longtime ironworkers' leader John Jarrett considered the two men most responsible for the creation of the Amalgamated Association of Iron and Steel Workers, the ironworkers at the Columbus Rolling Mill had long been fearful of what they called the "Aggression of Combined Capital."[4] But, angered that they had been forced to lose a day's wages and at seeing the welfare of the community threatened, the ironworkers held a special meeting to voice their grievances against both the striking railroaders and the unruly crowd. Using a vocabulary drawn heavily from the producerist and republican traditions, the ironworkers acknowledged the validity of the railroaders' complaints and expressed sympathy for their plight but criticized them for resorting to a strike. "[S]trikes," they declared, "tend to create a spirit of discord and hatred," threatening the welfare of the community and making it more difficult for capital and labor to resolve their disputes. The ironworkers reserved most of their bile, though, for the crowd, which they condemned for using "force and threats of violence," creating conditions that would make it harder for railroaders and management to reach a settlement, "subject[ing] the laboring classes to the ridicule and contempt of all honorable and law-abiding citizens," and threatening to destroy "the best form of republican government." The Columbus ironworkers concluded that the city's workers, like all good citizens, should rely on the ballot to redress their grievances: "the difficulties existing between capital and labor . . . can only be rectified by proper and judicious legislation."[5]

The unfolding of the 1877 railroad strike in Columbus suggests three distinct methods or strategies that Ohio workers adopted to confront the growing power of capital during the Gilded Age—collective economic action, popular or mass protest, and political mobilization. While these three strategies were not mutually exclusive and workers did employ all three (sometimes simultaneously), organized workers in Ohio saw political mobilization as the most legitimate method of affecting industrial change and solving what those at the time referred to as the "labor problem." They would have certainly agreed with Samuel Gompers's assessment that the nation's workers "looked at industrial problems from the point of view of American citizens and turned instinctively to political activity for reform."[6]

The Gilded Age's most pressing political problem, at least in the eyes of most Ohio trade unionists, was what the Columbus ironworkers called the "difficulties existing between capital and labor" and the "Aggression of Combined Capital." "Year after year," declared the Cincinnati-based Iron Molder Union of North America, "the capital of this country becomes more and more concentrated in the hands of the few; and in proportion as the wealth becomes centralized, its power increases and the laboring classes are impoverished." Labor leaders worried that this "rapid concentration of wealth" and the "massing of machinery in immense workshops" would rob producers of the wealth they had created, destroying the "possibility of the workman becoming his own employer" and transforming republican government into an aristocracy.[7]

Starting in the 1850s and continuing after the Civil War, Ohio and much of the Industrial Midwest and Northeast witnessed a profound reordering of industrial production—small, locally owned shops and manufacturers that relied on the skill of workers to produce goods for local markets began giving way to large, corporately financed factories that sought to undermine the skill and power of workers and sell goods to a regional or national market. This change was rooted in the development of railroads. Railroads lowered transportation costs, allowing for the geographical expansion of markets and a more intensive utilization of economies of scale, especially the use of machinery and the division of labor, to drive down per unit costs. Railroads also pioneered new forms of capital accumulation, forms that would be emulated by manufacturers in the decades following the Civil War and would allow them to build enterprises on a scale never imagined at the time Ohio became a state. Those producers without access to capital for machinery and expansion often found their products driven out of the marketplace.

The concentration of capital did not proceed evenly throughout the state. In many areas and in many industries, manufacturing continued to be dominated by local producers using traditional production techniques, but large corporations and their factories became increasingly conspicuous in the state's economic and political life. Their influence and power extended far beyond the numbers of workers employed, goods produced, and revenue generated. Cleveland's Standard Oil, for instance, used threats of increasing the output of its own cooperage and importing barrels from other cities to force Cleveland barrel makers to lower prices, in effect dictating terms to scores of small producers and their employees who were not formally under the company's control.[8]

Large corporations also threatened the state's republican institutions. Gilded Age Ohio was rife with political corruption. Streetcar and utility magnates bribed city councilmen to receive franchises. Contractors bribed municipal and county officials for public works contracts. And businesses bribed the general assembly to secure friendly legislation or undermine attempts at greater regulation.[9] The state's most conspicuous bribery episode involved the Ohio General Assembly, the election of a U.S. senator, and the world's largest corporation, Standard Oil. In 1884 Oliver Hazard Payne, the treasurer of Standard Oil, secured a Senate seat for his father, Henry B. Payne, a Democrat, by dispensing large amounts of cash to members of the Ohio General Assembly. Newspaper charges that John D. Rockefeller and Standard Oil had bought the seat, a general assembly investigation launched by Republicans after they had regained the majority, and the U.S. Senate's refusal to look into the episode kept the issue before voters for at least a decade and contributed to the widespread belief, especially among trade unionists, that corporations had corrupted Ohio's political system.[10] Corporations were not the only ones offering bribes, but their access to money made them the most prominent player in the boodle system.

The concentration of capital took hold first in the large cities before spreading to industrial towns and rural areas. Historian Steven Ross has calculated that in 1870 50.6 percent of Cincinnati's manufacturing workers labored in shops of fewer than fifty employees and 33.2 percent worked in shops with more than a hundred employees. But ten years later these numbers were reversed, as 34.8 percent of Cincinnati factory workers toiled in shops with less than fifty employees and 49.6 percent labored in shops with more than a hundred workers.[11] Nowhere in Ohio was the mid-nineteenth century's growth of industry and concentration of capital more apparent than in Cleveland. In 1850 Cleveland was scarcely more than a regional banking and commercial hub for prosperous farmers of northeast Ohio's Western Reserve. The city's population stood at just over 17,000, and Cleveland's Cuyahoga County ranked eighteenth among the state's eighty-five counties in terms of industrial output. But the development of railroads, the acumen of business leaders such as John D. Rockefeller, proximity to the oil fields of northwestern Pennsylvania, and the city's strategic position between the coalfields of Ohio and Pennsylvania and Lake Superior's iron ranges fueled spectacular growth, especially in the refining, chemical, and iron industries. Between 1860 and 1870, the amount of capital invested in shops, mills, and factories increased fivefold and the number of manufacturing employees more than doubled. By 1870 the city's population stood at 92,829, and Cuyahoga County ranked second in the state in terms of industrial output.[12] Although the city had over 1,100 shops and factories, two firms—the Cleveland Rolling Mills with 2,700 employees and Standard Oil with 2,500 industrial workers—employed over half of the county's 10,069 factory workers enumerated in the census. In other words, a majority of the city's industrial workers labored in plants with at least 2,500 employees.[13]

Organized workers in Ohio had ambivalent feelings about the concentration of capital. Most Ohio workers, at least those who were male, hoped one day to open a shop or factory of their own and gain the type of economic independence that had long been prized as the cornerstone of liberty in the American republic. As a Cleveland labor federation declared in the early 1870s, "[W]e believe that there should be no antagonism between capital and labor. . . . [I]n this country every workingman should consider that he has a chance to become an employer himself." Most Ohio workers thought that wage labor should be a temporary condition that would enable them to accumulate the money needed to achieve their independence. This type of mobility had characterized antebellum Ohio. In pre–Civil War Cincinnati, according to historian Steven Ross, "[e]arnings were sufficiently high and the costs of starting a new business were sufficiently low that ambitious journeymen frequently found themselves able to save enough money to start a small shop."[14]

Workers feared, though, that the concentration of capital and the rise of big business were making it more difficult to escape a life of wage labor, robbing workers of the independence necessary to be good citizens. The intensification of the division of labor and the increasing use of labor-saving machinery gave employers powerful tools that could be used to undermine the skill and wages of workers. During the 1870s annual wages for industrial workers in Ohio's two largest cities actually declined. In Cincinnati, they fell 14.4 percent, from $417 in 1870 to $357 in 1880, and in Cleveland they dropped from $451 to $388 (14.0%). Only in Columbus did industrial workers see wages rise over the course of the decade, from an average of $341 in 1870 to $342 in 1880. Not all of this decline can be attributed to the concentration of capital (the decade also witnessed a slight contraction in the supply of currency that, with a rapid increase in the volume of goods produced, worked to fuel price and wage deflation), but workers argued that the volume of currency was being manipulated for the benefit of big business and Wall Street bankers.

While wages were dropping (or in the case of Columbus remaining stagnant), the cost of opening a shop or factory was climbing. In 1870 the average capitalization of the state's 22,773 factories and shops was $6,232, but ten years later the number of shops had declined to 20,699 and the average capitalization had increased 46.5 percent to $9,128. In the cities, the capitalization of manufacturing establishments was even higher. In Cleveland, the average capitalization increased 37.2 percent to $16,298; and in Columbus, 109.5 percent to $13,566. For some unknown reason, between 1870 and 1880, Cincinnati actually witnessed a slight decline in the average capitalization of manufacturing concerns, but between 1860 and 1890 the average capitalization increased over 300 percent, from $9,109 to $27,632.[15]

Declining wages and the increased cost of opening a shop or a factory conspired to make it more difficult for wage workers to become capitalists themselves. Ross has argued that by 1880 conditions in Cincinnati had prevented "all but a small number of journeymen from rising to the top." Labor leaders called this new condition the "wage system," which Martin Foran, the founder and former president of the Coopers' International Union who represented Cleveland in the U.S. Congress for much of the 1880s, considered to be "a species of slavery in some respects more galling than chattel slavery." Not only did the wage system prevent the advancement of individual workers, it also threatened the American republic through the creation of an aristocracy.[16]

The ambivalence of Ohio workers toward corporations and big business can be discerned in the words used by the Columbus ironworkers, "Aggression of Combined Capital." Combined capital in and of itself was not the problem. Ohio workers could point to many examples of capitalists who treated their workers with dignity, providing both opportunities for advancement and wages to support families. During the Populist and Progressive eras, Ohio trade unionists would work closely with some industrialists—Tom L. Johnson, Samuel "Golden Rule" Jones, Thomas Fitzsimmons, and Jacob Coxey. Capital only became a problem when those who controlled it acted in an aggressive manner. Capitalists who abused their power through either the creation of monopolistic enterprises or the corruption of the political process or by depriving workers of just wages had to be stopped, and ways had to be devised to increase the opportunities open to wage laborers.

Although most Ohio trade unionists agreed as to the nature of the problems confronting the nation's workers—the concentration of capital into the hands of those who might abuse it and the creation of the wage system—and that political action was the best avenue through which to resolve these problems, there was little agreement as to the type of reform needed or the best strategy to be used to realize reform. Ohio labor organizations advocated a host of reforms that they hoped would eliminate the "wage system" and the most baneful effects of the concentration of capital. These ranged from land reform, the single tax, and the abolition of child and convict labor to hour and wage regulation and legislation that would make it easier to enforce corporate charters. Monetary reform in general—and greenbackism in particular—drew the most attention and support from Ohio labor leaders. Many Ohio trade unionists believed that an inflationist monetary policy and the elimination of national banks would encourage individual economic activity and prosperity by easing credit, increasing profits and wages, and ending Wall Street's stranglehold over the nation's producers.

Since most nineteenth-century trade unions were organized along craft or industrial lines, they were ill-suited to engage in political activity. The national government had little authority over labor matters, and most reforms required state or municipal action. Thus, carpenters in Ohio and carpenters in Michigan might belong to the same international union, but they operated in distinct political environments and could be of little help to one another when it came to political action. To assert their political power, Ohio trade unions formed federations at both state and local levels. These federations combined union locals within a jurisdiction (city, county, or state) to pressure lawmaking bodies to enact legislation in the interest of workers, executives to enforce laws in such a way as to benefit labor, and courts to offer labor-friendly interpretations of laws.

Most Ohio labor federations adopted nonpartisan political strategies. Union leaders reasoned that the attachment of most of the state's trade unionists to the traditional parties prevented the formation of formal alliances between labor and political parties. Labor leaders also feared that party officials would want unions to subordinate their concerns to those of the party, that the needs of labor would be sacrificed to political expediency.

As a Columbus labor leader warned, "We hold the balance of power, and by the proper use of that power, we can accomplish vastly more than anyone can possibly hope to accomplish by independent political action. . . . As organized bodies, [partisan] political action and the enunciation of political principles can only divide us, just what our enemies want to see." Instead, he urged labor federations to work "in support of friendly candidates and against obnoxious ones on the tickets of the dominant parties."[17]

Aware of this nonpartisan strategy, the major parties were often solicitous of the labor vote. With a vigorous two-party system, statewide elections in Ohio often hinged on a few thousand votes, and candidates often realized that labor's endorsement could mean the difference between victory and defeat. The major parties presented themselves as friends of labor. The Republicans pointed to their position on the tariff, telling workers that it protected American jobs and wages, while Ohio Democrats emphasized their anti-monopoly monetary policy and support for protective legislation. Candidates appeared before federations promising to enact beneficial legislation and appoint union members to positions like building inspector or mine inspector where they could protect the rights of workers.

Political parties also recruited labor leaders to run for office, and labor leaders, often motivated by personal ambition as well as the desire to work for labor interests, willingly obliged. In Cleveland in the early 1870s, for instance, the Republican party nominated John Fehrenbatch, the president of the national blacksmiths' union, to run for the general assembly, and Democrats put Robert Schilling, one of the leaders of the Coopers' International Union, on their slate. While Schilling was never elected and would leave both Cleveland and the Democratic party before becoming a leader in Wisconsin's Populist movement, Fehrenbatch served a term in the statehouse. Perhaps the most successful of the labor leaders turned politicians in Ohio was Martin Foran, a Democrat who served as a delegate to the state's 1874 Constitutional Convention, presided over Cleveland's police court, and spent three terms in Congress.[18]

The political parties put so much pressure on trade unionists by soliciting endorsements and recruiting candidates that federations banned officials and delegates from engaging in certain types of partisan activity. When the Cleveland Central Labor Union (CLU) was formed, the founders took steps to ensure that those who would place party loyalties over the federation would be kept out. The constitution forbade not only the discussion of partisan issues but also the election of a president. The founders feared that the office of president would attract trade unionists interested in using it as a springboard for a political career and that the parties would target a president for special favors. Instead, the chairmanship of CLU meetings rotated among the constituent unions.[19]

While trade unionists in the state's industrial cities had begun forming urban labor federations in the 1860s and 1870s, Ohio trade unionists took the first step toward the formation of a statewide federation that would lobby the general assembly in April 1884 when the Columbus Trades and Labor Assembly issued a call for delegates from the state's unions to meet in Columbus. The call made it clear that the new organization's primary mission was to secure favorable labor legislation, insisting that organized labor's "weight and influence . . . with our law-making bodies cannot be overestimated." When eighty-five delegates representing the state's urban labor federations, large local craft unions, and Knights of Labor assemblies met in June 1884, they formed the Ohio State Trades and Labor Assembly (OSTLA). The principal act of the new federation was the creation of a legislative board, "whose duty it shall be to prepare and urge passage of such bills through our State Legislature as will better protect honest toil."[20]

The OSTLA then called for the state general assembly to pass several measures to help not only union members but all of the state's workingmen and their families: the eight-hour workday; compulsory school attendance; prohibition of employment of children under fourteen years old; the end of the use of coal screens and the payment for all coal mined; the abolition of prison contract labor; equal wages for women performing equal work; a variety of factory and mine safety regulations; and a law making it illegal for employers to fire individuals for union membership. The OSTLA adopted a nonpartisan strategy that included banning "any person holding an elective or appointed office under either political party" from holding any official position in the federation.[21] As one of the OSTLA's founders would declare: "As workingmen, we can best ameliorate our condition—so far as legislation is concerned—by rewarding friends and punishing political enemies, it matters not [to] what party they belong."[22]

The OSTLA's efforts generally met with success in the general assembly. With the state's voters evenly split between the Republican and Democratic parties, most politicians realized that labor support could easily swing election results. Both parties pledged to pass much of the OSTLA's agenda. Within a few years the legislature passed bills regulating conditions in coal mines, establishing a system to inspect factories, and changing convict labor practices. The OSTLA's greatest legislative triumph came in April 1886 when after several setbacks it convinced the state legislature to pass the Haley Bill, which declared that "in any mechanical, manufacturing, or mining business, a day's work, when the contract is silent on the subject, or where there is no express contract, shall consist of eight hours." In 1887 the Ohio legislature prohibited payment of wages in scrip, tokens, checks, or any other instruments that were not redeemable for cash.[23]

The OSTLA's success in the general assembly continued into the Populist era. In 1890 the legislators passed a bill limiting the number of hours certain railroad workers could be on the job and requiring overtime pay for work beyond ten hours a day. Two years later, the general assembly passed a bill prohibiting employers from coercing union members into quitting their membership in a trades union and another requiring employers to pay their employees at least twice a month. In 1894 the general assembly sought to discourage the use of convict labor by making it "unlawful for any person, persons or corporations to expose for sale within the state of Ohio, without first obtaining from the secretary of state a license to sell any convict-made goods, merchandise or wares."[24]

The responsiveness of the two major parties to the demands of Ohio labor blunted efforts to form workingmen's parties. The mid 1870s witnessed the only statewide wave of third-party activity before the Populist era.[25] Ohio workers were feeling the effects of the depression that began in 1873. In Cleveland, labor leaders including Robert Schilling and Issac Cowans broke off from the traditional parties to form a local branch of the Greenback party in 1875. Two years later, Columbus trade unionists led by the ironworkers at the Columbus Rolling Mill responded to the railroad strike of 1877 and the nation's abysmal economic conditions by organizing a Greenback party in Franklin County.[26]

While trade unionists in Cleveland and Columbus turned to the Greenback party, Cincinnati's trade unionists turned to the socialistic Workingman's party. Although many of the party's leaders were recent immigrants from Germany and other European countries, the Workingman's party echoed many of the Greenback party's producerist concerns. The Workingman's party thought that "all legitimate property belonged to the producer" and called for the creation of industrial cooperatives. Support for the party was limited to a handful of activists, until the railroad strike of 1877 radicalized many of Cincinnati's workers. The party's local slate captured about 20 percent of the vote in both October and November of 1877.[27]

In the fall of 1877, the state's Greenback party and one branch of the Workingman's party (the non-Cincinnati branch) merged for the state's gubernatorial election. The party complained, "[L]abor, the creator of all wealth, is either unemployed or denied its just reward" and blamed politicians for creating the situation through "class legislation and the mismanagement of our national finances." The party's platform contained a number of planks that would remain popular in labor circles for the next fifty years: repayment of all government bonds "according to the laws under which they were issued" rather than with specie, the restoration of silver coinage, the enforcement of corporate charters, the adoption of a graduated income tax, the issuance of paper money directly by the national government, reservation of government land for actual settlers, and the abolition of the practice of paying wages in scrip. Stephen Johnson, the party's gubernatorial nominee, received 16,912 votes, just over 3.0 percent of the votes cast. The branch of the Workingman's party that refused to fuse with the Greenback party nominated Lewis Bond, who received 12,489 votes (2.3%), about two-thirds of which came from Cincinnati.[28]

The following year the rest of the Workingman's party merged with the Greenback party to form the Greenback-Labor party. In Ohio the party nominated a leader of the state miners' union, Andrew Roy, for the top spot on the ticket, secretary of state. Roy polled 38,332 votes (just over 6.5%) in a race the Republican candidate won by less than 3,200 votes. As in 1877 most of the Greenback-Labor party supporters came from the state's industrial centers and mining areas. In Columbus, Roy collected slightly more than 10 percent of the vote, while he received just over 28 percent of the vote in Cleveland.[29]

The rapid rise of the Greenback-Labor party from just over 3,000 votes in 1876 to close to 40,000 votes in 1878 caused concern among politicians from the traditional parties, especially the Democrats. Since 1868 the Democrats had been calling for many of the same reforms demanded by the Greenbackers, and party leaders saw Greenbackers as potential supporters. To win the Greenback vote the Democrats nominated Thomas Ewing, Jr., for governor in 1879. Ewing, whose father had served as secretary of the treasury during the Harrison and Taylor administrations, was the one Democrat who could command the respect of Greenback party leaders. He had been a steadfast supporter of paper money and had worked closely with the National Labor Union and Ohio trade unionists to bring about currency reform. Ewing's nomination split Ohio's Greenback-Labor party and spelled an end to the party in Ohio. The larger of the two factions endorsed Ewing and the Democratic platform, while the smaller faction insisted that the party retain its independence but refused to nominate a candidate to oppose Ewing. In the end, not only did Ewing lose the election, but the supporters of the Greenback-Labor party drifted back to the major parties. The miners' leader Andrew Roy became a Republican, while Robert Schilling rejoined the Democrats.[30]

The success of the Ohio State Trades and Labor Assembly's nonpartisan lobbying efforts and the willingness of both parties to co-opt labor's demands conspired to make Gilded Age Ohio trade unionists suspicious of third-party political activity. Additionally, both the Republican and the Democratic parties were elastic enough to make room for those of the producerist and labor republican traditions. From the OSTLA all the way down to the smallest of the local labor federations, Ohio labor organizations entered the 1890s determined to maintain their nonpartisan stance and to steer clear of the increasingly successful third-party wave sweeping the Great Plains.

Agrarian Radicalism and the Ohio People's Party

IN AUGUST 1891 MANY OF the nation's most prominent Populists gathered in Springfield, Ohio, for the inaugural convention of the Ohio People's party, and they were confident of success. The previous fall's elections had swept Farmers' Alliance candidates into office throughout the South and on the Great Plains. In Kansas the Populists controlled the statehouse and elected William A. Peffer to the U.S. Senate, while Farmers' Alliance–endorsed candidates sat in governors' mansions throughout the South. The Populists insisted that they could "Kansasize" Ohio. Peffer thought that Ohio had "precisely the same" conditions that had created the Populist success in Kansas. Kansas congressman "Sockless" Jerry Simpson insisted that the new party would hold the balance of power in the Ohio General Assembly and force the retirement of Republican senator John Sherman, the man most responsible for the demonetization of silver, the infamous "Crime of '73."[1]

Ohio was crucial in the Populists' plan to expand beyond the South and the Plains and create a national party that could challenge the dominance of the Democrats and Republicans. The state was at the center of the nation's political life during the Gilded Age. Three of the six men elected president between the Civil War and the turn of the century called Ohio home, while two others were born in the state. More important, if the party was to fulfill its promise to unite the producers of wealth and to defend workers and farmers from the greed of speculators, monopolists, and other non-producers, it had to do well in midwestern states like Ohio with large agricultural populations and major industrial centers. To ensure success in Ohio, the People's party sent a dozen stump speakers, including Annie Diggs, Ralph Beaumont, W. E. Farmer, H. E. Taubeneck, Robert Schilling, John F. Willits, and M. L. Wilkins, into the state.[2]

The Populists' confidence of success in Ohio proved misplaced, however. Not only did the People's party fail to elect a single member to the Ohio General Assembly, the party's 1891 gubernatorial nominee, John Seitz, received less than 3 percent of the popular vote. Historians trying to understand the failure of Populism in Ohio and the Midwest have offered two different interpretations for these dismal results. John Hicks, Richard Hofstadter, and others equate Populism with economic hard times and suggest that the People's party failed to take root in the Industrial Midwest because the region's relative agricultural prosperity bred contentment with the nation's political system. In the only published study of farmers and Populism in Ohio, R. Douglas Hurt agrees: "In the absence of severe economic problems, most [Ohio] farmers were too conservative to switch parties." In short, economic concerns tied the region's farmers to the traditional parties. This argument is consistent with what many politicians said at the time. For instance, John Sherman observed in 1895, "The prosperity in Ohio was a great aid to Republicans. . . . Prices were good and the farmers as a rule prosperous. This naturally made them regard with grim humor the talk of the Farmers' Alliance lecturers about poverty and distress."[3]

Others, most notably Richard Jensen and Paul Kleppner, argue that the loyalty of midwestern farmers to the traditional parties was not simply a function of economic concerns. Ethnic and cultural ties bound these farmers to both the Democratic and Republican parties, making the efforts of third parties difficult. As Kleppner writes, "The social norms connected with his [the midwestern voter] religious values were an integral part of his daily experiences. It was these that he defended through the agency of his partisan affiliation. As long as he perceived the party to serve this function, to sever that allegiance would have been as disruptive and wrenching an experience as religious conversion." Both Jensen and Kleppner suggest that the farm crisis of the 1880s and early 1890s was not severe enough in the Industrial Midwest to convince farmers to cut the cultural ties that bound them to the traditional parties.[4]

In his study of Populism on the Great Plains, Jeffrey Ostler suggests a different explanation. He argues that economic prosperity and the strength of cultural ties to the traditional parties do not fully explain the failure of Populism to take root in certain areas. Ostler argues that the success of Populism depended on the degree of party competition in a state. In Kansas and Nebraska, where the Republican party dominated in the 1880s, Populism flourished, while in Iowa, a state with similar economic conditions but marked by party competition in the 1880s, the People's party met with little success. Ostler concludes, "state political environments were crucial in determining whether agrarian radicalism took a third party turn."[5]

By examining the activities of Ohio farm organizations and the creation of the state People's party, this chapter argues that Ostler's findings apply to Ohio. The state's two-party system made it difficult for farmers to support the People's party even though agrarian radicalism did exist. Ohio farmers were deeply troubled by the increasing concentration of capital, big business's corruption of the political process, and the inability of workers and farmers to enjoy the wealth they had created. Their organizations, including the Ohio State Grange, the Ohio Farmers' Alliance, and the Ohio Farmers' Union, formulated a reform agenda to give voice to these grievances. For the most part, this reform agenda echoed the People's party platform and the Populists' critique of American political life. However, given Ohio's competitive two-party political environment, the farm organizations concluded that reform could best be accomplished by working through the existing parties.

Even though the state had the nation's second-largest agricultural population, farm organizations tended to be small in Ohio when compared to similar organizations on the Plains. According to the *Ohio Farmer*, membership in statewide farm organizations totaled about fifty thousand in May 1891. The Ohio State Grange and the Ohio Farmers' Alliance (affiliated with the Northern Alliance) each had about twenty thousand members, while the Patrons of Industry and the Ohio Farmers' Alliance and Industrial Union (affiliated with the Southern Alliance) together had about ten thousand members. While the region's economic prosperity may account for the low membership in national organizations designed to redress the farmers' needs, there are other factors. On the sparsely populated Plains, granges and alliances provided social activities for the area's geographically isolated farm families, while in more densely populated Ohio, granges and alliances had to compete with political parties, voluntary organizations, and nearby towns and cities for the farm family's attention. The state's farm organizations also had to compete with local, independent farm organizations, many of which predated the establishment of the Grange or the Alliances. There is no way to estimate the number of farmers belonging to local groups, but clearly they were more popular than the Grange or the alliances. For example, over ten thousand people regularly attended the Erie County Agricultural Society's annual picnic and close to five thousand attended similar events in Summit County.[6]

Despite the relative prosperity of Ohio farmers, the leaders of the state's farm organizations were deeply troubled by changes in the nation's political and economic life. Anger reached a peak in August 1890 when the editor of the *Ohio Farmer* convened a meeting of representatives of the state's farm organizations. He suggested that the decentralized and local nature of the farm organizations had robbed the state's farmers of their proper share of political influence, and he envisioned the meeting as uniting "all of the different farmers' organizations under one head for the benefit of agricultural interests." The new organization, called the Ohio Farmers' Union, received the endorsement of the Ohio State Grange, the Ohio Farmers' Alliance, and the Patrons of Industry as well as the Cincinnati-based *American Grange Bulletin*. Over a thousand farmers representing local granges, alliances, and hundreds of independent county farm organizations attended the meeting. Democratic and Republican papers alike called the meeting the greatest assembly of farmers in the state's history and suggested that all of the state's farmers would now speak with one voice.

A series of speeches kicked off the first Farmers' Union convention. John Seitz, a former Democratic legislator who had run for governor on both the Greenback and United Labor tickets, told the farmers that hard times "are the results of other interests being arrayed against the farmer and [these] are especially those of the capitalists." For Seitz, these interests were destroying American democracy by corrupting politicians, depriving workers of the product of their labor, and creating a new aristocracy. He told the crowd, "Wealth passes from the hands of those who produce to the 25,000 men who own half the wealth of this country." John Brigham followed Seitz. The grand master of the National Grange as well as a Republican candidate for Congress, Brigham sounded as radical as Seitz. He warned, "The farmers only ask to receive a fair reward for the results of their labor, and if they cannot receive it by peaceable methods then the time will come when they secure it by revolution." Like Seitz, Brigham rooted the problems of farmers in the state and national legislatures. He told the farmers they had to elect farmers to public office because the "bankers and professional men" who run the government are "not as much awake to the interests of agriculturalists as farmers would be."[7]

Brigham, the convention chairman, and the leaders of the Ohio Farmers' Union faced the daunting task of uniting these farmers for political action. Noting the strong ties between farmers and the existing parties, the *American Grange Bulletin* suggested it would take "a severe wrench to sever the connection." For nineteenth-century farmers steeped in the nation's republican traditions, political participation was a serious matter. They attributed the greatness of the nation to its political institutions and saw themselves as the guardians of this American greatness. This need to strengthen and defend the nation, in turn, fostered an intense devotion to party. Kleppner estimates that in 1888 47.5 percent of rural Ohio voters cast their ballots for the Democratic party, while 48.7 percent voted for Republicans. In the last half of the 1880s, Democrats dominated in the western counties along the Indiana border, while the Republicans did well in the counties of northeast Ohio's Western Reserve and the Appalachian counties along the Ohio River in the southeast part of the state. Given the divisions among Ohio farmers, the *American Grange Bulletin* suggested it would be impossible to create a farmers' party. But "[i]t ought not to be a difficult matter to get them [Ohio farmers] earnestly to work in their party organizations to secure a fairer representation of farmers in their representative bodies," the paper argued. Brigham understood the difficulties associated with uniting the farmers for political action. He told the convention, "we are here . . . not to antagonize especially any political party, nor to endorse or bolster up any political party. . . . we are here as farmers, with the idea that it is possible for us as farmers to do something in the way of influencing state and national legislation." In order to accomplish this goal, Brigham suggested, "We must keep in the background, if we can, those questions over which we will quarrel and divide and wrangle, and from which no good can come."[8]

At the convention, delegates from the Knox County Alliance tried repeatedly to discuss the creation of a new political party. Fearing an effort to organize a political party would divide the farmers and destroy any chance of united action, Brigham ruled the Knox County delegates out of order each time they broached the subject. Brigham's use of the gavel was so heavy-handed that the *Columbus Post-Press* charged him with "gross violations of parliamentary law and usage." The convention's final declaration simply stated, "Can this position [political reform] best be reached by the formation of a farmers' party or by making our influence felt in the control of the existing parties? It is the sense of this convention that we should first thoroughly test the latter and hope we shall not be compelled to resort to the former."[9]

The decision to forgo the creation of a farmers' party, though, did not indicate that the state's farmers were content with their political situation. The Farmers' Union's declaration of principles expressed traditional

Not all agrarian activists worked through the traditional parties. The *Plow and Hammer,* an Alliance paper from Tiffin, demanded the creation of a new party, and several local farmers' organizations took its advice. In early September the Knox County Farmers' Alliance formed a county ticket. The Knox County farmers noted that the "influence of liquor interests" and the "corruption of our local legislature by the lobby" had forced farmers and workers to bear an "unequal and unjust" tax burden. The Knox County party offered a twelve-plank platform to reform both the county and the state governments. Among the demands were tax reform, prohibition of speculation, reduction of interest rates to no more than 5 percent, regulation of the liquor trade, the end of alien landownership, the restriction of immigration, reduction in the price of schoolbooks, and reduction of the salaries for public officials.[15]

The Knox County Farmer's Alliance was not alone in organizing a new political party. In Wood County a convention of farmers echoed the complaints of the Ohio Farmers' Union: "The farmers must henceforth be a factor in politics and not a patient bearing ass, content with an occasional thistle, but a wide awake, intelligent, courageous, directing power." But the Wood County farmers insisted that the only way to accomplish this was to offer their own slate of candidates for local office. In Jefferson County, alliance men met in Steubenville and formed a "people's party." The Jefferson County Alliance men did not offer a complete platform as they were concerned only with taxes. They called for a "reduction of county official salaries, and thus a reduction of taxes to the already burdened taxpayers." Nine other counties produced alliance tickets.[16]

Not only did alliances offer slates for county and township offices, they ran candidates for Congress. In Lima the Knights of Labor and alliance men nominated John Smith, the vice president of the state alliance, for the U.S. House of Representatives. W. H. Likins, president of the Ohio Farmers' Alliance, ran for Congress in the eighth district on both the Prohibition and "People's party" tickets. In the third district S. H. Ellis, the master of the state grange, ran under a Farmer-Labor banner. Isaac Freeman, the overseer of the Ohio State Grange, ran in the fourth district. In six other congressional districts the local alliances fielded candidates.[17]

Third-party activists asserted that both parties had aligned themselves with speculators, corporations, and bankers to rob the producers of wealth of their just reward. The candidates portrayed themselves as the defenders of the producing classes. Likins called capitalists and politicians from the major parties "maggots that are feasting on the hard earned labor and sinew of the land." The candidacy of alliance men, Likins continued, "will teach the producer that neither of the old parties will give them correct and pure legislation so long as money, rum, and corrupt partisan demagogues rule supreme." John Seitz criticized the government's railroad subsidies as creating a "dozen railroad kings" who have been able to "accumulate mightier fortunes than the house of the Rothchilds," while the farmer and the worker toil in poverty. The *Plow and Hammer* portrayed the election as a replay of the Federalist-Republican contest of ninety years earlier. Like the earlier Federalists, the leaders of the Democrats and Republicans believed that "the better policy was to have . . . power concentrated in the hands of the few; the masses must be governed; the well born and the wealthy to govern the rabble; legislation for the rich and they to take care of and keep the poor in subjection." The paper saw the alliance's political movement as the embodiment of the ideas of Jefferson and Madison: "a government of the whole people; the poorest citizen to have equal rights and privileges with the wealthiest."[18]

For the state's farmers in 1890, the paramount issue was tax reform. Although the state's constitution required that all forms of property—including "all moneys, credits, investments in bonds, stocks, joint stock companies, or otherwise; and also all real and personal property"—be taxed at a uniform rate, in practice this was not done. Stocks, bonds, bank accounts, and personal property were easily hidden from assessors and thus escaped taxation. One legislator called the state's tax system "a game of hide and seek," noting that in Cincinnati's Hamilton County, the value of personal property appearing on the tax duplicate declined 23 percent from 1865 until 1885, a period of robust economic growth. On the other hand, the farmers' main source of wealth, land, could not be hidden. At a time when unprecedented fortunes were accumulating in urban areas, farmers were paying a disproportionate share of the state's taxes. For example, in 1890 Toledo's Lucas County paid about the same in taxes as mostly rural Muskingum County even though Lucas County had twice the population and over three times the bank deposits.[19]

The election of 1890 proved a disaster for third-party tickets. While a handful of Farmers' Alliance candidates were elected to township office, at the county level not a single third-party candidate succeeded. As table 2.1 shows, the Highland County Alliance ticket fared the best, receiving close to 12 percent of the popular vote. Third-party congressional candidates fared just as poorly, with none of the eight candidates polling more than 4 percent of the vote and only two receiving more than 2 percent. Only in the eighth district did the third-party candidate possibly affect the result of the election. Likins received 1,436 votes in a race decided by 194 votes.

TABLE 2.1—Third-Party Candidates in 1890 County Elections

County	Votes received	Total votes	Percentage
Darke	300	9,150	3.3
Delaware	70	6,400	1.1
Highland	800	6,700	11.9
Jefferson	360	6,500	5.5
Knox	300	6,800	4.4
Licking	20	9,400	0.2
Logan	300	5,850	5.1
Pickaway	400	6,200	6.5
Seneca	140	9,450	1.5
Union	90	5,650	1.6
Williams	580	6,050	9.6
Wood	35	9,150	0.4

Source: Report of the Ohio Secretary of State, 1890, 287–347. The "votes received" and the "total votes" are rounded averages as in most cases there were six candidates on the county slate.

Not only did farmers running on third-party tickets fare badly, so did farmers on major party tickets. Republicans Brigham and Wilson lost by 1,702 and 2,132 votes, respectively, while Democrat Smith lost by 3,754. As each of these candidates had the support of farm organizations and did not face competition from a Farmers' Alliance candidate, the losses demonstrated how hard it would be for farmers to win seats in the national legislature.[20]

Three months after the election of 1890 both the Ohio State Grange and the Ohio Farmers' Alliance held their annual statewide conventions. Both organizations and their leaders responded to the election in the same way: they praised the farmers' newfound activism and predicted a responsive legislative session. More important, the two agrarian groups formally rejected any involvement with the third-party movement and committed themselves to reform through the traditional parties.

TABLE 2.2—Third-Party Candidates in 1890 Congressional Elections

Candidate (district)	Votes received	Total votes	Percentage
Seth Ellis (third)	447	41,307	1.1
Isaac Freeman (fourth)	198	41,800	0.5
John Smith (fifth)	684	38,288	1.8
C. Storer (seventh)	33	34,620	0.1
W. H. Likins (eighth)	1,436	36,070	4.0
H. W. Rhodes (eleventh)	955	31,041	3.1
J. Junkins (fourteenth)	30	36,052	0.1
D. T. Adams (fifteenth)	414	37,825	1.1

Source: Report of the Ohio Secretary of State, 1890, 246–51.

Despite the losses of farmers running on both third-party slates and on the major tickets, many Grange and Alliance leaders saw the campaign and the election of 1890 as producing the desired results—the creation of a general assembly sympathetic to the needs of the farmers. Henry Talcott, the treasurer of the Ohio State Grange, suggested that the political activities of the farmers had changed the political climate as "[o]ffice holders and the press are now all in favor of the farmer." B. F. Swingle, lecturer for the Grange, declared, "Great reforms are anticipated in the future, ballot reforms, legislative relief, proper representation in proportion to our interests are all foreshadowed in the future if we are true to our interests." Even the Grange's lobbying arm felt that the farmer's newfound activism would be strong enough "to compel these officials to do their duty."[21]

Many Ohio farm leaders also interpreted the results of the election of 1890 as a warning against the formation of a political party. Reminding farmers of the "battle scars" of Brigham and Alliance candidates in the last election, Talcott declared it to be "difficult and dangerous . . . to attempt to create a new party" and concluded that reform "can be accomplished best by the exercise of level headed counsel on the part of grangers with their present party associates." Grange Master Seth Ellis, perhaps disappointed with his own showing in the election, abandoned the idea of third-party action and told farmers to reform the existing parties to bring about relief for the farmer. Alliance President Likins, also a casualty of the previous election, told farmers to work through the existing parties to "[b]reak down partisan lines, help to educate and elevate our brother and sister to a higher state of manhood and womanhood. Make no radical demands; discountenance office seekers of every name, tribe or calling; shun the politician; attend the conventions; see that good men are nominated and stop voting for bankers, lawyers, railroad attorneys, stockholders in Standard Oil companies, and millionaires and you will fill the mission this great alliance system set out to accomplish." The Ohio State Grange reiterated its nonpartisan policy; and the Ohio Farmers' Alliance announced that it would work through the existing parties but warned, "in the event that the demands of our state and national legislators are unheeded, we shall co-operate with other reform organizations and all those desiring political reform, in a call for a mass convention to form a people's party that shall enforce our demands with the ballot."[22]

Despite the decisions to forgo the creation of a third party, Ohio farm leaders remained critical of the state's and the nation's political climate. John Brigham asserted, "There needs to be a great many political funerals in both political parties. It is very difficult to discover which of the parties furnishes the most obedient servants of Wall street and monopoly." The most outspoken critic continued to be Farmers' Alliance president Likins. For Likins, the troubles of the farmers were rooted in capital's corruption of politicians, who were too fond of "silken couches, the store of gold and the applause of men who worship present success." But he predicted that "in the better and fairer days that are coming the life of the selfish and cruel time server shall be deemed an awful failure." The Farmers' Alliance convention declared, "corporate monopolies . . . absolutely control . . . the general government, state legislatures, executives and courts . . . [and] have robbed the farmers of millions and made millionaires by the thousand; have taken millions from labor without giving adequate equivalent therefore, and virtually placed capital above labor." The abandonment of third-party action did not entail a moderation of views. Ohio farm leaders felt that, given the state's vigorous two-party system, working with the major parties offered the best chance for reform.

At their conventions, the Ohio State Grange and the Ohio Farmers' Alliance reiterated the legislative demands of the Ohio Farmers' Union. The most important of these was passage of the Rawlings Bill, which would make manufacturers bear a greater share of the state's tax burden. The organizations also called for the adoption of the Australian ballot; a reduction in the salaries of state and county officials; a lowering of the cost of schoolbooks; and approval of a constitutional amendment to allow for the initiative and referendum.[23]

Ohio farmers were not alone in their enthusiasm for the farmers' newfound political activism. Plains Alliance men were agitating for the creation of a national third party, while Southern Alliance men continued to believe that activity through the Democratic party offered the best chance for success. Partisans of these two views met in Ocala, Florida, in December 1890 as part of the convention of the supreme council of the Southern Alliance. The Kansas delegation, which had left the Plains Alliance for the Southern Alliance the year before, pushed for the creation of a new party, while southerners thought it was possible for the alliance to capture the Democratic party at the national level. Texas Alliance leader Charles William Macune worked out a compromise. There would be a national convention of "organizations of producers" on the eve of the 1892 national campaign at which time delegates could consider the creation of a third party. Radical third-party men at Ocala rejected the compromise. Wanting immediate action, they called for reformers to meet in Cincinnati in May 1891 to form a new party.[24]

In January 1891, the Ohio General Assembly began a new session. Farmers serving in the legislature immediately formed a bipartisan caucus dedicated to enacting the Farmers' Union platform. The thirty-six-member Farmers' Independent Caucus made the passage of tax reform, in the form of the Rawlings Bill, its first priority. The Rawlings Bill required the state's manufacturers to pay taxes on their inventories. Although some farm legislators disagreed on certain provisions of the Rawlings Bill, all of them pledged themselves to support its passage. Commenting on this caucus, the *Ohio State Journal* predicted, "recent political developments added to the growing and united strength of the farmers' organizations, have impressed the general assembly with the merits of bills they have overlooked in the past." Immediately legislators on both sides of the aisle introduced legislation demanded by farmers: the abolition of gambling and speculation in agricultural commodities; the exemption of mortgaged property from taxation to the amount of the mortgage; the election of the dairy and food commissioner; the adoption of the Australian ballot; and restriction of hunting on private property.[25]

When the legislature was about to adjourn in late winter, it looked as though the general assembly was not going to pass tax reform or the farmers' other demands. Urban legislators held up tax reform arguing that it would drive Ohio factories to other states, and the *Ohio Farmer* predicted, "the present legislature would not pass a single measure that would relieve the farmers from paying more than their fair share of taxes." The paper went on to threaten that "the farmers will undoubtedly show their hands at the ballot box the coming fall. It is to be hoped that this will not come in the shape of a farmers' party." The equally conservative *American Grange Bulletin* sounded a similar alarm suggesting that the farmers could follow the Kansas example and abandon the two major parties. One Farmers' Alliance activist even declared his desire to see the Rawlings Bill defeated as it would drive Ohio farmers into a third party.[26]

On April 18, 1891, the Ohio General Assembly blunted the third-party movement by passing the Rawlings Bill. Although the final bill was not all that the farmers had hoped, the *Ohio Farmer* considered "it is very much better for farmers than the old bill." The paper attributed passage to the fact that "the demand for legislation was so great that it could not be ignored." Voting on tax reform did not break down along party lines. Legislators from rural districts tended to vote for the Rawlings Bill, while the opposition came from the industrial centers. The general assembly also passed several other measures demanded by Ohio farm organizations: the Australian ballot, the direct election of the dairy and food commissioner, cheaper schoolbooks, and a reduction in the salaries of county officials. The actions of the general assembly were so sympathetic to the state's farmers that the *Cincinnati Enquirer* complained of the "tendency of the country people this year to go against the towns."[27]

The Ohio General Assembly's passage of most of the farmers' political agenda made the state's farm leaders wary of the upcoming Cincinnati conference and the creation of a new party. They no longer saw the existing parties as hostile to the concerns of farmers and increasingly characterized the urban politician, regardless of party, as the chief enemy of the farmer. Likins announced his opposition to sending Ohio Farmers' Alliance delegates to the Cincinnati conference: "[I]f a third party is organized or an independent ticket placed in the field at that convention, our hopes of success in the future will be blasted." Other Ohio farm groups—Southern Alliance, Patrons of Industry, and the Grange—refused to send delegates to the Cincinnati conference.[28]

The Cincinnati convention of third-party proponents opened on May 18, 1891, with over 1,417 delegates. Although the Farmers' Alliance was the strongest voice at the convention, reformers of all stripes—Bellamy Nationalists, Knights of Labor, Union and United Labor party activists, single taxers, and trade unionists—were granted credentials. To no one's surprise, the Cincinnati convention created a new political party and named it the People's party. Fearing that the new party would not succeed without southern support, the convention adopted the Southern Alliance's Ocala platform and created a committee to attend the third-party meeting in St. Louis called by Southern Alliance president Leonidas Polk.

Because the convention was held in the state, Ohio had the convention's second-largest delegation with 317 delegates. Only Kansas with 407 delegates had a larger representation. While there were a number of Ohio Farmers' Alliance leaders present, including Seitz, Crawford, J. H. C. Cobb, H. F. Barnes, and T. R. Smith, urban reformers dominated the Ohio delegation. Of the 317 Ohio delegates, over 100 were from Cincinnati's Hamilton County, while another forty delegates represented Cleveland's Cuyahoga County. The Ohio delegation took the first step toward the creation of the state's People's party by calling for reformers to meet in Springfield on August 5 and 6. The convention's call stated, "We . . . declare our adherence to the doctrine proclaimed by Lincoln that this should be 'a government of the people, by the people and for the people,' that peace may reign and prosperity be established." The call also asserted that the leaders of the traditional parties "blind their eyes to the inequities now being inflicted on our people by the monied interests of the land."[29]

The Ohio Farmers' Union was scheduled to meet the week after the Cincinnati convention, and the call to form an Ohio People's party was pushed to the top of the meeting's agenda. On the eve of the Farmers' Union meeting, the *Ohio Farmer* published the results of a poll of the state's farmers. The paper printed questionnaires for both alliances, the Grange, and the Patrons of Industry asking members if they were "in favor of independent political action by farmers this fall?" and other political questions. The *Ohio Farmer* asked farmers not affiliated with one of the organizations to send in a postcard with answers to the same questions.[30]

Although the poll's methodology was less than scientific, it suggested that Ohio farmers supported independent political action by a margin of more than two to one. The state's branch of the Southern Alliance and the Patrons of Industry did not return the surveys, but the *Ohio Farmer*, noting that these two organizations generally favored the creation of a farmers' party, estimated that at least two-thirds of their members endorsed independent political action. The paper's editor, an opponent of independent political action, conceded that a majority of all of the state's farmers, not just the ones responding to the survey, probably favored the creation of a farmers' party, but he feared that, without the unanimous support of the state's farmers, a farmers' party would be easily overwhelmed by urban and industrial interests.[31]

TABLE 2.3—Reponses to *Ohio Farmer* Poll concerning
Third-Party Participation

Farm Group	Favors third party	Opposes third party
Independent Farmers	862	794
National Alliance members	4,008	1,552
National Alliance (prorated)	14,000	4,500
Grange (voting as granges)	60	43
Grange (prorated)	2,857	2,048
Total (prorated)	**17,719**	**7,342**

Source: Ohio Farmer, May 28, 1891.

At the start of the Farmers' Union convention the state's most prominent farm leaders, including Ellis, Brigham, and Likins, announced their opposition to aiding the new party. The farmers' nonpartisan pressure had transformed an indifferent general assembly into a body sensitive to the demands of the farmers. Ellis, Brigham, and Likins feared that third-party action would jeopardize the farmers' newfound political strength by alienating the traditional parties. Moreover, the leaders feared that the endorsement of the People's party would destroy the unity that had pressured the general assembly into action. While all of the farmers could unite behind a nonpartisan platform, the endorsement of a third party would alienate a sizable number of farmers who would remain loyal to the traditional parties. Brigham listed the demands that the Farmers' Union had made in 1890, "the Rawlings tax bill, the Australian ballot bill, school books at cost, restriction of fees and salaries of public officers, reduction of railroad rates, and the election by the people of the food and dairy commissioner," and concluded, "every demand we made was granted except for one—the reduction of railroad passenger rates." Ellis agreed with that assessment: "Most of the legislation we asked for from this body [Ohio General Assembly] we got." Likins declared that although he had supported independent political action for over a decade he now felt that Ohio farmers were not ready for third-party action. At no time did opponents of third-party action criticize the ideals of the People's party or suggest that its complaints were not valid. Indeed, Likins, Brigham, and Ellis simply felt that the reforms demanded by the People's party could best be achieved through the traditional parties.

Not all Farmers' Union delegates opposed an alliance with the new party. These delegates portrayed the existing parties as too corrupt for the people to trust. John Seitz suggested that, even though the general assembly passed the farmers' program, the members of the legislature could not be trusted. He told the convention, "We want men who love the truth and will fight for the right." Another delegate declared, "The people want Jacksonian democracy and Lincoln republicanism, and can get it only through a new party." T. R. Smith, a state Grange official, told the convention, "It is a fact that under both political parties, in less than twenty-five years a thousand men have become millionaires on the basis of nothing, and a million men who were in good circumstances have become poor as church mice." In the end, much to the surprise of the state's major newspapers, the Farmers' Union refused to endorse the People's party—by the smallest of margins. Sixty-three delegates voted for independent political action, while sixty-four delegates voted against endorsing the new party. Despite the defeat, supporters of the People's party vowed to continue without the aid of the Farmers' Union and the state's farm organizations.[32]

The Ohio People's party's first convention opened August 5, 1891, in Springfield. Draped behind the stage were banners reading "Seven hundred millionaires: the result—9,000,000 mortgaged homes, 15,000 business failings per annum, 1,500,000 tramps and millions of paupers" and "The voice of the people is the voice of God. Then let the voice speak and the nation prosper." The convention attracted over 500 delegates. The *Dayton Journal* reported that the new party drew most heavily from the Republican ranks as more than 300 of the delegates were former Republicans. Between 125 and 150 delegates left the Democratic party to attend the convention, while 30 to 40 former Greenbackers and a scattering of former Prohibitionists made up the rest of the contingent.[33]

Convention chairman Hugh Cavanaugh, a longtime Knight of Labor from Cincinnati and Union Labor party activist, opened the meeting by declaring, "there appears to be no question paramount to the one who shall succeed the gentleman from Mansfield [John Sherman] in the United States Senate." For Cavanaugh, Sherman represented all that was wrong with the American political and economic system. Not only had Sherman turned a blind eye to the suffering of the "10,000,000 people in the United States who do not receive enough to eat in any day of the year," he was "contaminated by the descendent of the money changer and shylocks who were scorned out of the Temple and found lodgement on Wall Street." Cavanaugh insisted that, if the party produced an honest slate, the state's workers and farmers would flock to it. Other convention speakers stressed the European and Jewish domination of the nation's financial and political systems. Robert Schilling, the national secretary of the People's party and a former Cleveland labor leader, asserted that "the entire United States is controlled by British capital," while J. H. C. Cobb, an early favorite for the party's gubernatorial nomination, announced, "it is the Rothschilds . . . who control the legislation in this country."

The convention ratified a platform affirming the party's allegiance to the ideals enunciated at the Cincinnati conference. Additionally, the platform included a number of state demands: restriction of the ability of politicians to change city charters and the requirement that voters approve all charter changes, initiative and referendum, the "suppression of gambling in futures and all agricultural and mechanical products," the direct election of U.S. senators, enforcement of laws prohibiting the adulteration of food, free schoolbooks and compulsory education, the prohibition of child labor, the abolition of contracting out prison labor, the revocation of the charter of the Standard Oil Company, and the eight-hour day. In an effort to attract Prohibition party voters without alienating the party's more liberal elements, the platform demanded state control of the liquor trade. The backers of the plank, which was based on a proposal by Edward Bellamy, insisted that the removal of the "profit-motive" would make the problems associated with liquor evaporate.

The selection of a candidate for governor presented problems for the delegates. Given the party's emphasis on Ohio General Assembly races in order to defeat Sherman and its willingness to concede the governor's race to the major parties, the party had difficulty finding a top-flight candidate. The convention's first choice was Alva Agee, the young president of the Ohio Farmers' Alliance and Industrial Union (Southern Alliance). Agee declined the nomination fearing that voters would confuse his nomination with a Southern Alliance endorsement of the People's party. Newspapers speculated that A. J. Warner, a former Democratic congressman from Washington County and one of the nation's leading free silver advocates, would receive the nomination, but Warner wanted to maintain close ties to the state's Democratic party in hopes of convincing it to come out for the free coinage of silver. Warner was probably angling for a seat in the U.S. Senate. If the Populists held the balance of power in the general assembly, he would become the logical person for the Populists and the Democrats to rally behind. One alliance delegate proposed that the party nominate Prohibition party candidate John Ashenhurst as a way to bring fusion between the parties. Although the new party and the Prohibitionists agreed on almost every issue except the liquor question, delegates from Cleveland and Cincinnati threatened to walk out of the convention if Ashenhurst was nominated or if fusion was seriously contemplated. Other names circulated before the party chose veteran Greenback and former Union Labor party gubernatorial nominee John Seitz. The party saw Seitz, a farmer from Seneca County, as an experienced campaigner who could draw both the farm and the labor vote, yet no one considered him a top-flight candidate. The rest of the slate was composed of laborites and Bellamyites from urban areas.[34]

Fearing the new party would draw support from farmers, the Republicans, especially those associated with the Sherman-Hanna faction, denigrated the new party and asserted that it was "organized in the interests of the Democrats" as part of a "plot" to steal the election of 1892. The *Ohio State Journal* called the party a "grotesque political pygmy" composed of "fad planks." The *Athens Messenger* declared the new party to be "moved and managed and manipulated as completely by Democratic Bourbon politicians of the South as was ever a set of puppets" and suggested the "existence within the farmers alliance of a secret and independent body pledged to carry out their views by violence and bloodshed."[35]

The other faction of the Republican party tried to work with the Farmers' Alliance during the summer and fall of 1891. Led by former governor Joseph Foraker, these Republicans sought to capitalize on the unpopularity of John Sherman among farmers in order to place Foraker in Sherman's Senate seat. Populists and Alliance men throughout the nation blamed Sherman for the demonetization of silver in 1873—the famous "Crime of '73"—and considered him to be the main architect of the financial policies that had brought ruin to the American farmer. They accused Sherman of being at the center of a European conspiracy that sought to "enslave" the American people through the manipulation of the currency. The *Cincinnati Enquirer* noted that in county Republican conventions "the Foraker people are hand in glove with the Alliance people." Not only did Foraker believe that the Farmers' Alliance could help him win control of the state's GOP, he thought that the People's party would win some seats in the general assembly and that its support could be crucial to his election to the Senate. Despite working with the Farmers' Alliance, Foraker had little sympathy for the group. Privately he confessed that he had "little patience for the Simpson-Peffer crowd" and that he did not "like seeing Jerry Simpson and that class attacking Sherman because of his financial views." Foraker concluded that the triumph of Farmers' Alliance ideals "would be a calamity both to the country and the end of Republicanism."[36]

The Democrats, on the other hand, were more sympathetic to the new party's demands and hopeful that the People's party could cut into the Republican's farm support. Like the People's party, the Ohio Democrats had endorsed the free coinage of silver, a lower tariff, and most of the reforms demanded by the Ohio Farmers' Union. The Democrats and the People's party were so alike that the astute Sherman remarked, "The Democratic platform of Ohio had unfortunately committed that great party to the ideas of the new party calling itself the People's party."[37]

Not surprisingly, Democrats flooded county People's party conventions in hopes of persuading the new party to simply endorse local Democratic tickets. In Columbus's Franklin County so many Democrats attended the county nominating convention the organizers declared that those who refused to sign a pledge to support the ticket had to leave. Of the roughly one hundred people in the hall about two-thirds promptly exited. In Youngstown's Mahoning County the People's party's organizers announced that only those who support "the principles of the People's party and are in favor of independent political action" could participate in the party's proceedings.[38]

During the campaign, representatives of the Farmers' Alliance and Grange distanced their organizations from the People's party. The Farmers' Alliance issued a "manifesto" asserting its political independence from the Populists. Joshua Crawford, the Alliance's secretary, told farmers that the "Alliance is not a party organization. . . . It is not [working] in the interests of any party." Seth Ellis, grand master of the Ohio State Grange, declared, "The grange, the church or any other organization has no right to dictate how people use their ballots. . . . I don't belong to the People's Party, but belong to the people and did not have anything to do with the late convention."[39]

The Republicans nominated one of their rising stars, William McKinley, for governor. McKinley had been a congressman from Canton and chairman of the U.S. House Ways and Means Committee until the Democrats gerrymandered him out of office. A leading proponent of the protective tariff, McKinley kicked off the campaign by attacking the incumbent Democratic governor James Campbell and the Democrats on the tariff and currency questions. McKinley told the citizens of Ohio that the free coinage of silver at a ratio of sixteen to one would contract the currency as people would horde their gold dollars. Like the Populists, McKinley played on fears of British domination of the American economic system by portraying free traders as pawns of the British. He assured Ohioans that the tariff would aid in boasting wages at home and finding markets abroad.[40]

The Democrats nominated Campbell, a wealthy Butler County lawyer. Although the Ohio Democratic platform had declared for the free coinage of silver, important elements within the party—including U.S. senator Calvin Brice and those close to former president Grover Cleveland—opposed the plank. Fearing that a campaign emphasizing silver would damage party unity, Campbell and the Democrats sought to downplay the currency issue and centered their campaign on the tariff. The convention's resolutions declared that "we accept the issue tendered to us by the Republican party on the subject of the tariff . . . confident that the verdict of the people of Ohio will be recorded against the iniquitous policy of so-called protection."[41]

During the campaign, it was often difficult to differentiate the Populists from the Democrats. Not only did both parties endorse the free coinage of silver and a lower tariff, they employed similar rhetoric, using traditional producerist arguments and playing on the themes of monopoly and British domination of the American political system. During the campaign Columbus's Democratic mayor declared, "[W]e have a constitutional government corrupted by millionaires and politicians. We see legislators, judges and other officials using their places for private gain. We see capitalists and speculators bribing the lawmakers and lobbying for schemes to enrich themselves." He questioned, "what is there to hinder the growth and accumulation of wealth until the disposition between the insignificance of the common laborer and the gigantic power of the capitalist is still more monstrous?" Allen Thurman, a former U.S. senator who had received the party's 1888 vice-presidential nomination, played on these same fears. He attacked McKinley as the agent of "Intrenched monopoly" and the Republicans as assisting "England in her attempt to establish monometallism." Campbell, himself, accused the Republicans and their tariff policy of creating a government "of monopoly, by monopoly, and for monopoly." He also raised the specter of British domination by telling the citizens of Ohio that the tariff benefited a select group of "capitalists who live in England" and invested in protected American industries.[42]

People's party speakers tried unsuccessfully to shift the emphasis of the campaign away from the tariff and currency questions. William Farmer, the former head of Texas's Knights of Labor, told a Columbus crowd that the "tariff is not the leading issue of to-day in this country" and enumerated the reforms spelled out in the People's party platform. H. F. Barnes, the chairman of the Ohio People's party, declared, "it will matter very little whether we have free trade or protection, as the money power will control our industries and plunder the products under protection or free trade." Peffer informed a Cleveland crowd that, "The free coinage of silver would be but a drop in the bucket which eventually must be filled." The People's party's attempts to turn the campaign away from the tariff and silver did not work. The *National Labor Tribune* declared that "the issue, shorn of the red fire of rhetoric, is 'tariff'" and later insisted that "the Ohio election is regarded all over the country as a test of the protective policy as formulated in the McKinley act in Congress."[43]

Through their use of the press and party workers, the major parties were able to make the tariff and, to a lesser extent, the free coinage of silver the defining issues of the campaign and, thus, were able to marginalize the People's party. There was no effective difference between the People's party and the Democratic party on these two issues and no reason for workers or farmers to abandon the Democratic party for the People's party. Moreover, if a Republican was going to abandon the party over the tariff or the free coinage of silver, it made more sense to go to the party that stood the best chance of winning—the Democrats.

Compounding the inability of the People's party to shift the focus of the election away from tariff and currency was a lack of funds. The traditional parties used money to print campaign literature, pay speakers fees, provide travel money, as well as to pay newspaper editors for support and to buy votes. As Warren G. Harding, then a young newspaper editor, declared, "campaigning without funds [is] very hard sledding." At the Springfield convention, the Populists collected only about a hundred dollars for the fall campaign. Seitz and the other People's party candidates had to dip into their own pockets to finance speaking tours. At most campaign appearances, a hat was passed in order to pay for the speaker's food, lodging, and transportation. The existing parties, on the other hand, had tremendous financial resources. Republican leaders, including Hanna, Sherman, and Foraker, spent tens of thousands of dollars apiece in hopes of securing the nominations of allies and getting out the vote in the general election. The Democrats, led by Campbell and Brice, also distributed tens of thousands of dollars to party activists.[44]

The election of 1891 was a disappointment for the Ohio People's party. Not only did the party fail to elect a single member to the general assembly, Seitz fell far short of gaining the 75,000–100,000 votes expected. In the end Seitz received 23,472 votes or 2.9 percent of the 795,629 votes cast. The big winners were Republicans McKinley and Sherman. In defeating Campbell by 21,511 votes, McKinley kept his political career alive. By recapturing the general assembly, the Republicans controlled the election of Ohio's next senator and, amid charges of vote buying, elected Sherman over Foraker.[45]

The Populists polled best in the predominately agricultural counties of the western and northern parts of the state. In these counties, the party won 3.4 percent of the vote. In Mercer and Defiance Counties, heavily agricultural counties along the Indiana border, the Populists won close to 15 percent of the vote. In the state's urban counties the People's party polled 2.9 percent of the vote with the highest totals in Akron's Summit County (7.1%), Cincinnati's Hamilton County (4.3%), Cleveland's Cuyahoga County (3.5%). In Toledo's Lucas County and Dayton's Montgomery County, the party polled less than 1 percent of the vote. The People's party vote was the lowest (1.7%) in the Appalachian counties of the southern and eastern part of the state. These counties were dotted with small farms, coal mines, mills, and factories.

Adding insult to the poor results was the fact that the Prohibition party, whose platform mirrored the People's party platform except on the liquor question, outpolled the People's party in the non-urban counties. The Prohibition candidate for governor, John Ashenhurst, did nearly as well as the Populist candidate, polling 20,200 votes (2.5%) to Seitz's 23,472 (2.9%). The Prohibition party received 2.9 percent of the vote in the predominately agricultural counties, 3.1 percent in the Appalachian counties, and 1.6 percent in the urban counties.[46]

The failure of the People's party to elect a single member of the Ohio General Assembly only served to reinforce the decision of the Ohio farm organizations to forgo participation in the People's party. The passage of the Rawlings Bill in the spring of 1891 produced a backlash. Many of the state's manufacturers, urban politicians, and trade unionists vowed to reverse the legislation, and Ohio farmers were looking for allies for the coming fight. With no voice in the general assembly, the People's party made a poor ally for the farmers. The simple fact is that third-party politics was the refuge for those with nothing to lose, and, with the general assembly's passage of most of the Farmers' Union demands, the state's farmers thought they had something to lose.

Not surprisingly, in the winter of 1891–1892 the Ohio State Grange and both alliances refused to revisit the question of political participation with the Populists. A Farmers' Alliance official told the state convention, farmers "must stay out of party politics" and vote for the best candidates regardless of partisan affiliation, while one of the state's Southern Alliance officials insisted that "in no sense can the order be partisan or nominate a party ticket." The Ohio State Grange's lobbying arm, the executive committee, told farmers to ignore the People's party, declaring that "we can generally accomplish our purposes best by acting within the lines of the two great parties." Unlike a year earlier, the farm organizations did not bother to threaten third-party action if the two major parties proved unreceptive to the farmers' demands.[47]

While the Ohio Constitution called for biennial sessions of the general assembly, meeting in the winter of odd numbered years, legislators met in a special session in the winter of 1892 to address a number of outstanding issues. The holding of a special session angered farm leaders. Manufacturers, bankers, and trade unionists saw the session as an opportunity to repeal the Rawlings Act, and urban legislators pushed the issue to the top of the legislative agenda. The state's manufacturers claimed that by taxing the inventories of factories the Rawlings Act was putting the state at a competitive disadvantage with its neighbors and driving manufacturers from the state. Many of the state's trade unions joined the fight to repeal the Rawlings Act. Not only did the unions fear the loss of jobs, but echoing the arguments of Henry George they argued that taxing production and improvements to land was fundamentally wrong. By taxing inventories, the trade unionists claimed, the state was in essence taxing production rather than encouraging it.

In the legislative battle over the repeal of the Rawlings Act, the anti-repeal forces marshaled their resources and turned back their opponents early in the session by winning a vote to send the bill to the agricultural committee rather than the manufacturers and commerce committee. The agricultural committee, dominated by the Farmers' Independent Caucus, killed the measure by refusing to allow it to come to a vote. Like the 1891 battle to pass the Rawlings Act, the contest to repeal the measure did not break down along partisan lines. Urban legislators, regardless of party, generally favored the repeal while rural legislators of both parties fought any attempt to weaken the Rawlings Act. In spite of losing both the 1891 and 1892 battles, those hoping to repeal the Rawlings Act promised to bring the issue up in 1893 when the legislature elected in 1891 began its session. The farmers' success during the 1892 special session functioned much like it had in 1891—to convince the farm organizations that urban legislators, rather than the traditional parties, were the real roadblocks to reform.[48]

The miserable showing of Seitz and other Populist candidates in the 1891 election, as well as the party's failure to secure the support of farm organizations, demoralized the state's People's party. The party's 1892 convention proved to be a series of frustrations. While the 1891 convention had attracted close to five hundred delegates, just over two hundred delegates attended the 1892 convention, which was held in Massillon, the hometown of one of the party's few wealthy supporters, Jacob S. Coxey. On the eve of the convention, the party held a mass meeting with a series of speakers and musical entertainers. Although the party's officials made a point of inviting the city's industrial workers to attend the festivities, only about one dozen attended.[49]

Convention delegates spent most of their time discussing the wisdom of merging with the state's Democratic party. After all, a number of delegates noted, there were few differences in the two parties' platforms, and the combined totals of the Populists and Democrats in 1891 would have been enough to defeat McKinley and the Republicans. A delegate from Medina County formally proposed that the Democrats and Populists merge, with the People's party naming one-third of the Democrats' presidential electors in the upcoming elections. In the end, two reasons convinced the Populists not to pursue fusion with the Democrats. First, the Populists felt that the Democratic party, led by Calvin Brice in Ohio and Grover Cleveland, the probable nominee for president, was too corrupt or beholden to financial interests. Second, and perhaps most important, the Populists doubted that the Democratic party would be willing to fuse on terms favorable to the Populists.

During the convention, the delegates heaped as much criticism on the state's farm leaders as they did on Wall Street manipulators, British bankers, and the two main parties. Convention speakers insisted that the party would prosper if it had the support of the state's farm organizations. The delegates believed that a majority of the state's farmers would have supported the People's party in 1891 had it not been for the opposition of the "so-called" leaders of the Ohio State Grange, Farmers' Alliance, and Farmers' Union. The party attached to its platform a resolution denouncing Seth Ellis, W. H. Likins, and John Brigham for betraying the state's farmers by steering their organizations away from the People's party.

The People's party had trouble securing a nominee for the top spot of the state ballot, secretary of state. Like the year before, none of the more notable Populists allowed their names to be considered by the convention. In the end, the convention prevailed on Solon C. Thayer, a Stark County milk dealer, to run. As a condition of his nomination, Thayer insisted that the party reimburse him for the time that he was away from his job while campaigning. The near-destitute party agreed to pay Thayer two dollars a day plus expenses during the campaign. Although other Ohio politicians, including William McKinley and James Campbell, received secret payments from their parties during campaigns, the public disclosure of this financial relationship opened the People's party to the ridicule of the partisan press. The rest of the ticket was made up of relative unknowns. As one newspaper noted, the Populists' ticket was "as crisp and new as it is possible for a Treasury note to be."[50]

The 1892 election did not go well for Thayer, presidential nominee James B. Weaver, or the others on the Populist slate in Ohio. At the county and township levels the Ohio People's party did not elect a single candidate, and Weaver collected only 14,850 votes. On the state level, the percentage of voters casting their ballots for the Populists declined 41 percent from the previous year (from 2.9 to 1.7%). The steepest decline was in the state's urban counties where the percentage of Populist voters was cut almost in half (from 2.9 to 1.5%). In the predominately agricultural counties the Populists received just under 2 percent of the vote as opposed to 3.4 percent a year earlier. In the Appalachian counties, the decline was less precipitous from 1.7 percent to 1.5 percent.

Most discouraging for the Ohio People's party was the fact that the election stripped the party of its third-party status as it finished fourth behind the two major parties and the Prohibition party. John Bidwell, the Prohibitionist candidate for president, outpolled Weaver, 26,012 votes (3.1%) to 14,850 (1.7%). While the Prohibitionists were only able to attract 1.9 percent of the vote in urban counties, the party collected 3.7 percent of the vote in the Appalachian counties and 3.4 percent of the vote in the predominately agricultural counties. Rather than the People's party, agrarian third-party activists increasingly saw the Prohibition party, with its anti-urban message, as the most attractive vehicle through which to voice their discontentment.

The election of 1892 did nothing to convince the state's farm organizations they had made a mistake by refusing to work with the People's party. The poor showing suggested that whatever support the party had among the state's farmers was rapidly fading, and the party's lack of influence in the general assembly made it a poor ally. Reflecting the growing belief that urban legislators rather than the traditional parties were the main impediments to reform, the Ohio State Grange and the Farmers' Alliance continued to call for farmers to exercise nonpartisan political action. T. R. Smith, the grand master of the state grange and a former People's party supporter, told farmers that a farmers' party was unnecessary as long as farmers voted for the best candidate regardless of party affiliation. He declared, "our partisan shackles must be broken, or set so loosely around our shoulders that we are not bound to vote for the devil if he should be nominated by our party." The secretary of the Ohio Farmers' Alliance reported that at the organization's annual meeting "no time [was] wasted in discussing party questions" and that the organization was placing "justice" over "party."[51]

The state's farmers and their organizations approached the January 1893 opening of a new legislative session with both hope and fear. They were hopeful because they considered the legislators to be generally sympathetic to the farmers' cause. T. R. Smith insisted that the Ohio General Assembly has "never before paid such deference to our [the farmers'] expressed will as now," while the *Ohio Farmer* praised the state legislature "as willing to look after the interests of the farmers." But the farm leaders were also apprehensive. The state's manufacturers and urban legislators promised to launch a bid to repeal the Rawlings Act, the cornerstone of the farmers' legislative triumph in 1891.[52]

The Ohio General Assembly did not disappoint the farmers in the winter of 1893. Farmers serving in the legislature reorganized the Farmers' Independent Caucus and announced their intentions to pass legislation favored by the state's farm organizations. Not only did the much anticipated attempt to repeal the Rawlings Act fizzle, but the legislature created a special commission to study the state's tax code and make recommendations to equalize the burden. The general assembly also considered the Nichols Bill to further reform the state's tax code. This bill sought to increase the revenue collected from gas companies, electric utilities, telegraphs, oil pipelines, street railway systems, and transfer companies by having the value of the franchise included in any assessments. While the *Ohio Farmer* called passage of the bill "the most important matter that has come up [before the legislature] or will come up this winter," urban politicians, especially Joseph Foraker and Marcus Hanna, worked feverishly to prevent passage. The pressure of the farmers proved to be too much as the general assembly passed an amended version of the Nichols Bill. In deference to Hanna, who owned a street railway in Cleveland, and Foraker, who served as general counsel for Cincinnati's main streetcar company, the general assembly excluded street railways from the bill.[53]

During the winter of 1893, the Ohio General Assembly continued to take actions demanded by the state's farmers. The legislature passed a constitutional amendment altering the makeup of the general assembly to increase the political power of rural districts at the expense of urban areas. The amendment provided that each of the state's eighty-eight counties would have a representative in the lower chamber regardless of population. As the number of legislators in the House of Representatives would remain the same, the measure would entail the loss of five legislators from urban counties and the addition of five rural legislators. The *Ohio Farmer* boasted that the measure would break the "grip of the political boss" and cleanse the state's political machinery. As changes to the state constitution needed to be ratified by the voters, the measure was sent to the state's electorate where it was defeated. Yet, the amendment's initial passage by the general assembly signaled to the state's farmers that the legislature was on their side.[54]

Despite minor quibbles, the *Ohio Farmer* praised the general assembly for enacting "many good laws." The paper reflected the growing anti-urban sentiments of many farm leaders when it declared, "as great a percent of moral level-headed men as any preceding legislature, and a larger number of farmers, and it is a notable fact that not many of the doubtful measures considered by this assembly originated with the members outside of the cities. Observation has led us to believe that a greater number of country members in the legislature would be to the advantage of the general public."

At the conclusion of the session, the *Ohio Farmer* insisted that there were too many good legislators to list.[55]

While the Ohio General Assembly was passing legislation demanded by the state's farm organizations in the winter and spring of 1893, the People's party's fortunes continued to descend. The January 1893 meeting of the party's state executive committee was a comedy of errors. First, the state committee forgot to inform national People's party chairman Herman Taubeneck of a change in the meeting's date. Taubeneck arrived on the original date, missing the meeting. Second, most of the meeting's time was devoted to a petty dispute between state party chairman H. F. Barnes and the executive board over $28.25. Barnes maintained he was entitled to the money as compensation for expenses, while the board insisted that the money should be placed in the party's treasury. Although the amount appeared insignificant, the party only had slightly more than ten dollars in its coffers and more than thirty-six dollars in bills waiting to be paid. Executive committee meeting members collected about fifty dollars amongst themselves, which they used to pay off the outstanding bills and leave the party with a balance of about $20.00.[56]

That spring, the dispute between Barnes and the state's executive committee reached a climax. Barnes resigned over the issue and refused to give the party's records to the executive committee. The records contained the only list of the names and addresses of county People's party chairmen and secretaries as well as local activists. Without this list, the party's organization would become useless. To reassemble these records, the new chairman of the executive committee, George Flummerfelt, used the pages of the *Plow and Hammer* to ask county parties to "report the name and address of the chairman and secretary of the county committee as soon as they see this letter." Flummerfelt ended the letter by invoking the memory of the Revolution, "The men of '76 had their Benedict Arnold and we have ours, and his action has done more harm to the movement in Ohio, but our cause is just and will prevail, as did that of our forefathers."[57]

Then, just when the *Plow and Hammer* was about to pronounce it "dead," the Ohio People's party twitched back to life. But it did so not as a vehicle of agrarian protest but of urban labor reform. Never again would the Ohio People's party be associated with farmers.

3
Gas and Sewer Populism
The People's Party in Cleveland

ON SATURDAY, JUNE 25, 1892, thousands of citizens of Cleveland vented their growing frustrations with the concentration of economic power on the city's most visible monopolies—the streetcar lines. Trouble had been brewing for most of the year. Attempts in the state legislature to extend the terms of the franchises by ninety-nine years, anger over fare increases and service problems, and rumors of municipal corruption had set many Clevelanders against the lines.[1] But it was the firing of union activists and the subsequent strikes against two lines—the Newburgh and Broadway line and the East Cleveland line—that produced a series of mass protests on a scale the city had never before witnessed. The largest confrontation began when a streetcar from the East Cleveland line passed by Public Square in the middle downtown. There a group of four to five hundred men set upon the car, throwing mud and debris at the driver and dislodging the car from the rails. Soon the crowd swelled to over three thousand and began molesting the Newburgh and East Cleveland cars that came through Public Square, derailing most of them and sending the scab drivers fleeing for their lives. The crowd, which according to newspaper reports did not contain any of the striking drivers or conductors, was aided in its effort by the drivers of streetcars on other lines that shared the tracks. These drivers stopped in front of cars from the striking lines, making it less dangerous to remove the cars from the rails. The confrontations only came to an end when the operators of the striking lines shut down and Mayor William G. Rose led a battalion of police onto Public Square.[2]

That night, on Public Square, strike supporters held the largest mass rally in the city's history. The conservative *Cleveland Leader* estimated the crowd at ten thousand, the *Plain Dealer* thought that more than fifteen thousand people were in attendance, but others put the number as high as twenty-five thousand, almost 10 percent of the city's total population. Angered at the violent nature of the protests earlier that afternoon, rally organizers—all leading trade unionists associated with the People's party— sought to channel the frustration of the population into political reform. Chaired by the president of Iron Molders Local 218, Peter Witt, the meeting heard from a who's who of the city's leading labor-Populists—Edmund Vail, Robert Bandlow, David Rankin—before passing a resolution denouncing the corporations holding municipal franchises and calling for municipal ownership of the streetcar lines and all other utilities: "[S]uch corporations cannot be depended upon either to keep their faith with their men or their obligations to the public. . . . we hereby demand that our city administration proceed at once to forfeit the franchise of said corporations and operate the same as a branch of the public service."[3]

The rally on Public Square set in motion the alliance between Cleveland's labor movement and the People's party. During the next round of municipal elections, Cleveland's Central Labor Union (CLU) and the Populists would be working hand in hand in the attempt to take control of the city's government. Initially built around demands for the public ownership of utilities, the alliance would come to embrace a wider set of reforms embracing changes at all levels of the federal system. Cleveland's labor–Populist alliance, like others throughout the state, would come apart after the fusion of 1896, with trade unionists and other reformers splitting over support for William Jennings Bryan. But the demand for public ownership of utilities would animate labor's involvement in Cleveland politics well into the Progressive era.

Strikes like the ones on the Newburgh and East Cleveland lines would be important catalysts in the creation of labor–Populist alliances in Ohio. Each of Ohio's major urban labor federations and the state's coal miners joined with the People's party only after a major work stoppage or series of labor confrontations. Strikes whipped up emotion, mobilized people for action, and brought out into the open competing visions of employment relations. Perhaps just as important, the strikes forced elected officials— both Republicans such as Mayor Rose and Governor William McKinley and Democrats such as President Grover Cleveland—to choose sides. Invariably in early and mid 1890s Ohio, these politicians lined up against the labor unions. Feeling betrayed by the major parties, trade union leaders looked to the People's party and its anti-corporate platform for salvation.

The roots of the People's party in Cleveland predate the establishment of the national People's party at the May 1891 Cincinnati convention. The founders of the Cleveland-area People's party had been involved in earlier third-party efforts, most notably the Union Labor party and the Edward Bellamy–inspired Nationalist party. But these parties had all but disappeared from Cleveland by 1890. Union Labor party candidates had garnered fewer than three hundred votes in the late 1880s, and the Nationalists even fewer in 1890. The successes of Farmers' Alliance candidates on the Great Plains in the fall of 1890, though, excited Cleveland-area reformers, giving them renewed energy. In February 1891, Wade Shurtleff, the leader of the local Nationalists and an officer in both Knights of Labor District Assembly 47 and the local musicians' union, announced the formation of a new party. Shurtleff told the city's trade unionists, Knights of Labor, and reform clubs that they "could most rapidly advance the interests of labor by following the example set by the Farmers' Alliance and other labor organizations of Kansas and voting unitedly against both the old corrupt political rings." He called on the organizations to send delegates to a convention to select candidates for the upcoming municipal election.[4]

Although the Nationalist party issued the call, the city's leading Democratic newspaper, the *Plain Dealer*, insisted that the Franklin Club was the real force behind the movement. Organized by followers of Henry George and Edward Bellamy and modeled after Benjamin Franklin's Junto society, the Franklin Club stood at the center of Cleveland's labor and municipal reform movement and functioned as a free forum for the exchange of progressive ideas. The club had the sort of cross-class leadership that would characterize the city's People's party. Although the Franklin Club had no official membership roll or elected officers, the informal leadership included physicians L. B. Tuckerman and C. E. Woodbridge and factory owner Tom Fitzsimmons. But most of the leaders came from the ranks of labor, among them David Rankin, Peter Witt, Edmund Vail, Max Hayes, and Robert Bandlow. Like most of Cleveland's labor leaders, these men were dual unionists, maintaining ties to both the Knights of Labor and the craft unions. According to Hayes, the Franklin Club served as a "post graduate course" for the leaders of the city's labor movement, many of whom had little formal schooling. There they discussed public events, debated the ideas of Karl Marx, Daniel DeLeon, Bellamy, George, and other progressive thinkers, and honed their public speaking and debating skills.[5]

The new party's first meeting in Cleveland was a disappointment. Only 108 delegates representing twenty-two of the city's labor organizations and reform clubs attended. Those assembled condemned the enactment of "class legislation" and denounced the Democratic and Republican parties as "agents of the classes." There was "no hope of wresting these political machines from the plutocrats," they insisted. The only answer was for "the wealth-producing classes of Cleveland [to] strike unitedly at the ballot box as the farmers of Kansas have." The convention refused to take any concrete action such as creating a party structure or selecting a ticket for the spring's municipal elections, hoping that another meeting in March would be able to generate "more enthusiasm."[6]

Attendance and enthusiasm at the March meeting was not much better. Nonetheless, the party selected a ticket, ratified a platform, and took the name the Citizens' party. It nominated Henry C. Wolf, a jeweler, for mayor. The rest of the slate was selected in a pattern that the People's party would follow in subsequent elections. Citywide slots went to professionals and businessmen associated with the Franklin Club. This was because laborites would have had difficulty securing the necessary bond to serve as treasurer or auditor and did not have the legal training necessary to serve in a judicial post. Trade unionists received nominations for nearly every city council slot, which were selected by wards. The platform focused on the corruption of the city's government by contractors and public utilities. It called for municipal ownership of the street railways and other utilities (an action that required the approval of the Ohio General Assembly), the abolition of the contracting system for public works, and the creation of a civil service system that would have experts rather than political appointees in charge of running city departments.[7]

The Cleveland Central Labor Union's response to the new Citizens' party was cautious. The CLU clearly sympathized with the aims of the new party, but the labor federation remained committed to its policy of nonpartisanship. When Franklin Club members asked the trade unionists to join the third-party movement, the CLU's directors tabled the motion, never bringing it up for consideration. In the week following the Citizens' party's formation, the lead editorial in the CLU's newspaper, the *Cleveland Citizen*—edited by Max Hayes of the Franklin Club who had participated in the formation of the Citizens' party—sang the praises of the American Federation of Labor's renunciation of partisan politics: "Instead of making the organization a political one and demanding twenty reforms at once, the Federation . . . attends purely to trades interest. A great deal of its prestige is based upon the fact that it does not advise workingmen how to vote or for whom, and therefore its course is conservative, safe, and substantial." The same edition reprinted excerpts of a recent speech by AFL president Samuel Gompers warning against all types of partisan activity under the headline "Wise Words": "As for your political parties, I say a plague on all of them. . . . We are looking to the welfare of people, not to the welfare of parties."[8]

Despite their commitment to nonpartisanship, the leaders of the CLU supported the Citizens' party and its platform. Not only were many of the Citizens' party leaders, including Witt, Bandlow, and Hayes, active in the CLU, but the central body had close ties to the Franklin Club. The new party's platform mirrored, almost to the letter, the CLU's municipal platform, and in an editorial just after the Citizens' party's first organizational meeting, the *Citizen* praised the growing third-party movement among farmers on the Plains and called for urban workers to follow suit. Praising the Farmers' Alliance's "spirit of reform, which is necessary to make this a government of the people," the *Citizen* continued:

> Laugh if you like at the man with the hayseed in his hair, but he sees the light. He realizes that industrial reform must come through political action, and that every question affecting labor is necessarily a political question. It took the farmer many years to find this out, but he now understands it and is hunting for b'ar. . . .
>
> The farmer is in the saddle, and only awaits the word to storm the citadel of Wrong and Oppression! Where is the tradesman?

Throughout the municipal campaign, the *Citizen* ran articles touting the reforms demanded in both the CLU platform and the Citizens' party platform. Thus, while the CLU was reluctant to have any organizational ties to the Citizens' party, it urged the city's workers to embrace the party's ideals and the ideals that would inform the founding of the People's party.[9]

The campaign pitted the Citizens' party mayoral candidate Wolf against two veteran Cleveland politicians. The Republicans nominated William G. Rose who had served a two-year term as mayor beginning in 1877. The Democrats ran John Farley, who had sat on the city council in the 1870s and served as director of public works during much of the 1880s. Neither Rose nor Farley had much support in the labor community. When local coopers struck the city's largest corporation, John D. Rockefeller's Standard Oil Company, to protest a 20 percent reduction in wages in 1877, Rose had ordered the police to break up the rallies of strikers and mobilized the police force to protect Rockefeller's interests. Since that time, Rose had maintained close ties to the Rockefellers and the city's other leading capitalists. Reformer Frederic C. Howe would later call "Honest John" Farley "a big, raw-boned, profane Irishman of substantial wealth." He had made his money as a contractor, using his position as director of public works to win large contracts from those seeking municipal franchises or other government projects.[10]

The Republicans took the challenge of the Citizens' party seriously, thinking the new party might hold the balance of power or take enough votes from one of the candidates to determine the outcome of the race. In order to ensure that the Citizens' slate drew more from the Democrats, the Republicans distributed fake "Citizens' Committee" literature calling on the trade unionists to cast their ballots for Rose. It turned out that Rose had little to fear from either the Citizens' party or the Democratic challenger as the Republican candidate collected over 53 percent of the vote. The Citizens' party candidate, Henry Wolf, won only 314 of the over 34,000 votes cast, hardly an auspicious start for the new party.[11] Shortly after the April municipal election, representatives of the farmers' alliances, labor groups, and reformers met in Cincinnati to form the People's party. Cleveland's Citizens' party was well represented at the meeting, sending a delegation of twenty-five, and the municipal party transformed itself into the local arm of the People's party.[12]

The *Citizen*'s coverage of the Cincinnati convention and emerging Populist movement suggests that both the paper and the CLU were trying to work out their relationship to the new political movement. The leaders of the CLU shared the Populist's critique of American economic life. In spring 1891 the *Citizen* reprinted both the Hazard and Buell circulars, which were widely circulated in Populist circles to provide "proof" that British capitalists and Wall Street bankers were conspiring to deprive American producers of the wealth they had created. The Hazard circular purported to be a private communication written by an agent of "English capitalists" during the Civil War. It detailed a plan to deprive American labor of economic freedom:

> Slavery is likely to be abolished by the war power, and chattel slavery destroyed. This, I and my European friends are in favor of, for slavery is but the owning of labor, and carries with it the care of the laborer; while the European plan, led on by England, is capital control of labor by controlling wages. This can be done by controlling the money. The great debt that capitalists will see to it is made out of the war, must be used as a measure to control the volume of money. To accomplish this the bonds must be used as a banking basis. We are now waiting to get the secretary of the treasury to make his recommendation to Congress. It will not do to allow the greenback, as it is called, to circulate as money for any length of time, for we cannot control that.

Populists cited the Buell circular to prove that current banking laws were part of a conspiracy to deny Americans access to money and opportunity. Purportedly written by James Buell, secretary of the National Bankers Association, the circular warned bankers, "To repeal the law creating national banks, or restore to circulation the government issue of money, will be to provide the people with money and will therefore effect your individual profits as bankers and lenders." Although the Hazard and Buell circulars have since been proved fraudulent, they proved to the leaders of the CLU that, "when brave men were fighting gallantly on the field to save the union, the bankers of this country were conspiring to rivet upon the government a banking system that would bring millions of dollars into their coffers directly and give them a hold upon the government for a half a century."[13]

Despite the *Citizen*'s embrace of much of the Populist critique of American economic life, the paper did not support all of the Populist's remedies. It argued that both the free and unlimited coinage of silver at sixteen to one and the sub-treasury plan amounted to class legislation. An editorial in the *Citizen* recognized the "fact that the currency of this country is insufficient for its business exigencies" but added that "it is hard to disguise what is apparent to all—that the clamor for unlimited silver coinage comes from the men who own the silver mines. Mine owners are so disinterested in that matter that they are willing to accept one dollar for eighty cents worth of silver." Moreover, the paper concluded, the free coinage of silver "would not increase the circulating medium to the volume needed to relieve the financial distress of the country." Rather than advocating the use of silver or any other metallic currency, the *Citizen* called for "Uncle Sam to issue his own currency, repudiate the national debt, and dethrone the national banking system." Greenbacks would give the people through their elected representatives control over the nation's financial system, while the free and unlimited coinage of silver would give silver mine owners the ability to manipulate the nation's currency.[14]

The *Citizen* considered the sub-treasury plan to be both impractical and solely for the benefit of one segment of the nation's producers. The paper argued that if the sub-treasury system were to become law, "we do not see how the government could refuse to issue certificates for warehoused lumber, clothing, iron, steel, copper, coal, furnishings, dry goods, hardware or, in fact, any commodity of value." Later, the *Citizen* suggested, "to denounce class measures in one breath and advocate the Sub-treasury plan in the next is a good example of the devil rebuking sin."[15]

In addition to greenbacks, the leaders of the CLU saw Henry George's single tax as the way to rid the nation of "wage slavery" and to preserve essential American rights. Generally opposed by farmers (who feared higher taxes) and ignored by the Populists, the single tax promised to assess all land at a uniform rate regardless of improvements. By taxing improvements on a property, George insisted, states and localities were taxing labor and discouraging production. A uniform tax rate, single-tax advocates argued, would end land ownership for speculative purposes by making such practices financially impractical. This in turn would make land available to those willing to put it to productive use, giving opportunity to the urban unemployed and stopping the migration of rural youth to the city. As the *Citizen* insisted:

> The two factors land and labor create all wealth. . . . If a man is debarred from taking advantage of either the primary two elements, he cannot produce wealth; and to that extent he is barred from life, liberty and the pursuit of happiness. . . . Everyman is made a slave who is forbidden to apply his energies to the earth and its products. . . . Slavery may be imposed in two ways, either by taking possession of the laborer's person, or by taking possession of the land and its products.[16]

Despite the CLU's embrace of nonpartisan political action and its opposition to key portions of the Populist platform, local conflicts pushed the Cleveland labor movement into an alliance with the party. Business interests, especially public contractors and utility owners, dominated the city's government. Not surprisingly, the city's two most influential political figures were utility owners. Republican Marcus Alonzo Hanna controlled the city's second-largest streetcar line, the Little Consolidated, while Democratic congressman Tom Loftin Johnson controlled the largest, the Big Consolidated. Neither man was above using his political influence to help his business interests. As Hanna's biographer, Herbert Croly, wrote, "The municipal government of Cleveland . . . was as corrupt as that of the average American municipality. The council, to whom was entrusted the grant of franchises, was composed of petty local politicians whose votes had to be secured by some kind of influence. . . . A street railway company that applied for and needed a particular franchise had to purchase this influence or else go out of business." Johnson characterized Cleveland's government in similar terms: "The city government belonged to the business interests generally, but as the public utility companies had more use for it than other kinds of business enterprise had, they paid the most attention to it. They nominated and elected the councilmen and of course the councilmen represented them instead of the community."[17]

The tension between the city's labor community and Cleveland utilities came to a head in the late spring and summer of 1892. In mid May, the drivers and conductors of the East Cleveland Street Railway Company walked off the job after the company fired three employees for membership in the local streetcar workers' union, a Knights of Labor Assembly that belonged to the CLU. In addition to the reinstatement of the fired men, the strikers demanded a ten-hour workday and an increase in wages to twenty cents an hour. After only six hours, the company agreed to rehire the dismissed workers, reduce the workday to ten hours, and increase wages to eighteen cents an hour for drivers and nineteen cents for conductors. Peace between the company and its workers did not last long, however. Less than a week later, the company began hiring "regular extras" at twelve and a half cents an hour, instituting a two-tiered wage structure that increased tensions on the line.[18]

The agreement between the East Cleveland Street Railway Company and the streetcar workers' union had repercussions for the city's other street railway lines. On these lines, drivers and conductors were already unhappy. Having to work from twelve to sixteen hours a day at about fifteen cents per hour, drivers and conductors on the other lines demanded to be brought up the East Cleveland standard. When other companies refused to increase wages and shorten hours, the streetcar employees joined the local union in droves. So many wanted to enroll, the *Citizen* reported, "that it is simply impossible to handle them at one meeting place."[19]

Tensions boiled over on June 20, 1892, when the employees of the Broadway and Newburgh line walked off the job to protest the firing of three union leaders for minor infractions of company rules. Insisting that the streetcar line was seeking to break the union, the strikers demanded the same wages and hours as the East Cleveland workers, the rehiring of the dismissed workers, and recognition of the local. At the beginning of the walkout, the strikers insisted that the strike would be peaceful. As one of the leaders declared, "What we need is unity. To acquire unity we need the sympathy of the people and to win that we must be gentlemen."[20]

The strikers' hope for peace, though, was not realized. The company hired Pinkerton detectives, brought in replacement drivers and conductors from Buffalo, and secured an injunction enjoining the strikers from interfering with the operation of the line. On the third day of the strike, the company tried to resume operations. When the first car left the barn, strikers and onlookers stopped the car, disconnected the horses, turned the car around, and pushed it back into the barn. The strikers and their allies threatened the replacement driver, who promptly ran away. After a few more tries ended with similar results, the company ceased operations for the day. The victory was short-lived, however, as the police arrested fifteen strikers for violating the injunction, and a local judge levied fines of between one hundred and two hundred dollars apiece.

The drivers and conductors of the East Cleveland line joined the walkout, hoping to force the company to live up to its earlier agreement and wanting to show their sympathy for the Newburgh men. The East Cleveland line then also hired replacement workers and secured a judicial order enjoining the strikers from interfering with the operation of the line. Violence broke out on June 24 when the company began running cars with replacement drivers. The first car out of the barn was loaded with police intent on preventing a disruption of the line, but subsequent cars left the barn without such protection. The strikers ran buggies ahead of the unprotected cars to alert sympathizers and to warn off potential riders. Along the route, residents rushed from their homes and businesses to heckle the driver and the police. Crowds formed at every major intersection, and many threw rocks and bottles at the cars. The police responded in kind. One account summed the day up in simple terms: "Women threw stones [at the cars], heads were broken by police, and several of the rioters were arrested."[21] The next day, the trouble continued with most of the action taking place on Public Square.

The CLU organized a mass meeting on Public Square to voice support for the strikers and to protest the actions of the police on the night of June 25. The *Citizen* called the rally "the largest demonstration of its kind known in the history of this city."[22] Populist leaders, including Witt, Dr. C. E. Woodbridge, Robert Bandlow, Edmund Vail, and David Rankin, took center stage and dominated the proceedings. The speakers saw the strike as just one of the symptoms of a larger malady confronting the nation—the concentration of capital and the rise of the wage system. They called on the residents of Cleveland to rise up to confront these threats. E. B. Bennett, the head of the local carpenters, reminded the crowd that "in 1861 thousands of brave men went to the front to save the country" and that now they should be willing to do the same. "This was the land of the free and the home of the brave," he continued, "but it is now the land of the rich and the home of the slave."[23]

Rather than setting up boycotts of the street railway lines or contributing to the strikers' defense fund, the speakers called for a political solution. Arguing that the street railway companies oppressed their workers and threatened the well-being of the community, the meeting passed a resolution demanding that the "city administration proceed at once to forfeit the franchises of said corporations [the street railways] and to operate the same as a branch of the public service." In editorials, the *Citizen* agreed, declaring that only the municipal ownership of the street railways would ensure that the street railway workers were accorded their rights as workers and citizens.[24]

At the public rally, the organizers announced another meeting on Public Square three days later if the strikes were not settled. When the CLU leaders applied for a permit for the second rally, Mayor Rose refused, claiming that he feared a violent confrontation. Insisting that such fears were unfounded, the CLU accused Rose of working with the city's capitalists to deprive the strikers of their rights to speech and assembly and insisted that in any conflict between American liberty and the interests of the streetcar companies that liberty should prevail.

The Franklin Club conducted the second rally on Public Square despite Rose's refusal to grant the permit. It is not clear if the Franklin Club conducted the rally in order to shield the CLU and the labor organizations from the legal repercussions of holding the rally without a permit or if the Franklin Club sought to sponsor the meeting hoping to attract workers to the People's party. What is clear, though, is that Cleveland's Populists worked closely with the CLU during the strike. As Peter Witt later declared, "The strongest supporters of the strikers in this contest were the populists."[25]

Two days after the second public rally, the street railway workers settled their strikes. The streetcar lines reluctantly agreed to wage increases, the ten-hour day, and the reinstatement of the dismissed workers, but they refused to grant a closed shop or even recognize the union. This refusal troubled Cleveland's labor leaders, who feared that the relationships between the streetcar lines and the workers would continue to be marked by hostility and that the lines would be looking for an opportunity to roll back the gains made during the strike. Additionally, these leaders saw the community's mass support of the strikes as a sign of widespread dissatisfaction with the city's administration, the city's streetcar companies, and the concentration of economic power more generally.[26]

The strike and its aftermath forced CLU leaders to reconsider their policy of nonpartisanship. Labor needed an administration that would remain neutral during labor disputes or come to the aid of workers, neither of which was likely with a Democratic or Republican mayor when the major parties were so beholden to the public utility corporations. The strike also strengthened the bonds between the Populists and the CLU. The groups had worked together and ultimately won a series of concessions from the streetcar lines. More important, the conflict reinforced the conviction of CLU leaders that municipal ownership of public utilities offered the only long-term answer and that the people of Cleveland who had rallied to the aid of the strikers would support such a solution. Since the People's party was the only political faction advocating municipal ownership, a labor–Populist alliance seemed logical.

Soon after the streetcar strike of 1892, the pages of the *Cleveland Citizen* were filled with articles, letters, and editorials advocating Populist ideals and suggesting that the city's workers should look to the People's party to improve their lives. The first direct advocacy of the People's party by a CLU official occurred in the fall of 1892 when Max Hayes used the *Citizen* to urge workers to support the People's party and its presidential candidate, General James Weaver. Hayes compared the platforms of the People's party and the CLU and suggested they were virtually identical. He pointed to only two substantive differences: the CLU opposed the sub-treasury program, and the Populists were not on record as supporting the single tax. Hayes was careful, though, to make it clear that the paper's endorsement should not be construed as a formal CLU endorsement of the People's party.[27] It would be five more months before the CLU would do that.

The Populists and the CLU formalized their alliance in the winter of 1893. With a substantial overlap in the leadership of the local People's party and the CLU, the alliance was consummated with little difficulty and an ease suggesting it had been well planned. In February 1893, the Central Labor Union announced its intention to run a candidate for mayor and called on the city's "labor unions and industrial organizations" to convene to nominate a slate. Twenty-eight locals—including locals traditionally wary of political action such as the carpenters, typographical workers, iron and steelworkers, and bakers—sent delegates to the meeting. The *Plain Dealer*, which generally mocked political enterprises not associated with the Democratic party, was impressed by the quality and quantity of the turnout. "The enthusiasm and excitement which prevailed throughout the convention," the paper declared, "showed the earnestness and sincerity of purpose felt by most of the members." From the outset the meeting was run by trade unionists who were active in the People's party. Robert Bandlow presided, while David Rankin, Peter Witt, and Bandlow were the principle speakers.[28]

At every turn, the convention pursued a moderate course. The speeches were relatively tame, emphasizing the need for workers to have a voice in local government. Rather than demanding a list of reforms that might alienate potential supporters, the convention stressed that the first step to reforming city government entailed the election of officials who could not be bought by public service corporations, would treat all citizens impartially, and promised to enforce the city's and state's labor laws. Fearing that the nomination of a whole slate would open the movement up to criticism and provoke controversy over places on the ticket, the convention decided to nominate only a mayoral candidate.

While a number of labor leaders and Franklin Club members, including Rankin, Bandlow, Woodbridge, and Tuckerman, were mentioned as potential mayoral nominees, the convention unanimously nominated Edward S. Meyer. The *Plain Dealer* considered the nomination of Meyer as something of a surprise. A lifelong Republican who had never been associated with labor politics, Meyer had served a term as Cleveland's corporation counsel, a position similar to city attorney. In that position, Meyer had impressed trade unionists by challenging the prerogatives of many of the city's public utilities. Meyer had led the fight against the supplier of natural gas for the city's street lights and forced the company to reduce the price it charged both the city and many customers by two-thirds. Witt would later insist that the labor movement nominated Meyer simply because he was "an anti-corporationist." The convention appointed a committee to inform Meyer of his nomination and to convince him to accept it.[29]

A week after the CLU's nomination of Meyer, the city People's party met to nominate a slate for the upcoming municipal election. Presided over by the same men who had conducted the CLU's meeting, the People's party also nominated Meyer. While the CLU's convention had been reluctant to nominate a whole slate of candidates, the People's party showed no such compunction, fielding a ticket composed mostly of trade unionists. The CLU's vice president received the nomination for police judge, while the nominees for city council were, with a singular exception, trade unionists associated with the CLU.[30]

For the next couple of weeks, Meyer seemed unable to decide if he should run. Calling the nominations by the CLU and the People's party the greatest honor of his political career, Meyer "declined," but he left the door open by announcing that he would happily serve if elected. Moreover, he did not object when both the People's party and the CLU filed the thousand signatures required for his name to appear on the ballot. But it was only when the city's leading Republican paper, the *Cleveland Leader*, published a series of articles attacking him in the week before the election that Meyer officially accepted the nominations and began actively campaigning for office.[31]

Meyer and other People's party candidates attacked the city's public utilities, especially the city's street railways. Dr. L. B. Tuckerman, the only non–trade unionist running for city council, called public utilities the worst form of monopoly and insisted that a vote for Meyer and the People's party slate was a vote against "a monopoly of land, a monopoly of labor, a monopoly of money, and monopoly in general." Meyer's speeches called for the professionalization of city departments, the removal of partisanship from the administration of public laws, a program under which city workers rather than private contractors completed public projects, and the Ohio General Assembly to pass legislation to allow the city to assume control of the city's street railway lines. By the end of the campaign, any distinction between the CLU and the People's party had vanished, and until the fusion of 1896, the two organizations would be synonymous.[32]

In spite of his late entry into the campaign, Meyer fared well for a third-party candidate. He received 6,092 of the 37,683 votes cast (16.2%), finishing well behind Robert E. Blee, the Democratic candidate who received 43.2 percent of the vote, and the Republican candidate, who received 39.2 percent of the vote. The Republicans charged that Meyer's candidacy garnered enough Republican voters to swing the election to the Democrats, but a *Plain Dealer* analysis showed that Meyer had polled best in traditionally Democratic working-class wards, which had gone for Farley two years earlier. Anger at the Republican administration's actions during the streetcar strike probably accounted for the fall off in that party's vote. The *Plain Dealer* reluctantly admitted that the CLU had "delivered the votes" to Meyer and that the People's party had enough supporters to be a factor in the city's politics.[33]

The CLU and the People's party were generally pleased with the results. Only two years before, the party's mayoral nominee had received just 314 votes, so Meyer's total was nearly twenty times the 1891 vote. The *Citizen* noted that the party received this support "despite the cracking of the party lash, despite the opposition of every street railway monopoly in the city, despite the opposition of every boodler, heeler, ward worker, and boss in the city, and despite the fact that there was no party organization." The election convinced the leaders of the CLU that they had made the right decision by throwing in with the People's party.[34]

Cleveland's municipal election also revitalized the nearly dead Ohio People's party. Populist leaders realized that the party's hopes resided with urban and industrial workers rather than with the state's farmers. The party's leadership passed from the hands of agrarian reformers like John Seitz to the Populists associated with Cleveland's CLU. Later that spring, Cleveland's Populists began planning for the fall's gubernatorial contest. From this point forward, urban and labor interests would control the People's party in Ohio.[35]

Ohio's Republicans met in June 1893 and nominated the incumbent McKinley for governor. The party promulgated a typical Republican platform.

It denounced the actions of the Democratic-controlled U.S. Congress and the Grover Cleveland administration, while praising the efforts of Governor McKinley and the Republicans who controlled the Ohio General Assembly. Like most state platforms, the Republicans' effort barely touched on state issues, devoting most of its attention to the tariff and money question. The Republicans praised the McKinley Tariff as "the best exemplification of the principles of protection and reciprocity that has found expression" and favored "honest money composed of gold, silver, and paper, maintained at equal value."[36]

Although most political observers had interpreted Grover Cleveland's 1892 election as a major defeat for protection, McKinley was not about to let the issue die, even though it had little to do with issues the person elected governor would in fact confront. McKinley had built his reputation as his party's tariff expert and to have abandoned the issue would have damaged both his presidential aspirations and the party's chances of retaining control of the Ohio General Assembly and governor's office. As such, McKinley and Ohio's Republicans were determined to make the tariff the cornerstone of their 1893 campaign. As early as February 1893, McKinley was attacking the Democrats' tariff plank and telling audiences that the party would fight its coming battles on the basis of the tariff. The keynote speaker at the state Republican convention, Congressman Charles Grosvenor, praised the McKinley Tariff as a "marvel of wisdom" and the "wisest tariff legislation the country has ever seen." Making 130 speeches in eighty-six of the state's eighty-eight counties, McKinley stressed the benefits of the tariff and paid only passing attention to either the currency question or the issues he would face as governor—taxation, liquor and prohibition, municipal affairs, home-rule for cities, industrial relations, agricultural affairs.[37]

The Democrats were only too happy to center their campaign on the tariff and avoid other thorny issues. Opposition to the McKinley Tariff, they thought, had propelled Grover Cleveland into the White House in 1892 and would deliver them control of the state's government. The convention chairman called the argument that protection led to higher wages "a delusion and a snare" and insisted that the profits of protected corporations had become "lodged in the pockets of employers." In an obvious attack on McKinley, he went on to denounce "the leading advocates of the doctrine of taxation for the protection of capital" and blamed protection for the current depression. The Democrats chose their best expert on the issue, Lawrence Neal, to run against McKinley. A Chillicothe lawyer, Neal had led the free trader forces at the Democrats' 1892 convention in Chicago and authored the platform's tariff plank. That plank called protection a "robbery of the great majority for the benefit of a few" and insisted "the Federal Government has no Constitutional power to impose and collect tariff duties, except for the purpose of revenue only." The platform singled out the McKinley Tariff as "the culminating atrocity of class legislation."[38]

As they did in 1891, the Democrats avoided the monetary question. Except for its endorsement of the Democrats' 1892 monetary plank, the state platform was conspicuously silent on the issue, even though just days earlier President Cleveland had called a special session of Congress to repeal the Sherman Silver Purchase Act. The Democrats knew that the issue had the potential to tear the party apart. While President Cleveland was arguing that the limited coinage of silver allowed under the Sherman Silver Purchase Act had driven gold from the market, other Democrats were calling for the unlimited coinage of silver to increase the currency supply and end the "stringency" gripping the nation. In Ohio, free silver advocates—led by *Cleveland Plain Dealer* publisher Liberty Emery Holden—introduced a resolution condemning the Republican party for demonetizing silver and calling for the free and unlimited coinage of silver at sixteen to one, but Democrats who feared that the plank would displease President Cleveland joined hard-money Democrats to defeat the measure.[39]

While the state's Democrats and Republicans wanted to fight the election of 1893 on the tariff question, the state's Populists insisted that the paramount issue of the day was the money question and criticized "the hypocrisy of the sham battle over tariff schedules." Reenergized by the party's strong showing in Cleveland's municipal races that spring, Ohio's Populists saw the currency shortage and the resulting unemployment associated with the Panic of 1893 as clear evidence of the need both to increase the money supply and to free the nation from the grip of bankers. The party's 1893 platform began by denouncing both Democrats and Republicans as "servile tools of the money power" who had surrendered "the treasury administration to the control of British bankers and their Wall Street agents and allies."

Unlike the two previous Ohio People's party conventions, which had openly fretted about the lack of farm support and condemned the leaders of the Ohio State Grange and Farmers' Alliance, the 1893 convention ignored the farmers and turned its attention to urban workers and organized labor. Cleveland Populists were largely responsible for writing the party's platform, which was divided into national and state sections. Other than the obligatory endorsement of the Omaha platform, the national section dealt entirely with the money question. Reflecting the party's new urban bias, the platform warned of the gold standard's "deadly consequences for the industrial classes," making no mention of its impact on the state's farmers. To avoid these consequences, the Populists demanded both the free and unlimited coinage of silver at sixteen to one and that the government issue "full legal tender paper money . . . in volume sufficient to restore and maintain normal and healthy prices." Additionally, the platform called for the abolition of national banks.[40]

Most of the state section of the platform dealt with urban concerns and reflected the Populist demand for an expansion of the state and municipal governments to counteract the influence of corporations. Planks called for the municipal ownership of street railways, gas and electric plants, and all other natural monopolies, the end of the contracting system on public works, and home rule for the cities. Other planks sought to purify the electoral system (the initiative and referendum and women's suffrage) or increase educational opportunities for needy children (compulsory school attendance and free schoolbooks for public school students).

The party nominated E. J. Bracken, a well-connected Columbus labor leader, for governor. Bracken's credentials were impressive. A lasterer by trade, he was a leader of Columbus's Phoenix Assembly 2960 of the Knights of Labor, a former officer of the Columbus Trades and Labor Assembly, a longtime member of the Ohio State Trades and Labor Assembly's three-man legislative committee, the editor of a small Columbus labor newspaper (the *Sun*), and the legislative correspondent for the Cleveland CLU's *Citizen*. Bracken was also someone who would appeal to those who had supported Ohio's People's party since its inception, as he had attended the inaugural convention of the Ohio People's party and presided over the creation of the Franklin County People's party in Columbus. His being from Columbus, party leaders insisted, would help attract trade unionists and voters outside of Cleveland. Populist leaders knew that Bracken stood little chance of being elected, but they reasoned that, with the resources of Cleveland's CLU, including the *Citizen*, the party would fare much better than it had in its short past.[41]

The 1893 election proved a disappointment for Bracken and the Ohio Populists, as McKinley easily won reelection. Bracken garnered just 1.9 percent of the vote, only a slight increase over the 1.7 percent that Weaver had polled the year before. In the state's ten most urban counties, Bracken collected 2.2 percent of the vote, whereas Weaver only polled 1.5 percent. Cleveland's Cuyahoga County led the way with 4.5 percent of the voters casting their ballot for the Populist ticket. The party would not substantially increase its vote until the following fall.[42]

Following the 1893 election, two men emerged as the leading voices of both Cleveland's People's party and the Central Labor Union, Max Hayes and Peter Witt. For the next thirty-five years, these two men—sometimes as allies but more often as rivals—would be at the center of the city's working-class politics. The twenty-eight-year-old Witt, son of a refugee of Germany's Revolution of 1848, had been an iron molder and president of Local 218 until he was blacklisted in 1893 after leading a successful strike. Unable to return to his vocation, Witt devoted more time to spreading the gospel of the single tax and Populism, especially after his election as president of the CLU in 1894. Frederic C. Howe later described Witt as the *"Enfant terrible* among [Cleveland] radicals." Howe explained, "He respected no man because of his position. His language was vitriolic, his facts accurate, and his attacks cut to the quick." Democratic congressman Tom Johnson, also a single-taxer, was one of those subjected to Witt's wrath, when Witt and other Populists tried to disrupt a campaign event in 1894. Johnson, running for reelection, caught Witt off guard, though, inviting him to the platform and engaging in a spirited debate. The rivalry between Witt and Johnson would not last long. The two men would become allies during Samuel "Golden Rule" Jones's gubernatorial bid in 1899.[43]

Around 1894 Max Hayes stepped from the shadow of his mentor and fellow typographer, Robert Bandlow, to assume a greater role in both the CLU and Cleveland's People's party. Born in rural northern Ohio, Hayes worked as an apprentice printer in Fremont, Ohio, before moving to Cleveland in 1883 and getting a job with the *Cleveland Press.* Hayes founded the *Citizen* in January 1891 and became its editor in 1892. By 1894 Hayes had gained the confidence and the stature to take a more forceful role in Cleveland's labor movement, working behind the scenes to push through much of the Populist agenda. Unlike Witt who was prone to provocation and passion, Hayes was cautious, relying more on reason and consensus building. Until the 1930s Hayes and Witt would contend for the leadership of the city's working classes.[44]

Unlike their counterparts in Columbus, Cincinnati, or the coalfields of eastern Ohio, Cleveland trade unionists were mostly spectators during the calamitous events of 1894. The nationwide coal strike had little effect on the city, the contingent of Coxey's army that passed through was quickly hurried along, and the American Railway Union's strike lasted but a few days in the city. The CLU participated in John McBride's efforts that fall to move the state's labor movement into the People's party, and Cleveland laborites supported the Populist nominee for secretary of state. But mostly there was not much to do on the local front for Cleveland's Populists.

In late 1894, though, Cleveland trade unionists confronted what the *Citizen* called "a serious menace" threatening the People's party—the efforts of People's party national chairman Herman Taubeneck and other party officials to abandon the broad-gauge Omaha platform in favor of a narrow one emphasizing only the free and unlimited coinage of silver at a ratio of sixteen to one. To accomplish this, Taubeneck called for party activists to meet in late December in St. Louis. The *Citizen* insisted that the free coinage movement was similar to the high tariff movement. Both were led by monopolists who promised prosperity for labor but in the end would refuse to share any increase in profits with workers: "The disinherited, the landless, and propertyless masses have no more to gain from the free coinage of silver than from a protective tariff. . . . No one is so foolish as to believe that in event of the enactment of a free coinage law large capitalists would divide the spoil with their employees." In the weeks leading up to the St. Louis conference, the *Citizen* talked of little else, opening its pages up to local activists and prominent Populists who shared its view. Harry Thomas summed up the feelings of the most radical of Cleveland labor-Populists when he declared, "I think that it is about time the People's party drop the silver plank in their platform and adopt instead a plank nationalizing the means of production, distribution, and exchange."[45]

After midwestern trade unionists and their allies defeated those seeking to trim the Omaha platform in St. Louis, Cleveland Populists were confident that success lay ahead. They had good reason to be hopeful, especially as it pertained to the upcoming mayoral election. The party's 1893 candidate, Edward Meyer, had received about six thousand votes (16%), and this was before the events of 1894 led to the dramatic increase of support for the state's Populists. If Cleveland's Populists could double the 1893 vote as the Populists did statewide in 1894, the party could seriously compete with the two older parties.

Additionally, the city's Democratic administration had done much to alienate its traditional working-class constituency. Under the effective control of director of public works John Farley, the Democratic administration was essentially conservative in outlook. Farley had grown wealthy through his control of the bidding process for city public projects, and he used this money and access to jobs to build an effective organization. Perceived as simply a pawn of Farley, Mayor Robert Blee had incurred the wrath of the city's trade union leaders for a series of decisions he made as mayor. He ignored petition after petition sent by the unemployed and organized labor demanding public works projects. He rejected demands that the city itself oversee public projects, rather than letting the jobs out to contractors. He called out the militia to ensure that sewer workers striking against a city contractor did not congregate on Public Square or disrupt the hiring of replacement diggers. He directed the city's police to attack with clubs a group of May Day marchers demanding that the city employ those out of work. When a branch of Coxey's army under the command of "General" Jeffries arrived in Cleveland demanding public employment for the unemployed, the police drove the marchers from Public Square. Under Farley's direction, the city council also refused to consider a CLU request for a minimum wage on public projects and that city contractors be required to hire union labor.[46]

Dissension within the local Democratic party and speculation of a bolt if Blee was renominated also fueled the Populists' hope. Like many local Democratic organizations, Cleveland Democrats were split between those sympathetic to President Grover Cleveland and those who described themselves as anti-monopolists. Farley and Blee led the pro–Grover Cleveland forces, supporting the president's effort to repeal the Sherman Silver Purchase Act and actions during the Pullman strike and boycott. This faction also opposed the public ownership of municipal utilities and efforts to eliminate the contracting system on public works. Led by former congressman Tom Johnson (a former streetcar magnate who had become a single-taxer), Johnson's aide Charles Salen, and former congressman and union leader Martin Foran, the anti-monopoly wing occupied the opposite end of the political spectrum on both local matters and national policy. Johnson and his allies saw government as an instrument to improve the lives of the city's citizens and sympathized with a number of the reforms advocated by the Populists and city's labor leaders, including municipal ownership of public utilities, the end of the contracting system for public works, and monetary reform.[47]

The Cleveland CLU thought that reform forces had a real chance to capture city hall in the spring of 1895 and, much as it had in 1893, called on Populists, Socialists, Prohibitionists, Knights of Labor, trade unionists, and reform clubs to unite on a single platform that might draw sympathetic Democrats and Republicans. The labor leaders maintained that divisions within reform forces had kept the Democrats and Republicans in power. As the *Citizen* declared: "So long as reform roosters continue planting their spurs into each others' bodies, the cunning politicians have nothing to fear." Not only would unity end the internecine sniping, it would attract thousands of additional voters who had avoided third parties for fear they could not win.[48]

The CLU leaders understood that uniting the reform forces would be difficult, but they maintained that the differences could be bridged. Hoping to avoid thorny issues that had little to do with municipal affairs, such as currency, tariff, and the collective ownership of the means of production, the *Citizen* insisted the party limit its platform to those local issues that enjoyed the broad support of reformers. Additionally, the paper suggested that the labor unions and political parties send their most open-minded representatives, men who were willing to compromise rather than those who insisted on party doctrine.[49]

The response to the CLU's call was enthusiastic. Fifty-six labor unions, reform clubs, and political parties sent over 150 delegates to the convention. Although most of the delegates were Populists, representatives of the Socialist Labor party (SLP) and a scattering of Prohibitionists also attended. Additionally, a number of local unions that had traditionally avoided politics sent delegates. In spite of the *Citizen's* insistence that the individual parties send their most open-minded representatives, the conference proved "tempestuous," with much squabbling over the platform's details. As the *Citizen* remarked, many of the delegates "seemed to have become imbued with the notion that it was their duty to wrangle and split hairs over mere trifles." The most vocal and dogmatic delegates represented the relatively small Cleveland section of the SLP—no more than a few dozen members. Believing that politics were merely a propaganda tool rather than the path toward reform, the delegates of the Cleveland section insisted that the platform reflect their party's emphasis on the "class struggle" and denounce the meddling of middle-class reformers. Since they had little faith in the electoral process, they were unwilling to compromise on the platform.[50]

Even though the convention was marked by conflict, the *Citizen* was pleased with the results. Led by the CLU's Witt and Hayes, the Populists were able to defeat the Cleveland section at every turn, ensuring that the party embraced only those reforms that enjoyed wide support among the workingmen. Witt told the convention, "a class movement has never amounted to anything" and that the party should welcome all who want to free workers from the wage system. Even Robert Bandlow, who was more sympathetic to the idea of "class struggle," insisted that if reformers refused to compromise among themselves they would have no hope of defeating the "plutocrats." In the end, the convention's nominee for mayor was Thomas Fitzsimmons, a Populist and longtime Franklin Club member who owned a factory manufacturing iron and steel shafting. As the *Citizen* insisted, "his standing in this community among workers and employers is of the very best."[51]

Not only did the Populists secure the nomination of Fitzsimmons for mayor, they were able to dictate the convention's platform. The platform called for municipal ownership of public utilities, public service divorced from politics, the eight-hour day on public works projects, the abolition of the subcontracting system for public work, weekly pay for city employees, equal pay for men and women, the simplification of municipal laws, the revision of public salaries, and the initiative and referendum. The convention defeated proposals to add a plank demanded by the Cleveland section calling for the collective ownership of the means of production and a plank demanded by the Prohibitionists calling for the suppression of the liquor trade on the grounds that these were not municipal issues.[52]

Two days after the labor convention, the Cuyahoga County People's party met to nominate a local ticket. Most assumed they would simply endorse the actions of the labor convention, but a number of Populists not associated with the CLU dissented. Led by a lawyer close to the American Bimetallic League, E. D. Stark, the dissenters wanted to distance the party from the radicals who attended the labor convention and argued that the local People's party should support only those who supported the Omaha platform. Moreover, the dissenters insisted that the local People's party privilege the demand for the free and unlimited coinage of silver over all other reform. Those associated with the CLU easily overcame the dissenters, and the Populists nominated Fitzsimmons and the rest of the labor convention's slate. A handful of dissenters, though, left the party.[53]

The *Plain Dealer* sided with Stark. It suggested that the People's party made a strategic blunder when it allied itself with the radicals, especially those in the Cleveland section, who attended the labor convention. The presence of "the kind that believe in throwing bombs and that every man who employs another is an arch fiend" in the Independent Labor party would alienate voters from the other parties who would be inclined to vote for the Populists due to their monetary planks.[54]

During the campaign, the Independent Labor–People's party focused most of its attention on the Blee administration's failure to provide work for the city's unemployed. To publicize their plight, Bandlow organized a march of one thousand unemployed men to city hall. First, they visited the department of public works to demand that the city immediately spend the two million dollars set aside for public improvements. After being refused, they asked the director of public charities to provide food for their families. When this request was denied, the marchers asked to be put in jail. Bandlow asked, "Is it right that criminals have work and live, while honest men have not and starve?"[55]

Other aspects of the campaign went poorly. The Democrats remained united in their support for Blee's reelection. Farley worked out a deal with the anti-monopoly faction that kept the party together until the eve of the election. In return for Johnson, Foran, and Salen's support, Farley promised to use his influence with the state's Democratic senator, Calvin Brice, and

President Cleveland to secure the city's most lucrative patronage post, the city's postmastership, for Salen. Although this deal fell through on the eve of the election, it kept the anti-monopoly faction from bolting and possibly supporting the Independent Labor–People's candidate.[56]

Like the Independent Labor–People's party, the Republicans centered their campaign on the corruption of Farley's department of public works and the city's public utilities. The Republicans nominated Robert McKisson—a thirty-two-year-old, mostly unknown city councilman—for mayor. Untarnished by any association to the local Republican organization, McKisson ran as an outsider and a reformer and appropriated important parts of the People's party platform. Railing against business's corruption of the city's government, McKisson openly criticized the city's streetcar companies, called for increased spending on public works, and insisted that public projects be completed by city employees. Moreover, McKisson demanded that the police department become a professional rather than a partisan organization and that the city reclaim public lands along the river and lakefront being controlled by private corporations. McKisson attacked not only Farley and Blee but also his own party leader, Marcus Hanna, for being greedy and indifferent to the suffering of the city's workers. At times during the campaign, it was difficult to differentiate between McKisson and Fitzsimmons. They employed similar rhetoric and called for many of the same reforms.[57]

Unable to differentiate himself and his message from the Republican candidate, Fitzsimmons captured less than 6 percent of the vote, a far cry from the 16 percent the party had captured two years earlier. Cleveland voters backed McKisson's reform campaign instead, electing him by a landslide. As historian Ronald Weiner has noted, McKisson's victory "signaled the apparent triumph of the working class" agenda.[58]

As would be the case in most Ohio elections, the Populists did best when their message and platform could be clearly distinguished from those of the Democrats and the Republicans. But when one of the major parties promised many of the same things as the Populists, the People's party did not stand much of a chance. The Democrats and the Republicans had access to money, daily newspapers, and sophisticated campaign organizations. Since the Populists had only a slight chance of actually winning, voters reasoned that the major party would have greater opportunity to enact reforms. Disappointed with the results of the election, the *Cleveland Citizen* chided the city's workers for failing to support Fitzsimmons and the labor ticket. The paper insisted, though, that it would continue to work with the People's party, as it was the only hope for labor's salvation.[59]

TABLE 3.1—Results of Cleveland's 1895 Mayoral Election

Candidate (party)	Votes	Percentage
McKisson (Republican)	25,058	54.3
Blee (Democratic)	17,850	38.7
Pinney (Prohibitionist)	580	1.3
Fitzsimmons (Independent Labor/Populist)	2,653	5.8

Source: Cleveland Leader, April 6, 1895.

Preparing for the campaign of 1896, Cleveland's labor-Populists threw their support behind Eugene Debs for the presidential nomination and continued to work against those who wanted the People's party to concentrate on the silver issue. The *Citizen* asserted that a ticket with Debs at the top and Kansas senator William A. Peffer in the second slot not only would symbolize the union of industrial workers and farmers but would also deliver the White House to the nation's producers. As national party leaders kept up efforts to concentrate on the silver issue, the Cleveland People's party remained steadfast, instructing its delegates to the national convention to defend the broad-gauged reforms found in the Omaha Platform and ensure that the party's nomination went to someone who would reject any effort to fuse with either of the two major parties.[60]

But the efforts of Cleveland labor-Populists went for naught, and the People's party's nomination of the Democratic candidate, William Jennings Bryan, split the city's labor movement in two. From 1893 through early 1896, Cleveland's labor leaders had worked hard to unite reformers of all stripes under the banner of the People's party. Traditional Populists, single taxers, Socialists, Bellamy nationalists, and trade unionists alienated from the traditional parties worked together under a broad municipal platform flexible enough to accommodate a wide variety of thought. This alliance, however, proved too tenuous and fractious to survive the nomination of Bryan. The larger of the two factions, led by Max Hayes, Robert Bandlow, and the leadership of the CLU, called for reformers to join the SLP; the smaller faction, led by David Rankin, Edmund Vail, and Peter Witt, supported Bryan and would closely align itself with the Johnson-Salen-Foran wing of the local Democratic party to form the core of the city's Progressive movement.

Although Hayes praised Bryan as a fighter for labor and predicted that he would easily defeat McKinley in the fall, he saw the People's party nomination of Bryan as a betrayal of the "greatest political revolt that this country has ever known" and blamed this betrayal on the middle-class "bosses" of the People's party, who "had the smell of office in their nostrils." The free coinage of silver, he asserted, was simply another scheme to enrich bankers, speculators, mine owners, and the debt-ridden middle class who would keep all of the benefits accrued from an expanded currency and "not come forward with a raise of wages on a silver platter." Bryan's nomination was further evidence, he concluded, that only members of the working class could be trusted to work for true reform.[61] According to those who would join the Socialist Labor party, the disintegration of the People's party was a blessing; it would usher in a better political movement that would sweep away corporate capitalism, the real cause of the nation's labor problems. An editorial in the *Citizen* declared:

> The destruction of the present organization of the People's party is neither
> a loss nor an end to a struggle. . . . The coming third party will draw the lines
> of class interests more clearly and the propaganda will be better understood
> because no attempt will be made to be all things to all men. It will be a great
> class conscious politico-labor movement that is world-wide in its sweep and
> that no human power can successfully oppose. It is the child of want and
> proposes to destroy the barbarous competitive system and substitute therefor
> a co-operative commonwealth.

Realizing that refusing to back Bryan and demanding the creation of a "cooperative commonwealth" was neither politically expedient nor practical in the short term, those who refused to support Bryan likened themselves to the abolitionists who refused to compromise with the peculiar institution. "Chattel slavery was wrong; wage slavery is wrong," Hayes said simply. The nation's workers should not be sidetracked by the "'half-loaf,' 'one-thing-at-a-time' humbuggery" of the Bryanites.[62]

Hayes and his allies turned to Daniel DeLeon's Socialist Labor party. The salvation of labor could only be achieved by "nationalizing the tools of production and distribution, and abolishing the element known as profit." While Hayes considered socialism to be part of a world-wide movement, he blasted the notion that it was un-American or of "foreign importation." "Socialism is truly Americanism," he insisted. When they founded the government, the Revolutionaries of '76 "established a great cooperative enterprise—a socialistic institution—in which it was expected that all men would be free and equal." The independence and freedom promised by the Revolution had been destroyed by the "hurry to grasp the empty shadow of riches."[63]

Peter Witt, Edmund Vail, David Rankin, and those labor leaders who worked for the election of Bryan were much more pragmatic than Hayes, Bandlow, and those who followed them into the SLP. They too had opposed the emphasis on silver and fusion with the Democrats before the 1896 Populist convention, but after the convention they threw their support behind Bryan. Witt told the *Plain Dealer*, "I am a Populist from the ground up. I preferred Debs, but I like Bryan. I will take my coat off and work night and day for his election." Labor leaders like Witt thought Bryan's victory would break the hold of Wall Street bankers over the nation's financial system and provide greater economic opportunity by increasing the supply of money and credit. Although they preferred greenbacks to silver, these Populists-turned-Bryanites reasoned that the free coinage of silver was a good first step. Perhaps more important, they thought that working with the Democrats offered the best chance for accomplishing reform and destroying the "money power." Only Bryan could beat William McKinley, whom they saw as simply a pawn of Marcus Hanna and Wall Street speculators. As David Rankin stated simply, the Democrats "can win and the socialists can't."[64]

The differences between those Populists who supported Bryan and those who turned to the SLP were not limited to strategy. The Bryanites did not feel that the nation's economic system was fundamentally flawed, just that it had been perverted by the concentration of the nation's wealth into the hands of a few who had corrupted the nation's political system. The Bryanites called for a series of reforms to free the nation's workers from the grasp of these corporations and corrupt politicians. These reforms included the free coinage of silver and the expansion of the nation's currency, stricter laws to regulate trusts, an end to labor injunctions, the direct election of U.S. senators and president, and tax reform. The SLP, on the other hand, insisted on the complete overthrow of the capitalist system. The *Cleveland Citizen* argued that the main difference between the two factions was that the Socialists were prepared "to fight the whole of capitalism instead of merely the money power."[65]

Within Cleveland's Democratic party, the former Populists began working with the Bryan wing of the party to unseat the pro–Grover Cleveland leadership. However, Farley outmaneuvered them at every turn. His ties to ward politicians and the city's business community provided him with too much ammunition. In the spring of 1897 Cleveland's Democratic party nominated Farley for mayor. Led by Peter Witt, David Rankin, and Edmund Vail, angry former Populists bolted from the Democratic convention, resurrecting the city's People's party. With the support of a number of Bryan

Democrats, including Martin Foran, the Populists nominated a whole slate of candidates for office including Tom Fitzsimmons for mayor. The platform resembled the ones that the Populists had run in 1893 and 1895 with demands for municipal ownership of the public utilities, the end of the contract system for public works, an eight-hour day for public employees, and salaries for public officials (rather than fee-based compensation).[66]

Even though they had supported the reforms in the Populist platform for years and expressed admiration for Fitzsimmons and other Populist candidates, the *Citizen* and the Central Labor Union refused to support the People's party slate. The *Citizen* insisted the People's party was not class-conscious enough. Instead, at the urging of Hayes and Bandlow the CLU formally endorsed the SLP's candidate, Edward Larsen, for mayor. The Socialist Labor party "is the only [party] that favors the abolition of the capitalistic wage-system in all forms," the *Citizen* explained.[67]

Neither Fitzsimmons nor Larsen was able to attract much support. Fitzsimmons garnered slightly more than three thousand votes, 5.5 percent of the fifty-five thousand votes cast. Larsen captured just under a thousand voters, less than 2 percent of the total. Fitzsimmons's candidacy did, however, have a dramatic effect on the election. Republican incumbent Robert McKisson squeaked by with a narrow victory. As the *Citizen* observed, "McKisson can thank the fates that Fitzsimmons was the third candidate and prevented the radical silverites from going to the big boss."[68]

The 1897 municipal election proved the last appearance of the Populist party in Cleveland politics. Believing that the defection of the Populists and a handful of Bryan Democrats in the spring had cost them the mayoral election, Democratic leaders worked hard to reunite the party by courting the former Populists and their allies. That fall, Cleveland's Democrats placed several former Populists on the local slate, including labor leaders Edmund Vail and William Pate, who were nominated for the Ohio General Assembly. The Democrats were so solicitous of former Populist labor leaders that the *Citizen* noted dryly that the city's Democratic party had been "populized."[69]

Arguing that the Central Labor Union could only support candidates who opposed the capitalist system, the *Citizen* refused to endorse Vail and Pate that fall, calling on trade unionists to vote for the SLP slate instead. The endorsement prompted the first challenge to the CLU's partisan activism in years. Angry members of Iron Molders Local 218, the home of a number of influential Populists-turned-Bryanites (including Peter Witt), charged that the labor federation had become "the headquarters of the Socialist Labor Party" and the *Citizen* "the storm center for propagation of that doctrine." The CLU, Local 218 pointed out, had been established on the principle that partisan politics had no place in a trades' assembly. The molders were not alone in criticizing the federation for its relationship with the SLP. The machinists, other iron trades' locals, and the sewer workers' union backed the molders' motion to recommit the CLU to nonpartisanship. The iron workers' demands, though, did not reflect any deep-seated commitment to nonpartisanism but rather an aversion to the SLP. After all, the machinists and the iron workers had supported the federation's alliance with the Populists and were working closing with the Bryan faction of the Democratic party. Hayes and Bandlow defended the alliance between the CLU and the Socialists, insisting that the labor federation had an obligation to work for the abolition of capitalism and that the Socialist Labor party was the only party pledged to that goal. In the end, CLU delegates voted to support both the positions of Hayes and Bandlow and an alliance with the SLP.[70]

The Democratic party's nomination of former Populists in 1897 and in 1898 did not ensure that former Populists would stay in the fold. When the Democratic party again nominated Farley to run against McKisson for mayor in the spring of 1899, Witt, Rankin, and many former Populists refused to support him. But they were unwilling to resurrect the Populist party for another try. After briefly flirting with the idea of supporting McKisson, who had largely failed to follow through on his reform agenda, or nominating Charles Salen on a Bryan-Democratic ticket, the former Populists sat out the election. They seemed to be foundering.[71]

While the Populists-turned-Bryanites stood on the sidelines, a number of prominent Republicans, including Marcus Hanna, supported Farley's campaign. McKisson had angered Hanna by challenging his bid for a seat in the U.S. Senate and by setting up a political machine that rivaled Hanna's local operations. To punish McKisson for these transgressions, Hanna used what was left of his political operation in Cleveland to help out Farley, including a secret twenty-thousand-dollar contribution in the campaign's final days. This support enabled Farley to squeak out a narrow victory.[72]

As the historian Shelton Stromquist has argued, soon after Farley's election, two events changed dramatically the nature of labor politics in Cleveland. The first was a violent, disruptive streetcar strike lasting from June until well into the fall that energized the city's working population and prompted them to challenge the existing economic order. The second was the gubernatorial candidacy that fall of Toledo's Samuel "Golden Rule" Jones, which channeled workers' discontent into politics.[73]

The strike began in the spring soon after the Cleveland Consolidated Street Railway Company—commonly called the Big Consolidated or the Big Con—issued new rules requiring motor men and conductors to work longer hours and to run faster routes. Although Tom Johnson had once owned a considerable part of the Big Con, he had sold his interest to Henry Everett after he was defeated in his bid to return to Congress in 1894. By April 1899 several pedestrians had been hit and killed by streetcars speeding to maintain the grueling schedule. The popular outcry against the company and its employees was swift and unprecedented. Newspaper editorials and politicians called upon the company and employees to operate the cars in a safe manner. On the streets crowds threatened to lynch speeding drivers. The Big Con blamed the accidents on the carelessness of both individual motor men and pedestrians; the employees maintained that the speedup and changes in work rules forced them to operate the streetcars in an unsafe manner. While the company agreed to relax the speedup and the accident rate declined, tensions between the company and the employees remained high as motor men and conductors were forced to work from twelve to sixteen hours a day, six days a week.[74]

To redress their grievances, 519 of the company's 900–1,000 employees organized a local chapter of the Amalgamated Association of Street Railway Employees of America. No longer would they be "treated as a portion of the machinery of the car which they operated," an observer noted. The new local made no immediate demands but set about to organize the rest of the Big Con's employees and to prepare to fight for better conditions.[75] The management of the Big Con prepared for a strike, though. Not only did the owner, Henry Everett, make arrangements for the importation of strikebreakers, he built special dormitories to house them so they would not have to leave company property during any unrest. Confident of his preparations and unwilling to relinquish control over the operations of the line, Everett steadfastly refused to meet with the union.

Everett's refusal to recognize the union or even negotiate with his men and the changes in work rules prompted the motor men and conductors to launch a strike on the morning of June 11, 1899. That afternoon two train cars of strikebreakers arrived from Buffalo. When the strikebreakers began operating the streetcars, chaos ensued. Strikers and sympathizers attacked the cars with stones and bottles as the cars left the barns. Crowds blocked streetcar lines by placing boulders, timber, or large boxes over the tracks. Newspapers blamed the strikers for the violence and conflict, but the public sided with the strikers. Throughout the city, shop owners, workers, and others boycotted the Big Consolidated and patronized smaller streetcar lines or rode wagons supplied by enterprising farmers and teamsters.[76]

In late June, strikers and the Big Consolidated reached an agreement. It required the Big Con to hire back 80 percent of the strikers, segregate the strikebreakers who remained employed, and implement a less grueling work schedule. But after the strikers returned to work, Everett refused to make any changes. "Mr. Everett has been a very busy man and has not had time to put the new schedules into effect and to carry out terms of the settlement," one of his subordinates explained. Additionally, the Big Con began firing those workers most closely associated with the union. Twenty-seven union members, including all of the leaders, were discharged. The conductors and motor men voted to resume the strike in mid July.[77]

The resumption of the strike brought a dramatic increase in the level of violence. The strikers continued to enjoy the support of a broad cross section of the city's population. Newspaper accounts suggest that Clevelanders from every class and ethnic group supported the strike. Throughout the city, citizens and strikers attacked streetcars operated by non-union men. When a streetcar appeared at a major intersection, hundreds, if not thousands, of protesters blocked the tracks, threw bottles and rocks at the streetcars, and assaulted non-union drivers. Protesters dynamited cars and other company property, prompting Farley to ask the governor to send in the state militia. The *London Spectator* observed that the strike looked more like a civil war than a labor dispute.[78]

The strikers tried to distance themselves from the roving crowds, dynamite, and attacks on strikebreakers, pointing proudly to the fact that only one of the hundreds arrested for rioting had been a striker. Instead, the strikers organized a highly effective communitywide boycott of the Big Con. "Working men generally, and the merchants of all classes, joined in boycotting with little hesitancy," one observer noted. The strikers secured omnibuses and wagons to help the citizens stranded by the boycott. Ridership on the Big Consolidated fell to no more than a handful on its most traveled routes. A reporter observed that the "cars of the Big Consolidated are running practically empty."[79]

Buoyed by their success, the strikers and sympathizers sought to stigmatize those who continued to patronize the Big Con. Spotters identified riders and followed them home. Organizers circulated the names of those who refused to observe the boycott, and sympathetic merchants denied their goods and services to the offenders. The boycott was so effective that an editorial in *Harper's Weekly* declared, "Persons who ride on the boycotted cars find it difficult to buy the necessities of life. They are obliged to resort to subterfuge to obtain food and drink." Occasionally signs would be posted at the offenders' homes declaring "scabs live here."[80]

Populists-turned-Bryanites Peter Witt, David Rankin, and Edmund Vail took the lead in organizing the boycott, protest rallies against the Big Consolidated, and picnics and fundraisers for the strikers. In their speeches, Witt and Rankin rarely spoke in terms of class. Rather they characterized

Those violating the labor movement's boycott of the Big Consolidated line were subjected to insults and violence. From *Harper's Weekly*, August 12, 1899.

Everett and the Big Con as threats to the whole community and solicited
the aid of shopkeepers, workers, professionals, and even sympathetic
factory owners. The Central Labor Union and the Socialist Labor party, on
the other hand, did not take an active role in the strike, except to tell people
to "vote the Socialist Labor ticket and down with capitalism and the old
parties." Tellingly, the *Citizen* devoted only limited space to discussions of
the strike. The front page of the August 12 issue devoted five times more
front-page space to Cleveland SLP's spat with Daniel DeLeon and the party's
national office than it did to the strike. Hayes, Bandlow, and the rest of the
CLU's leadership insisted that true reform could only come by voting for
the SLP. As Eugene Debs wrote in the *Citizen*, "The key to the situation is in
the ballot. . . . Do you suppose for one instant if Robert Bandlow were the
governor of Ohio, Max Hayes in the legislature, and Issac Cowans mayor of
Cleveland, you would be in your present plight." All three men were on the
SLP ballot for the upcoming election.[81]

Despite public sympathy and the initial success of the boycott, the strike
failed. By the fall, Everett had paid off the owners of the omnibuses and wagon
teams that had provided alternative transportation, forcing boycotters to walk to

their destinations. Cooler weather forced Clevelanders back onto the streetcars. The strike, however, was not officially ended until May 1900. Three hundred workers returned to work on terms very favorable to the Big Consolidated. Although the strike had petered out, it had mobilized Cleveland's workers who were increasingly unhappy with the city's administrations and politicians.

One of the few politicians to side openly with the strikers was Toledo mayor and independent candidate for governor Samuel "Golden Rule" Jones. A former Republican and factory owner, Jones enjoyed the support of Toledo's workers and spoke a language that echoed much of the Populist message. Historian Chester McArthur Destler even identified Jones and his protégé Brand Whitlock as the leaders to the movement to incorporate Populist ideals in municipal government.[82]

In the late summer of 1899—in the midst of the streetcar strike—Jones launched an independent bid to become governor. His Cuyahoga County campaign managers, Peter Witt and Thomas Fitzsimmons, who had helped the streetcar employees organize their boycott, arranged for him to speak at a picnic for the strikers. There he chastised the management of the Big Con for "degradation of American citizens to the level of serfs" and Cleveland's government for allowing the city "to be used for the profit of private corporations."[83] In his campaign for governor, Jones endorsed the reforms Populists had demanded, including government ownership of monopolies and mines, the eight-hour day, and a state program to provide work for the state's unemployed. Employing Populist rhetoric, he also called for the "end of the present social order known as competition" and the creation of a cooperative economic order. As he told one Cleveland-area labor leader, "I am trying, the best I know how, to lead the people into the great truth of Brotherhood, Socialism—for me they are synonymous terms." Jones said he was reluctant to use the term "socialism" on the campaign trail, though, for fear it would alienate voters. The cornerstone of Jones's campaign was a call for an end to political parties and partisanship—which he thought had allowed corporations to corrupt the nation's political system, undermine the "brotherhood of man," and encourage class strife.[84]

Jones's candidacy nearly destroyed Cleveland's Democratic party. By the fall of 1899, the local Democratic party, which had triumphed that spring, was supported only by anti-Bryan men and party stalwarts who continued to support Farley. Those who had abandoned Farley in the spring and those in the Bryan wing of the party rallied to the Jones campaign. With McKisson out of the way, Hanna's supporters returned to the Republican fold. The chances of the Democratic gubernatorial nominee, *Cincinnati Enquirer* publisher John McLean, were so dismal in Cleveland that the party stopped holding public meetings and rallies.[85]

Despite, or maybe because of, this increasing Democratic support for Jones, Cleveland's Central Labor Union openly mocked the possibility of a Jones campaign, charging that it was part of a Republican scheme to win the votes of the working class. The *Citizen* predicted that "if Jones runs he will hardly receive more votes than Coxey received" in 1897. To counter Jones, Ohio's Socialist Labor party, which was controlled by those associated with the CLU, nominated Robert Bandlow for governor. The *Citizen* insisted that Bandlow was the only candidate to oppose the wage system and able to serve the needs of the state's workers. Later, the paper declared, "All this talk of Jones carrying Cuyahoga County is nonsense. We are positive that the SLP will beat him out in many precincts and wards, and quite likely in the city." The *Citizen* could not have been more wrong, though. Not only did Jones outpoll the SLP in Cuyahoga County, he outpolled the Republicans and Democrats combined. Jones captured a whooping 32,599 votes (55.8%) while Robert Bandlow received 1,085 votes.[86]

As Shelton Stromquist has argued, the streetcar strike and Jones's electoral success in Cleveland led to a realignment of the city's Democratic party. Following the election, the city's leading Democratic paper reported, "the great mass of people who voted for Jones are now aware of their power and will cause further trouble to leading political parties." The main casualties were John Farley and the anti-Bryan wing of the Democratic party, while former congressman Tom Johnson, a close personal friend of Jones, was the big winner.[87] Running for mayor in 1901, Johnson appealed to the city's working class, sounding much like his friend from Toledo. He railed against the greed of corporations, especially the ones doing business with the city, advocated the municipal ownership of street railroads and other public utilities, pushed for the end of the contracting system for city projects, and urged the enactment of Henry George's single tax. Basically, Johnson adopted the platform of Cleveland's Populist movement. While the CLU refused to support Johnson, a number of Populists-turned-Bryanites, the most important being Peter Witt and Edmund Vail, did. Witt and Vail canvassed working-class and immigrant neighborhoods for Johnson as they had for Jones in 1899, providing crucial links between Johnson and the city's workers. Johnson, winning with the support of much of the city's working class, brought to the city what political scientist Kenneth Finegold calls "municipal populism."[88]

After his triumph in 1901 and his success as Cleveland's mayor, Johnson would stand at the center of the state's Progressive movement, bringing into the Bryan wing of the Democratic party like-minded young politicians and labor activists from around the state. As Oscar Ameringer, a Columbus labor leader who would become one of the nation's most prominent Socialists, later boasted, "I was one of Tom L. Johnson's young men. Newton Baker,

Mayor Tom L. Johnson, shortly before his death, with his two most important aides, Peter Witt (left) and Newton Baker. From Tom L. Johnson, *My Story* (1911).

later Woodrow Wilson's Secretary of War, was another of them. Peter Witt, the iron molder and for a third of a century one of the leading lights in the municipal government of Cleveland, was another. Frederic C. Howe, who ended as a New Dealer and who was as clean and sincere as they make them, was still another." Others included Toledo mayor Brand Whitlock and Cincinnati single-taxer Herbert Bigelow.[89]

Ironically, Johnson's occupation of the mayor's office, his long tenure in that position, and Democratic control of the city's government removed the main challengers to the dominance of Hayes and Bandlow within Cleveland's labor community and allowed the Central Labor Union to continue its embrace of socialism. Witt and Vail, the most articulate challengers to the Socialists, took positions in the Johnson administration and removed themselves from CLU debates. Perhaps more important, Johnson's pro-labor policies allowed the CLU to disengage itself from municipal affairs and local partisan politics. Unlike labor organizations in other large cities, Cleveland's central body did not have to cut political deals and endorse candidates to ensure that city contractors hired union labor or that labor laws were enforced. This freed Hayes, Bandlow, and the leaders of the CLU to continue their uncompromising advocacy of socialism at the national level.

Hayes, Bandlow, and other Central Labor Union activists were never happy within the Socialist Labor party. Like many others, they chafed under the autocratic and dogmatic rule of party leader Daniel DeLeon. By 1899 Hayes and Bandlow had found that life in the SLP was no longer tolerable. DeLeon was insisting that party members abandon membership in trade unions associated with the American Federation of Labor (AFL) and join rival unions set up under the aegis of the Socialist Trades and Labor Alliance. Hayes and Bandlow considered this type of dual unionism to be destructive to both socialism and the trade union movement. Along with Morris Hillquit and Job Harriman, Hayes and Bandlow created a rump Socialist Labor party—the so-called Rochester faction, named after the city in which the faction had its first meeting in 1900. The next year the Rochester faction would merge with Eugene Debs and Victor Berger's Social Democratic party to form the Socialist party, which would rapidly eclipse the SLP in terms of popular support. The leaders of the Socialist party—Eugene Debs, Victor Berger, Tommy Morgan, Max Hayes—were a diverse lot, but they did have one thing in common—they were all former Populists from the Industrial Midwest. Hayes would play an important role in the party, becoming what historian David Montgomery called, the Socialists' "most prominent spokesman with the AFL."[90]

4 Government by Injunction and Labor Populism in Cincinnati

ON JULY 13, 1894, federal judge William Howard Taft sentenced American Railway Union organizer Frank W. Phelan to jail for violating an injunction not to interfere with the operation of the Cincinnati Southern railway, which was under federal receivership. Taft declared that Phelan's main offense was "his interference with the operation of the Southern road by the instigation and maintenance of the boycott and strike." Taft acknowledged that workers had a right to organize unions and even to strike for increased wages, but he insisted that what Phelan was doing was different. The purpose of the strike was not for the immediate benefit of those doing the striking, but to aid people with no "natural relation" to Cincinnati Southern railroaders—those striking the Pullman Sleeping Car Company. "It was the motive of quitting and the end sought" that made the strike illegal. "Certainly, the starvation of a nation cannot be the lawful purpose of a combination," he declared. To make matters worse, Taft maintained that Phelan had engaged in that "terrorism which is so effective for discouraging new men from filling the strikers' places." Taft admitted that the evidence that Phelan had advocated terrorizing replacement workers was suspect and that the charges against him were of the type "hard to prove in court," but the judge nonetheless used the terrorism finding to justify the harsh six-month jail sentence.[1]

Although some scholars have maintained that Taft's decision promoted trade unionism (in that it affirmed the right to organize and strike for better conditions), the trade union leaders and workingmen of Cincinnati did not see it that way.[2] For them, it was just another indication of the judiciary's hostility toward the labor movement and its attempts to disrupt worker solidarity. The state and federal judiciary had already invalidated many laws designed to aid Ohio workers, interpreted others in ways to mitigate their effectiveness, and employed the conspiracy doctrine to limit the use of boycotts and other trade union activity.[3] A disproportional number of these decisions arose out of disputes in Cincinnati—one undermining the effectiveness of an anti-union coercion bill, another ruling that secondary boycotts constituted an unlawful conspiracy in restraint of trade, and still another rendering the state's eight-hour-day law meaningless.[4] Cincinnati trade union leaders interpreted the conviction and imprisonment of Phelan in light of these other decisions, arguing that "the last bulwark of the rights of the people, the United States Judiciary" had been pressed "into the service of monopoly." More than anything else, the hostility of the court system pushed Cincinnati's labor movement into a formal alliance with the People's party.[5]

Unlike their counterparts in other Ohio cities, Cincinnati's trade unionists entered the Populist era with a long history of third-party political activism. The Workingmen's party had flourished right after the Civil War, electing General Samuel F. Cary to the U.S. Congress. In 1877 the Greenback-Workingmen's party had captured about 20 percent of the vote. Ten years later, Cincinnati-area Knights of Labor working through the United Labor party (later the Union Labor party) almost captured the mayor's office, coming within 682 votes of victory. These forays into third-party politics came with a price, however. After each episode the city's labor movement had nearly collapsed, mostly from political infighting and the efforts of the major parties to undermine potential rivals for the workingman's vote. By the early 1890s Cincinnati's trade union leaders were both fearful of third-party political action and enticed by its possibility for reform and personal advancement. But until they rebuilt their movement, questions concerning an alliance with the Populists were relegated to the background.[6]

The Populist party in Cincinnati got off to an inauspicious start. In March 1891 reformers, Socialists, and trade unionists met to form a party and nominate a slate of candidates for the upcoming municipal election. Although the *Cincinnati Commercial Gazette* argued that there was only a "sprinkling" of trade unionists present, the *Cincinnati Times-Star* characterized the new organization as a "labor" ticket and a "workingman's party." Adopting the name "Citizens' party," the 150 delegates declared that politicians from the two major parties had betrayed the interests of the people and were manipulated by the city's "monopolists, trusts, and corporations." To purify city politics and restore democracy, the party called for home rule for cities and the municipal ownership of gas, electric, and street railway franchises. The new party drew up a slate of candidates for office that included Gustav Tafel, the Democratic nominee for mayor, and Theodore Horstmann, the Republican nominee for city solicitor.

The selection of candidates provoked controversy. Led by United Labor party veteran and Knights of Labor executive board member Hugh Cavanaugh, the delegates associated with the rapidly declining Knights of Labor District Assembly 48 argued that, by nominating candidates belonging to the traditional parties, the Citizens' party would attract few voters and do little to change the status quo. The Knights argued that only by nominating "new names" could the party gain the trust of the voters and be sure that those elected would not be tools of capitalists. The controversy was so disruptive that the party rescinded its nominations but vowed to continue as a party.[7]

Although a number of the Citizens' party leaders, including Frank Rist and Louis Benjamin, were active in the Cincinnati's Central Labor Council (CLC), the central body steered clear of any formal affiliation with the new body. The CLC had emerged as the city's leading labor federation following the United Labor party's rapid collapse after the 1887 municipal election, and it had a formal policy prohibiting partisan activity. As the first issue of the CLC's newspaper, the *Cincinnati Chronicle*, declared: "The CLC is a purely labor concern. Politics and religion are entirely excluded from the deliberations of the council." When the Citizens' party was forming, a few delegates asked the CLC to lend its support, but after "a lengthy discussion" the trade unionists, according to their minutes, "concluded that the CLC as a body take no definite action concerning the matter, leaving that to each local or individual member."[8]

Despite its refusal to join the third-party movement, the CLC was hostile toward the two major parties and saw political reform as the only way to redress the problems facing the nation's workers. It clearly supported the ideals of the Citizens' party and the nation's growing third-party movement. The central body's declaration of principles called the existing industrial system "wrong and immoral" as it allowed "idlers to roll in luxury" while "wealth producers live in poverty." The CLC's declaration continued:

> It is self-evident that as the power of capital combines and increases the political freedom of the toiling masses becomes more and more a delusive

farce. There can be no harmony between capital and labor under the present industrial system, for the single reason that capital, in its modern character, consists very largely of rents, interest and profits wrongly extorted from the producer, who possesses neither the land nor the means of production, and is therefore compelled to sell his arms, brains, or both, to the possessor of the land and the means of production, and at such prices as an uncertain and speculative market may allow.

The CLC blamed this injustice on politicians from both parties who had allowed the "ruling moneyed classes" to profit from "high rents, costly transportation, gigantic corners in grain and other provisions, and by monopolizing the issue of money." The CLC demanded a series of reforms that were similar to those demanded by the People's party and the nascent Citizens' party—the eight-hour day, the prohibition of the contract system for public works, the enforcement of all labor laws, the issuance of greenbacks directly from the government, and the abolition of conspiracy laws and "all class privileges."[9]

The CLC's reluctance to join the new third-party movement can be attributed in part to the organization's small size and fragile nature. It is not clear how many trade unionists belonged to unions affiliated with the CLC in 1891, but the numbers were small. The previous year the organization voted down a measure to count its total membership for fear it would "expose our weakness in numbers." Probably no more than two thousand workers belonged to unions affiliated with the CLC. Hoping to establish itself as the sole labor body in the city, the CLC avoided actions that could alienate potential members and detract from its efforts to unite with other labor bodies such as the Building Trade Council and the once powerful Knights of Labor District Assembly 48. Working with the Citizens' party and making the central body a partisan organization would undoubtedly have done that.[10]

Cincinnati's third-party movement was given a boost when those leaders of the Farmers' Alliance pushing for the formation of a third party chose the city to host the convention that would establish the People's party. Although Cincinnati was selected because it had hosted the convention to create the Union Labor party and was centrally located, the decision was a boon for the local movement. The convention's organizers were liberal with credentials for fear that no one would show up, and about one hundred Cincinnatians attended. The rousing speeches and presence of thousands of enthusiastic activists and reporters encouraged local party officials to believe in the vitality of the new movement. Following the convention, the Citizens' party transformed itself into the local People's party and its leaders began predicting that the party would poll between fifteen and forty thousand votes in Cincinnati's Hamilton County in the fall elections.[11]

Despite the CLC's official reluctance to join the new party, the trade unionists who led the CLC began vying with Cavanaugh and the Knights of Labor for control of the local People's party. The conflict between the trade unionists and the Knights had little to do with People's party issues or strategy. It continued a mostly personal rivalry dating back to the mid 1880s. The trade unionists won the initial battle when the Hamilton County People's party elected CLC founder Frank Rist to the party's chairmanship. The rivalry again erupted on the eve of the state People's party convention as Rist and those associated with the CLC initially opposed the state central committee's plan to make Cavanaugh the convention's chairman. To appease Rist and his allies (and to appeal to voters in the state's largest city), the state executive committee promised that the lieutenant governor's slot would go to a Cincinnati trade unionist.[12]

Cincinnati trade unionists were active at the state People's party's August 1891 convention. The *New Nation*, a Bellamyite publication, reported that 137 Cincinnati trade unions would be represented at the Springfield meeting, but that number was a gross exaggeration—there were not that many trade unions in the whole city. The *Times-Star* reported that the Building Trades Council as well as the printers, metalworkers, shoemakers, and tinworkers unions sent official delegations to the convention. A number of trade unionists associated with the CLC, including D. P. Rowland, W. H. Stevenson, and Rist, began campaigning for the lieutenant governor's nomination. Although Stevenson of the Bricklayers' Union was a proven vote-getter (as the United Labor party's mayoral nominee in 1887 he had polled almost 37 percent of the vote), the state's People's party selected Rist. At the convention, the CLC founder promoted himself by passing out cards declaring, "Frank L. Rist for Lieutenant Governor means 40,000 votes in Hamilton County and the [election of] the legislative ticket."[13]

Rist was not alone in thinking that the new party would poll well in Cincinnati. Soon after the inaugural state People's party convention, former governor Joseph B. Foraker wrote a political ally about the anxiety that the city's Labor Day parade had created among local Republicans: "One gentleman estimated the number in the procession at 15,000. I think that he must surely have been mistaken, but, however, that may be, our people are considerably disturbed by it, since the impression seems to be prevailing among them, that they will nearly all vote for Sites [Seitz] and the straight labor [People's party] ticket."[14] Both Rist's enthusiasm and Foraker's fears proved misplaced, though. When the votes were counted, Populist gubernatorial candidate John Seitz polled only 3,182 votes in Hamilton County or about 4.3 percent of the total vote.[15]

In 1892 and 1893 Cincinnati trade unionists enjoyed tremendous success in organizing new workers and building membership in the CLC. In a number of highly publicized labor disputes, trade unionists won union recognition, substantial wage increases, and improved working conditions. In April 1892 Cincinnati's two thousand union carpenters threatened to strike unless the Builders' Congress agreed to a pay increase to 33 1/3 cents per hour by May 1. Shortly before the deadline, the Builders' Congress granted the pay increase as well as time and a half for overtime and double time for Sunday. Plasterers avoided a strike after the Contracting Plasterers' Association agreed to hire only union members, raise wages to 40 cents per hour, and reduce the workweek to fifty-three hours. In September 1892 Brewery Workers Local 12 won a five-year fight with the local Beer Brewers' Association. The agreement provided for a union shop, the right of workmen to live and board where they choose, a limitation on the number of apprentices, a reduction in the workweek to 55 1/2 hours, weekly pay, 25 cents per hour for overtime, and an arbitration system for grievances.[16]

While local unions gained members, the CLC focused on uniting all of the city's labor organizations under its banner. Insisting that divisions within the labor movement had robbed workers of their influence over political affairs, the CLC called for Knights of Labor craft assemblies, the Amalgamated Council of Building Trades (which already worked with the CLC on political matters through a standing joint committee), the Carpenters' District Council, the Furniture Workers' Council, and the Machinery Trades Council to work with the CLC to form a single central body. After several meetings and the drafting of a proposed constitution, the merger movement fell apart due to the fear that the CLC leaders would dominate the new organization and push other leaders aside. The surprising result was that the failed merger brought new members to the CLC, as many locals sought affiliation in the CLC as well as the more craft-oriented councils. This created a system in which a carpenters' local, for instance, would work through the CLC on political and municipal matters but through the Building Trades Council on issues directly involving the construction trades.[17]

The successful organizing drives and strikes increased the number of Cincinnatians belonging to unions, while the merger drive increased the number of Cincinnati locals affiliated with the CLC. By fall 1893 membership in CLC-affiliated unions numbered just under twenty thousand. This membership growth gave CLC leaders increasing confidence in the political power of the central body. Whereas the two thousand or so members the CLC had claimed in 1891 would make little impact in local election, the twenty thousand in 1893 equaled about one-third of the city's electorate.[18]

The most immediate concerns of Cincinnati trade unionists revolved around the corruption of municipal affairs involving utility companies and others seeking municipal favors. As in Cleveland and other major cities, Cincinnati's public utility companies and contractors regularly bribed local politicians to secure contracts, franchises, and favorable legislation from the city. Historian Zane Miller has referred to Cincinnati's government in the early and mid 1880s as "a chaotic political system based upon unorganized bipartisan political corruption." By 1892 this unorganized corruption had given way to the much more efficient, organized corruption under the local Republican machine led by George "Boss" Cox and former governor Joseph B. Foraker. To secure political favors, utilities and contractors paid large sums to Cox, Foraker, and the Republican party. For example, Andrew Hickenlooper, the owner of the Cincinnati Gas, Light and Coke Company, which supplied manufactured gas for city streetlights, agreed to pay Cox thirty-five hundred dollars, four times a year, for his help. Payments to Foraker took on a more legitimate appearance. Since he was a lawyer, utilities and contractors simply placed him on retainer.[19]

This corruption pushed the CLC into a more active role in city politics. Issue after issue of the CLC's newspaper, the *Chronicle*, contained complaints about the "boodle ring" composed of "the gas company, electric light combine, Consolidated street railroad company, and corrupt politicians." The *Chronicle* accused the Consolidated Street Railway of "charging exorbitant fares and furnishing slow and inadequate facilities." Declaring that "the power of boodle has been too great," the paper protested the granting of a million-dollar contract to the "electric light combine" and fought the construction of a new waterworks on the grounds that the cost of the "stealage" would be borne by the workingman's pocketbook. The *Chronicle* called on trade unionists to exercise vigilance to ensure that the municipal government functioned in the "interests of the people instead of machine politicians."[20]

Not only did utility franchises exploit their monopoly position by charging Cincinnatians inflated rates and providing poor service, the CLC maintained that each of these franchises sought "to make slaves of its employes" by refusing to recognize unions, harassing union members, paying low wages, requiring workers to work more than eight hours a day, and ignoring labor laws. The CLC scored the city's board of administration for giving the contract to build a large viaduct to a company that brought in outside workers willing to work at half the standard rate. The CLC also carried on a two-year battle to force the Consolidated Street Railway to comply with a state law requiring the installation of vestibules on each car for the protection of drivers and conductors. Not only did the company ignore the law, the county prosecutor refused to take action against the company's transgression of the law.[21]

Particularly offensive to the CLC was an incident involving the Edison Light Company. Despite a state law forbidding employers from coercing employees to quit membership in labor unions, the company dismissed six employees for belonging to the Electrical Workers' union. The dismissed employees promptly filed suit in the local police court, where the judge found the company to be in violation of the law, ordered the workers' reinstatement, and fined the company's superintendent one hundred dollars plus court costs. Edison Light appealed the ruling to Hamilton County's common pleas court, where the company's lawyer, former governor Foraker, willingly admitted that the employees had been fired for belonging to the union. He insisted, though, that the law was an unconstitutional restriction on the right of the company to engage in commerce. The judge upheld the constitutionality of the law but did so in a manner that greatly mitigated its effectiveness. The judge declared that an employer may discharge an employee "for any reason, but shall not attempt to coerce him to quit the labor organization." In other words, an employer could fire a worker who had joined a union, but the employer could not apply other forms of pressure to convince a worker to resign from a union. The ruling infuriated the CLC and local trade unionists. The *Chronicle* suggested that the effect of the ruling was as dangerous as if the court declared that "the Declaration of Independence and the Constitution of the United States are unconstitutional."[22]

To rein in local franchises, the CLC called for the Ohio General Assembly to pass bills giving municipal governments greater control over franchises and the authority to operate them if necessary. In other words, the CLC wanted the state to allow cities to own and operate streetcars, gas and electric companies, and other public service utilities. Not only would this improve service and reduce costs to consumers, it would rid the city and state of corruption. The *Chronicle* declared, "The ownership of light and transport facilities of this city should be vested in the people, where it rightfully belongs, and such men as [telephone and streetcar magnate] John Kilgour, Andy Hickenlooper, etc will be deprived of their incentive to bribe members of the Legislature and city boards."[23]

Not only did the state legislature refuse to heed the calls for municipal ownership, in that same session it passed legislation exempting street railways from certain state taxes at the insistence of Foraker and his rival for the leadership of the state's Republicans, Marcus Hanna. As one state representative later wrote, Foraker and Hanna managed Ohio's legislature like a "private estate" in the interest of an "oligarchy of business bosses."[24]

To challenge the general assembly's decision to grant the exemption, its refusal to allow public operation of utilities, and its subservience to business interests, the CLC organized the Direct Legislation League of Hamilton County, an organization dedicated to adding the initiative, referendum, and recall to the state constitution. "Our system of representative legislation is rotten," CLC leaders insisted, and they hoped that direct legislation would provide a method for solving many of the problems facing trade unionists. Perhaps most important, direct legislation would allow trade union leaders to rally members attached to one of the major parties for political action and to form alliances with sympathetic groups—farmers, educators, and the like. It would also allow the labor movement to bypass the general assembly, where one or two powerful members had held up much needed reform—like the eight-hour day, mechanics' lien, weekly pay laws, municipal home rule, and public ownership of utilities. Additionally, the CLC hoped that direct legislation would make it less likely that corporations or other powerful interests would try to corrupt the legislature. If the people could invalidate a bad law or enact a good one, then corporations would be less willing to corrupt the legislative process.[25]

Although the Direct Legislation League was not officially connected with the People's party, the roster of its officers reads like a who's who of Hamilton County Populists. Rist served as the organization's president, E. M. Davis held the vice presidency, and Louis Benjamin was the secretary. Other officers included People's party leaders E. P. Foster and J. R. Jacobs. Of the league's officers only Foster, a minister, was not active in the CLC. The Direct Legislation League allowed the CLC to coordinate political activity with the People's party without breaking its policy of nonpartisanship. In this way, the Direct Legislation League served as a crucial intermediary step in the CLC's evolution from nonpartisanship to a formal alliance with the People's party.[26]

The financial difficulties associated with the Panic of 1893 compounded the CLC's frustration with the political environment in the city and the state. The panic hit Cincinnati particularly hard. According to the state's Bureau of Labor Statistics, "almost every man it seems was out of work" in the wards populated by the city's industrial workers during the fall of 1893. Families quickly depleted what savings they had been able to accumulate, which forced women and children into the labor force and further deflated the cost of labor. As a state official observed, "strong, able-bodied men remained in enforced idleness while the wives and children supported them by taking in washing and scrubbing."[27]

Drawing heavily upon the Populist critique of the American economic system, the CLC blamed the financial crisis on a conspiracy of European capitalists and Washington lawmakers. Particularly offensive to the leaders of the CLC was Grover Cleveland's proposal to repeal the Sherman Silver Purchase Act, which had allowed a limited coinage of silver.

> [F]oreign capitalists . . . have in the past secured legislation by our Congress which has robbed the American producers of millions of dollars at one fell swoop. And still again we are met with a demand that our coinage laws be so amended as to demonetize our silver dollars and establish the gold standard of coinage to conform to the idea of the Bank of England and the Rothschild. Once this scheme is effected the masses of the people of the United States will have descended one more step toward absolute slavery.

To combat this conspiracy, the *Chronicle* called for Cincinnati workers to "rise to the full dignity of their manhood" and "throw off the yoke of the thieving statesmen and financiers who now do our law making and banking."[28]

A *Chronicle* editorial on the eve of the 1893 election reveals the growing closeness between the CLC and the People's party. Although the paper insisted that the "CLC has wisely forbidden the introduction and discussion of partisan politics on its floor and through the *Chronicle*," it praised the People's party as the "only party whose platform approximates the declaration of principles promulgated by the CLC." Noting that the People's party's legislative ticket was composed mostly of "faithful and energetic delegates and officers of the CLC," the paper argued that only the election of Populists would assure "honest and just laws" and an economical administration.[29]

Over the next year, the CLC would move fitfully into a formal alliance with the Populists. Representatives of the People's party and the CLC began discussing joint action for the spring 1894 mayoral election, but the discussions were overtaken by another political development. A growing number of business and civic leaders came to believe that rampant corruption associated with Boss Cox's dominance of city hall had caused higher taxes and inefficient services, and church and moral reformers disliked the wide open nature of the town, which they asserted was run from Cox's downtown saloon. To unite the anti-Cox forces, a committee of six business and civic leaders, three Democrats and three Republicans, formed a new Citizens' party. The leaders of the Citizens' party chose Theodore Horstmann, whom the Citizens' party had contemplated nominating in 1891, as their standard-bearer in the upcoming mayoral election. The choice was politically shrewd. The incumbent corporation counsel, with a long record of battling both Cox and the city's utility companies, Horstmann had already won citywide election and had ties to the city's large German community. Rather than promising a wide range of reforms, the Citizens' party simply guaranteed that their ticket would provide a "clean administration of city affairs."[30]

Horstmann's nomination caused problems for the People's party. Party officials had been expecting the formation of the Citizens' party for several months and had several heated and unresolved discussions about the relationship between the two groups. Soon after the Citizens' party nominated Horstmann, the city People's party held its convention to nominate a slate for the upcoming municipal election. Discord broke out as soon as the meeting began, and the party divided into two factions. Led by CLC leaders Thomas Butterworth, Rist, and Benjamin, the larger of the two factions urged the party to endorse Horstmann. They argued that the Citizens' ticket offered the best chance of winning the election and freeing the city from the corruption of the Cox machine. The other faction, led by minister E. P. Foster and shopkeeper Zadoc Griffiths, insisted that the party should nominate its own candidate. Foster and Griffiths maintained that the People's party's nominee should support the Omaha platform and that long-lasting reform could only come through a permanent organization. The non-labor faction, the smaller of the two, bolted after the party nominated Horstmann, ensuring that the People's party would have two mayoral candidates. The rump faction nominated John L. Grover, a former Republican with close ties to the African American community, for the party's mayoral nomination.[31]

Although a number of prominent Democrats, including *Cincinnati Enquirer* publisher John McLean, urged the city's Democrats to support Horstmann, so-called Cox Democrats insisted that the party nominate its own candidate and prevented Horstmann's nomination. With neither Horstmann Democrats nor Cox Democrats wanting a strong candidate, Cincinnati's Democratic party, on the verge of collapse, nominated Isaac Miller, a weak candidate with little support either inside or outside the party. Like Horstmann, Miller ran as a reformer and promised a clean administration, but he was unable to generate much enthusiasm during the campaign, and newspapers and the other campaigns dismissed any possibility of his election. Horstmann supporters feared that Miller would divide the anti-Cox vote and keep disgruntled Democrats from voting for the Citizens' party.[32]

Labor's animosity toward Boss Cox and the Republican-controlled city government was so great that the CLC decided it would endorse a mayoral candidate for the first time in its history. Although a small number of CLC delegates supported Grover's candidacy on the grounds that he was the only candidate to support the People's party's Omaha platform and the municipal ownership of public utilities, the majority of the delegates voted to endorse Horstmann, insisting that he was the only candidate who could beat Cox's nominee, Congressman John Caldwell. The CLC declared:

> Whereas, the political bosses have obtained such complete control of our municipal affairs that the will of the people can no longer be expressed in their respective party conventions, and the corruption among our city officials is such that large corporations can violate their contracts, under which they hold valuable public franchises from the people, and defy the law at will. . . .
>
> Resolved, that we, the members of the Central Labor Council representing twenty thousand workingmen, heartily approve the action taken by a committee of citizens in putting a Citizens' ticket into the field, holding that such action was not only justifiable, but imperative, under prevailing circumstances, and we hereby endorse the whole ticket and ask all union men and friends to give their unqualified support to the Citizens' Ticket and especially to Theodore Horstmann for Mayor, in order that the gang of boodlers which now infest the city may be ousted by an overwhelming majority and honesty in municipal government take the place of corruption; be it further.[33]

During the campaign, the labor-led People's party faction and the CLC worked closely to secure Horstmann's election. They scheduled a series of mass meetings in which the heads of a dozen local unions made five-minute speeches urging workers to support Horstmann and the Citizens' party slate. During the campaign, Horstmann touted the support of Rist, Benjamin, Cavanaugh (now active in CLC), and other CLC and Populist leaders, making sure they occupied prominent places on the podium and invoking labor's endorsement as proof that he was a man of the people. As historian Zane Miller has noted, Horstmann's candidacy was "overwhelmingly popular among the workingmen."[34]

Throughout the campaign, the laborites avoided class rhetoric. Not only did they support a reform effort begun by business and civic leaders and the nomination of a lawyer, they portrayed the fortunes of business leaders and workers as intertwined. The *Chronicle* blamed the city's low wages and high unemployment on the high taxes caused by Cox's corruption of the city's administration. The city's high tax rate, the paper argued, "has driven many of our largest manufacturers from the city, and in that manner thousands of our citizens, with families depending upon them, were thrown out of employment and forced to compete with their more fortunate brethren."[35]

Despite his support among workers and others dissatisfied with Cox, Horstmann was unable to overcome Cox's formidable machine, however. Cox kept his party workers in line and secured the support of a number of Democratic leaders with the promise of contracts and city jobs. Additionally, Democratic nominee Isaac Miller drew enough of the anti-Cox vote to ensure the election of Cox's candidate.[36]

Although Horstmann lost the election to Cox's candidate, the contest offered some hope to labor forces and the People's party. In little more than six weeks, the anti-Cox forces were able to find a candidate, organize a campaign, and collect over a third of the vote in a three-way race. Although the Citizens' party took the lead in much of this, the Populists and the CLC played important roles in mobilizing workingmen—the very people who, Zane Miller suggests, formed the core of Horstmann's supporters. The election witnessed the eclipse of the Democrats as the main challengers to Cox's regime, suggested a dissatisfaction with the traditional parties, and convinced trade unionists that a third party could do well in Cincinnati. While moving the CLC and the People's party closer, the municipal election of 1894 did not see the two organizations consummating a formal political alliance. This would not come until the late summer, after the city and the nation witnessed the turbulent events of spring and summer 1894.

Soon after the start of the American Railway Union's (ARU) boycott of Pullman sleeping cars in late June 1894, Cincinnati-area switchmen reluctantly agreed to participate.[37] Their reluctance stemmed from the fear that area railroads would simply replace them, as there were, according to one striker, a "good number of unemployed switchmen looking for work." Their fears were realized on the second day of the boycott, June 28, when the Cincinnati, Hamilton, and Dayton Railroad fired its switchmen for refusing to handle Pullman cars. Thirty-five hundred Cincinnati-area yardmen and switchmen immediately walked off their jobs in a sympathy strike. With the exception of the Pennsylvania Railroad, all of the city's rail yards were shut down, essentially stopping the movement of freight—but not passengers—through Cincinnati.[38]

From the outset, F. W. Phelan, an ARU organizer who had recently arrived from Oregon under orders from Eugene Debs, warned the strikers to act responsibly: "We have no malice toward the railroad companies. We are fighting to put down corporation rule as shown in the actions of the Pullman company. If any man gets drunk or interferes with company

TABLE 4.1—Results of Cincinnati's 1894 Mayoral Election

Candidate (party)	Votes	Percentage
Caldwell (Republican)	26,667	45.6
Horstmann (Citizens'/People's/CLC)	19,912	34.1
Miller (Democrat)	11,657	19.9
Grover (People's)	216	0.4

Source: Cincinnati Enquirer, April 3, 1894.

property or with scabs who the officials may hire, he will be discharged and if he gets thrown into jail, he will have to get himself out."[39] Despite this plea, federal judge William Howard Taft intervened on July 2. One of the roads shut down by the strikers, the Cincinnati, New Orleans, & Texas Pacific Railroad (commonly called the Cincinnati Southern), was in receivership. After the railroad's engineers refused to work with "scab" switchmen, Taft, at the request of the receiver, enjoined Phelan, ARU president Eugene V. Debs, and the strikers from interfering with the operation of the line: "Any act to intimidate the men operating it is forbidden. The trains of that line are going to run, whether certain men approve their running or not."[40] The following day, at the request of the Cincinnati Southern's receiver, Taft ordered the arrest of Phelan and the leaders of the ARU for impeding the operation of the railroad. Not only did the receiver present affidavits from detectives posing as railroaders, which asserted that Phelan had threatened violence against those remaining at work during the strike, he asserted that the strike was part of a conspiracy by Debs, Phelan, and other ARU officials to stop the railroad from doing business.[41]

The arrest of Phelan and other strikers outraged the CLC and its leaders. At a special meeting, the CLC passed resolutions supporting Phelan and the strikers. The resolutions insisted that the first amendment guarantee of freedom of speech protected both Phelan when he called for workers to join the strike and strikers when they yelled at strikebreakers. Rist declared, "The present fight of the ARU is the fight of every labor organization in this land, and every laboring man."[42]

Cincinnati newspapers speculated that CLC leaders and members were so angry they would launch a general strike in an effort to protest the prosecution of Phelan and other ARU leaders and to pressure city and state leaders to take action. Such a strike did not happen, but the CLC did organize a series of mass meetings urging the city's workers to organize for political action. The day after Phelan's arrest, fifteen hundred strikers marched from strike headquarters to Workman's Hall, the CLC's meeting place, where they were joined by thousands of members of Cincinnati's working class. Protestors jammed inside the hall, while over two thousand supporters were turned away and waited in the streets. Those inside heard speeches from CLC president T. J. Donnelly and a host of others detailing the "contemptible" actions of George Pullman, William Howard Taft, and Grover Cleveland. For Donnelly these actions were not surprising, given that "capitalists and boodlers" controlled the state's and the nation's governments. He insisted that government had deprived labor of weapons in its fight against capital and the only solution was for workingmen to vote with the same enthusiasm with which they went on strike. E. S. Denny of the Iron Molders' Union echoed this call for political action, telling the crowd, "The working man [has] produced all the wealth in the country and is only prevented from enjoying his just share of the same by corrupt and capitalistic legislation." Phelan gave a brief defense of his actions before concluding that workers themselves were to blame for the current unrest—"workingmen have failed to intelligently use their votes and by petty diversions and bickering have allowed the enemy to get elected." The workingmen must cut their ties with the traditional parties and unite politically if they are going to change the situation. On each of the next four nights, the CLC organized smaller rallies in every part of the city. The protests were to culminate on July 9 as the CLC rented the Music Hall for what it hoped would be the largest mass meeting in the city's history. One CLC leader predicted that over fifty thousand would attend the protest.[43]

Cincinnati was so tense on the eve of the Music Hall rally that civic leaders feared the city was on the verge of a riot such as it had seen in 1884. Cincinnati police began making preparations, and Mayor Caldwell even wired Governor McKinley, requesting that the state militia send 250 stands of arms to the city's police and asking that troops be readied to enter the city if needed. McKinley did not send the arms, but the *Commercial Gazette* assured readers that the police department's Gatling gun "is stored in the police armory, and conveniently placed near it are 10,000 rounds of Springfield cartridges."[44]

The Music Hall event lived up to its billing as the largest protest meeting in the city's history. Over six thousand workers paraded from city hall to the Music Hall. Along the route, tens of thousands of supporters cheered the protesters, following them to the rally. Workers and citizens jammed the hall, and thousands more were turned away. Inside, the CLC officials railed against the nation's railroads, corporations generally, the policies of the Cleveland administration, especially Attorney General Richard Olney's use of federal troops to defeat the boycott, and the corruption of the whole political system, but most of the venom was reserved for Taft and the use of the labor injunction.[45]

On July 13, Taft found Phelan guilty of violating the injunction enjoining him from interfering with the Cincinnati Southern and sentenced him to six months in the Warren County jail. Since the trial was on contempt charges, there was no jury, a fact that outraged the city's workingmen, who insisted that Phelan had a constitutional right to be judged by his peers. To make matters worse, the evidence that Phelan had threatened violence against strikebreakers, Taft admitted, was inconclusive—"threats are hard to prove"—but he concluded that Phelan had engaged in "that secret terrorism which is so effective for discouraging new men from filling the strikers' places." Soon after Phelan's conviction, the strike petered out and the defeated workers returned to work.[46]

Phelan's conviction and the defeat of the ARU exacerbated the tensions between the CLC and the traditional parties and prompted the CLC to enter a formal alliance with the People's party in the late summer of 1894. In late August CLC president Thomas Donnelly issued a manifesto calling on the city's trade unions and reform organizations to send representatives to an organizational meeting for a new political party: "We demand the unconditional emancipation from the thralldom of capital and ask *for freedom, equality, and fraternity.* And knowing that the people's arsenal of strength is the ballot-box, we hereby call upon all liberty-loving and patriotic citizens to sever their affiliations with the Plutocratic parties, and aid in the advancement of a movement which will secure justice and righteousness, fraternity and equality to all." Donnelly insisted that the new movement would be built upon three principles: (1) that the "great resources of life and wealth" were created for the "free and equal use of all mankind," (2) that all wealth is the product of labor, and (3) that wealth ought to be the servant of labor rather than its master. Such a movement, Donnelly promised, would "relieve the masses from the sordid grasp of a relentless and soulless despotism, a despotism that enthralls labor, prostitutes government, corrupts the laws, defies justice, and robs the people."[47]

The principal speaker at the CLC's meeting was United Mine Workers president John McBride, who had just announced his intention to form an Ohio labor party and to merge the party with the People's party. McBride, who had worked closely with ARU leaders during both the spring's nationwide coal strike and the summer's Pullman boycott, told the workers that the use of labor injunctions had taken away labor's main weapon in its confrontation with capital. Only through the formation of an independent labor party and the reform of the nation's political system, he told the crowd, could trade unionists free themselves from the chain of slavery. Although McBride's speech was met with great enthusiasm, the crowd went wild when Donnelly read a letter Phelan had written from his jail cell: "The unwarranted and illegal usurpations of authority by the tools of monopoly as represented by the Republican and Democratic judges of the Federal Courts during the mine and Pullman strikes, have shown the workers that their supposed friends are their worst enemies . . . join the forces of that party whose principles every true reformer holds dear to heart—the People's party."[48]

The delegates to the CLC's meeting voted overwhelmingly to work with the People's party in the upcoming election and passed a platform that contained many Populist demands, including the initiative and referendum; greenbacks; the single tax; public ownership of all mines, public utilities, and means of communications and transportation; compulsory education; the eight-hour day; and a massive investment in public works to provide "productive labor for the unemployed." Shortly afterward, the Hamilton County People's party met and endorsed the CLC's platform as its own. The convention also produced a slate of candidates for office. Heading the ticket were two CLC activists. Typographer and CLC president T. J. Donnelly received the party's nomination for Congress in the first district, while shoemaker Robert Wheeler received the nomination in the second district. The party also nominated CLC members for county clerk, sheriff, and the board of control. The CLC in turn endorsed the People's party slate of candidates, noting that many of the nominees "have held or are still holding positions of honor and trust in the CLC." The era was over in which the CLC remained formally nonpartisan but coordinated activities with the People's party through interlocking boards. All pretenses were dropped, and labor and the People's party consummated their alliance.[49]

The CLC participated in McBride's successful effort to unite Ohio labor forces and the state's Populist party in the late summer. The CLC endorsed the Populist candidates for state office, including secretary of state candidate Charles Martin, who headed the ticket. Horstmann's strong showing that spring and the seeming disarray of the local Democratic party had given CLC leaders hope that Martin and the rest of the slate, especially Donnelly and Wheeler, would do well in the city, maybe even winning a few offices. But this hope was misplaced. The city's voters gave Martin only about 6 percent of the vote. Martin ran best in the newly emerging industrial areas just north of the city's core, gathering about 10 percent of the vote in this area. The next year, Jacob Coxey, the People's party gubernatorial candidate, did even worse, collecting less than 5 percent of the vote.[50]

The poor showings of Martin and Coxey confounded and angered CLC leaders. One even went so far as to declare the bulk of the city's workingmen to be "ignoramuses" and that any trade unionist who voted for one of the traditional parties suffered from "stupidity and ignorance." The editors of the *Chronicle*, Frank Rist and Thomas Donnelly, offered a different explanation. Most of the city's twenty thousand trade unionists, they insisted, supported the CLC's alliance with the People's party, realizing that the party's platform best represented their needs and that the party's candidates were the most sympathetic to their concerns. But Cincinnati workers did not think that the Populists could win, and therefore they "throw their vote away by voting for one of the old parties."[51]

The results in Cincinnati were nearly identical to the ones in Cleveland and Columbus (see next chapter) for both statewide elections. These three cities were not very similar, though, in terms of industrial development or the composition of their working class. Cincinnati, which developed in the early nineteenth century with mixed industry, had a working class composed largely of older immigrant groups—mostly Irish and Germans. Cleveland developed its industry after the Civil War and attracted more southern and eastern European immigrants to work in the steel and refining/chemical industries. Columbus never achieved the level of industrialization of the other two cities, but its biggest industry—railroads—tended to attract native-born workers. What the cities did have in common was that they were in the same state and their voters cast ballots in the same two-party system.[52] Historian Jeffrey Ostler in his study of Populism in Iowa, Kansas, and Nebraska has shown that this type of two-party system presented a structural impediment to the success of the People's party and other third parties. The two older parties—with tremendous advantages over a new one in terms of money, newspaper resources, tradition, incumbency, and electability—had the ability to define the main issues of the campaign (whether it be the tariff, the money question, or imperialism), and on these issues the two parties always disagreed. The Republicans, for instance, would not spend the time or resources to trumpet their tariff position if that position was endorsed by the Democrats. This left little room for the People's party to maneuver or appeal to voters. As People's party chairman Herman Taubeneck declared, "No new party can be successfully organized until the discontent becomes intense and all existing parties decline to take up the new issue."[53]

Despite the poor showing of Populist candidates in Cincinnati and the structural barriers to the party's success, the leaders of the CLC remained committed to the alliance, insisting that they have "always advocated the People's party, believing it better for the workers than the other two parties, and shall continue to advocate that which it considers to be the best for organized labor." Donnelly and Rist remained confident that, if the old parties continued to oppress labor, there would be a "solid phalanx" of workers joining the Populists. "Our advice to our fellow workers is," they concluded, "Vote the People's party ticket."[54]

CLC leaders opposed the attempts by the People's party national leadership in 1895 and 1896 to shed the party's 1892 Omaha platform in favor of one emphasizing the free and unlimited coinage of silver at the ratio of sixteen to one. Led by James Weaver and Herman Taubeneck, party leaders reasoned that neither of the old parties would be willing to endorse free silver, thus giving the People's party a unique and popular position on what people were rapidly considering the most important issue of the day—the money question. The leadership added that other planks on the Omaha platform, such as sub-treasury, government ownership of railroads and telegraphs, and the abolition of alien landownership, would alienate many of those who might otherwise support free silver.[55] The CLC leaders affirmed their support of free silver, seeing it as a way to counter "the restless assault of the money power upon the liberties of the people." But they realized that the "free coinage of silver is not going to benefit the man who has nothing but his labor to sell" and insisted that the Populists retain their Omaha platform. In keeping with its middle-of-the-road position, Cincinnati labor leaders urged that the People's party nominate Eugene Debs for president: "There is no man that the people could put up who so thoroughly represents the working classes as does Debs. With Debs at the head of the Populist ticket, that party would stand a very good show of winning the presidential campaign."[56]

After the Populists' national convention nominated the Democrats' free silver candidate, William Jennings Bryan, the leaders of the CLC were disappointed, but they quickly went to work for the Nebraskan. The *Chronicle* insisted that the coinage of silver would free the nation from "gold monometallism," which was bringing "great injury to all classes of citizens." The newspaper praised those who wrote the Democratic platform as being "in the front rank as reformers and the enemies of corporations, trusts, monopolies and the bondholders" and told readers "if they would be honest, if they would be true, if they would be just, they would vote for William Jennings Bryan for President of the United States."[57]

Following the advice of the state People's party's executive committee, Cincinnati's Populists met with the local Democratic party in the late summer of 1896 to consider the nomination of a joint local slate. Hamilton County's Democratic party was on the verge of collapse, bitterly divided between Bryan silverites, monometallists, and even a few "Cox Democrats." The party had not fared well in the 1894 mayoral contest, with the nominee receiving only about 20 percent of the vote, while the CLC and Populist candidate had received 34 percent. So the Populists entered negotiations from a position of strength, demanding one of the county's two congressional nominations and several other slots on the ballot. At first Democratic officials refused to give one of the congressional nominations to a Populist, but after Hugh Cavanaugh, the People's party chief negotiator, threatened that his party would nominate a full slate, the Democrats backed down. The Democrats nominated CLC president Thomas Donnelly in the first congressional district and other "prominent labor leaders" to lesser offices.[58]

During the campaign, the CLC worked hard to get Bryan and Democrats, especially those who had been associated with the People's party, elected. The *Chronicle* transformed itself into a Democratic campaign organ, working on behalf of the whole Democratic slate and castigating Republican candidates as having "championed every measure in the interest of corporations, pools and trusts." Hugh Cavanaugh traveled the state, escorting Bryan on his campaign tour. When Bryan spoke in Cincinnati and nearby Covington, Kentucky, CLC leaders, including Donnelly and Cavanaugh, occupied conspicuous places on the podium. Bryan tailored his speech to the interests of labor: "Let me state to you a reason for the opposition of some of these railroad presidents which they themselves do not suggest. They oppose our platform, not so much because it declares for free coinage—they can stand free coinage. They object to it because we demand that instead of summoning an army to settle labor troubles that we shall have arbitration to settle them." Two weeks later, Eugene Debs appeared at a labor-sponsored event campaigning for Bryan. Debs also linked Bryan's candidacy to the hostility of the court system, the Pullman boycott, and the arrest of Frank Phelan in the city two years before: "The Democratic party declares . . . against government by injunction. We are opposed to government by injunction, not because we are opposed to the law, but because we are in favor of the law. Government by injunction is arresting the citizen and condemning him to trial without a jury trial." On the eve of the election, the *Chronicle* published the whole Democratic slate and told readers "to vote for Bryan of Nebraska for president of the United States."[59]

The election of 1896 did not go well for Bryan and the Democrats in Cincinnati. McKinley won 60 percent of the vote in Hamilton County, and the CLC leaders running on the Democratic ticket were overwhelmed by their Republican opponents. The defeats were especially frustrating to the editors of the *Chronicle* who complained that "a big majority of workingmen evidently do not want one of their number to be elected to office." Donnelly's poor showing, the paper continued, showed that the city's workingmen "would rather be represented in Congress by a willing tool of monopolies and corporations and a follower of a political boss than an honorable young workingman."[60]

Reeling from a string of electoral defeats culminating in the election of 1896 and increasingly suspicious of middle-class reformers, the CLC began distancing itself from the Democratic party and partisanship in general. The *Chronicle* quoted Karl Marx: "All political parties, may they be what they will and without exception, can only passingly enthuse the workers for a time." Later editorials blasted the Democratic party for losing interest in labor reform, the Republicans for being the tools of monopolists, and the Socialist Labor party for dual unionism and trying to build "wonderful structures of air."[61]

The municipal elections of April 1897 gave the CLC an opportunity to sort out its new political orientation. Middle-class reformers and "good government" business leaders joined forces to challenge George Cox's Republican machine, much as they had done in 1894. Unlike the earlier election, though, the local Democrats officially joined the anti-Cox movement. Running under the banner of the Fusion ticket, the Democrats and the reformers nominated Gustav Tafel for mayor in part because they hoped he could win the labor vote. Tafel, whom many trade unionists and Populists had supported for mayor in 1891, had flirted with the Populist party since its beginnings. But rejecting the type of cross-class political action that Richard Schneirov found in Chicago, the CLC declined both to join the Democratic-led Fusion party and to support the candidacy of Tafel. The CLC was clearly unwilling to become the tail of a middle-class kite. Warning that the Democrats were just as corrupt as the Republicans, the *Chronicle* announced, "Trade unionists have learned by the past if they have learned anything, that their only hope lies in themselves and that if they are ever to get the recognition they are by every right entitled to, they must have a sounder basis of support than a few ephemeral reformers, mugwumps, and disgruntled gangsters." On the eve of the election, the paper told its readers that the election of "a few self-styled reformers . . . is nothing to be enthusiastic about" and that "changing bosses" would not benefit the city's workers.[62]

The remnants of the Hamilton County People's party—led by CLC leaders Donnelly, Rist, and Ernest Weier who had given up on the local Democrat party after the disastrous results of 1896—refused either to nominate a local slate or to endorse the Fusion ticket. The Populists realized that the nomination of a slate might draw votes from the Fusion ticket and throw the election to the "boodlers, corruptionists, and thieves" nominated by the Cox machine. But, like the CLC, the Populists were also uncomfortable with the Fusion party, which contained a number of anti-labor business leaders.[63]

Much to the surprise of Cox and the Republican party, Tafel won by a landslide, capturing over 55 percent of the popular vote. While business leaders and reformers rejoiced over the victory, the CLC continued to distance itself from the political scene. During the fall of 1897, the *Chronicle* was conspicuously silent. There was no mention of the governor's race or the local legislative contests other than a small blurb listing the trade unionists seeking office. After the election the *Chronicle* justified its new political strategy: "The K of L and the ARU are not the only wrecks that strew the sea of the past, but they show the folly of trade organizations' allowing themselves to be led into strange [political] paths by over-zealous officers . . . they [union leaders] must keep their organizations intact or retard the final emancipation."[64]

Instead of concentrating on political action, the *Chronicle* told unionists to work toward goals that would improve the daily lives of workers and their families. It declared that trade unions should "[a]gitate for a shorter work day; insist upon the label and keep your organization's strength, that means men live to strive for better things. A starving man can never think or act." This new emphasis on improving the immediate material circumstances of its members rather than the promise of reform through partisan activity did not entail a change in goals as much as it did a change in methods. The paper kept telling its members that labor's agitation and educational programs would lead to their "final emancipation," the "new abolition" of wage slavery. In June 1899, the CLC ratified a political platform that continued to embrace much of the Populist agenda. The leading planks called for the abolition of national banks, the government to issue greenbacks, the municipal ownership of utilities and public service franchises, national ownership of railroads, telephones, and telegraphs, the abolition of child labor, women's suffrage, and the eight-hour day.[65]

When Tafel came up for election in 1900, CLC again refused to support him and the *Chronicle* barely mentioned the mayoral campaign. A number of factors probably contributed to labor's nonpartisan stance. First, the

Tafel administration had accomplished little during its three years in office. Labor had hoped that Tafel would fulfill his promises of a more efficient and honest government but instead saw an increase in taxes and little regard for the condition of workers employed by city contractors. Second, the anti-Cox coalition was supported by some of the city's most anti-labor businessmen, including a "scab tobacco manufacturer," a "rat printer," and a "scab teamster." The paper said that if these men controlled the local government "a sign would appear at the City Hall and the Courthouse declaring 'No Union Men Need Apply.'" Third, the Republicans chose a candidate, Julius Fleischmann, who was friendly toward labor. Calling workmen "the very backbone of all cities and all governments," Fleischmann campaigned hard to win labor's support.[66]

Fleischmann won handily, and during his first term Cox's Republican machine and the CLC cemented an informal alliance, at least as it pertained to local matters. Fleischmann was liberal with his appointment of union members to city offices. For example, the mayor's five appointees to the building inspector's office all carried union cards. Two were plumbers, while the others belonged to the carpenters, plasterers, and the typographical unions. He also launched a number of bond-funded public improvements, including a new public hospital, public baths, playgrounds, and an expansion of the park system, which created construction jobs for the building trades without substantially raising taxes.[67]

Not only did the Fleischmann administration provide jobs and other direct benefits to labor, it also launched an ambitious program to improve public education. For years the CLC had been lobbying for a series of improvements in the city's public school system. Not only did the CLC see compulsory public education as a means to eliminate competition from cheap child labor, trade unionists saw free public education as essential to the American ideal. By providing opportunity, education could mitigate distinctions in class and allow the children of workers to compete with the children of the upper crust. The mayor helped build new schools, introduced free kindergarten, and lobbied the general assembly for free textbooks for all public school students.

Perhaps more important for cementing labor's alliance with the Cox machine, Fleischmann presided over a period of relative prosperity for the city's workers. The superintendent of the state's Free Public Employment Bureau reported that during Fleischmann's first year in office the area finally emerged from the economic downturn that had begun in the late summer of 1893. Not only did the bureau have problems finding skilled workers, especially in the building trades, to fill employers' requests for help, the number of unemployed unskilled workers decreased dramatically. The superintendent told the legislature that he was downright "cheerful" about the employment prospects in the city.[68]

Fleischmann was not the only Republican working to gain the support of the city's labor movement. None was more conspicuous than Cox's top lieutenant, August Hermann. A former member of the printers' union, Hermann used his position on the board of the waterworks to help the cause of labor. In 1900 Hermann and the CLC worked together to secure municipal ownership of the city's waterworks. In early 1903, he won praise from the CLC and the Building Trades Council for ensuring that the expansion of the waterworks would be performed by union labor. In the words of the *Chronicle*, "August Hermann brought his influence to bear once more in favor of organized labor."[69]

By the mayoral election of 1903, the CLC's support for Fleischmann and the Cox Republican machine was unmistakable, creating a working-class alliance. As in 1900 middle-class reformers of both parties organized the anti-Cox forces. Leading the way was the Committee of Twenty-six, a group of lawyers dedicated to ending corruption and boodle in the city that Lincoln Steffens called the "worst" governed in America. The Committee of Twenty-six attracted the city's disorganized Democrats, independent Republicans, and the ministers of the evangelical alliance into the Citizens' party to challenge the Cox machine.[70]

The Citizens' party's platform called for honest, efficient, and progressive government and attacked Cox and the Republican incumbent Fleischmann on two fronts—the corruption of Boss Cox's Cincinnati and the failure of the police force to enforce certain laws. The Citizens' party could not have picked a candidate more alienating to Cincinnati's labor movement and working class than its candidate, Melville E. Ingalls, a Democrat and the president of the Big Four railroad. A New England–born Protestant who railed against the excesses of gambling and the saloon, Ingalls regarded Bryan as a "blight" on his party. Moreover, he had to fight the impression that he was anti-immigrant and the tool of Wall Street railroad interests. Rumors persisted throughout the campaign that he had once declared that $1.12 a day was enough for any workingman and that $1.50 a day would cause the workman to "make a fool of himself" by either gambling it away or spending it in a saloon.[71]

Supporters of the Citizens' party spoke a language of class. By calling for a government of experts and businessmen, the reformers were asserting that the prerogatives of government belong to the middle class. By portraying working-class neighborhoods as hot beds of gambling, drinking, and assorted forms of vice, the Citizens' party suggested that the lower classes were cancers on the city. By campaigning against the saloon, an institution central to the lives of many workers, the reformers promised the replacement of working-class culture with bourgeois values.

Like the Citizens' party, Fleischmann and his supporters spoke a language of class, but they, unlike the Fusionists, championed the poor and laboring classes. Fleischmann turned the Citizens' party's and Ingall's attacks on his administration for its lax enforcement of liquor, gambling, and vice laws into attacks on working-class Cincinnatians, asserting that those in the working and lower classes were citizens both hardworking and honest. Telling his opponents that "politics and religion are two entirely distinct institutions," Fleischmann defended the lower and working classes from the imposition of middle-class Protestant values. Fleischmann reminded the city's working class, "It is the innate nature of the average 'reformer' to desire to reap the benefit of the labor and brain of his neighbor" before enumerating the anti-labor businessmen who supported Ingalls and the Citizens' ticket.[72]

In the days before the election, the labor movement made its support for Fleischmann and the Republican slate clear. The *Chronicle* told its readers, "Julius Fleischmann stands for fair wages and hours" and that under his administration Cincinnati's "citizens as a whole have had better times, less friction, and [the city] has progressed faster than ever before." Ingalls and the reformers, the paper insisted, were long on theory and short in practice. The paper also called for the reelection of the Board of Public Service, which set the labor standards for most city projects. The *Chronicle* and CLC officials praised the Cox-dominated Board of Public Service. The paper even suggested that the Board of Public Service contributed to the success of the city's labor movement:

> Cincinnati is justly regarded by the national labor leaders as the best organized city of its class in the whole country. Chicago may be more militant, San Francisco more conscious, Cleveland more radical, but this city for harmony and effectiveness beats them all. Organized labor in this town gets there without any wire drawn theory or broken heads. One big reason for this is the attitude of the Board of Public Service. This city has been a good pacemaker in the matter of wages and hours. When a grievance arises this board has never been called in vain. They have always been open to free and full discussion of any point of controversy. They as a body have always been friendly to organized labor and have never refused to meet it halfway. What is more to the point, they have never cut the wages of women or manual laborers. In other words, the five present members have made it impossible to become a labor martyr. You don't have to die in this town or break heads or go into the newspapers—just talk it over with these five men and presto, it is all over."[73]

The *Chronicle* ran brief, favorable profiles of thirty-seven candidates for municipal office. Of these candidates, thirty-four were identified as Republican. The party affiliation of the other three was not listed.[74]

As Zane Miller has noted, the reelection of Fleischmann signaled the completion of a realignment of Cincinnati municipal politics. Cox and the Republican party came to power in the late 1880s and early 1890s by polling well in the middle-class neighborhoods of the hills overlooking the central city. In those years, the Democrats polled best in the lower- and working-class neighborhoods of the center city and the West Side. By 1903 these formerly Democratic working- and lower-class wards were giving Fleischmann and the Cox machine their greatest support, while Ingalls and the Citizens' ticket did their best in the middle- and upper-class areas known as the Hilltops.[75]

While Cincinnati's labor movement found itself in a de facto alliance with the Cox machine and the Republican party at the local level, it continued to advocate what had been the Populist agenda at the state and national level. Not only did the CLC join the statewide labor effort on behalf of Samuel "Golden Rule" Jones's 1899 gubernatorial bid, but after 1900 Thomas Donnelly and most CLC leaders attached themselves to the Tom Johnson/Bryan faction of the state Democratic party. In fact, Donnelly coordinated labor's efforts at the 1912 Ohio Constitutional Convention, where the labor movement along with the disciples of Johnson rewrote much of the state constitution along lines that had been advocated by the state's labor-Populists.[76]

5 Middle-class Reform and Labor's Embrace of Populism in Columbus

IN 1893 CONGREGATIONALIST MINISTER and prominent social gospeler Washington Gladden published *The Cosmopolis City Club*, a thoroughly fictionalized account of the recent municipal reform effort he had helped to lead in Columbus, Ohio. Gladden portrayed the unreformed city as chaotic, corrupt, and filled with Sabbath breaking, gambling, prostitution, and drunkenness. The problem was that the votes of the lower and working classes had empowered machine politicians who catered to hedonistic appetites rather than to the needs of the city as a whole. Gladden's protagonists felt that the municipal government needed reforming in such as way as to empower the business community. As one fictional reformer declared, "The educated men, the professional men, the active businessmen of our cities, are the men to whom the political leadership of our community belongs; we shall never have good government until these men come to the front and take hold of it." The heart of Gladden's novel describes how a group of mostly business leaders and professionals successfully banded together to restructure the city's government in such as way as to decrease lower- and working-class political power and increase the ability of the business class to rule the city.[1]

The reform effort in Columbus resembled the one described by Gladden in one fundamental way—the business leaders pushed through a municipal structuring that gave them increased power over municipal affairs. But the story as told by Gladden omitted several important details. The Columbus business community pushed for reform not to curb vice but in the wake of a streetcar strike and an unprecedented display of the Columbus Trades and Labor Assembly's (CTLA) power. The municipal reform movement in Columbus played a critical role in the labor movement's embrace of Populism by severing the traditional ties between the CTLA and the Democratic party and convincing trade unionists that the Populists' warnings of efforts to rob producers of their political and economic rights had validity.[2]

Although it had an official policy of nonpartisanship, the CTLA entered the Populist era in a de facto alliance with the Democratic party. Whereas in Cleveland and Cincinnati the leaders of the central labor federations worked with the People's party early on, the most prominent men in Columbus's labor movement—John McBride, Patrick McBryde, William Mahon, and Louis Bauman—were active in the Democratic party and, in many cases, used their connections to labor organizations to secure jobs and political office. In return for labor's support, Columbus Democrats generally aided labor whenever possible. The relationship was so beneficial that even CTLA president S. P. Ewing, a member of the Republican party at least when it came to national or state affairs, extolled the "pleasant relations" between organized labor and the Democratic-controlled municipal government.[3]

The undisputed leader of the city's Democratic party at the beginning of the 1890s was the aging Allen G. Thurman. Active in Democratic politics since the Civil War, Thurman had served in the U.S. Senate and on the Ohio Supreme Court. Since the late 1870s, Thurman had been a stalwart in the greenback/anti-monopoly wing of the Democratic party. His standing among radicals was such that a Greenback-Labor convention in California even passed a resolution calling for him to receive that party's presidential nomination. In 1888 the Democratic party nominated him to be Grover Cleveland's running mate. As Cleveland biographer Allen Nevins explained, Thurman was placed on the ticket so that "Labor, Anti-Monopoly, and Greenback agitation would subside." In the early 1890s, Thurman sounded much like a Populist, attacking Republican gubernatorial candidate William McKinley's tariff policy as a part of a conspiracy to aid "intrenched monopoly" and leading the monetary reformers at the state's Democratic conventions. His activities on behalf of the nation's producing classes had won Thurman the respect of Ohio trade unionists. Even the Cleveland Central Labor Union's *Citizen*, which rarely had anything positive to say about politicians from either of the two major parties, praised Thurman as one of the nation's few politicians who had tried to stop the "hand of greed [from] fastening its vile clutches upon the wealth producers of this land."[4]

Following Thurman's lead, the city's most prominent Democrats spoke in a language that echoed both the concerns of the city's workers and the party's anti-monopoly tradition. Mayor George Karb told a labor crowd in September 1891 that the concentration of capital threatened the ideals that Americans had died for during the Civil War and the American Revolution. "Instead of kings and lords," he said, "we have a constitutional government, corrupted by millionaires and politicians. We see legislators, judges and other officials using their places for private gain. We see capitalists and speculators bribing the lawmakers and lobbying for schemes to enrich themselves." The president of Columbus's Democratic-controlled city council insisted in 1890 that "the unscrupulous and avaricious employer" has caused the "products of labor to be unevenly distributed."[5]

Not only did the city's Democratic leaders speak in a language that appealed to Columbus's labor community, they also sided with organized labor during strikes and other confrontations with employers. The most dramatic example occurred during the June 1890 streetcar strike, in which nearly 300 of the city's 350 streetcar drivers, conductors, and barn workers walked off the job demanding that the city's streetcar monopoly pay higher wages and end arbitrary punishment. The workers, who had been averaging just under twelve cents an hour for a twelve-hour day, demanded fifteen cents an hour for an eleven-and-a-half-hour day and changes in work rules that would allow for meal breaks. City and county Democratic officials quickly rallied behind the strikers and promised to use the municipal structure to aid the strikers. The city's police chief, John E. Murphy, declared that he considered the strikers' cause to be "just" and that the department's officers were "in sympathy with the strikers." Murphy initially refused to order the police to remove strikers from company property, insisting, "the men wear the company's badges and claim they have neither been paid off [n]or discharged." Officers harassed strikebreakers, often arresting them on a variety of pretexts ranging from disorderly conduct and vagrancy to assault. In one instance, the police filed fraud charges against a strikebreaker who took money from strikers to quit work but showed up to drive a car the next day. When the streetcar company secured injunctions enjoining the strikers from damaging property or interfering with the operation of the cars, the county sheriff refused to serve the injunctions, claiming, somewhat disingenuously, that he did not know who the enjoined men were or where they could be found. Former Democratic congressman George Converse volunteered to serve as the strikers' attorney during the dispute, while a Democratic judge organized a relief fund for the strikers' families. The *Cincinnati Commercial*

Gazette reported that Democratic mayor Philip Bruck "encourages the strikers by an open manifestation of his sympathy for them and his hostility toward the company." The biggest boost to the strikers came from the Democratic-controlled city council, which passed a resolution urging the streetcar company to meet the strikers' demands or face revocation of its franchise on the grounds that it had failed to provide the daily service required by its charter during the strike's first days.[6]

Public sympathy for the strikers was strong. One city councilman suggested that 90 percent of the city's residents supported the strikers and opposed the company. When the company attempted to run cars, strikers and supporters often blocked the tracks coming out of the company barns and disconnected the horse teams from the streetcars. Those streetcars that made it out of the barns were greeted by residents who pelted the drivers with debris and used stones to block the movement of the cars. On the fourth day of the strike, a few streetcars finally made their way downtown where crowds numbering close to five thousand streamed into the streets surrounding the cars and lifting them from the tracks.[7]

Facing a hostile public, three hundred striking workers, an unsympathetic police force willing to harass strikebreakers and unwilling to protect streetcars attempting to operate, and a city council threatening to revoke its charter, the Consolidated Street Railway Company quickly abandoned its efforts to run the streetcars with strikebreakers and agreed to the strikers' demands. The agreement, brokered by Bruck and the leaders of the city's business community, gave the strikers the pay increase and changes in work rules they demanded. The strikers viewed the agreement as a complete victory, and E. K. Stewart, the general manager of the railway company, agreed, complaining that with the police department working "hand in hand with the strikers," it was impossible for the company to win the strike.[8]

Given the close relationship between organized labor and the city's Democratic party, it is not surprising that the People's party had an inauspicious start in Columbus and Franklin County. Unlike in Cleveland and Cincinnati, where trade unionists led third-party efforts before the formal establishment of the People's party, in Columbus the local Populist party was formed only after the executive committee of the state People's party appointed a committee led by trade unionists E. J. Bracken and William Bentz to get things moving. In fact, local Populists had to meet twice in the summer of 1891 in order to organize the Franklin County People's party. In July Democrats flooded the Knights of Labor Hall, where the first meeting was held, hoping to convince the party simply to endorse the local Democratic slate. The local People's party organizers had to adjourn,

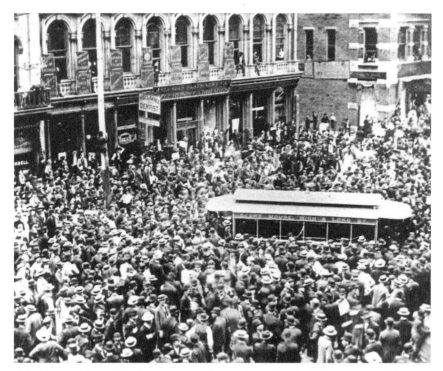

Columbus residents dislodge a streetcar during the strike of 1890. Courtesy of the
Columbus Metropolitan Library.

inviting those willing to pledge support to the new party to reconvene at a
later date. Newspapers suggested that nearly two-thirds of the 150 people
who attended the first meeting were Democrats hoping to prevent the new
party from fielding an independent slate.[9]

When the Franklin County People's party reconvened in August, the
Democrats again tried to take over the party, but organizers insisted that only
those who would sign a pledge to support the party's ticket and platform
would be allowed to participate. Of the more than one hundred people in
attendance, only thirty-four people, seven of whom were women and thus
ineligible to vote in Ohio elections, signed the pledge. After expelling the
Democrats from the hall, these thirty-four people set about nominating a
local slate.

Led by Ohio State Trades and Labor Assembly official and Columbus labor
editor E. J. Bracken, the Franklin County People's party split the slots on the
local ticket between labor unionists and members of the Farmers' Alliance.
Most of the unionists, including Bracken, were active in Local Assembly

2490 of the Knights of Labor. Although a mixed assembly, LA 2490 (or the Phoenix Assembly, as it was commonly known) contained mostly workers from the iron trades—rollers, puddlers, molders, and chainmakers—and was one of the most active locals in the CTLA. During the 1880s the Phoenix Assembly was the only Columbus-area labor organization to flirt with third-party politics, and some of the individual members had founded the local chapter of the Greenback party in 1877. In addition to Bracken, Phoenix Assembly members Tim Shea and Lafayette Mann were placed on the party's ballot.[10]

While the streetcar strike of 1890 had reminded the city's labor leaders and workers of the benefits of a close relationship with the Democratic party, it had alarmed and mobilized the business community. Businessmen and the Republican party looked on in horror as the police refused to oust strikers from company property, failed to protect those attempting to operate streetcars during the strike, and allowed crowds to hurl insults and debris at non-striking drivers. Nothing irritated the business leaders more than hearing that the police department was in "sympathy" with the strikers. One prominent businessman, active in the Republican party, insisted that for the city government "to stand by apathetically and allow laws to be violated, and men's rights to be disregarded is to invite and encourage lawlessness." He continued that it was the duty of the police department to protect the property of the streetcar company and to ensure that strike supporters did not interfere with the operation of the cars. The president of the Columbus Board of Trade agreed, suggesting that the mayor, police chief, and city council's actions during the strike threatened the property rights and peace of the entire community. Since the actions of the mayor and the city council had been extremely popular with the community, the city's business leaders and their Republican allies had little hope of electing a more sympathetic mayor or council and had to look elsewhere for a solution to their dilemma.[11]

The concerns of the business community echoed complaints the city's moral reformers had been making for years. Led by Washington Gladden, moral reformers argued that the police had shirked their duty by allowing the operation of saloons on Sundays and past midnight and by turning a blind eye to gambling and prostitution. Since the moral reformers realized the difficulties of electing officials willing to enforce unpopular laws, they had been advocating changes to the city's municipal code that they hoped would compel the police department to enforce the law. Gladden placed most of the blame on the decentralized structure of the city's government. Popularly elected five-member boards governed the city's departments, and the mayor was mostly a figurehead with a few judicial duties. Gladden argued that this system not only allowed police board members to escape individual responsibility for failing to enforce the laws, but that the proliferation of offices encouraged the election of petty politicians. Talented individuals, he maintained, grew frustrated trying to make changes in the cumbersome system and working with politicians who placed individual or party needs over those of the city. Gladden wanted the structure of the city's government to resemble that of the federal government, with the mayor solely responsible for the enforcement of laws and the administration of city affairs. Such a plan, Gladden insisted, would also encourage more talented and responsible individuals to seek office.

While Gladden had been calling for municipal reform for half a decade, his plans had largely been ignored by business leaders until the streetcar strike of 1890 convinced them that such reform might have merit. In late 1890 the Board of Trade invited Gladden to present the details of his plan to its members. Impressed with his ideas, the Board of Trade formed a committee to work for the implementation of such a plan. As Ohio cities received their charters from the Ohio General Assembly, state legislators rather than Columbus residents determined the city's governmental structure. The Board of Trade began lobbying the general assembly, but these efforts got nowhere as the general assembly's Democrats, fearing the reform was nothing more than a thinly disguised Republican attempt to undermine the city's Democratic administration, held enough seats to ensure that the measure did not receive the necessary two-thirds majority.[12]

The legislative elections of 1891, however, gave the GOP an overwhelming majority in the general assembly and renewed the Board of Trade's hope for a new charter from the legislature, which would not meet until January 1893. To build momentum for reform and to fend off criticisms that the charter movement did not have popular support and was simply a partisan attempt to undermine the Democratic administration, the Board of Trade announced that it would organize a special plebiscite to allow the citizens of Columbus to select a commission to draw up a new charter. Only about a thousand of the city's residents (less than 5 percent of the electorate) voted in the Board of Trade's extralegal election, and the resulting charter commission was dominated by Republicans and Board of Trade leaders. Not surprisingly, the charter commission simply proposed a charter based on the federal plan advocated by Gladden and the Board of Trade.[13]

As the Board of Trade's agitation for a new charter was in full swing, the streetcar workers launched another strike in November 1892. Although the action was prompted by the dismissal of a conductor who refused to accept a plugged dime, trouble had been brewing between the company and the drivers for months. The conductors' main complaint involved the company's use of "shortage slips." If receipts turned in by a conductor did not match the number of tickets sold, the company gave the conductor a shortage slip, and the difference was deducted from the conductor's pay. The conductors charged that the company was intentionally miscounting the money and unjustly deducting pay. In one publicized incident, a conductor reconciled his receipts and tickets in the presence of an attorney before turning them into the company but was nonetheless given a shortage slip. In an effort to demonstrate the union's power, the workers demanded the immediate reinstatement of the driver dismissed for refusing to take the adulterated coin.[14]

As in 1890 the strikers had the support of the general public. The Consolidated Street Railway Company had remained very unpopular with the citizens of Columbus. A few days before the strike, the company had nearly set off a riot by tearing up a street without getting the necessary permission from the street's residents or the city. Residents brandished shotguns and turned water hoses on the company's contractors before the police arrived to separate the parties. The company's officers were later arrested for violating an injunction enjoining them from continuing work on the line. The public's animosity toward the streetcar company continued during the strike. Like in 1890, large crowds gathered along the streets to harass non-striking drivers and to ridicule company officials.[15]

This time, however, the police, the mayor, and other public officials did not side openly with the strikers. The Board of Trade's agitation following the 1890 strike had changed the city's political climate. The voters of Columbus no longer controlled the future of the city's administration. The fate of Mayor George Karb and the Democrats at city hall rested in the hands of the Board of Trade and its Republican allies in the Ohio General Assembly. As soon as the strike began, Karb assured the city that he would do his "duty as an executive officer," while Police Chief Murphy warned that "men wanting work will receive the protection that the law affords them." The dispute was settled before the strikers and the police had a chance to test each other's resolve. The strikers and the company agreed to submit the dispute to arbitration, with Karb serving as the arbitrator. While Karb found in favor of the dismissed employee and ordered his reinstatement, the strike revealed labor's changing relationship with the Democratic party. No longer could the city's labor movement count on the support of Columbus's Democratic officials, and labor leaders started moving closer to the People's party. William D. Mahon, the head of the local streetcar workers, for example, left the Democrats for the People's party soon after the strike.[16]

In January 1893, during the opening days of the legislative session, the Republican-controlled Ohio General Assembly took up the municipal charter proposed by the Board of Trade. The leaders of the CTLA held a mass meeting to criticize both the new charter and the legislature's meddling in municipal affairs. CTLA leaders understood that the new charter's purpose was to undermine the working class's political power and to make the municipal government more responsive to the demands of the business community. Former CTLA president Louis Bauman called the new charter a scheme to disfranchise the people, while E. J. Bracken saw it as another example of the businesses' conspiring to control the political system. Many of the trade unionists thought that some sort of municipal reform was needed to cleanse the city's politics but advocated the adoption of the initiative and referendum—rather than the federal plan—as a way of bringing this about. They insisted that municipal reform come from those living in the city rather than from a body of corrupt legislators, few of whom were beholden to the voters of the city. The Columbus labor movement, though, held little sway among those serving in the general assembly, and the Board of Trade's measure easily passed.[17]

The unwillingness of the police and the Democratic mayor to side with strikers during the 1892 streetcar strike and anger over the new charter increased labor's support for third-party politics. CTLA leaders were nearly all members of the People's party with the arrival of Mahon and other disaffected Democrats, and these leaders took steps to bring the organizations together in ways that did not violate the CTLA's nonpartisan policy. As a first step, the CTLA adopted its first ever municipal platform. Written by Populists Mahon and Oscar Freer, the platform called for municipal ownership of utilities and street railways, an eight-hour day for city workers, direct legislation, the end of the contracting system for public projects, weekly pay, equal pay for women, and simplification of the municipal code. The labor federation insisted that their members should only vote for candidates who pledge themselves to that platform.[18]

A few days later, Columbus's Populists adopted the CTLA platform as their own and fielded a slate to run in municipal elections for the first time. Led by Bracken and Mahon, the People's party convention insisted that monopolists and capitalists had captured the city's government, seeking to use it for their own gain. The three nominees for citywide office were active trade unionists, as were most of the nominees for city council, including CTLA treasurer Martin Krumm and past president Louis Bauman. From the outset of the campaign, mayoral nominee William Bentz, the leader of the local patternmakers' union, conceded that he had little chance of getting elected as long as the other two parties were dominated by the "money power." Nonetheless, he insisted that the campaign was worth waging for "educational purposes." He predicted that the party would only attract two hundred votes but added that this would be a good start.[19]

Unfortunately for the People's party, issues surrounding the American Protective Association (APA) dominated the mayoral election. The APA asserted that there was a papal plot to take over the United States and dedicated itself to attacking any perceived source of Catholic power in the nation. The organization's members distributed a number of documents that they alleged supported their claims. One such document, purported by the *Columbus Record* and other APA newspapers to be an encyclical from Pope Leo XIII, claimed that, since Christopher Columbus had discovered America, the land belongs to the pope and that on September 5, 1893, the feast of Ignatius Loyola, the pope would assume control over the nation, by force if necessary. The "encyclical" further asserted that once the Catholic Church ruled the nation, "it will be the duty of the faithful to exterminate all heretics found within the jurisdiction of the United States."[20]

In Columbus, the APA was especially powerful and functioned much as an auxiliary to the Republican party. Not only did one of the organization's leading spokesmen, the Reverend Adam Fawcett, use Columbus as his base of operations, but five local chapters boasted that they had over a thousand members apiece. In late 1892, newspapers reported that the organization had about eight thousand members in Columbus and was growing rapidly. Bands of APA members attacked Catholic priests on the streets, and Catholics physically confronted prominent APA figures. Rumors that a local Catholic priest was about to receive a shipment of rifles and bayonets in anticipation of the feast of Ignatius Loyola prompted the APA to launch a campaign to purchase weapons and form a Protestant militia.[21]

In many ways, the campaign against the APA resembled the struggle over municipal reform, with religion becoming a surrogate for class. In Gladden's novel all of the protagonists with a single exception had Anglo-Saxon names—Payne, Tomlinson, Harper, Hathaway, and Hamlin. The exception, Morison, was a protestant minister, lest readers think he might be Irish Catholic. Of the protagonists only Sam Hathaway, a carpenter, was not a member of the business or professional classes, but he, after offering a few sage words, fades to the background when the others begin the important work. The corrupt politicians, on the other hand, had names associated with those who made up a large share of the city's mostly German Catholic and Irish working class—Schneider, O'Halloran, Flynn, Mulloy, Schwab, Dugan, Murphy, and O'Kane.[22]

During the mayoral campaign, the two major candidates and the city's newspapers talked of little except the APA. In the month before the election, Fawcett stirred up the public with a series of inflammatory speeches. Before crowds of as many as three thousand people, he insisted that the APA flag be flown over city hall. The Republican candidate, John Hayden, spent most of the campaign denying rumors that he agreed with Washington Gladden's denunciations of the APA and attacking Karb's management of the police force, a reputed bastion of Roman Catholicism. While not openly attacking the APA, Karb assured voters that his administration would not discriminate against Roman Catholics and argued that the city had the finest police force in the nation. With a campaign centered on the APA and the place of Catholicism in the city, the Populists could make little headway as they saw the real issues of the campaign as revolving around efforts of the business community—rather than papists—to control city hall. Likewise, with large numbers of the working class seeing the Democratic party as the defender of their faith, there was little chance of these voters forsaking it for a party whose standard-bearer acknowledged he had little chance of winning. The People's party's mayoral candidate received only 155 of the 20,000 votes cast, and Karb won reelection in the closest race in decades.[23]

The financial distress associated with the Panic of 1893 hit the city hard, though, causing the public to lose interest in the fight between the APA and its critics. Although there were no reliable estimates of the city's unemployment rate, contemporary sources estimated that one in five Columbusites was without regular work. As one railroader told the *Columbus Dispatch*, "I have been running out of this town twenty-one years and I never saw so many tramps than I have in the past week. I say tramps; they ought not to be called tramps, for the great majority of them are men just as good as you or I, except they are less fortunate. I never saw so many idle men in my life in this city."[24]

Not only did the unemployment rate go up, those with jobs saw their hourly wages drop and the number of days worked decline. The Ohio Bureau of Labor Statistics reported that 20 percent of Columbus workers saw their wages decline in 1893, while only 1.5 percent saw their wages go up. Of the city's major occupation groups, only the brewery workers did not see their number of working days cut. At the city's largest factory, for example, 360 saddle hardware makers toiled forty fewer days (over six weeks) in 1893 than they had in 1892. The Bureau of Labor Statistics data, though, does not reveal the true depths of the crisis as only the most prosperous and stable firms tended to supply employment information to the state.[25]

With the onset of the financial crisis, the CTLA increasingly adopted the Populist critique of the American financial system. In mid August, the CTLA held a meeting to discuss the financial crisis and declared, "The American people no longer tolerate a system of finance which permits the social, industrial and commercial interests to be dominated by foreign governments and capitalists; that the full and unlimited coinage of silver be restored to the people; that the present national, state and private banks be abolished and that the issue of [paper] money be exercised exclusively by the government." A mass meeting of city workers two weeks later blamed "the widespread disaster, idleness, and untold suffering" on the financial manipulations of "designing persons." The thousand workers present at the later meeting passed a resolution demanding the passage of legislation to "secure the free and unlimited coinage of gold and silver and provide for the issue of paper money in such an amount as will increase our currency to an amount not less than $40 per capita."[26]

Although the CTLA did not officially endorse the People's party or local labor leader E. J. Bracken, its gubernatorial candidate, during the fall 1893 campaign, the two organizations worked so closely during the campaign that the *Dispatch* started referring to the People's party as the "Labor party" and denouncing CTLA initiatives to relieve unemployment by the construction of large public works projects as "Populist schemes." CTLA president William D. Mahon toured the region on behalf of the People's party. The CTLA also invited Populist candidates, but not Democratic or Republican candidates, to address their meetings. Sentiment for the Populist party ran so high in the CTLA that when prominent labor journalist and scholar George McNeill came to town on an American Federation of Labor-sponsored speaking tour and warned the CTLA "to keep out of [partisan] politics," he was practically booed off the podium.[27]

At the height of the gubernatorial campaign, on October 25, the streetcar workers launched another strike against the Consolidated Street Railway. Trouble between the company and workers had been brewing since the summer when the company fired several union members and reinstituted its practices regarding shortage slips. The immediate cause of the strike centered on the dismissal of two union members for what the streetcar workers considered to be trivial violations of company rules. The employees saw the firings as part of a company strategy to break the union, while the company insisted it had a right to enforce work rules as it saw fit. The union demanded the reinstatement of the two workers and company recognition of the union.

From the outset the strike went badly for the workers. The financial crisis had created a pool of unemployed willing to work under almost any condition, and the reform movement created a police force willing to protect the strikebreakers. At the outset the police chief told a gathering of strikers to return to work and announced that the department would not tolerate any interference with the operation of the cars or harassment of strikebreakers. The police department lived up to the chief's promise. Not only did the police officers arrest scores of strikers trying to disrupt the operation of the cars or harassing strikebreakers, they also refused to allow strikers and sympathizers to congregate in public. Able to run its cars and recruit replacement workers, the Consolidated Street Railway Company quickly resumed operations and announced the firing of the strikers. Both the strike and the union were broken.[28]

The 1893 streetcar strike completed labor's alienation from the Democratic party in Columbus. The municipal reform movement had transformed the city's government and police force into tools of the business community. During the 1890 streetcar strike, the police force had announced its sympathy with the strikers and refused to intervene. In 1892 the police force had taken a more neutral stand and announced it would enforce the law. But now, in 1893, the police force sided with the company. Not only did the police chief advise the workers to return to their jobs, but the police force refused to allow the strikers to assemble on city streets. To compound problems, even though the changes in the municipal code were inspired by business leaders and the Republican party, it was labor's traditional ally, the Democratic party, that held power during the period.

The end of the streetcar strike was not the end of labor unrest in the city but just the beginning. In the spring and summer of 1894, Columbus witnessed what one newspaper called an "epidemic of strikes." In the city's small manufacturing sector, employers responded to the financial crisis that began in the late summer of 1893 by demanding wage reductions. They argued that only by lowering costs and prices could they capture enough business to keep their plants operating. Although workers at a number of factories agreed to reductions, the chain makers and wagon makers walked off the job but were unable to stop the reductions. The epidemic was not limited to the city's manufacturing sector, though. Bricklayers, hod carriers, and tailors also struck to protest wage reductions, but they were able only to limit the amount of the reductions. Although it did not involve Columbus workers, the nationwide coal strike of the spring of 1894 (discussed in Chapter 6) also affected the city. As the United Mine Workers' headquarters was in the city, the strike captured the attention of the city's workers and added to the growing impression that public officials were working closely with corporations to undermine the prospects of organized workers.[29]

The strike that had the most dramatic effect on the city's workers was the strike of the Hocking Valley Railroad that members of the American Railway Union (ARU) began in late June 1894 at the height of the Pullman boycott. With its headquarters and main yards in Columbus, the Hocking Valley Railroad connected the rich coalfields of southeastern Ohio to markets along the Great Lakes and had a long history of anti-union activity. The company had suffered a rough winter and spring in 1894. Not only did the panic cut the demand for coal, the line's most important freight, but the miners' strike had idled much of the line. Moreover, because of the financial crisis, many of the railroad's customers were paying in promissory notes rather than hard currency. The company responded to the crisis by reducing wages 10 percent and delaying payments to workers. Some Hocking Valley workers had not been paid for three months. Perhaps emboldened by the Pullman boycott, the Hocking Valley yardmen and switchmen, members of the ARU, struck to restore the 10 percent wage reduction and to gain the immediate payment of back wages. The local chapters of the railroad brotherhoods—conductors, engineers, and firemen—agreed to honor the ARU pickets, declaring that they would not operate trains assembled by scabs. At the outset of the strike, the ARU also expressed willingness to submit the dispute to arbitration.[30]

On the strike's first day, the ARU's local organizer, Mark Wild, counseled nonviolence, telling the strikers to avoid confrontations with non-union workers. The railroad, meanwhile, sought an injunction from the Franklin County common pleas court enjoining the ARU and Wild from conspiring to disrupt the operation of the line. While the initial request was denied on procedural grounds, two days later the judge enjoined Wild and the local ARU leadership from taking any action designed to disrupt the operation of the railroad. Federal judge William Howard Taft also issued an "omnibus injunction" enjoining the ARU strikers from "entering upon, impeding, interfering with or in any other way interrupting by word or act the operation" of several railroads, including the Hocking Valley.[31]

While the Hocking Valley Railroad was arguing in court that it was illegal for workers to "conspire" to impede the operation of a road, the company and the managers of the other Columbus rail yards announced the formation of a "mutual benefit association." The purpose of the organization, according to one of the organizers, was "to keep one another posted on the character of the men who are employed or might come up for employment." The strikers and the city's labor community quickly denounced the new organization's efforts as nothing more than a blacklist, and they questioned why it was legal for corporations to conspire to deny economic opportunity to individual workers while it was illegal for individual workers to conspire to withhold their labor from a corporation. Insisting that the use of the labor injunction had perverted the nation's constitution, Columbus trade union leaders concluded that corporations now enjoyed greater rights and liberties than the workers they employed. The president of the CTLA later declared, "if you raise your hand and say you have rights, you are shot down like a dog, or else arrested for violating an injunction placed on you by the courts."[32]

Support for the strikers was strong both in the city's labor community and among the working classes. The Columbus Trades and Labor Assembly attracted thousands to a series of mass meetings to support the strikers. At these meetings, Populist leaders associated with the CTLA were at the forefront. Noting that British stockholders owned the Hocking Valley Railroad, E. J. Bracken told the crowds that the strikers were fighting a British conspiracy to enslave the American worker. John Gayton, one of those who found themselves on the railroads' blacklist, denounced the "tyranny of organized capital against the working classes." After the CTLA called for local merchants to refuse to sell to non-striking railroaders, the *Columbus Post-Press* reported that landlords were asking for union cards, lunch counters were refusing to serve meals to the scabs, and that barbers denied service to anyone suspected of remaining in the employ of the Hocking Valley Railroad.[33]

The most important support for the strikers came from the United Mine Workers of America (UMWA). During the miners' strike earlier in the year, ARU members had worked with strikers to halt the flow of non-union coal from West Virginia and Virginia, and during the Hocking Valley strike the miners returned the favor, agreeing to curtail production of the railroad's main freight. After meeting with Wild, United Mine Workers officials announced that "not a pound of coal would be dug by the four thousand miners of the [Hocking] valley" as long as the strike lasted. UMWA president John McBride denounced the injunction enjoining Hocking Valley strikers as a threat to American liberties: "These injunctions are directed at everyone and forbid free thought, not to mention free speech. They are directed at every labor leader in the country and through them organized labor."[34]

Despite the support of the city's labor community and working class, the strike went badly for the ARU. The threat of imprisonment, the readiness of unemployed railroaders to take the strikers' positions, the police protection of non-striking workers, and the decision of the Brotherhood of Locomotive Engineers chief P. M. Arthur to order his men to cross the ARU picket lines allowed the company to resume operations, on a limited basis. On the verge of defeat the ARU accepted an agreement brokered by McBride and Hocking Valley coal operators anxious to resume normal operations. The company recognized the union and agreed to negotiate a new wage scale. As part of the agreement, the company stipulated that ARU organizer Wild would not be rehired. Realizing that the situation might worsen, Wild insisted the strikers agree to the settlement, and he became a local labor hero. Soon after he was elected president of the CTLA and announced that he was casting his lot with the People's party.[35]

The Hocking Valley Railroad strike combined with the national events of the summer of 1894 to push the Columbus labor community into a formal alliance with the People's party. Six weeks after the conclusion of the strike, Columbus labor leaders Bracken, Wild, and Mahon met with John McBride and UMWA officials to plan the formation of a state labor party, which they intended to merge with the state's Populists. The call for the labor party's convention, issued by McBride, noted that partisan action was the only remedy available to labor. Capitalists had rejected labor's preferred remedy, conciliation and arbitration; and the injunction had taken away labor's second option, the strike. This left politics as labor's only alternative, McBride insisted. With the two major parties controlled by "concentrated corporate wealth," McBride declared that the People's party offered the best chance to free labor from corporate bondage.[36]

Calling the formation of the new party the most remarkable upheaval in Ohio politics since the formation of the Republican party, the *Columbus Post-Press* predicted it would "revolutionize state politics" and worried that every labor union in the city would support the movement. At its regular meeting, the CTLA took up McBride's call. CTLA president Wild opened the discussion, insisting that the organization's rule forbidding partisan activity was no longer feasible. By making it impossible for workers to strike, the injunction, Wild insisted, forced labor to use the only weapon it had left, the ballot, to "free ourselves from the chain of slavery." After a brief discussion the delegates voted overwhelmingly to endorse the new party and to send delegates to the convention. Of the CTLA's eighty delegates only two voted against working with the Populists; and the alliance between the People's party and the Columbus Trades and Labor Alliance was formalized.[37]

During the fall campaign the CTLA, which had served as host of McBride's labor convention, and CTLA leaders worked hard for the People's party and its candidate for secretary of state, Charles Martin. The CTLA and the Central Populist Club held a series of rallies in Columbus neighborhoods featuring speeches by Mark Wild (who was running for county recorder), Tim Shea, William Mahon, John McBride, and Patrick McBryde (secretary treasurer of UMWA). Most of the speeches criticized traditional politicians and officeholders—Grover Cleveland for his monetary policies and actions during the Pullman boycott, William McKinley for his liberal use of the state militia against striking miners, and the federal judiciary for the use of injunctions—before extolling the virtues of the state People's party platform, especially the plank calling for the collective ownership of the means of production. William Mahon, for example, placed the abolition of private ownership of the means to production and the overthrow of the "wage system" alongside the abolition of the divine right of kings, the abolition of aristocratic privilege, and the abolition of chattel slavery as transformative events in the progress of human civilization. Collective ownership of the means of production, he insisted, will end "strikes, lockouts, idleness, starvation, riots, and bloodshed" and allow the people to assume control over their government and to enjoy the wealth they produce. As one speaker concluded, the liberation of the working class could be accomplished by voting the "straight People's party ticket in November."[38]

The leaders of the CTLA were disappointed with the election returns, however. Martin and the other People's party candidates won about 6 percent of the vote in Columbus, with the working-class wards of the South and Near North Sides giving the party about 10 percent of the vote. Still the news was not all bad. The 1,373 votes Martin received in the city represented a vast improvement over the 155 votes for the 1893 mayoral candidate. CTLA president Mark Wild told the city's trade unionists that the election represented a positive "step" and that soon those in the workshops would recognize the necessity for united political action through a workers' party. Additionally, the votes represented less than the margin between the triumphant Republicans and the defeated Democrats in the city, and one newspaper insisted that Populist showing had cost the Democrats several local offices. For the first time, the Populist vote had affected the outcome of a race.[39]

When the local People's party met in the spring of 1895 to plan for the municipal campaign, activists denounced the efforts of national party leaders Herman Taubeneck and James Weaver to focus the party's platform on the silver issue for the 1896 presidential campaign. Weaver and Taubeneck insisted that neither the Democratic nor the Republican party would support the free and unlimited coinage of silver at a ratio of sixteen to one, and if the People's party adopted a one-plank silver platform (jettisoning more radical reforms that might alienate voters), voters would flock to the party. The Columbus Populists unanimously objected to such a move, calling for the national party to stand by the broad-based reforms of the Omaha platform and adopt a "Middle of the Road" position (that is, forgo fusion with either Democrats or Republicans). The city's Populists had long embraced the free coinage of silver, but only as part of a broader platform, which included greenbacks, direct legislation, and government ownership of monopolies.

Although the city's Populists were in agreement as to the direction of the national platform, they divided when it came time to select candidates for the municipal elections. During the fall elections of 1894, several non-laborite Populists had chafed at the arrival of so many trade unionists. These non-laborites called themselves the "old-timers," although none of them had been active in the founding of the local party in 1891. The old-timers insisted that the unions subordinate their trade union activities to the party's interests. In other words, they felt that trade unions should simply serve as forums to convert members to the People's party. When it came time to choose candidates for mayor and other citywide offices, the old-timers "packed" the meeting hall with many who had never shown any prior interest in party matters. The old-timers pushed for the nomination a downtown merchant, George Twiss, for mayor, setting off a firestorm. Trade unionists, led by Wild, Bracken, Max Weitzenecker of the chain makers' union, and Lloyd Jenkins, president of the local typographers' union, accused Twiss of being hostile to labor. One trade unionist reported that Twiss had declared that the Homestead strikers were no better than anarchists and should have been shot on the spot. Jenkins also attacked Twiss's supporters for ignoring requests to use union printers for party material. The trade unionists in turn nominated D. E. Williams, a former Democrat who, while working in the city's accounting department, had exposed the misuse of funds by both Democrats and Republicans. Williams, however, declined to allow his name to be placed in nomination, and the trade unionists were unable to prevail on anyone else to oppose Twiss, enabling the old-timers to push through their man. The party's trade unionists immediately announced they would not stand by the party's candidate.[40]

After the Populist nominating meeting, the city's leading trade unionists distanced themselves from Twiss's nomination and the local People's party. Jacob Stroezel, an ironworker and former secretary of the CTLA, announced that he would no longer be the party's candidate for justice of the peace, and Tim Shea, a former CTLA president and Populist candidate for sheriff, resigned from the party's executive committee. Shea even threatened to support the Democratic candidate and warned the Populist executive committee that he could take a large portion of the labor vote with him. At its biweekly meeting, the CTLA voted down a motion to support Twiss and the Populist slate and announced that none of the candidates were worth supporting.[41]

The day after the CTLA voted to withhold support from Twiss's candidacy, Williams had a change of heart and announced he would run for mayor as an independent. At his announcement, Williams was joined on the podium by unionists E. J. Bracken and J. W. Doherty of the ARU. Bracken insisted that Williams was the only candidate who could rally the city's trade unionists and rid the city of the corrupt influence of city contractors and utility owners. Other trade unionists, including Wild, Jenkins, and Gayton, were quick to support Williams's candidacy, and the CTLA's political committee promptly endorsed him.[42]

Unlike Twiss, Williams appealed to a broad segment of the city. Not only did he pick up the endorsement of the Prohibitionists, he garnered some support from the "liberal" wing of the local Republican party. Led by the social gospel minister Washington Gladden, these Republicans supported the municipal ownership of public utilities, the removal of party politics from municipal affairs, and civil service reform. Some of the liberal Republicans' support for Williams can be attributed to their disdain for the regular Republican candidate, Oliver Evans, whom they considered a pawn of Jerry Bliss, the Board of Public Works director. Most important, though, Williams picked up the support of the *Columbus Dispatch*, a nominally Republican paper with close ties to Gladden and the liberal Republicans.[43]

The Democrats nominated Cotton Allen, a wealthy businessman from the Grover Cleveland–wing of the party. Allen enjoyed a good reputation with his workers and did not associate with the contractors and franchise holders that those in the labor movement considered the prime sources of boodle. Yet Allen and the local Democrats did not champion the reforms demanded by the CTLA and the city's workers. Allen simply insisted he would run the city as a business and be a good steward of the taxpayers' money.

After Williams announced his candidacy, the CTLA worked hard to convince the People's party to force Twiss to withdraw in favor of Williams. Most of the pressure came from the CTLA-dominated Central Populist club. Led by Bracken, Wild, Gayton, and Doherty, the club argued that Twiss's continued candidacy both endangered labor's support for the local People's party and destroyed any chances to build the type of reform coalition needed to challenge the Democrats and Republicans for control of city hall. Moreover, the laborites complained that—since the CTLA's decision to support the People's party in the late summer of 1894—many non-laborite Populists had resented the labor body's role in People's party affairs and had taken steps to drive labor out. The old-timers flooded the Central Populist Club meeting in order to support Twiss's candidacy, somewhat disingenuously insisting that the party should support only those candidates who supported the Omaha platform as well as the 1894 Ohio People's party platform. They also labeled Williams's Populist supporters "fusionists" and likened them to those who would do away with the Omaha platform. The meeting proved so contentious the papers expressed amazement that fistfights did not erupt.[44]

It remains unclear whether Twiss did withdraw from the race, but the Central Populist Club endorsed Williams. The loss of the Central Populist Club's support so crippled Twiss's candidacy that the *Columbus Dispatch* doubted he would attract more than a handful of votes. The CTLA continued to campaign for Williams suggesting that he was the only true Populist candidate for mayor. At Williams's campaign appearances, trade unionists dominated the crowd and applauded his calls for municipal ownership of streetcars and utilities, reform of the tax system so that assessments reflected the real value of property, and abolition of the contracting system for public projects.[45]

On the eve of the election, Williams's supporters were hopeful he could win the mayor's office. His crowds had been enthusiastic. He had the support of the CTLA, the *Dispatch*, and many of the city's most influential citizens, including Washington Gladden, but still the odds were stacked against him. The Democrats were able to hold onto the mayor's office, although Williams attracted over 11 percent of the popular vote. His 2,599 votes were roughly double what the Populist candidate for secretary of state had polled five months before. The split in the People's party did not last long. The poor showing of Twiss and the much better showing of Williams vindicated the position taken by those associated with the CTLA. That summer, CTLA Populists led the Franklin County delegation to the state People's party convention and worked hard for gubernatorial nominee Jacob Coxey.

The city's trade unionists used Labor Day celebrations to champion Coxey and the rest of the People's party 1895 slate. A jurisdictional dispute caused the city's labor movement to hold two celebrations, but both heard what the *Ohio State Journal* called "red hot Populist" speeches. At the CTLA's picnic, Cleveland labor-Populist David Rankin told the audience that the "struggle through the ages between the producing and non-producing classes . . . must ultimately be settled at the ballot" before predicting that the laboring classes will find their salvation through the election of Debs to the presidency in 1896. Patrick McBryde, the secretary treasurer of the UMWA, reminded the rival celebration of the gaping disparity in wealth between bankers, corporationists, and speculators and the nation's producers, who represent "98.6 per cent of the population, [yet] own just 30% of the wealth." To save the republic, McBryde continued, wealth needed to be more evenly distributed, and the labor movement was the only force strong enough to make the

TABLE 5.1—Results of Columbus's 1895 Mayoral Election

Candidate (party)	Votes	Percentage
Allen (Democrat)	10,747	47.9
Evans (Republican)	8,968	40.0
Williams (Independent/CTLA/Central Populist Club)	2,599	11.6
Twiss (People's)	117	0.5

Source: *Columbus Dispatch*, April 6, 1895.

government pursue policies to do this. McBryde ended by reminding trade unionists to shun those from the traditional parties "as you would a snake."[46]

Columbus trade union Populists were disappointed with Coxey's showing in Franklin County, where he collected just over eight hundred votes, but they quickly turned their attention to fighting the continued efforts by Herman Taubeneck, James Weaver, and other national Populist leaders to focus the party's platform on the silver issue.[47] Most of the city's labor leaders supported the free coinage of silver at a ratio of sixteen to one, but they declared that the national People's party should maintain the type of broad-based reform embodied in the Omaha platform and avoid actions that could lead to fusion with either of the major parties. When the Franklin County People's party selected its delegates to the party's national convention in St. Louis, it instructed them "to have the three cardinal principles of finance, transportation, and land, with the addition of the initiative and referendum and imperative mandate incorporated into the St. Louis platform." The *Ohio Populist*, published by the Franklin County People's party and edited by the CTLA's Oscar Freer, called for the nomination of Kansas senator William Peffer (the only member of the People's party's congressional delegation to oppose the emphasis on silver) for president, and Debs for vice president. The paper explained, "Of all the populists who have figured prominently in public life, none have 'wobbled' less than Senator Peffer. None have been more fearless and outspoken in defense of the whole principles laid down in the Omaha platform. Not once has he ever dodged, apologized, or 'flunked.' He has stood squarely on the whole populist platform, and has bravely defended it in its entirety."[48]

Even after Bryan received the Democratic nomination on a free silver platform and local party leaders realized it was a forgone conclusion that the People's party would also nominate Bryan, the Franklin County Populist party refused to give in. It instructed its delegates to oppose any effort to fuse with the Democrats and to "reaffirm the principles incorporated in the Omaha platform." The party continued, "We do not propose to surrender any of the principles of the People's party or endorse any principles of the Democratic or Republican parties."[49]

Although they had opposed the Populists' nomination of Bryan and the prospects of fusion with the Democrats, once those things had happened, the leaders of the CTLA, including E. J. Bracken, Tim Shea, and Louis Bauman, embraced them, leading the local People's party and the city's labor movement into a de facto alliance with the Democrats. Although the Franklin County People's party continued to function as an independent political party through 1897, it would never again nominate an independent slate of candidates and endorsed the Democrats' actions at every turn. Within the Democratic party, the former Populists allied with the Bryan wing of the party. Led by Allen W. Thurman, the son of the late senator and vice-presidential nominee, the Bryan wing of the party had much in common with the Populists, supporting many of the same reforms, including the free and unlimited coinage of silver, the end of the labor injunction, the institution of a graduated income tax, and a number of laws to protect employees on the job. Columbus's most prominent labor leader, John McBride, who had returned to the city after losing his reelection bid in December 1895, became a vocal supporter of Bryan, opening a labor bureau to disseminate information for the campaign.[50]

Unlike most large cities in the Industrial Midwest, Columbus was actually a Bryan stronghold. During the campaign, between thirty-five and fifty thousand people showed up on the state capitol grounds to hear the Democratic candidate, making this the largest crowd of the entire campaign. Bryan's coattails helped local Democratic candidates in their electoral bids. The most important of these Democrats, at least from labor's standpoint, was John Jacob Lentz, an insurance executive and recent convert to free silver who was narrowly elected to the U.S. Congress. In his two terms in the House, Lentz often campaigned with Bryan and became the labor movement's most outspoken congressional advocate, forcing a very public investigation of the imprisonment and abuse of members of the Western Federation of Miners in Coeur d'Alene, Idaho. During the hearings, Lentz led an eight-day grilling of Idaho governor Frank Steunenberg, accusing him of violating the constitutional rights of the miners and their families.

Lentz's activities became so popular among laborites and western radicals that when the remnants of the Populist party met in 1900 to nominate Bryan again for the presidency, Lentz received substantial support for the vice-presidential nomination.[51]

Following Bryan's national defeat in 1896, Thurman, Bryan Democrats, and their former Populist allies focused their attention on the April 1897 municipal election and efforts to purge the party of those who had refused to support Bryan. At the top of their list was incumbent Democratic mayor Cotton Allen, who was again seeking the party's nomination. Not only had Allen refused to campaign for the Nebraskan, he had declined to support those local Democratic candidates who had endorsed the free coinage of silver, including Lentz. Many prominent Democrats believed that Allen had actually committed the ultimate heresy—voting for Republican candidate William McKinley.[52]

During the spring of 1897, free silver Democrats and their Populist allies used the threat of an independent Populist ticket in that April's municipal election to wrest control of the party from Allen and the anti-Bryan wing of the party. Congressman Lentz argued that the party must nominate a ticket that the Populists would support in the upcoming municipal race. Likewise, the Jackson Club, led by Thurman, insisted that the nomination of a gold Democrat, especially Allen, would cause the city's Populists to nominate their own candidate who would receive the support of a good number of free silver Democrats. Both men argued that Populist votes had cost many on the local Democratic slate victories in 1894 and 1895 and that the removal of the local Populist slate was the only way to achieve victory. The arguments of Lentz and the Jackson Club worked as the party purged all of the gold Democrats, including Allen, from the spring's municipal ballot and nominated a slate composed entirely of those who had enthusiastically supported Bryan. So as not to alienate Gold Democrats completely and to forestall a bolt, the Bryanites nominated Samuel Black for mayor. A moderate and recent convert to silver, Black was one of the few Democrats who still retained the support of both factions. The Bryanites were so successful in their takeover of the Franklin County Democratic party that the *Ohio State Journal* sarcastically observed it was the Populists who had swallowed the Democrats.[53]

The efforts of the Bryanites worked. Not only did the Populists refuse to nominate their own slate, the citizens of Columbus elected Black mayor, defeating the Republican nominee, Emmett Tompkins. Black garnered 12,383 votes (50%) to Tompkins's 11,956 (48.6%), with the remainder divided between Prohibitionist and Socialist candidates. Black ran well in the working-class wards of the South Side and the Near North Side, while Tompkins polled well in the middle-class wards of the East Side and far north areas. Bryan Democrats, pointing out that an independent Populist ticket would have collected more than the 430 votes that gave Black and the party's other candidates their victory, insisted that the decision to jettison Allen and other gold Democrats had paid off.[54]

The Populists' alliance with Black and the city's Democratic party paid dividends to the city's workers and the labor movement. The Black administration and other Democratic officials appointed a number of former labor-Populists-turned-Democrats to positions in the city government. The mayor named Tim Shea sanitation officer and Louis Bauman building inspector. The party selected E. J. Bracken, the former Populist gubernatorial candidate, to oversee a committee to provide relief to the city's unemployed. While not glamorous, these positions gave labor leaders a significant amount of power and influence. Building inspectors could make work difficult for non-union contractors, while sanitation officers had the power to shut down businesses on any number of pretexts.[55]

Not only did the city's Democratic officials appoint former labor-Populists to official positions, they expanded the city government in ways demanded by the Populists. In the summer of 1897, the city launched a public works project designed to provide relief to the city's unemployed. The city council appropriated $60,000 for the city's unemployed to work at between $1.00 and $1.25 a day. The project, overseen by Bracken, was not designed to achieve long-term reform, but simply to allow the city's unemployed to survive until the end of hard times. The creation of the public works project had the added benefit of boosting the daily wage for unskilled workers by establishing $1.00 a day as the going rate for day labor. For the first time in its history, the Columbus municipal government took efforts to promote employment at a living wage.[56]

Other Populist demands were enacted. At the CTLA's behest, the city council passed an ordinance requiring that contracts for city improvements go to those employing union labor and that eight hours a day constituted a day's work on the projects. The city's school board rejected a bid for desks on the grounds that the bidder had recently replaced his unionized workers with newly arrived non-unionized immigrants. Instead, the contract went to a firm employing union labor. Local Democrats also used their influence to ensure that work at a private auditorium, where the state Democratic convention was to be held, would be performed by union labor. During the spring and summer of 1897, the city's police force began enforcing the 1893 state law prohibiting the intimidation of union workers for the purpose of convincing them to quit a union. The police chief ordered the arrest of the superintendent of a bicycle factory after the CTLA secured affidavits from a number of employees detailing threats made against union workers.[57]

Given the increasingly friendly relationship between city hall and the CTLA, it is little wonder that what remained of the local People's party in the summer of 1897 considered it "inexpedient to place an independent ticket in the field for election this coming fall." Led by trade unionists Tim Shea, E. J. Bracken, Louis Bauman, and Oscar Freer, the Franklin County People's party again endorsed fusion with the Democrats as "a valuable means of the Populist party to get before the people." The party instructed its delegates to the state convention to fight against the nomination of an independent Populist slate. Columbus Democrats rewarded the Populist action by placing a number of trade unionists on its local ticket, including E. J. Bracken who won a seat in the state legislature.[58]

Despite the obvious benefits the labor community received from the Black administration, the CTLA and the Bryan wing of the Democratic party were not enthusiastic about renominating Black in 1899. He had alienated voters in the heavily German and working-class wards of the South Side by enforcing city ordinances requiring saloons to close at midnight and on Sundays. The Black administration had also failed to deliver on promised city projects, including improvements to the levee protecting the Near West Side and the construction of a new water-storage reservoir. Most important, the Jackson Club and its allies in the CTLA did not trust Black on the silver question and feared he might work against Bryan's nomination in 1900. Ultimately, though, Black did get the nomination.

The Republicans nominated Samuel Swartz, the city's police judge, for mayor. Swartz was one of the few Republicans who had run well in the working-class wards on the South and Near North Sides. Wanting to become the first Republican mayor elected since 1885, Swartz enthusiastically courted the city's labor community, bringing in several labor leaders to campaign for him, including John Jones, a former president of the Ohio State Trades and Labor Council, and Tom Lewis of the UMWA. He also rented the Trades Assembly Hall for a number of campaign functions.

In the weeks leading up to the election, the *Ohio State Journal* charged members of the Black administration with pocketing over $140,000 of the city's money. Rather than ignoring the charges, which were typical for turn-of-the-century municipal elections, Black provided city council with obviously doctored financial statements and escalated the issue. The fraudulent documents fueled the fire, allowing Swartz to become the first Republican elected mayor of Columbus in fourteen years.

Following Black's loss and the election of the labor-friendly Swartz, the ties that bound the city's trade union movement to the Democratic party started to erode. With the loss the Democrats could not use the lure of public jobs and legislation to keep the support of the city's labor movement, and this freed the CTLA leaders, who had never been entirely comfortable within the Democratic fold, to pursue a more radical course. The CTLA's platform contained a number of planks—the elimination of the contract system for public improvements, the eight-hour day for all public employees, and the "municipal ownership of gas and electric light plants, telephones, and all street railroads"—that Black and many local Democrats had refused to support. Additionally, the CTLA's platform continued to call for the "collective ownership of the means of production," the abolition of the wage system, and a host of other reforms associated with its alliance to the People's party and earlier anti-monopoly politics. In distancing itself from the Democratic party, the CTLA began pursuing policies it knew would not pay immediate dividends but hoped would help restructure economic life.[59]

Soon after the spring's municipal election, the CTLA jumped on the Samuel "Golden Rule" Jones bandwagon. Jones, the pro-labor mayor of Toledo who won reelection in 1897 as an independent after the Republican party refused to renominate him, was toying with the idea of running for governor. In the late spring 1899, Jones let Ohioans know he would be willing to make an independent bid for governor, if the people of the state drafted him.[60]

To convince Jones to run, the CTLA organized a convention of Ohio labor groups in June 1899, much like the one John McBride had convened in the late summer of 1894. Although most of the four thousand delegates were from Columbus and Toledo, almost every section of the state was represented. Before Jones arrived, the convention ratified a platform containing most of the demands the Ohio People's party had supported. The delegates insisted on government ownership of monopolies and public utilities, the eight-hour day, compulsory education, equal pay for equal work, abolition of the "sweating system," and the end of government by injunction. When Jones began speaking, the convention's delegates began chanting "the next Governor of Ohio, the next Governor of Ohio." Jones devoted most of his speech to the evils of partisanship and called for the state's workers to avoid all political parties, but he also called for the end of the "present social order known as competition" and the creation of a cooperative commonwealth. Although Jones refused to use the word in public for fear of alienating voters, he told labor leaders there was no real difference between what he and the "Socialists" were fighting for.[61]

Soon after the convention, Jones formally committed to an independent bid for governor. In Columbus, CTLA officials John McNamee and James Cannon coordinated the Jones campaign, and he launched the campaign season with a speech at the CTLA's Labor Day picnic in which he railed against partisanship and the abuses of the competitive system. Cannon and McNamee, both former Populists, had assumed larger roles in the CTLA after Mahon moved to Detroit, Wild left the city in the wake of bribery allegations, and Bracken devoted attention to legislative affairs. The pair organized meetings and rallies on Jones's behalf and kept him informed of their activities in Columbus. Although Jones did not do as well in Columbus as he did in Cleveland or Toledo, where he won a majority of the votes, he polled well for a third-party candidate, winning the support of over 10 percent of the city's votes. His candidacy might have been the basis of another labor-based third-party movement in the city and state, but the Toledo mayor had left behind no party apparatus. He had campaigned against partisanship, refusing to allow his candidacy to be used to rally labor and reform forces into a new political party.[62]

After the defection of so many trade unionists to the Jones campaign in 1899 and the defeat of Congressman Lentz's reelection bid the next year, the city's Democratic party redoubled its efforts to convince CTLA leaders to return to the fold. Local party chairman Thurman, who had not been entirely upset with labor's support of Jones because it undermined his hated rival, Democratic candidate John McLean, insisted that the party had to appeal to the city's labor movement in order "to hold Democratic workingmen in line with their party." To that end, the party gave several slots on its legislative ballot to CTLA officials—including Bracken, Cannon, McNamee, and Oscar Ameringer—in 1901 and 1903.[63]

But not all labor leaders chose to return to the Democratic fold in the wake of the Jones candidacy. Led by longtime CTLA official and former Populist Oscar Freer, a small band of Columbus trade unionists and reformers formed the Columbus section of the Socialist Labor party (SLP) in late 1899. Freer predicted that "organized labor acting in co-operation with the Socialist political body" would "establish an industrial commonwealth," which would free workers from wage slavery. The Columbus section, though, was never comfortable with DeLeonism and the SLP's efforts to form a trade union federation to rival the American Federation of Labor and would soon become a branch of the Eugene Debs and Victor Berger–led Social Democratic party. The Social Democrats party put forth a municipal platform that was nearly identical to the ones offered by the Populists of the mid 1890s: municipal ownership of utilities, abolition of the contracting system for public works, civil service, direct legislation, compulsory public education, and the eight-hour day for public workers. Like elsewhere in the Industrial Midwest, Populism served as the midwife to Columbus's socialist movement.[64]

Over the course of the first decade of the new century, the Socialists and the Democrats vied for the support of CTLA leaders. But as anti-Bryan forces assumed more influence in the Franklin County Democratic party, the CTLA's support for the Socialists increased. For example, Oscar Ameringer, a musicians' union official and editor of the CTLA's newspaper, made the switch in late 1903. Ameringer had become a supporter of Bryan in 1896, while playing the clarinet in William McKinley's campaign band in Canton, and boasted of being one of Tom L. Johnson's young men. After moving to Columbus and moving up in CTLA circles, Ameringer received the Democratic nomination for the Ohio General Assembly in 1903. Upon receiving the nomination, Ameringer, at the insistence of the local party officials, went to Cleveland to solicit financial support for the county ticket from Johnson. Johnson informed Ameringer that the Columbus's conservative Democrats were using him—"You are doomed my boy. The deal is made. The county offices are to go to their Democratic friends, the state offices, including your office, to their Republican friends." Soon after his defeat, Ameringer joined the Socialists, with whom he would be associated until his death. For Ameringer and many of Ohio labor leaders, the differences between Jones-and Johnson-style reform and that proposed by the Socialists were so small that local circumstances often determined party affiliation.[65]

By 1906 most of the city's labor leaders had followed Ameringer's lead. Late that year, socialist control of the CTLA was so strong that the American Federation of Labor found a pretext to revoke the body's charter and set up a rival, the Columbus Federation of Labor, in hopes that it would be more amenable to Gompers and the federation's conservative leadership. The two bodies would merge in 1909, keeping the name Columbus Federation of Labor but electing a leadership dominated by Socialists.[66] Rather than embracing liberalism or any other ideology that privileged the rights of property, the Columbus labor community followed the path of Eugene Debs (albeit more slowly)—Populism to Bryanism to Socialism.

6 The United Mine Workers and Ohio's Labor–Populist Alliance

ON AUGUST 2, 1894, from his office in Columbus, United Mine Workers of America (UMWA) president John McBride called for Ohio trade unionists to form a political party and to merge that party with the Populists. He explained that recent labor troubles had "convince[d] honest, ardent advocates of labor's cause that corporate power, when aided by the executive, judicial, and military arm of the state and national government, can and will override the rights of our people and oppress wage workers." McBride insisted that labor's preferred methods of dealing with labor disputes—negotiation and arbitration—had been "spurned" by employers and that the right to strike had been taken away by the use of injunctions. The only weapon left to workers was the ballot. Since it was "evident that labor cannot hope for relief at the hands of either the Republican or Democratic party," labor must "join hands politically with the People's Party."[1]

Delegates representing practically every organized trade in the state answered McBride's call, showing up in Columbus on August 14 and 15 to forge a statewide labor–Populist alliance. UMWA took the lead in these actions, but the Columbus Trades and Labor Assembly hosted the meeting, and the president of Toledo's Central Labor Union presided over the convention. The labor federations of Cincinnati and Cleveland, which had already formed labor–Populist alliances at the local level, sent large delegations. Those assembled issued a platform, calling for the power of the government to be "expanded as rapidly and as far as the good sense of an intelligent people and the teachings of experience shall justify, along the lines of the collective ownership by the people of all such means of production and distribution as the people may elect to operate." The convention also demanded the abolition of the national banking system; government issuance of greenbacks; the free and unlimited coinage of silver; government ownership of telephones, telegraphs, railroads, and mines; taxation to force the end of landholding for speculative purposes; compulsory education; an effective law to end the importation of contract labor; direct legislation; end of child labor; the eight-hour day and employer liability for job-related injuries; and women's suffrage. The platform was nearly identical to the political program being considered by the unions affiliated with the American Federation of Labor (AFL) and the platforms that had been issued by labor–Populist alliances in Illinois and Wisconsin just a few weeks earlier.[2]

When the Populists showed up in Columbus the next day for their annual convention, they readily accepted the labor platform (with additional planks calling for liberal pensions for those who fought for the Union during the Civil War and endorsing the Omaha platform), effectively consummating the state's labor–Populist alliance. The two conventions came together to produce a slate of delegates for the upcoming election. The top spot on the ticket went to Charles Martin, a longtime Knight of Labor and Populist who was especially close to McBride and the UMWA leaders. The convention ended with a parade through the streets of the city, ending at the state capitol where Jacob Coxey and John McBride, old friends from Massillon, addressed the crowd of nearly twelve thousand people. Led by Coxey and McBride—the newspapers dubbed them the "Massillon Twins"—the Ohio People's party took on the trappings of a major party for the first time and threatened to upset the state's political system.[3]

Nearly four months later, delegates at the AFL's annual convention elected John McBride president, sending Samuel Gompers, a fierce defender of the federation's nonpartisan orientation, into temporary retirement. Upon taking office, McBride announced his desire to see the federation create a "union of labor men" that would "place a presidential candidate in the field" in 1896. For those who had been following McBride's political activities, his intentions were clear: the creation of a national Populist–labor alliance.[4]

McBride and the state's coal miners had taken a different path to Populism than those coming out of the state's urban labor federations. The urban federations had been established to coordinate the political activities of trade unionists of different crafts to give workers a voice in municipal affairs. In other words, the urban federations were created for political action. UMWA, on the other hand, was formed to improve the economic lives of miners by representing them at the bargaining table. At its founding in Columbus in January 1890, the organization had dedicated itself to increasing wages, reducing hours, and improving conditions in the nation's mines. Like other trade unions fearful that political disputes would divide workers, the United Mine Workers had a policy mandating nonpartisanship.[5] But the events of 1894—especially the nationwide coal strike but also the Pullman strike and boycott and the arrest of Jacob Coxey for petitioning Congress for action to put people back to work—convinced the leaders of the union that the lives of miners could never be improved at the bargaining table, that the nationalization of the nation's mines offered the only practical solution to the problems facing miners, and that only a political alliance with the Populists could lead to nationalization.

In the late 1880s and early 1890s, the most pressing problems facing the miners' union and the coal industry were, in the words of John McBride, "too many mines and too many miners." In Ohio and much of the bituminous coal belt stretching from Western Pennsylvania into Iowa, there were few barriers to entry into the mining industry. Coal was plentiful and easily accessible. As one early miners' union official noted, in the eastern half of Ohio one could start digging on the side of almost any hill and find marketable coal. Small mining operations proliferated. Throughout the 1870s and 1880s, some operators sought to rationalize production by forming syndicates or buying out smaller competitors, but these efforts did little to alleviate the excessive competition that characterized the industry. Just as mines proliferated, so did miners. Although using experienced, skilled miners made mines safer and more efficient, unskilled laborers could easily dig coal. Thus, mining communities attracted large numbers of unskilled workers whose very presence kept wages low.[6]

In such an environment, it made little sense for the UMWA to seek changes at individual mines, and the union pursued what historian David Brody has called "market unionism." An operator agreeing to decent wages, the abolition of the company store, a small screen over which coal is passed before weighing, and safety improvements could not compete on the open market with operators paying low wages, using large screens, and refusing to invest in safety equipment. To escape the pernicious effects of this competitive environment, the miners' unions sought an effective industry-wide agreement that would set wages for each region based on the ease of mining and the transportation costs to market. Many operators liked the idea of such agreement too, seeing it as the only way to rationalize an industry plagued by cutthroat competition.[7]

Although forerunners of the UMWA had secured a "joint interstate agreement" with the largest of the nation's operators in 1886, this did not translate into improved conditions for miners. Most of the nation's coal mining operations remained outside the agreement. Operators and miners who participated in the interstate agreement tended to be located in the region stretching from Western Pennsylvania to Illinois where access to inexpensive transportation systems—railroads and barges on the Great Lakes and the Ohio River and its tributaries—made competition especially fierce. But these miners and owners feared that cheap coal from non-union areas in Virginia, Tennessee, and West Virginia or from operators who refused to join the agreement would undercut the scale. Thus, the participants in the joint interstate agreement kept the scale relatively low. In 1890, after the agreement had been in operation for four years, the Ohio Bureau of Labor Statistics found that the average state miner earned just $324 per year. University of Chicago professor and reformer Edward Bemis compiled statistics from the 1890 U.S. census and found that 79 percent of a sample of five hundred miners from Ohio, Indiana, West Virginia, Pennsylvania, and Alabama earned less than the $500 that he calculated a family needed to live decently.[8]

Thus, at its birth in January 1890, the UMWA viewed the market, rather than coal mine operators, as the greatest threat to the welfare of the nation's miners. The UMWA saw mine operators as potential allies in its efforts to escape the competitive system that kept operator profits small and forced them to slash wages in order to survive. Many large coal operators—including William Rend and Marcus Hanna, who controlled Ohio's two largest mining companies—saw the miners' union as the only force capable of bringing stability to the chaotic industry. As a statement issued by one of the forerunners of the UMWA and a group of operators insists, "Apart and in conflict labor and capital become agents of evil, while united they create the blessings of plenty and prosperity, and enable a man to enjoy the bounteous resources of nature intended for his use and happiness by the Almighty."[9]

While the primary strategy of the UMWA focused on the creation of an industry-wide agreement to insulate wages and the price of coal from the competitive market, the miners also saw political action as essential to the success of their union and the improvement of their lives. Like an industry-wide agreement, legislation could help the miners overcome the effects of the market by requiring all of the operators in a given jurisdiction to improve work conditions. The miners sought legislation to regulate the size of screens, improve safety conditions, require regular inspections, and require the coal to be weighed by a man of the miners' choosing.

While the economics of the industry forced miners to seek state legislation, geography gave the miners a great deal of political leverage. In Ohio, mines tended to be concentrated in the thinly populated hills of the eastern portion of the state where miners and those dependent upon them made up a significant percentage of the electorate. Both Democrats and Republicans believed that the votes of miners were crucial to success in a dozen counties, including Perry, Hocking, Athens, Jackson, Stark, and Tuscarawas, and that these counties held the key to controlling the general assembly. To win miners' votes, both parties courted union leaders, offering them slots on the ticket or appointed office.[10]

Nearly every Ohio miners' union leader had ties to the Republican or the Democratic party by 1890. Republicans included Chris Evans, who served as president of the Ohio Miners' Union in the late 1880s and as secretary of the AFL in the early 1890s; W. T. Lewis, who had been master workman of the Knights of Labor National Trade Assembly 135; Michael Ratchford, a member of the executive board of the UMWA's District 6, which included nearly all of Ohio; John P. Jones who was president of both the Ohio Miners' Union and the Ohio Trades and Labor Assembly in 1890; and UMWA president John Rae. Influential Democratic miners included W. C. Pearce, secretary of the Ohio Miners' Union; Nial Hysell, a member of the Ohio Miners' Union executive board, who served as speaker of the Ohio House of Representatives from 1889 to 1891; Robert Watchorn, the UMWA's secretary treasury; and, most important, John McBride, the president of the Ohio Miners' Union for much of the 1880s who had represented Stark County for two terms in the Ohio House of Representatives.[11]

The creation of the UMWA in January 1890 ended half a decade of internecine struggle between the Knights of Labor National Trade Assembly 135 and the National Progressive Union of Miners and Mine Laborers and its predecessors, which had undermined the unity of the nation's coal miners and hampered attempts to expand the joint agreement to include more mines and more miners. Although the UMWA included only about 20,000 (about 10,000 of whom were in Ohio) of the nation's 192,000 soft coal miners at its inception, the organization's influence went beyond mere numbers. Almost all of the major operators in the nation's most productive bituminous coal region, an area stretching from Western Pennsylvania through Illinois, observed the UMWA-negotiated scale. The merger increased the expectations of both union leaders and mine operators that the joint operating agreement could be expanded geographically to the benefit of the entire industry.[12]

Enthusiastic about the UMWA's potential to improve the lives of the nation's miners, the officers of the new union met with the AFL's executive council in the winter of 1890 and agreed to participate in the AFL's eight-hour campaign. The AFL sought to devote its resources to help two strong unions win the eight-hour day in the hopes that success would help the movement for the shorter day spread to other industries and across the nation. The first part of the AFL's campaign succeeded when the United Brotherhood of Carpenters instituted the eight-hour day on May 1, 1890. Shortly thereafter, the AFL and UMWA agreed to a May 1, 1891, deadline for the institution of the eight-hour day in the nation's coal mines. While the primary purpose of the eight-hour day was to provide relief to the nation's workers, the miners told the operators that the reform was mutually beneficial as it would help curtail production, which in turn would increase the market price for coal, and end periodic shutdowns during which mine property decayed. Moreover, since the eight-hour day would be established industry-wide, the added costs would not alter the industry's competitive balance and could be passed along to the consumers. In short, the miners saw little reason for the operators to oppose the movement and many reasons for operators to support it.[13]

At the February 1891 annual meeting of operators and miners held to negotiate the scale for the upcoming year, the UMWA pushed the eight-hour day to the top of the agenda. Seventy-eight operators who employed seventy-five thousand miners attended the meeting as did seventy-three miner delegates representing thirty-five thousand miners. Although a few operators, most notably William Rend, supported the eight-hour movement, most operators shocked UMWA representatives by adamantly opposing the miners' demand. Some operators insisted that the setting of hours and other working conditions was among the prerogatives of the operators and that the conference could only negotiate issues dealing directly with wages, such as the scale and screen size. Other operators took a more paternalistic attitude, arguing that a long workday benefited the miners who would otherwise spend their extra time drinking or gambling. One operator declared that "the most prosperous man is the one who works ten hours a day." Still other operators conceded the benefits of the eight-hour day but doubted that it could be implemented industry-wide and feared it would place the operators who did adopt it at a competitive disadvantage.[14]

Stunned by the operators' refusal even to discuss the eight-hour day, the UMWA walked out of the joint conference before negotiating a scale for the upcoming year. At their annual convention the following week, the union leadership announced plans for a nationwide miners' strike to force the operators to capitulate. The union's officers believed that, with the assistance of organizers sent by the AFL, nearly all of the nation's soft coal miners would walk off the job. By allowing work to resume only at mines that granted the eight-hour day, the miners' union would reward those operators who shortened the day. Those operators agreeing to the union's demand would profit from the decreased supply, while those who refused to grant the increase would watch prices climb while their mines sat idle. The union's leadership called for the strike to start on May 1, 1891, the day chosen by the AFL to inaugurate the eight-hour-day movement in the coal industry.[15]

Almost immediately after the convention, local and state union leaders announced their opposition to the planned strike. They doubted whether the miners were ready to endure such an action. Times had been lean, and the miners had not been able to build up the food and cash reserves necessary to withstand a long conflict. Without such reserves the miners might be forced back to work before achieving the eight-hour day. Local leaders also argued that the timing was wrong for a strike. Although May 1 had symbolic meaning for the AFL and other labor organizations, the date occurred at a slack time in the cyclical demand for coal. Many operators would be happy to see their mines sit idle, while the market price of coal climbed, enabling them to sell their stockpiles at higher prices. Those opposed to the strike also feared that many organized and all of the unorganized miners would not join the strike. Under these conditions the local and state officials feared that the strike not only would fail but would also destroy both the union and all chances of expanding the joint agreement. Without the support of the state and local union officials, the UMWA's leadership had no choice but to postpone the strike.[16]

Called by one observer "a chapter of accidents," the failure to establish the eight-hour day set off a period of chaos in the mining industry. Before the 1891 interstate conference, the miners generally believed that the interests of the miners and the operators were in harmony, but the refusal of the majority of operators even to consider the request for the eight-hour day caused the miners to reexamine that assumption. The miners were genuinely shocked that most of the operators opposed the eight-hour day, which the miners saw as a way to lessen overproduction and to root out pernicious competition. The UMWA increasingly saw operators as obstacles rather than as allies in their efforts to improve the circumstances of miners.[17]

The collapse of the 1891 joint conference before a settlement on scale sent the industry's wage structure into disarray. Instead of negotiating a scale for the entire region stretching from Western Pennsylvania to Illinois, miners and operators in each region had to reach agreements for the upcoming year. Since coal from one region was competing with coal from the other regions, each region sought a competitive advantage. In well-organized areas, like Ohio's Hocking Valley, the miners and operators simply extended the existing scale for another year, but in less organized areas the operators demanded and won lower scales. This placed coal from well-organized areas at a competitive disadvantage, and Ohio operators began demanding reductions in the scale in order to meet the competition. In spite of the nation's general prosperity and an unusually harsh winter, which increased demand for coal, the real wages of the miners fell by 5–7 percent in 1891.[18]

Compounding the weakening of the interstate agreement, Ohio miners also failed in their attempts to secure legislation from the Ohio General Assembly. In 1889 Pennsylvania and Illinois had passed laws regulating the size of the screen coal passed over before it was weighed. Although operators sold the coal that fell through the screen, they paid the miners only for coal that was large enough to pass over the screen. Trying to limit an exploitative process, Ohio miners demanded that the state's general assembly pass a similar measure. The bill would make operators pay miners for more of the coal they removed from the earth and eliminate the competitive advantage that the state's coal had over coal from Illinois and Pennsylvania. Although the bill easily passed the Ohio House of Representatives, the UMWA's lobbying efforts got nowhere in the Ohio Senate, where the influence of the state's mine operators was too powerful to overcome. One of the bill's sponsors, Cuyahoga County senator John P. Green, accused the state's coal operators of offering him five hundred dollars to kill the bill and suggested that many of his colleagues had accepted similar offers.[19]

Following the failure of the eight-hour movement, the deterioration of the interstate agreement, the inability to secure passage of a screen law, and a fall in wages, miners began seeing the operators as much as the market as obstacles to improvements in their lives. Although most Ohio mine union leaders remained committed to the two major parties and believed that mine operators' and miners' interests were in harmony, they increasingly shared the Populists' fears that the concentration of wealth was destroying individual economic opportunity and that capitalists were corrupting the nation's political system in order to deprive workers of the product of their labor. John P. Jones, the president of the UMWA's District 6 and a devoted Republican, told the state's miners that the concentration of wealth "imperils the liberty that our fore-fathers fought and died for." For Jones it was clear that "the most illiterate among us perceive that the concentration of power and control of opportunity must in a very short time increase dependency to an extent never equaled in a civilized country. . . . Unless something is done to arrest this iniquitous concentration of wealth, a few plutocrats will own the whole of this country within a quarter of a century." Democrat John McBride, the former president of the Ohio Miners, echoed these concerns. McBride insisted that the concentration of wealth and the rise of large corporations worked to "crush the manly hopes of labor, trample humanity to death, and make our republican form of government seem but a mockery." He called for the nation's miners to use the ballot to pass laws limiting the growth of "corporate and concentrated wealth," regulating the introduction of labor-saving machines, and suspending the laws giving special privileges to the wealthy. By checking the concentration of wealth, McBride believed, workers "will hasten the day of their deliverance by the realization of Edward Bellamy's beautiful vision."[20]

The miners' increasing embrace of Populist ideas and the People's party was clear at the January 1892 convention of UMWA District 6, the most powerful of the union's districts. Covering all of Ohio except for a few dozen mines in Meigs County, District 6 contained more than half of the UMWA's dues-paying members. In spite of the poor showing that gubernatorial candidate John Seitz and the rest of the Populist slate had made that November, John Fahey, the secretary treasurer of Sub-District 9, called for Ohio miners to join the People's party. He told the miners that the Democratic and Republican parties had become too corrupt, that they would "die and fall of their own weight," and that miners should cast their lot with the Populists. The Ohio miners must have agreed with Fahey, as they voted to send him and newly elected District 6 president John Nugent to St. Louis for the convention that formally created the People's party.[21]

Given the failures in 1891, it was not surprising that UMWA membership dropped from close to 17,000 at its founding in 1890 to 13,955 in 1892, with 9,645 (69.1%) from Ohio, and that President John Rae and Secretary Treasurer Robert Watchorn announced they would not seek reelection in February 1892. The miners elected John McBride and Patrick McBryde to take their places. McBride, who had just concluded a term as the commissioner of the Ohio Bureau of Labor Statistics, had a long history as a leader of miners. Along with Illinois's Dan McLaughlin, he had been the guiding force behind the creation of both the 1886 interstate agreement and the UMWA. McBryde had been one of the leaders of the Knights of Labor National Trade Assembly 135 and, like McBride, was active in Democratic politics.[22]

Unlike their predecessors, who had agreed to launch the eight-hour movement without securing the support of local officials or allies among the operators, McBride and McBryde were cautious men who placed the reestablishment of the interstate agreement above all other concerns. McBride worked diligently among the operators, while McBryde led the efforts to organize the miners. McBride was unable to convince operators from the competitive coal belt running from Western Pennsylvania into Iowa to reestablish an interstate accord, but by the spring of 1892 he had cobbled together a semblance of an agreement. Miners' representatives and operators met by states and regions to set wage scales, but these conferences generally respected the differentials that had been negotiated in the 1890 agreement. State-by-state agreements made it difficult for the miners to improve their situations, as individual state conferences were unlikely to take any action such as increasing the wage scale, which would change the industry's competitive balance. The most that such agreements could deliver was stability within the status quo.[23]

While District 6 had sent representatives to the People's party St. Louis convention, the UMWA did not actively support the party's presidential nominee, General James Weaver, or local Populist candidates that fall. The *United Mine Workers Journal* followed its nonpartisan policy and remained silent during the election. District 6 president John Nugent was the only important union official to work with the Populists, and his participation provoked criticism at the state's convention in early 1893. Led by former District 6 president John Jones, a number of delegates with ties to the Republican party complained that Nugent had used his position in the union to advance the Populist cause. Nugent was able to withstand a censure motion by claiming that he campaigned as an individual rather than as a union official.[24]

Most other union officials continued to work with the major parties during the presidential election of 1892. McBryde, McBride, and Nial Hysell campaigned for Grover Cleveland and the Democratic ticket. McBride even defended Democratic vice-presidential candidate Adlai Stevenson from charges that he had treated his employees poorly as an Illinois mine operator. John Jones and Michael Ratchford, who were close to Massillon area-operator Marcus Hanna, worked on behalf of Benjamin Harrison and the Republican slate. During the campaign, both Cleveland supporters and Harrison partisans traded charges that the others were violating union rules by mixing politics with union affairs.[25]

In late 1892 and early 1893 conditions had improved for the nation's coal miners. An interstate agreement had been cobbled together, which improved the region's coal market. The market price of coal rose close to 10 percent. With the rise in demand for coal, miners worked more days and saw an increase in annual income. Historian Richard Jensen provides data suggesting that the miners' wages, adjusted for inflation, rose over 4 percent in 1892. The union's paid membership increased 45 percent (from 13,955 to 20,187) over the course of twelve months. More than half of the members were from Ohio. The UMWA leaders were guardedly optimistic about prospects for miners in the coming year. John McBride told the nation's miners that "the future appears bright and full of promise." Patrick McBryde insisted that market conditions were the best they had been in a number of years. District 6 president John Nugent boasted of the "material progress" that Ohio miners had made in 1892 and predicted continued improvement.[26]

While union leaders were pleased with improving market conditions, they were angered over political developments and what they considered to be the increasing hostility of many of the operators. In early 1893 union officials again lobbied the Ohio General Assembly to pass an anti-screen bill. As District 6 board member R. L. Davis insisted, the use of the screen perverted the natural order as it robbed those who produced wealth and rewarded "the idlers, the drones sometimes called capitalists." Like a similar measure two years earlier, the bill had little trouble passing in the House of Representatives. Operators, though, mounted a fight in the Senate. The operators did not dispute the claims of the miners or attack the purpose of the bill. Instead they asserted that the anti-screen law would violate the state constitution by breaching "the right of contract" and that it amounted to class legislation. Rumors circulated that a number of operators spent lavishly to persuade senators to oppose the bill. In the end the Senate defeated the bill, which was supported by only six of the body's thirty-four members. The defeat of the screen bill provoked an outcry from union officials. The District 6 board issued a "manifesto" complaining that the "rights of capital are of far greater importance than the honest and fair treatment of the laborer" and attributing the defeat to collusion between the Republican party, which controlled the general assembly, and the operators, including Republican party leader Marcus Hanna. John Nugent urged the miners not to forget the Senate's insult and to punish those legislators at the next election.[27]

Any optimism the UMWA had left after the failure of the screen bill came to an end late in the summer of 1893 as a financial panic gripped the nation. The panic devastated the nation's miners and mine operators. As factories throughout the nation shut their doors, the demand for coal dropped precipitously. Exacerbating the drop in demand, the panic hit during the summer when demand for coal traditionally declined and operators increased their stockpiles in anticipation of winter. While mines with long-term contracts continued to operate, mines producing coal for the open market had trouble finding customers. As operators were loath to close mines for fear that miners would simply pack up and leave the area, most mines continued to work a day or two a week. Miners from throughout the state wrote the *United Mine Workers Journal* complaining about the lack of regular work.[28]

At the beginning of the panic, the miners did not blame the mine owners for their situation. Instead, they blamed the nation's monetary system and the actions of Wall Street and British bankers for their economic ills. A circular signed by the District 6 executive board simply asserted that "many mines are now idle because operators cannot secure money." While the Democratic administration and Republican leaders in Congress called for the repeal of the Sherman Silver Purchase Act and the temporary demonetization of silver, the miners called for an expansion of the nation's currency supply. Former UMWA president John Rae organized a mass meeting that called for the free and unlimited coinage of both gold and silver as well as the "issue of paper money in such amount as will increase our currency to an amount not less than forty dollars per capita."[29] Sherman Glasgow, a District 6 official, advised the miners to join with the Farmers' Alliance and the Knights of Labor to reform the nation's monetary system. District 6 executive board member William H. Crawford rooted the nation's economic woes in the concentration of wealth and in capital's control of the nation's banking system. The economic system, he insisted, had so "reversed the true order of nature" that "actual producers are made slaves to non-producing capitalists." He called for the abolition of the private banking system and the issuance of greenbacks.[30]

In the Hocking Valley, currency-short customers bought coal from operators on credit. This squeezed the operators, who had to pay their miners while waiting for payment from their customers. To solve their own cash shortage, in early August the operators asked the UMWA for permission to pay miners with notes of credit. Noting that "[m]any miners are now idle because operators cannot secure money to pay their employees," the UMWA felt it had no choice but to accept the offer. After the Hocking Valley miners agreed to accept notes instead of cash, operators in Pomeroy and other regions of the state demanded similar concessions.[31]

By late September, the use of notes began taking a toll on the state's miners. Many merchants refused to take the notes for fear that the coal companies would not survive the panic or that the notes could not be redeemed in the near future. Alex Johnson, an UMWA delegate to a joint convention of Ohio miners and operators, complained that a Nelsonville

TABLE 6.1—Wages of Miners at Rendville Mine 3, from May 1893 to April 1894

Month Year	Average daily wages per man ($)	Average number of days worked	Average monthly wages ($)
May 1893	1.96	11.75	23.12
June 1893	1.63	10.25	16.74
July 1893	1.85	14.75	27.33
August 1893	1.78	11.50	20.57
September 1893	1.79	21.50	38.55
October 1893	1.67	23.25	38.92
November 1893	1.55	18.50	28.76
December 1893	1.41	16.50	23.36
January 1894	1.65	10.00	16.53
February 1894	1.27	13.50	17.18
March 1894	0.95	19.50	18.58
April 1894	1.32	12.50	16.53

Source: United Mine Workers' Journal, April 26, 1894.

businessman had told him that a note with a face value of "twenty some odd dollars and 27 cents" was worth about twenty-seven cents. Those merchants who accepted the notes discounted them between 10 and 20 percent. R. L. Davis, a member of the District 6 executive board, suggested that the companies issued the notes as part of a scheme to force the miners to use company stores. Though the miners insisted that economic conditions had improved enough to allow the resumption of cash payments, the operators ignored the union's plea and continued to issue notes.[32]

The panic also set off cutthroat competition throughout the Ohio Valley. Mines in Western Pennsylvania and West Virginia were especially hard hit. These mines had supplied Pittsburgh-area iron and steel mills, which had quickly closed after the start of the panic. Pittsburgh-area coal operators responded by slashing wages and prices in hopes of finding new buyers. This, in turn, had repercussions throughout coal markets, destroying the wage agreements that McBride and McBryde had worked so hard to reestablish and forcing miners to accept wage reductions. UMWA officials in Ohio did not fault the state's operators for falling wages. Instead, they blamed Pittsburgh-area operators and miners. District 6 president John Nugent complained of the "invasion of our markets," and McBride told the state's miners that they should accept a lower scale in order to punish Pennsylvania miners and operators for trying to secure market share "by unfair practices and at the expense of Ohio miners."[33]

District 6 board member Richard L. Davis collected wage statistics showing the effects of the panic and price competition on his fellow miners at Rendville Mine 3 (see Table 6.1). The situation at other mines was even worse. New Straitsville miners earned an average of just $20.33 a month from May until December 1893. This was $6.84 less per month than those at Rendville made.[34]

The state's miners were reluctant to agree to a lower scale. One Hocking Valley miner told a *New York Times* reporter, "I have never seen as discouraged a set of men as the miners in this neighborhood have been since the last reduction was made. They know it matters not how steady they work: they cannot make enough money to keep a small-sized family in the necessary food, and they have concluded if they are to starve they prefer doing it all at once and not by degrees." In a letter to the *United Mine Workers Journal*, a North Industry miner put it more succinctly: "[I]t is better to starve above ground idle than to starve under ground working."[35]

The events surrounding the Panic of 1893—unemployment and poverty caused by the drop in demand, the intrusion of Pennsylvania and West Virginia coal into Ohio markets, President Cleveland's efforts to repeal the Sherman Silver Purchase Act, continued payment of notes to miners, demands to lower the scale, and collapse of the interstate agreement—radicalized Ohio coal miners, and they increasingly looked to the People's party for deliverance. When the state's miners met in early 1894, they endorsed the AFL's political program. Introduced at the 1893 AFL Convention by Chicago machinist Tommy Morgan, the political program would have committed the AFL to the creation of a producer-based political party. The program included the reforms demanded by the Omaha platform (with the exception of the sub-treasury plan) as well as a plank calling for the collective ownership of the means of production and distribution. As Morgan was at the forefront of efforts to build a Populist–labor alliance in Illinois, most observers saw ratification of the political program as an endorsement of the Populist party. Debate over Morgan's program proved so contentious that the 1893 AFL convention postponed voting on the program until the following year. During that time, the convention asked local and international unions to vote for or against the political program.[36]

Not only did Ohio miners endorse the political program at the 1894 District 6 convention, they also elected a number of officers associated with the People's party. The two main candidates for president, John Nugent and A. A. Adams, both had extensive ties to the Populists. Nugent had attended the party's St. Louis convention in 1892 and campaigned for Weaver that fall, while Adams ran for public office earlier in the year on a joint Populist–Socialist Labor party slate in Perry County. When the votes were counted, Adams narrowly defeated Nugent and vowed to take the union in a "radical direction." Three of the five miners elected to the state executive board were outspoken proponents of the People's party, and there is evidence suggesting that a fourth, Richard L. Davis, was also a Populist.[37]

Shortly thereafter, at the national UMWA convention, the union voted overwhelmingly to endorse the AFL's proposed political program. McBride told the convention that "radical reforms are needed in our industrial system." The endorsement of the political program was the "only way to deal a death blow to tyranny and oppression as practiced upon the wage workers . . . and administer a telling and lasting rebuke to legislative imbecility and administrative corruption," he declared. "[T]he people must either own or control the means of production and distribution or be subjected to the dictation, as they now are, of those who own and control these two powerful agencies." At this time, McBride was not willing to endorse the People's party, but he did call for workers to form "an independent political movement."[38]

At the same convention, the miners voted to launch a nationwide strike on April 21, 1894. The purpose of the strike was to create a shortage in order to increase the market price of coal. As the price of coal rose, the UMWA hoped that operators would be willing to increase wages and reestablish the interstate conference to stabilize the entire industry for the benefit of both miners and operators. As the convention told the nation's miners, "The interests of home, family, and organizations; the interests of the coal trade and the prosperity of mining communities demand that you do your duty."[39]

Although less than 10 percent of the nation's soft coal miners belonged to the UMWA, nearly all of the nation's miners supported the strike, much to the elation of UMWA officials. Initial reports indicated that 160,000 of the nation's 184,000 miners walked off the job. In Ohio and the rest of the bituminous coal belt, at most a handful of miners continued to work. The largest concentration of non-striking miners was found in southern West

Virginia and southwestern Virginia, where about 10,000 miners continued to produce coal.[40]

UMWA leaders realized that for the strike to be successful the flow of coal from non-striking mines and existing stockpiles had to be stopped. Only a severe shortage and a dramatic rise in coal prices would convince operators to reestablish a scale high enough to allow miners to provide for their families. To stop the production of coal, the UMWA sent organizers to the non-striking areas to convince the miners to join their effort. To stop the transportation of coal from the non-union mines to industrial markets, McBride met in Columbus with Eugene Debs, the head of the American Railway Union (ARU). Debs and McBride hammered out a cooperative agreement between the two industrial unions. During the UMWA strike, the ARU would refuse to carry non-union coal and, if the ARU went on strike, the UMWA would refuse to provide coal to fuel scab trains.[41] It was just the beginning of a busy summer for both men and their unions. For the next several months, members of both the ARU and UMWA would be aiding each other. In fact, the unprecedented cooperation between members of the two unions makes it difficult to understand the miners' strike and the subsequent Pullman boycott and strike as discrete events.

The first weeks of the strike were generally quiet. Ohio operators, with the exception of a few in the Massillon region, supported the strike and the strikers. The collapse of the scale and the invasion of low-priced Pennsylvania coal into Ohio markets had hurt them too. The managers of a couple of Hocking Valley mines even put miners to work making improvements around mines and paid them union scale. The Perry County mining village of New Straitsville put hundreds of miners to work repairing streets, bridges, and public buildings. Ohio operators made no effort to bring in strikebreakers and announced their willingness to participate in a new interstate agreement and to increase wages. The *Pomeroy Weekly Tribune Telegraph* declared, "The strike has been a remarkable one in the apparent perfection of its organization, the peaceful methods used and the extent of the territories it covers. There has been no violence or riots in this part of the country."[42]

On May 14, 1894, operators representing three hundred mines met in Cleveland with UMWA officials and miners from fourteen states and territories to reestablish a scale and to end the strike. The miners argued that the market price of coal had improved enough to allow the operators to pay the scale they had agreed to in the spring of 1893. Most operators, though, insisted that the miners accept a lower scale, maintaining that the dollar had increased in value since the last agreement and that miners should accept the lower scale for the good of the industry. A few operators even opposed the reestablishment of a scale at any level. One UMWA official blamed several greedy operators for the failure of the conference: "Some of the operators hold large stocks of coal which they are beginning to dispose of at almost fabulous prices, and they are more than willing to see the strike continue until the coal piles are leveled."[43]

The actions of the operators angered the miners and convinced the UMWA leadership that a harmony of interest no longer characterized the mining industry. Leading the miners out of the conference, McBride accused the operators of being more interested in their individual profits than in the good of the whole industry. An UMWA resolution declared that, since the operators had "contemptuously" rejected the "hand of peace and conciliation" offered by the miners, any agreement was "utterly impractical."[44]

The failure of the Cleveland conference destroyed the peace that had characterized the strike. Confrontations between strikers and operators and between strikers and authorities became more pronounced. Most of the conflicts occurred in towns just north of the Ohio River where miners and ARU members tried to stop trains carrying coal from non-striking mines in Virginia and West Virginia to industrial areas along the Great Lakes. The strikers realized that, as long as the flow of coal continued, hopes of ending the strike remained remote. In Belmont County, Ohio, strikers and ARU members blocked a bridge and placed the coal cars on a side track. In Perry County, miners and railroaders burned a bridge to stop the movement of coal, and in Jackson County railroaders simply refused to attach coal cars to trains. Governor McKinley responded to these incidents and others by dispatching the state militia to protect the coal trains traveling through southern Ohio. McKinley mobilized so many troops that the state ran out of money to pay the soldiers' salaries.[45]

The miners and local government officials charged that mine operators colluded with local sheriffs to exaggerate the level of violence in order to provoke the intervention of state troops. A common pleas judge from Belmont County criticized the presence of the state militia, writing to Governor McKinley, "I do not see the necessity of this large force." The mayor of Corning, Ohio, two councilmen, and the president of the local miners' union wrote an open letter to the governor arguing that reports of miner violence were overblown: "The railroad men themselves refused to haul anymore scab coal, and they told the sheriff of Athens County so. . . . [M]iners paid strict attention to the advice given by our national officials and are determined to win this fight without resorting to any unlawful means."[46]

McKinley's actions angered the state's coal miners. When McKinley donated ten dollars to the Massillon miners' relief fund, the miners returned the money, declaring they did not want support "from the hand that assists in smiting them." A Massillon-area local denounced McKinley as "ever ready to aid and assist capital in crushing labor." When a Columbus paper reported that bankers with ties to Hocking Valley coal syndicates had advanced to the cash-crunched state the money needed to pay for the militia's strike duty and that the local board of trade had passed a resolution thanking the militia for their service, the *United Mine Workers Journal* responded, "We leave to our readers whether there seems to be anything incongruous in the above medley—bankers, boards of trade, militiamen, and the governor."[47]

Unable to convince the operators to agree to the restoration of the May 1893 scale and unable to stop the flow of coal from Virginia and West Virginia, the leaders of the UMWA realized that nothing could be gained from continuing the strike and that the problems plaguing miners and the coal industry required a political solution. Meeting with leading operators, McBride and the leaders of the UMWA acceded to a new scale that reduced payments to miners to nine cents a ton below the May 1893 scale. McBride advised the nation's coal miners to head back to work, insisting that continuing the strike would only bring more misery and hunger. Although many local leaders criticized the decision, almost all of the nation's coal miners heeded McBride's call and went back to work.[48]

After the conclusion of the coal strike, McBride found himself deeply involved with the Pullman boycott and strike. To support striking workers at the Pullman Sleeping Car Company, the ARU announced in late June 1894 that its members would not attach Pullman cars to trains or operate trains with Pullman cars attached. Determined to support the Pullman Company and to defeat the ARU, the General Managers' Association began firing those who refused to handle Pullman cars. When this did not work, the association began recruiting strikebreakers, hiring a private militia, and placing mail pouches on Pullman cars. When ARU members refused to handle mail-laden Pullman cars, the railroads' General Managers' Association used this as a pretext to induce U.S. attorney general Richard Olney to federalize its private militia. When this produced more conflict, Olney had federal troops break the strike. As if this was not enough, federal judges sentenced ARU president Eugene Debs to six months in prison for violating injunctions forbidding ARU members from interfering with the trains.[49] During the Pullman unrest, McBride and the UMWA lived up to their bargain with Debs and the ARU. Ohio miners—especially those in the Hocking Valley—stopped digging coal for the trains. Patrick McBryde assured strikers that the railroad "will not have a pound of coal to haul." Not surprisingly, McBride was the only union leader who answered Debs's pleas for support.[50]

The actions of President Grover Cleveland's administration during the Pullman strike was the final straw, convincing the leaders of the UMWA that the Democratic party no longer had much to offer workingmen. McBride, in particular, felt betrayed by Cleveland, who he had campaigned for just two years before. The time was right for labor to chart a new political course, and McBride called on the state's workers to join with the People's party.[51]

The Ohio People's party had undergone dramatic changes in 1894 even before McBride announced his intention to form a labor party and to merge it with the Populists. Not only had labor troubles and the hard times brought about by the Panic of 1893 increased support for the Populist cause, but the party had found a wealthy and charismatic leader—Jacob Coxey—around whom to rally. From the establishment of the Ohio People's party in 1891 until early 1894, Jacob Coxey had been a second-tier leader. A veteran Greenbacker and wealthy industrialist who owned a sandstone quarry and invested in race horses, Coxey had attended the Populists' 1892 St. Louis convention as an alternate and headed the local arrangements committee for the Ohio People's party 1892 convention in his hometown of Massillon. But Coxey had never been one of the party's principal leaders. Active in monetary reform circles, Coxey had developed a bond plan that, he asserted, would increase the amount of money in circulation and put the unemployed to work. The plan was relatively simple, calling for the financing of public works to end unemployment. Coxey wanted for the national government to issue five hundred million dollars in bonds to state and local governments to be used for building roads and making public improvements. The bonds, which would circulate as legal tender, and public works would provide work at $1.50 a day for the unemployed, stimulate other economic growth through improvements in infrastructure, and increase the money supply. The bonds were to be repaid with a 1 percent annual fee—the same rate that the government charged national banks—over the course of twenty-five years. Coxey insisted that Congress should give states and cities wanting to create jobs the same terms that it gave bankers seeking to make private profit.[52]

Coxey was able to convince the Ohio People's party in 1893 to support his plan, and that same year the AFL's national convention passed a resolution—introduced by his friend John McBride—endorsing it. Coxey even got Kansas senator William Peffer to introduce the program as a Senate bill in early 1894. These actions had little impact and generated only modest publicity until everything changed in the winter and spring of 1894. Angered at what he perceived to be congressional indifference to the plight of the nation's three to five million unemployed, Coxey and fellow monetary reformer Carl Browne came up with the idea of a march of unemployed men to the nation's Capitol to demand jobs and the enactment of his bond program. Calling his proposed march a "petition in boots" and the marchers an "industrial army," Coxey summoned the nation's unemployed to meet in Massillon to begin their march on Easter Sunday, March 25, 1894. Although only a little more than one hundred men began the march in Massillon, similar industrial armies formed throughout the nation with the intention of linking up with Coxey's contingent in the nation's capital.[53]

Thanks to Browne, an expert showman, Coxey's march attracted publicity out of all proportion to its modest size. Major newspapers dispatched reporters to travel with the marchers, documenting every day of the two-month ordeal. Coxey and Browne made great stories. Described by journalist Ray Stannard Baker as "mild looking and of medium size, with rounding shoulders, an oily face, a straw colored moustache, and gold bowed spectacles," Coxey appeared more like a scholar than the leader of a protest movement. Yet he had a flair for the dramatic. He would ride in an expensive carriage pulled by white horses and had named his youngest child "Legal Tender." Browne, in contrast, dressed much like the former carnival barker that he was. Baker described him as "strongly built with a heavy moustache, and a beard with spirals. He wore a leather coat fringed around the shoulders and the sleeves. A row of buttons down the front were shining silver dollars. Calvary boots, tight fitting, well polished came to his knees." In the words of historian Carlos Schwantes, "What Coxey and Browne essentially did was to create an unemployment adventure story that the press found irresistible."[54]

Although the march was generally uneventful and always peaceful, most of the press's coverage of Coxey, Browne, and their industrial army was negative. *Leslie's Weekly* complained that Coxey's "marauding columns" were spreading anarchism and communism. The *Nation* described Coxey's adventure as a "filthy eruption" of socialism. One commentator labeled the marchers as "worthless drifters as homeless and taxless as the aborigines who spent their money on tobacco, whiskey, and cards," and a health official warned that the marchers were "an un-American and unsanitary horde" spreading disease in its wake. The superintendent of the New York City police called Coxey's movement the greatest threat to the nation since the Civil War and insisted that it "should be stamped out just as the Great Rebellion was in 1861."[55]

Jacob S. Coxey, 1894. Courtesy of the Ohio Historical Society.

While the mainstream press was vilifying Coxey and the marchers, Populists and labor leaders supported their efforts. AFL president Samuel Gompers lobbied Congress to give Coxey's plan a hearing, while the *Journal of the Knights of Labor* praised the marchers as "serious, honest and determined" and as "absolutely right." Even the Socialist Labor party's Daniel DeLeon, who derided most middle-class reformers, praised Coxey. When an industrial army patterned after Coxey's movement passed through Cincinnati and Columbus, the labor federations of those cities appropriated funds to pay for food and housing, organized speeches and parades to support the marchers, and protested the efforts of authorities to restrict the activities of the marchers. Populist senator William Peffer introduced a motion calling for the U.S. Senate to form a committee to receive Coxey's petition, while Nebraska's Populist senator William Allen introduced a resolution defending the marchers' right to carry their petition to Congress.[56]

Coxey's march alarmed the citizens and authorities of the nation's capital. The *Washington News* called for government officials to "consider what could be done to avert the threatened invasion of the District by this swarm of human locusts." President Cleveland saw the march as an attack on his administration, while Democrats, Republicans, and even most of the Populists in Congress viewed Coxey as a crank and his "army" as potentially dangerous. After consulting with his cabinet, Cleveland decided to ignore the marchers and delegated the task of containing them to District of Columbia officials. District authorities, in turn, announced that they would rigidly enforce laws regulating vagrancy, parades, and the use of the Capitol grounds.[57]

As Coxey and his fellow marchers approached Washington, they were joined by two other industrial armies, one from Philadelphia and the other composed of local residents, bringing the total contingent to about five hundred. Coxey applied for and received a parade permit, but his request to speak on the Capitol's steps was neither denied nor granted. As the marchers entered the city and paraded to the Capitol, they drew thousands of spectators. When they arrived at the Capitol, the marchers stopped before entering the grounds. Coxey and Browne tried to make their way to the Capitol steps to deliver speeches but were promptly arrested. While legend has it that Coxey and Browne were arrested for walking on the grass, they were charged with displaying banners on the Capitol's grounds. In Coxey's case, the "banner" was a small badge pinned to his lapel. After telling them that they deserved a harsher sentence, a District of Columbia judge sentenced Coxey and Browne to twenty days in a local jail.

While politicians and newspaper editors associated with the major parties saw the arrest and imprisonment of Coxey as fitting punishment for a dangerous crank, many Populists and trade unionists viewed Coxey's arrest as symbolizing the government's indifference to the nation's unemployed and its willingness to trample the rights of those challenging the economic status quo. Populist leaders complained of the summary trial and Coxey's persecution for his political ideals, and trade unionists—from radicals such as Eugene Debs to the more conservative Samuel Gompers—complained that Coxey was prosecuted more for his ideas than for any violation of the law. Most trade unionists and Populists undoubtedly would have agreed with the words that Coxey had planned to deliver at the Capitol: "Up these steps the lobbyists of trusts and corporations have passed unchallenged on their way to committee rooms, access to which we, the representatives of the toiling wealth producers, have been denied."[58]

The notoriety and publicity associated with his march and arrest transformed Coxey into the undisputed leader of the Ohio People's party. While he was in jail, the Populists of Stark, Summit, and Columbiana Counties nominated him for a seat in the U.S. House of Representatives. Upon his release from prison, Coxey called on those who had marched to Washington to remain in the city to remind the politicians of the suffering of the nation's unemployed. In the hope of raising funds to feed and clothe the marchers as well as the participants in other industrial armies still making their way to Washington, Coxey launched a speaking tour. As most of his speaking engagements were in Ohio, the tour served to increase Coxey's popularity among the state's Populists. So when McBride announced his intention to form a labor party and to merge the party with the state's People's party, Ohio Populists had already found the type of leader they had been lacking since 1891—a wealthy, dynamic, well-known figure who could attract a crowd and was willing to spend money on the cause.[59]

The emergence of Coxey as a formidable figure in the Ohio People's party only increased labor's enthusiasm for the Populists, giving a boost to McBride's call for a labor convention. Local unions and urban labor federations sent over 250 delegates to the convention. Although the UMWA and Debs's ARU sent the largest contingents, there were delegates representing locals from almost every craft and trade. The central labor bodies of Columbus, Toledo, Zanesville, and Springfield endorsed McBride's move and dispatched members to the convention. Contingents from Cleveland and Cincinnati, where the central bodies had already endorsed the People's party, were especially strong. Attendance was so large that the attendees could not all fit into the Columbus Trades and Labor Assembly's Hall. The start of the convention was delayed as local delegates scurried to secure a room large enough to hold the delegates, journalists, and onlookers in attendance. Partisan papers that generally mocked the movement and had predicted the convention would draw but a handful of delegates conceded that the state's workers were "well represented" by "sober" delegates with "sincere motives."[60]

Unlike most labor meetings, the convention witnessed few disputes and little controversy. This was probably due to the fact that McBride made his intentions clear—the creation of a labor party and its merger with the People's party. Trade unionists who did not support these goals stayed home. The delegates elected Toledo Central Labor Union president John Braunschwiger as convention chairman and made a Knight of Labor from Tiffin, Charles Martin, convention secretary. Committees were selected and set off to work. The two most important committees were the resolutions committee, which would draft the convention's platform, and the merger committee, which would work out an alliance with the Populists.

The convention's platform and preamble reflected the trade unionists' desire to purify the nation's political system and expand the power of governments to allow them to check the abuses of corporations and to ensure national prosperity through the promotion of full employment. The preamble disputed the laissez-faire notion that unregulated competition promoted the common good, insisting that a republican government can only be built "on the love of the whole people for each other." This love had been destroyed by the "concentrated and corporate wealth," which had fostered an economic system built upon greed and want. To rekindle the ideal that the American people constituted "one united brotherhood," the convention first demanded that "the power of the Government should be expanded as rapidly and as far as the good sense of intelligent people and the teachings of experience justify along the lines of the collective ownership of the means of production."

Although such a formulation can be seen as a politically expedient attempt to satisfy both labor radicals and the more conservative supporters of the People's party, it also reflected the desire to balance traditional property rights with the welfare of the commonwealth. Unlike labor leaders such as Samuel Gompers who were schooled in European radical thought, Ohio trade unionists did not see a natural conflict between labor and capital. Rather, they thought that, in an ideal state, labor and capital operated in harmony. The rise of large corporations, which sought profit above all else, undermined this natural harmony, harming both the small producer and the wage laborer. By giving the government the power to distinguish between those owners of the means of production who benefited the community and those who threatened the community, the "collective ownership" plank, the labor leaders promised, would cure the nation's economic maladies. Individual entrepreneurs who did not exploit labor, like industrialist Jacob Coxey, would be allowed to continue operations, but those companies that exploited labor, consumers, and smaller competitors would be subject to government control.

The rest of the party's platform included traditional Populist demands: government issue of greenbacks and the elimination of private banks; the free and unlimited coinage of silver at a ratio of sixteen to one; government ownership of telegraphs, telephone, railroads, and mines; municipal ownership of public service franchises; abolition of alien landownership; prohibition of child labor; compulsory education; direct legislation; an eight-hour day; the end of the sweating system; inspection of factories and mines; the end to "undesirable immigration"; and women's suffrage. Only the plank to end "undesirable immigration" generated any controversy. Ernest Weier, a longtime Populist and printer from Cincinnati, asserted that the nation should remain "a harbor for the oppressed of all nations" and that the plank would hurt the party's chances among foreign-born voters. McBride countered that he was "willing to welcome to our shores all men who were honest and upright and would make good citizens," but that the nation should not allow in paupers and criminals. In the end McBride's view prevailed, as the delegates rejected Weier's motion to strike the plank from the platform.

After ratifying the platform, the convention adjourned for the day, and the merger committee met with the leaders of the Populist party. The merger committee—labor's delegation was led by McBride and the People's party's by T. J. Craeger, a Springfield printer who was also a delegate at the labor convention—had little trouble agreeing to a merger. The Populists needed the votes promised by the trade unionists, while the trade unionists needed both a party and allies. The merger talks were aided by the fact that there was a significant overlap of delegates for the two conventions. The only opposition to the merger came from members of the nearly dead Farmers' Alliance. Led by J. H. C. Cobb, the Alliance men feared that after merging with the laborites the Populist party would "fall into the hands of persons who will run it in the interest of either of the other parties." Republican newspapers insisted that McBride intended to fuse the parties with the state's Democrats. The fact that the state's Democratic Executive Committee was meeting in Columbus at the same time as the labor and Populist conventions fueled such rumors. Cobb and the Alliance men, though, were unable to convince the rest of the Populist convention of the potential threat posed by McBride and the laborites. The state's People's party, already dominated by trade unionists, saw an alliance with McBride's labor party as crucial to victory in the fall.[61]

The merger agreement provided that the Populists would accept the labor convention's platform (with the addition of planks supporting the Omaha platform and liberal pensions for veterans) and that the laborites would join the Populist convention for the nomination of a slate for the upcoming fall. The acceptance of the labor platform, even with the qualified call for the collective ownership of the means of production, generated little disagreement. Since the municipal elections of 1893, in which the labor-led Cleveland Populists collected 16 percent of the popular vote, trade unionists had emerged as the most important block within the Ohio People's party, and Coxey's presence only reinforced the dominance of urban and labor forces. As the *Ohio State Journal* remarked, the platforms of the two parties "are not that far apart."

Under the merger agreement, the labor delegates were to attend the Populist convention and vote as delegates at large, but when the two parties met the next day to nominate a slate of candidates for statewide office, the labor delegates were seated with their county delegations, thus depriving them of an independent vote. Although partisan newspapers charged that this was part of a Populist plot to deny a voice to the laborites, this does not appear to be the case. First, the laborites were assigned to their county delegations before members of the merger committee arrived at the convention to present the details of the agreement. The merger committee had been meeting in downtown Columbus well past midnight, while the convention convened early the next morning outside of the city. Not wanting to wait for the merger committee's arrival, convention chairman John Seitz integrated the labor delegates according to established party rules. Second, as almost all of the candidates were selected by acclamation, it made little difference how the delegates were seated or how votes were apportioned. Third, after the convention the laborites voiced no dissatisfaction with the procedures. As John McBride declared, "the labor delegates got all the recognition they asked for and a good deal more and are perfectly satisfied."

There was little controversy or even interest in the nomination of a slate of candidates for the fall's election. The Populists conceded that they had no chance of winning any of the statewide offices that were up for grabs. Instead, they pinned their hopes on congressional and local races, the candidates for which would be selected at local conventions. Adding to the lack of enthusiasm for the statewide races was the fact that the most important office coming available was that of secretary of state, hardly a position that inspired the faithful. Without dissent, the delegates nominated Charles Martin for secretary of state. The choice symbolized the alliance of Populists and trade unionists. Martin had close ties to leaders of both the Cleveland CLU and the UMWA, which had supported his failed attempt to unseat Knights of Labor general secretary John Hayes the previous winter. Martin had also served on the People's party's executive committee since its founding. The delegates nominated E. D. Stark of Cuyahoga County, one of the party's few lawyers, for the Supreme Court, while candidates for the board of public works and state school commissioner were selected to give the ticket geographical balance.

Ohio's Populists and commentators were much more optimistic about the party's chances in several congressional races. The *New York Times* even warned its readers to "expect some surprises from the [Ohio] Populist Party this November" before detailing several of the party's candidates. The party nominated Coxey for the seat from the eleventh district, which included Canton and a number of smaller industrial cities. James Brettell, an ironworker from Mingo Junction who served as an AFL vice president, ran for the seat in the district running along the Ohio River in the eastern part of the state. The *New York Times* thought that W. H. Crawford, a member of the District 6 executive board running in the Hocking Valley, had the best shot of any of the People's party nominees. The paper noted that UMWA "has 9,500 organized voters in the district" and "expected that the labor movement will . . . put in the Populist."[62]

Unlike the three previous conventions of the state's People's party, the 1894 convention took on the trappings of a major party's political convention and generated public excitement. On the evening of the convention's last day, Columbus's Central Populist Club, which was closely associated with the Columbus Trades and Labor Assembly, organized a parade followed by public speeches. Thousands crowded into the streets to watch Populist clubs from around the state march in formation. Many of the clubs wore special outfits, carried Chinese lanterns or canes, and marched behind bands. The parade ended at the state capitol, where a crowd of between eight and twelve thousand heard Coxey present the specifics of his bond plans and recount the details of his arrest and imprisonment. The proceedings so excited the *Topeka Advocate*, the main organ of Kansas Populism, that it praised the convention as "the most determined set of men that ever assembled . . . outside of Kansas."[63]

UMWA leaders toured the state campaigning for Martin and other People's party candidates. At a rally in Columbus, Patrick McBryde scored

President Cleveland for his monetary policies and actions during the Pullman boycott before attacking Governor McKinley's actions during the coal miners strike: "Someone told him three or four Hungarian miners were seen on a hill in the mining region, and he called out the militia. Someone else told him that the mules were loose in a certain mining region. He called out the militia. Some boys up at Massillon were playing base ball, and the governor was informed, and he called out a militia regiment." McBryde continued, "it makes no difference which of the two parties are in power," because each of them will oppress the workingman. The only solution was to "vote the straight Populist ticket." John McBride followed with a speech emphasizing the ways that the labor injunction had deprived workingmen of their rights to speech and assembly.[64]

The results of the election of 1894 disappointed the Populists. The party failed to "revolutionize" state politics as one Columbus newspaper had predicted. Statewide, Martin polled just under fifty thousand votes (6.5%), in a race in which the Republican candidate captured 54 percent of the vote. Although the Populists had not expected Martin to win, they had hoped for a better showing, at least 10 percent of the vote. In congressional and local races, the party did not have a single triumph.[65]

Despite these disappointments, Ohio's Populists did have a few reasons to be hopeful. The party had made sizable gains over the results of previous years and did quite well in a few areas. Martin tripled the vote General James Weaver had received in the state just two years earlier. Jacob Coxey, running for the eighteenth district's seat in Congress, captured 21 percent of the vote, more than quadrupling the percentage captured by any previous Populist candidate. As expected, the Populists ran well in the coal-mining areas of the eastern part of the state (see table 6.2).[66] The results were more encouraging in a number of smaller industrial cities. Here the Populists were able to climb out of the simple digits and, in some cases, capture over a quarter of the vote (see table 6.3).

Three months after the merger of McBride's labor party with the Ohio People's party, the AFL held its annual convention in Denver, Colorado. The convention promised to be divisive, as it was due to consider the political program that had been introduced in 1893 by Chicago machinist and People's party supporter Tommy Morgan. Adoption of the program would have committed the AFL to "independent political action." The AFL's constituent unions had overwhelmingly endorsed the political program over the past twelve months, with only four unions rejecting the program. Although supporters of the political program were called "Socialists," they were mostly Populists. During the summer and fall of 1894, the *Chicago*

TABLE 6.2—Percent of Populist Vote in the Selected Areas of the State's Six Largest Coal-Producing Counties, 1891–1894

Township/precinct (1890 pop.)	1891	1892	1893	1894
PERRY COUNTY				
Coal Twp. (3,747)				
East Precinct	3	6	10	22
West Precinct	1	3	6	16
Monroe Twp. (4,506)				
Buckingham Precinct	5	6	5	21
Corning Precinct	0	1	3	9
Rendville Precinct	1	4	2	15
Salt Lick Twp. (4,682)				
East Precinct	3	5	7	19
Middle Precinct	15	10	15	22
West Precinct	6	4	5	9
ATHENS COUNTY				
Trimble Twp. (4,966)				
E. Glouster Precinct	4	6	5	17
W. Glouster Precinct	4	6	12	35
Holister Precinct	1	4	20	38
Jackson Precinct	1	4	21	41
Trimble Precinct	4	10	13	18
York Twp.				
Bessemmer Precinct	5	7	9	33
Dover Twp.				
Millfield Precinct	3	0	9	16

Hocking County
Ward Twp. (5,090)	8	7	7	35

Green Twp.
Haydenville Precinct	10	1	2	33

STARK COUNTY
Lawrence Twp.
Canal Fulton Precinct 1	2	4	7	26
Canal Fulton Precinct 2	1	1	1	16
Lawrence Precinct	2	9	6	26
Youngstown Hill Precinct	6	6	36	55

JACKSON COUNTY
Coal Twp. (4,585)
First Precinct	3	4	2	11
Second Precinct	3	10	6	14
Third Precinct	6	5	6	34

BELMONT COUNTY
Pultney Twp.
Pultney Precinct	0	0	3	26

Richland Twp.
Glencoe Precinct	0	0	1	23

Source: Annual Report of the Ohio Secretary of State, 1894.

Tribune explained, the Socialists "in each of the larger bodies of the trade unions tried to pledge their respective organizations to the Populist party."[67]

But Gompers and his allies opposed key provisions of the political program. In opening the 1894 convention, Gompers told the delegates, "It would be ridiculous to imagine that wage-workers can be slaves in employment and yet achieve control at the polls." He believed that partisan politics would lead to "misery, deprivation, and demoralization."[68] Gompers

TABLE 6.3—Populist Vote in Selected Medium-Sized Industrial Ohio Cities, 1894

City	Population (1890)	Populist vote as % of total vote
Springfield	31,895	11.7
Akron	27,601	25.4
Canton	26,189	24.0
Sandusky	18,471	10.4
Lima	15,987	11.7
East Liverpool	10,956	17.6
Ironton	10,393	14.4
Massillon	10,092	18.0
Ashtabula	8,336	30.6
Alliance	7,606	13.7
Galion	6,326	20.0
Bucyrus	5,974	17.2
Salem	5,780	20.0

Source: Annual Report of the Ohio Secretary of State, 1894.

and his allies set out to defeat what they saw as the two most pernicious parts of the program—the call for collective ownership and the creation of a labor-based political party. Gompers used his power as chairman to limit debate, while his allies offered amendments designed to prevent the passage of the program. Early in the debate, Gompers and his allies won an important victory when delegates decided to vote on the planks individually instead of on the program as a whole. This allowed business unionists to focus their attacks. Adolph Strasser, a cigarmaker and longtime ally of Gompers, attacked the preamble, which called for the AFL to emulate British trade unionists by creating an independent labor party. Strasser told the convention that the preamble misrepresented the actions of the British labor movement as there was no independent labor party in Britain. He did not attack the idea of independent politics but just the characterization of British action. By asserting that the preamble mischaracterized the British situation, Strasser gave delegates who opposed independent political action but represented unions on record as supporting the political program justification to vote down the preamble. Strasser's motion carried 1,345 to 861, and the preamble was defeated.[69]

The delegates approved the first nine planks of the program with little opposition before turning to plank 10, which called for the "collective ownership by the people of all means of production and distribution." These planks included staples of the Populist agenda: compulsory education; initiative and referendum; the eight-hour day; sanitary inspection of homes, workshops, and mines; employer liability for workplace injuries; abolition of the sweating system; municipal ownership of public service utilities; and nationalization of telegraph, telephones, railroads, and mines. As soon as plank 10 was introduced, opponents rose to offer substitutes in the hope of diluting the amendment. In the end, the opponents of plank 10 were able to secure passage of a substitute that called for "the abolition of the monopoly system of land holding."[70]

Debate around the preamble and plank 10 proved so contentious that even those who supported them, including McBride's closest allies, feared their passage would splinter the AFL. N. R. Hysell, an UMWA delegate and close friend of McBride's, warned the convention that if it adopted plank 10 it "will break up the unions." Patrick McBryde told the convention that although he intended to vote for plank 10, he hoped to see it defeated. He feared that the opponents of plank 10 would not be able to accept defeat as well as its supporters could. William Mahon, the former president of the Columbus Trades and Labor Assembly who helped organize McBride's Ohio labor party, felt that transforming the AFL into a political party would have precipitated a split within the federation just as it had within the Knights of Labor. He declared, "I have been in independent politics and never lost an opportunity to get on the stand and plead for independent political action . . . , but [I] don't intend to do anything that will destroy this great machine."[71]

After the defeat of the original plank 10, the convention turned its attention to the election of a president. McBride had challenged Gompers in 1893, losing 1,222 to 1,314, but he had reason to be hopeful in 1894. By endorsing the political program and a labor–Populist alliance, McBride had differentiated himself from Gompers. Moreover, many delegates criticized Gompers for his inaction during the Pullman boycott. Other delegates viewed Gompers as too powerful and wanted to see new blood in the AFL. In the end, McBride defeated Gompers by a vote of 1,170 to 976. Although delegates voted for McBride for a number of reasons, it is clear that the most vocal supporters of the political program supported McBride, while the most outspoken opponents of the program voted for Gompers.[72]

John McBride officially assumed the presidency of the American Federation of Labor on January 1, 1895. At that time he declared his intention to steer the federation into partisan politics through an alliance with the People's party. He told reporters, "I trust and expect to see a great union of labor men before another year, and believe that we shall place a presidential candidate in the field" for the 1896 election.[73]

Labor Populism in Ohio and the Nation

BY THE END OF 1894, John McBride and Jacob Coxey—two old friends from Massillon—had helped transform the Ohio People's party into a labor party, bringing together the central labor bodies of the state's three largest cities, urban federations in dozens of smaller cities, and the state's most powerful union, the United Mine Workers of America (UMWA). Within the first week of 1895, the Populists picked up the support of the Ohio State Trades and Labor Assembly (OSTLA), which the state's trade unionists had established to lobby the Ohio General Assembly. Though the OSTLA did not formally endorse the party by name, it did ratify a platform that mirrored the Populist platform nearly word for word and called on the state's workers to mount an "aggressive campaign" on behalf of any political party that endorsed labor's platform.[1] The OSTLA, urban labor federations, and UMWA provided the Ohio People's party with newspapers, activists experienced in political mobilization, and legitimacy, and Coxey gave the party a charismatic leader with a national reputation and deep pockets. For the first time since its inception, the Ohio People's party took on the trappings of a legitimate political party.

But both McBride and Coxey were also looking beyond the state, hoping to replicate their experiences in Ohio at the national level. Coxey had his eye on the People's party presidential nomination for 1896. The *Cleveland Plain Dealer* declared, "He who takes Coxey for a fool is sadly mistaken. The chances are by no means small that Mr. Coxey will be their nominee for president and wage a vigorous campaign."[2] McBride had ridden the Populist boom to the presidency of the American Federation of Labor (AFL), defeating Samuel Gompers and expressing his desire to transform the federation into a partisan organization through an alliance with the Populists.

Neither man achieved his objective, however. The pair and the movement they led were beset by obstacles—electoral defeat at the hands of Ohio's Democrats and Republicans, national People's party leaders who wanted to purge the party of labor radicals, and the efforts of Gompers and his allies to keep the AFL out of partisan politics. But they survived until the disintegration of the Ohio People's party in the wake of the fusion of 1896. By the end of 1896, the most serious effort to create a national labor party was over. The AFL would never again come so close to aligning itself formally with a producer-based or class-based party. Even though their movement had collapsed, those labor leaders who had led their unions or federations into the People's party never changed their goals or renounced the ideals that had led to the labor–Populist alliance.

AT FIRST GLANCE, the results of the election of 1894 suggested that the People's party's future had never looked so bright. The number of voters casting their ballots for the People's party increased 42 percent over the 1892 results with close to 1.5 million votes for Populist candidates. Although the party increased in strength in the South, the gains were most dramatic in the urban and industrial areas of the Midwest. In 1894 Ohio Populists tripled their 1892 results with the largest increases in the industrial and mining areas. In Milwaukee the vote jumped from about 1,296 (2.5%) in 1892 to 9,479 (19%) in 1894. In Chicago, support for the People's party increased from about 2,000 (0.6%) voters in 1892 to close to 40,000 (12%) in 1894. In Minneapolis, the Populists garnered 35 percent of the vote, and in the Twin Cities the party tallied almost as many votes in 1894 as the party had received in the whole state in 1892. Communities in the coal belt running from Western Pennsylvania through Illinois gave as much as 55 percent of the vote to the Populists. Henry Demarest Lloyd declared, "the workingmen are rapidly coming to the conclusion to have nothing more to do with the old parties, that they will work with the People's Party." Since the creation of the party, People's party leaders considered these areas essential to their plans to expand beyond the mostly agricultural West and the South to create a national producer-based party that would unite the nation's farmers and urban workers.[3]

As in Ohio, the Populist parties in these states were dominated by urban and labor leaders who tended to be much more radical than the party's traditional followers. Men like Eugene Debs in Indiana, Henry Demarest Lloyd and Thomas Morgan in Illinois, and Victor Berger and Robert Schilling in Wisconsin saw within the People's party and the Omaha platform the type of ideas that they were convinced would attract urban workers and free them from the grasp of late-nineteenth-century industrial capitalism. These reformers insisted that the Omaha platform had been written primarily to attract farmers and sought to augment the platform with planks designed to attract urban and industrial workers. They wanted the party to extend the type of big government that they saw as inherent in the sub-treasury plan and the demand for government ownership of the railroads to areas that would aid urban workers. Or, as they would explain it, they wanted to democratize the nation's economic life by giving the people (through their governments) the power to control that property which threatened the commonwealth. In Illinois, Wisconsin, and Ohio, the People's party platforms included qualified calls for the collective ownership of the means of production. Those midwestern trade unionists who flocked to the People's party in the summer of 1894 and their allies were simply known as "Socialists" within both labor and Populist circles.[4]

Despite dramatic gains in Ohio and the rest of the Industrial Midwest and lesser ones in the South, the national leadership of the People's party was not pleased with the elections of 1894. Throughout areas of traditional Populist strength, especially the Plains and the Rocky Mountain states, the People's party lost ground. In Kansas the Republicans swept every state office, took control of the lower house of the legislature, and won all of the congressional seats except one. Kansas Populists were so demoralized they held a mock funeral for the movement. In Nebraska the Populists retained the governor's office but little else. Republicans took control of the governors' offices and the legislatures in Colorado, Idaho, South Dakota, North Dakota, and Minnesota. "We lost among the farmers," Ignatius Donnelly observed gloomily.[5]

The People's party leaders attributed the losses on the Plains and in the Mountain West to a number of factors. First, in many of these states the Populists had refused to combine with Democrats. Such fusions had allowed the Populists to achieve a measure of success in both 1890 and 1892, but in 1894 the Populists found that going it alone would be difficult. Second, state Democratic and Republican parties throughout the West and on the Plains had embraced the free and unlimited coinage of silver at a ratio of sixteen to one in an effort to win farmers' support. By latching onto what had been the Populists' most popular campaign plank in 1892, the major parties recaptured some of those silver enthusiasts who had defected to the Populists. Moreover, the adoption of free silver by Democratic and Republican state parties had left the Populists with no clear and distinct program. Third, the party was tainted by labor radicalism, especially after Colorado governor Davis Waite mobilized the state militia on behalf of strikers and Eugene V. Debs publicly embraced the party after his imprisonment.

The Populists faced another, related problem. One of the party's most important supporters was the American Bimetallic League, a lobby dedicated to the free and unlimited coinage of silver and funded by silver mine owners. In early December 1894, the American Bimetallic League suggested that it might form a political party dedicated exclusively to the free and unlimited coinage of silver at sixteen to one. Led by former Ohio congressman A. J. Warner, the Bimetallic League reasoned that, with both the Democrats and the Republicans dominated by their eastern wings, neither party would support the free coinage of silver in a national election and thus would alienate sizable constituencies, especially in the West and the South. However, these silver Republicans and Democrats would be hesitant to join the People's party because of its radical planks, including the sub-treasury plan, abolition of alien landownership, direct loans from the government, and the government ownership of railroads and telegraphs. By forming a party devoted exclusively to silver, the Bimetallic League hoped to capture silver Democrats and Republicans as well as Populists alienated by the radicals within the party.[6]

Despite the dramatic gains the People's party made in the Midwest among urban and industrial voters, the party's traditional leaders feared labor's growing influence in the party. Led by Herman Taubeneck and James Weaver, these leaders were philosophically opposed to the demands of the labor-Populists. They saw labor's demands as a threat to the sanctity of property and suggested they would undermine the nation's tradition of limited government. When Tommy Morgan tried in 1894 to convince the Illinois People's party to ratify a platform that was nearly identical to the one ratified by the Ohio People's party, Taubeneck told him, "If this is what you came to the people's party for, we don't want you. Go back from where you came with your socialism." Even leaders not as conservative as Taubeneck and Weaver were suspicious of the so-called Socialists. Ignatius Donnelly, for instance, called for the party to rid itself of the fanatics.[7]

To solve the many problems facing the party, Taubeneck and the party's national executive committee argued that the People's party must reformulate its platform to emphasize the free coinage of silver. Not only would a single plank platform appeal to more voters, Taubeneck argued, it would also forestall the American Bimetallic League's new party and alienate those trade unionists from the Industrial Midwest who had flocked to the party in 1894. To facilitate the trimming of the platform, the party invited hundreds of People's party activists to a conference in St. Louis at the end of December 1894. As Taubeneck told the press, the purpose of the party's conference was "to make known the fact that it has outgrown many of the 'isms' that characterized its birth and early growth." The Populists would now "take a stand on the financial question that will make it worthy of the support of those who . . . have not cared to support the party on account of its wild theories." In particular, Taubeneck wanted to eliminate the planks calling for the sub-treasury plan, direct government loans to the people, the abolition of alien landownership, and government ownership of railroads and telegraphs. By focusing the platform only on the free coinage of silver, Taubeneck thought that the Populists could preempt the formation of a silver party, attract free silver supporters alienated by the hard money policies of the traditional parties, undermine the midwestern labor radicals who wanted to expand the platform, and lead the party to victory in 1896.[8]

Ohio Populists, trade unionists throughout the Industrial Midwest, and their allies opposed Taubeneck's attempt to trim the People's party's platform. The *Cleveland Citizen* emerged as the most vocal critic of efforts to concentrate the platform on the free coinage of silver:

> The fact is becoming clearer each day that the silverites are not good Populists. . . . the mine-owners [pushing for free silver] are as mean a set of labor crushers as the Carnegies and Pullmans ever dared to be. They have repeatedly attempted to smash the organization of their employees. . . . While the miners injured their health and risked their lives in the bowels of the earth for treasures which the mine owners did not place there, and had no moral right to, the latter were rioting in luxury and playing the part of princes of wealth. The silver mine owners envy the Rothschild goldbugs, aspire to their fabulous riches, and would walk upon the neck of labor to reach the same goal.

John McBride also opposed the trimmers, deriding the free coinage of silver as a mere "palliative." Instead, he insisted that true reform would come when the national government issued greenbacks, eliminated the nation's private banking system, and took control of the nation's railroads and mines. These positions were hardly ones that would appease the mine owners who controlled the American Bimetallic League.[9]

Taubeneck and the People's party purposely excluded labor leaders and their allies—the most important of whom were Henry Demarest Lloyd and

Coxey—from the St. Louis conference. Lloyd insisted that the point of the conference was to "throw the radicals overboard." But Lloyd, Coxey, and a number of "Socialists" from the Industrial Midwest attended anyway. Led by Lloyd, they prevented Taubeneck and the executive committee from packing the conference committees and forced the debate over trimming the platform to the convention floor. On the floor, those who opposed the emphasis on the free coinage of silver and wanted the party to maintain the "broad-gauged" Omaha platform clearly predominated. Not only did the delegates reaffirm the Omaha platform, the conference's final address reflected the concerns of midwestern labor-Populists. Written by former Illinois senator Lyman Trumbull and brought to the floor by Lloyd, the conference's address pledged to "rescue the government from the control of monopolists and concentrated wealth," support government ownership of monopolies "affecting the public interest," limit "the amount of property to be acquired by devise or inheritance," and work for the free and unlimited coinage of silver at a ratio of sixteen to one. Additionally, Coxey convinced the conference to endorse his good roads and non-interest-bearing-bond plan, which was especially offensive to bimetallists because it privileged greenbacks over silver. In other words, People's party delegates affirmed the demands of the trade unionists from the Industrial Midwest.[10]

After the St. Louis conference, Taubeneck and his allies railed that "socialists," led by Lloyd, Coxey, and other midwestern labor-Populists, had "captured" the party. The *National Watchman*, the official paper of the Populist congressional delegation and closely associated with Taubeneck, insisted that the emphasizing of the silver issue was the only way to avoid "the destructive doctrines of the socialists." Shortly thereafter Taubeneck and the Populists serving in the U.S. House of Representatives and Senate, with the singular exception of Kansas senator William Peffer, signed a manifesto insisting that the party focus its energy on the money question.[11] As the *National Watchman* declared, "The time for Populism and Socialism to part has come." The paper urged, "Let us be conservative in order to secure the support of the business men, the professional men, and the well to do. These are elements we must use if ever success comes to our party. For every loud voiced socialist who declares war on us we will get a hundred of the conservative element in our society."[12]

Soon after the manifesto, the American Bimetallic League announced its intention to form a new party that had for "the principal planks of its platform the free and unlimited coinage of silver at a ratio of 16 to 1 and a demand that the money of the country shall be issued by the government itself." The league rejected the idea of fusion with the Populists because it considered them too radical to attract free silverites from the two main parties. In the words of the new party, "Republicans and Democrats could not unite with the Populists because the platform of that party contains declarations and the party advocates theories to which they cannot give their consent."[13]

Populist leaders understood the threat that a silver party posed to their party. Taubeneck tried to seize the initiative, declaring, "The People's party at its next national convention will declare in favor of making the money question the 'great central idea' with no other plank except those which add strength to this one. Those who desire to retard monetary reform by loading us down with other issues will, with the Socialists and Communists, go to the rear." James Weaver suggested a similar sort of alliance. For the rest of the year and into 1896, Weaver and Taubeneck played on fears of labor radicals as part of their effort to transform the People's party into a silver party.[14]

Even many of those who opposed Taubeneck's and Weaver's attempts to focus on the free and unlimited coinage of silver feared the increasing role of organized labor in the party and took steps to marginalize trade unionists within the party or push them out altogether. The party's most prominent "middle of the roader," Georgia's Tom Watson, had never been a strong supporter of trade unionists, especially those from the urban North. His *People's Party Paper* rarely expressed sympathy for the labor movement and would severely criticize workers who engaged in strikes and boycotts. In fact, during the Pullman boycott Watson had held Eugene V. Debs responsible for "paralyz[ing] the commerce of the country, incit[ing] insurrection, and redden[ing] the streets with innocent blood."[15] This dislike for organized labor intensified in late 1894 and 1895 as trade unionists and their allies took more prominent roles in the party. Like other Populist leaders, Watson seemed to take satisfaction in the fact that the Populist vote in Chicago declined in the spring 1895 municipal elections. He would later write, "In Chicago, the hot bed of Socialism, Democrats and Republicans get all of the votes. The Populists are nowhere. And yet Chicago will send a red-hot delegation to our next National Convention 'demanding' that our Platform be further twisted to suit their radical ideas."[16]

Some of Watson's ideas about the labor movement and its influence in the People's party can be deduced from a rambling and incoherent article that appeared in the *People's Party Paper* on November 29, 1895. The article called attention to the split of the AFL into "two great divisions"—those who wanted to transform the federation into a partisan organization and those who wanted to steer clear of partisan politics. It suggested that Eugene Debs, who was about to be released from prison, would attempt to reorganize the AFL's constituent unions along industrial rather than craft lines—much like the ARU and the UMWA, the two unions most closely identified with the Populist movement. Such a reorganization would "make it far easier" to transform the federation into a partisan organization. "It is understood," the article continued, "to be the purpose of the leaders to capture the machinery of the People's party."[17]

Soon after this article appeared, Jacob Coxey—one of the "Massillon twins," one of the "Socialists" who had "captured" the December 1894 St. Louis conference, one of Watson's competitors for a spot on the ticket in 1896—ventured into Georgia as part of a southern speaking tour. He arrived just as the Georgia People's party was convening its annual convention. There, a Knights of Labor organizer, whom the *People's Party Paper* called a "labor agitator," introduced a resolution inviting Coxey to address the gathering. The resolution passed, but Watson subsequently arranged to have the invitation withdrawn, setting off an acrimonious exchange that would fill the two men's newspapers for the next few weeks.[18]

During the convention and the subsequent exchange with Coxey, Watson made clear that he thought there was a secret socialist plot, a plot in which Coxey was playing a central role, to take over the People's party: "Socialists have opened fire on us and are moving all of their secret machinery against us. They do not come manfully and say that they are socialists. . . . They . . . [will] push the People's Party further and further, slyly but resolutely, until they [have] got it committed to their own radical and vicious doctrines." Watson added that Georgia Populists had rescinded Coxey's invitation because they had a duty to "open the eyes of the people to the stealthy approaches which the socialists are making to secure control of the People's Party."[19]

According to Watson, the Socialists had begun plotting as early as July 1892 because at "Omaha the wording of one plank was altered to make it capable of being construed into an attack on the private ownership of land." Despite the Socialists' action, southern Populists had voted for candidates standing on the Omaha platform "believing that our [Ocala] platform had not been altered at Omaha." Since Georgia Populists did "not believe in Socialism with the collective ownership of land, homes, and pocketbooks," Watson argued that the only logical step was to dump the tainted Omaha platform and reembrace the one that the Southern Alliance had drawn up in Ocala in 1890.[20]

After confronting Coxey, Watson wrote Marion Butler, a North Carolina Populist just elected to the U.S. Senate, "the Georgia Populists gave Coxey the cold shoulder and adopted the most conservative platform that the party has put forth. Speaking for myself, I do not hesitate to say that I will not go a step further toward Socialism and Radicalism than the Georgia platform goes. It is highly desirable, it seems to me, that those of us who favor this moderate and conservative course should begin to educate public sentiment in that line . . . to the end that the extremists shall not control our next National Convention." Butler's response to Watson has been lost, but in a subsequent letter Watson said that the two men were "in perfect accord." Watson also suggested that the North Carolinian take over the leadership of the party, since Taubeneck had proved incapable of controlling Coxey, Lloyd, and the Socialists. The party, Watson said, needed a chairman "who has nerve enough to rule with a rod of iron those hot-headed recalcitrants who want to load us down with extreme isms."[21]

Rather than welcoming midwestern trade unionists into the party, the leaders of the main two People's party factions—the trimmers and the middle-of-the-roaders—took steps to push them away. In order to protect the party from the "socialists," these leaders distanced themselves from the Omaha platform, Weaver and Taubeneck wanting to construct a platform based on silver and Watson and Butler reverting to Ocala. By the start of 1896, midwestern trade unionists and their allies had become the most forceful defenders of the Omaha platform.

SOON AFTER THE FALL ELECTIONS of 1894, political commentators of all stripes assumed that Coxey would be the Populist nominee for governor the following fall. Coxey was the logical choice. He had proved the party's best vote getter, receiving about 21 percent of the vote in his bid for Congress, including over 25 percent of the vote in both Akron and Canton.[22] Moreover his famous or infamous reputation guaranteed large crowds wherever he appeared. Not only would these crowds attract thousands of potential voters for Coxey, they would provide an audience for local Populist candidates who would be sharing the podium. Coxey's road program and his non-interest-bearing-bond plan—basically a greenbacks/public works program—also gave the party a platform that would be easily distinguished from that of the Democrats. Perhaps most important, the wealthy Coxey was willing to spend money on his election. Gone were the days when the party would have to scrape together two dollars a day so that its candidate could afford to run. For the first time since its inception, the Ohio People's party had a dynamic candidate with broad name recognition and the resources to mount an effective campaign.

Coxey realized at the outset that his prospects of being elected governor were slim, but he saw his candidacy as worthwhile nonetheless. He hoped that his name on the Populist slate would help attract enough votes to ensure the election of a dozen or so Populist candidates to the Ohio General Assembly, where the party could hold the balance of power and ensure that the state did not return Calvin Brice or any other "plutocrat" to the U.S. Senate. Perhaps more important, Coxey hoped the election might serve as a springboard to help him win the Populist nomination for president in 1896. A strong showing would make him attractive to the national party, which would need to do well in midwestern states such as Ohio if it was going to make an impression in 1896. Although he did not publicly admit until the summer of 1895 that he was "forced to consider [him]self a presidential possibility," Coxey's interest in the People's party presidential nomination was unmistakable.[23]

Coxey's gubernatorial campaign began early in 1895. By March he had established the Coxey Non-Interest Bond Bureau to publicize his greenbacks/public works program. At the same time, he established the Coxey Non-Interest Bond Club, with chapters throughout the state. Coxey hoped that these clubs, modeled after Lincoln Clubs and Jackson Clubs, would provide campaign workers and generate enthusiasm. In June 1895 he established a weekly newspaper, *Sound Money*, recruiting veteran Populist journalist Henry Vincent to serve as editor. Although Vincent got his start in Kansas where he had been instrumental in the creation of the Populist party, he had moved to Chicago in the early 1890s where he edited the *Chicago Searchlight*, working closely with Henry Demarest Lloyd and Thomas J. Morgan. Like Coxey and the labor leaders who supported the Ohio People's party, Vincent was considered a radical in Populist circles, putting public ownership of monopolies before the free coinage of silver on the party's agenda. As he told the readers of *Sound Money*, "[public ownership] guarantees to every American citizen that right and privilege to produce, and a protection in the enjoyment of that production."[24]

While most people believed that Coxey would be the Populist candidate for governor, the nominations of the two major parties were far from settled. The state's Republican party held one of the earliest conventions in that party's history when it met in Zanesville in late May. McKinley was not seeking renomination as he also had his sights set on a higher office. As it had been since the late 1880s, the party was deeply divided between the Hanna-McKinley-Sherman faction and the one led by Joseph B. Foraker. Each faction had worked hard that spring to ensure that county Republican conventions sent sympathetic delegations to Zanesville, but Foraker's forces controlled the convention from start to finish. Not only did the convention nominate a Foraker man, Springfield industrialist Asa

Bushnell, for governor, it took the unprecedented step of declaring Foraker to be the party's choice for the U.S. Senate seat that would be filled by the incoming general assembly. In a last ditch effort to secure party unity, the convention endorsed McKinley for the party's presidential nomination in 1896 and praised John Sherman's service in the Senate and to the nation.[25]

As the rivalry between the two factions was more over matters of personality and patronage than policy, there was little debate over the platform. Just as they had done since the early 1890s, the state's Republicans centered their platform on the issues of protection and money. The platform declared that by "restoring American wages and American products," the protective tariff would "serve the highest interests of American labor and American development." On the most talked about issue of the day, monetary reform, the party declared, "We favor bimetallism and demand the use of both gold and silver as standard money, either according to a ratio to be fixed by international agreement . . . or . . . as will secure the maintenance of the parity of value between the two metals." Lest people think that the Republican version of bimetallism was similar to the free and unlimited coinage of silver advocated by the American Bimetallic League, John Sherman elaborated:

> The policy now urged by the producers of silver, and by men who wish to pay their debts in money cheaper than they promised to pay, is the free coinage of silver. This means the single standard of silver and the demonetization of gold. . . . It confers no favor on producers of any kind, whether of the farm, [or] the workshop. . . . additional dollars would have only one-half the purchasing power of the gold dollars.

Sherman and the Republicans maintained that an ounce of gold was worth about twenty ounces of silver on the open market, which would make a gold dollar more valuable than a silver one if coined at sixteen to one. Consumers, at least those not living hand to mouth, would respond to this by hoarding their gold dollars and spending their silver ones, resulting in a contraction of the money supply. In formulating their platform, the Republicans expected the state's Democrats to reaffirm their 1894 declaration that "silver should be restored to the position that it occupied as money prior to its demonetization by the Republican party, and to that end we favor the unlimited coinage of silver at the legal ratio of 16 to 1 with equal legal tender power." Given that the currency question was the most salient political issue of the day, the Republicans were prepared and anxious to fight the campaign on silver.[26]

The Populists met soon after the Republicans. Even though the nomination of Coxey for governor was considered a foregone conclusion, the party's convention proved far from harmonious. The main point of controversy was the prominence of the free coinage of silver in the party's platform. National party chairman Herman Taubeneck's attempt to jettison the Omaha platform in favor of one emphasizing the free coinage of silver at a ratio of sixteen to one had polarized Populists throughout the nation. In Ohio Populists from the more agricultural districts, some of whom had been with the party since its inception, tended to emphasize the free coinage of silver, while Populists from urban and industrial regions generally favored a broad-gauged platform that included demands for greenbacks, government ownership of monopolies, women's suffrage, judicial reform, and direct legislation. Convention rules required that a representative from each congressional district served on each of the convention's committees, but a county's representation on the floor was apportioned according to how well the party did in the county in 1894. Since the People's party had done better in industrial and urban counties than in agricultural ones, the rules gave those wanting to emphasize the free coinage of silver disproportionate power in the convention's committees.[27]

Those wanting to emphasize the free coinage of silver, often called "one-plank men" or "trimmers," dominated the resolutions committee, forcing through a platform that reflected their beliefs. The first plank declared that the money issue was the most important political question of the day and pledged the party's support for the immediate free and unlimited coinage of silver at the ratio of sixteen to one. Only in the seventh plank did the proposed platform endorse the Omaha platform, and Coxey's greenbacks/public works program was relegated to plank 6. Gone were the more radical planks from the party's 1894 platform, which had been written by McBride and demanded by the laborites.

As soon as the report of the resolutions committee was read, Cleveland trade unionist David Rankin charged that "an effort was being made to smother the logical principles of the People's party and subordinate them to the silver issue." He proposed that the platform's first plank endorse the Omaha platform. Labor leaders and Coxey supporters followed Rankin's lead in denouncing the proposed platform and offering amendments. Coxey's followers insisted that his greenback/public works program be given a more conspicuous position in the platform. Max Hayes demanded the insertion of planks calling for the eight-hour day and the government ownership of all monopolies. Cincinnati laborites insisted on the inclusion of demands for the eight-hour day and the abolition of the labor injunction.

While opposed to the emphasis on the free and unlimited coinage of silver philosophically, the labor leaders and their allies also thought that emphasizing it would be a strategic blunder. Like the Republicans, they expected the Democrats to affirm their 1894 declaration in favor of the free and unlimited coinage of silver at a ratio of sixteen to one. If both the Democrats and the Populists ran on platforms emphasizing the free coinage of silver at sixteen to one, the labor leaders reasoned that the People's party would get lost. Instead they insisted that the party reaffirm the Omaha platform and fight for reform of the entire industrial system.[28]

The one-plank men and the trimmers did not go quietly. Led by E. D. Stark, a Cuyahoga County lawyer who was prominent in the American Bimetallic League, the free silver forces charged that Coxey and the trade unionists were weighing the platform down with so many "fads," "isms," and "whims" that the party's message was already getting lost. The one-plank men insisted that these planks had tainted the party with "socialism" and driven away potential voters. Not only did Stark maintain that the free coinage of silver would free the nation from the grasp of British and Wall Street bankers and provide economic opportunity for all Americans, he saw it as essential to the party's electoral success. Stark and his allies insisted that Ohio's hard-money Democrats, led by Brice and federal officeholders beholden to President Grover Cleveland, would control that party's state convention and nominate an "administration" candidate. By emphasizing the free coinage of silver, Stark thought that the People's party would be able to attract free silver Democrats and Republicans.[29]

Stark and his allies, though, proved no match for Coxey and the trade unionists. As the *Cleveland Citizen* observed, "the report of that one-idea platform was all that was necessary to drive the progressive reformers together." Led by Coxey and Cleveland-area labor leaders, those favoring a broad-gauged platform ignored the work of the resolutions committee and rewrote the entire platform on the convention floor. At the top of the platform, the convention endorsed the Omaha platform. This was followed by planks supporting Coxey's bond and good-roads plan and one demanding the "coinage out of paper of as many dollars . . . as will be sufficient to conduct the business of the country." In a blow to the "one-plank men," the party relegated the plank calling for the free coinage of silver to the fourth position on the platform. Other planks demanded the abolition of the national banking system, the release of Eugene Debs, the initiative and referendum, the eight-hour day, and the nationalization of all monopolies.[30]

After the passage of the platform, the convention set about to nominate a slate of candidates. To almost everyone's surprise, Coxey's nomination faced opposition. The Richland County delegation, which was dominated by Farmers' Alliance men claiming to speak for the party's agrarian supporters, charged that Coxey was too radical. They disliked his financial planks and did not think he held the free coinage of silver in high enough regard. To challenge Coxey, the Richland County delegation nominated Stark for governor. Stark received support from just 74 of the convention's 594 delegates (12%). Of his seventy-four votes, fifty-eight came from the heavily agricultural counties of west and northwest Ohio.[31]

After the trimmers attempted to write a one-plank platform and challenged Coxey's nomination, the broad-gaugers were in no mood to compromise concerning the rest of the slate. They controlled the convention floor and filled most of the remaining slots with trade unionists. John Crofton, the treasurer of the Cincinnati Central Labor Council and a member of the canvassers' union, easily defeated J. F. Lederer, a one-plank man belonging to the "conservative element of the party," for the party's nomination for lieutenant governor. Charles Bonsall, a veteran greenbacker and Knights of Labor organizer from Salem, received the nomination for auditor. The party selected William Gloyd, an officer in the Cleveland-based Brotherhood of Locomotive Engineers, to run for the Board of Public Works.[32]

Not long after the People's party nominated Coxey, the state's Democrats met in their annual convention. Like the national Democratic party, Ohio's Democrats were divided by the silver question. Led by Columbus's Allen W. Thurman, former congressman and American Bimetallic League president A. J. Warner, and *Cincinnati Enquirer* publisher John McLean, the free silver forces had captured the party's 1894 convention and pushed through a platform calling for the immediate free and unlimited coinage of silver at a ratio of sixteen to one. Believing the passage of the 1894 platform was a direct attack on him and the policies of President Cleveland, U.S. senator Calvin Brice sought to have the state's Democracy endorse the president's monetary policies at its 1895 convention. Enlisting the aid of the state's federal officeholders and other supporters of the Cleveland administration, Brice rallied the state's hard-money men and spent lavishly at county conventions to ensure that hard-money forces would be in the majority at the state convention.[33]

Brice's efforts paid off, as he was able to control the convention from its opening gavel until adjournment, dictating the party's platform. Most controversially, the platform's currency plank read:

> We hold to the use of both gold and silver as the standard money of the country, and to coin both gold and silver without discrimination against each

metal or charge for mintage, but the dollar unit of coinage of both metals must be of intrinsic and exchangeable value, or be adjusted by international agreement, or by such safe legislation as shall insure the maintenance of parity of the two metals and the equal power of every dollar at all times in the payment of debts.

Although the language of the platform suggested the party's support for bimetallism, Brice admitted that conditions placed on the coinage of silver were such that the platform essentially meant one word—"gold."[34]

Brice had little interest in who would be nominated for governor as long as the nominee was not a vocal silver supporter and would help elect the Democratic legislature essential to his reelection to the Senate. In an effort to heal the party's wounds, the convention nominated former governor James Campbell. Generally respected among the party's silver forces, Campbell had been elected governor in 1889 and had been considered a favorite for his party's 1892 presidential nomination until McKinley defeated him in 1891. Newspapers speculated that a win in 1895 would restore his status as presidential timbre in time for the 1896 campaign.[35]

The failure of the Democrats to endorse the free and unlimited coinage of silver at sixteen to one and both major parties' unwillingness to talk about what was arguably the most important political topic of the day—monetary reform—changed Coxey's campaign plans. The Populists could not ignore the support for free silver among the state voters and recognized the party's silver policy as a way to attract these voters. For the first time since the party's inception in 1891, the Ohio People's party had a platform plank with wide popular appeal that could attract voters from the traditional parties and that was not supported by either of the traditional parties. Although Coxey had opposed those who wanted the People's party to emphasize the free coinage silver and asserted that only the issuance of paper money would deliver the nation from the grasp of British and Wall Street bankers, he could not deny the value of the free coinage of silver as a campaign tool and was forced by circumstances to wage the campaign mostly on the silver issue.

Coxey's *Sound Money* increasingly portrayed him as the free silver candidate. "We cannot understand why," an editorial asked, "able and intelligent free silver men of both parties in Ohio do not throw aside their part shackles and unite on Mr. Coxey, the only free silver man in the field." Another editorial insisted, "We cannot see how our free silver democrats and republicans all over Ohio can vote otherwise than for [Coxey]." Still another asserted "that the removal of the restriction now resting on silver and the immediate placing of it on an equal footing with gold will destroy the monopoly of the monster gold trust." The paper even began quoting approvingly the previously hated Taubeneck on the currency question: "Our silver plank will bring ten new recruits to our ranks where the balance of our platform will bring but one. Whenever we abandon the contest for free silver, we are abandoning whatever hope of ever winning a victory."[36]

Other People's party speakers and writers emphasized the silver issue. Davis Waite told an audience in Canton that "the People's party alone proposes to change the financial system, which has reduced the common people to pauperism." State party chairman Hugo Preyer told Ohio farmers, "Both of the old parties have declared for gold money, of which there is not enough in the entire world to pay one third of the debts in the United States alone. By destroying the silver money of the country they have destroyed the value of your property and products by one half."[37]

Coxey turned out to be an enthusiastic campaigner. In the summer and fall he traveled the state making three or four speeches a day, six or seven days a week. Between Labor Day and the election day Coxey made over 175 speeches and spoke in eighty-four of the state's eighty-eight counties. Coxey was not the only Populist hitting the campaign trail in Ohio in the fall of 1895. Trade unions and Populist clubs also brought in stump speakers—William Peffer, Davis Waite, Robert Schilling, Annie L. Diggs, James Sovereign, and Ralph Beaumont—all of whom opposed Taubeneck's plan to emphasize the free coinage of silver.[38]

While his paper and speeches continued to stress that the People's party was the only party supporting the free and unlimited coinage of silver, Coxey told labor circles that his good roads and non-interest-bearing-bond program would "settle socialism." It would do this, he insisted, "By having the State purchase the railroads, waterways, telegraphs and telephones; townships build their own highways, municipalities their own street railways, electric light and gas plants, water works, and making all public improvements, and fixing a legal [wage] rate of not less than $1.50 a day for an eight hour day." Although Coxey appealed to self-identified Socialists, he resisted calling himself one because to do so would arouse "the prejudice of the American people who shrink from the word socialism when they actually do not know what the socialists want."[39]

Throughout the campaign, Coxey and the People's party received the support of the state's most powerful trade unionists. In Cleveland, labor leaders were disappointed with Coxey's increasing emphasis on the free coinage of silver, but as Max Hayes told the readers of the *Cleveland Citizen*, "The platform adopted is a radical one. It files notice of war upon the money

Ohio's 1895 gubernatorial race. From Coxey's *Sound Money*, November 2, 1895.

power all along the line. . . . It proposes that the masses shall take control of the public monopolies; that bank and bond robbery shall be destroyed; that denial of trial by jury is treason, and declares for many of other reforms." In Columbus, the split within the city's Populists appeared to heal as the city's trade unionists returned to the Populist fold. The trade unionists used Labor Day celebrations to champion the People's party. A jurisdictional dispute caused the city's labor movement to hold two separate celebrations, but both heard Populist orators exhort members to vote the party line. The Columbus Trades and Labor Assembly–dominated Central Populist club took the lead in the campaign by making arrangements for visits by Coxey and a number of other Populist stump speakers.[40]

When Coxey traveled throughout the state's coal mining regions, he was greeted by enormous crowds composed mostly of miners who had been without steady work for over six months. His Labor Day speech in Wellston, sponsored by Knights of Labor assemblies affiliated with the UMWA, attracted a crowd of between five and seven thousand to the town of three thousand people, and a speech to the Nelsonville Trades and Labor Assembly attracted close to four thousand miners, again far surpassing the population of that small mining town. Local UMWA assemblies also paid for a number of Populist stump speakers, including Davis Waite, Henry Vincent, and Iowa congressman E. H. Gillitte, to speak in the area. During the campaign former UMWA president McBride returned to the state for speaking engagements in Columbus, Cincinnati, Massillon, and the Hocking Valley in his capacity as AFL president. At every stop, McBride made clear his support for his friend Coxey.[41]

Cincinnati's labor community displayed the most enthusiasm for Coxey and the rest of the People's party slate, including CLC vice president John Crofton, the party's nominee for lieutenant governor.[42] On the eve of the election the CLC turned the *Chronicle* into a People's party campaign sheet. The biggest obstacle facing the People's party, the paper maintained, was the belief that workingmen would be throwing their votes away by voting for the People's party, but if workers started voting for the Populists, then other voters would see that the party had a chance of winning. Although the *Chronicle* conceded that the People's party would not win the election, the paper insisted that voting for the Populists was the only option for self-respecting trade unionists and that those who voted for the traditional parties were doing worse than throwing away their votes—they were aiding the oppressors of labor. A vote for the Democrats, the paper maintained, was a vote for Brice who as a railroad owner had fought the ARU, and a vote for the Republicans was a vote for Foraker who as a corporation lawyer had represented the city's monopolists. The paper concluded that the People's party was "the only party in this country that offers permanent relief for the present hard times, good wages for the working man, and freedom from monopoly."[43]

The *Chronicle* and the state's trade unionists were disappointed with the results of the election. Coxey received 52,675 votes (6.3%), only a few hundred more than Martin had received the previous year. Despite the disappointment with the results of the elections, the state's labor unions remained undeterred in their support for the People's party. The CLC's *Chronicle* editorialized:

> We have members of organized labor in this city [who] agree that the platform of the People's party was all right and the party should ride into power on it, but they say, "They have no show, and I don't want to throw my vote away," and they march right up and throw their vote away by voting one of the old party tickets. Yes, and worse than throwing their vote away—placing it where it counts against themselves. The advocates of political action by organized

labor must not get discouraged, but keep the hammer agoing and in time there will be a solid phalanx of workers and the result will not then be in long doubt.[44]

The failure of Coxey's candidacy to garner more support at the ballot box underscores the difficulty that the People's party faced when competing in states with strong two-party systems. Coxey could garner enthusiastic crowds, and commentators of all political stripes would comment on his popular appeal. But Coxey and his allies could not convince voters to cast their ballots for the party. The reason for this is simple. The Populists acknowledged that the man at the top of their ticket had little chance of winning, given the tremendous resources and traditions that the Democratic and Republican candidates brought to the campaign. Yet the party asked for voters' support anyway. Populist speakers and publications told voters that casting ballots for one of the traditional parties amounted to throwing away their votes, but in the minds of most voters checking the box next to a Populist candidate amounted to just that. In other words, election returns are not necessarily the best gauge of popular support for a third-party candidate or platform, especially in a strong two-party system where sometimes voters fear the election of a certain party or candidate. The Populists knew that the election results did not reflect the popularity of the party among voters, and this is what gave them hope.

AFTER JOHN MCBRIDE ANNOUNCED his desire to take the AFL into an alliance with the People's party, Joseph R. Buchanan, a self-described "labor agitator" whose columns ran in several Populist newspapers, wrote about the changing of the guard at the AFL: "McBride is generally credited with being a radical, but I doubt that there will be any change in the policy of the Federation on that account, especially as the executive council has to be taken into account."[45] Buchanan's prediction turned out to be prescient. Allies of Gompers still held nearly all of the seats on the federation's council, undermining McBride's presidency and constraining his attempts to steer the federation into partisan politics.

Soon after taking office, McBride, despite his radical credentials and convictions, announced a policy of moderation. Fearful of breaking up the fragile federation, he was constrained by the convention's failure to pass the preamble and plank 10. Aware that there had been "much speculation" and "great anxiety" concerning the direction the federation would take during his tenure, McBride assured the AFL's membership, "I shall be guided by the constitutional provisions of the American Federation of Labor, and in all important cases not covered by constitutional provisions, will be governed by my own judgment and the directing advice of the Executive Council." Contradicting fears that he was too radical, McBride told reporters that he was only a "limited socialist," explaining that the "government should . . . take charge of such productions as the people may elect to operate. That leaves the opening broad enough to admit or exclude anything." McBride insisted that forcing the AFL into politics would be "very foolish" and "almost suicidal" at this time. McBride, though, never indicated that he had retreated from his earlier beliefs or abandoned his desire to take the federation into politics.[46]

The composition of the AFL's executive council, as Buchanan noted, limited McBride's choices. Five of the six members of the executive council had supported Gompers at the 1894 convention and were committed to economic rather than political action. Led by first vice president P. J. McGuire, Gompers's allies kept a close eye on McBride to ensure that he did not overstep his authority. When McBride wrote an article supporting compulsory arbitration, they responded angrily. They noted that the federation's 1893 convention had rejected compulsory arbitration. A concerted effort to move toward the establishment of a political party surely would have provoked more than an angry letter from McGuire.[47]

Scandal also limited McBride's effectiveness as AFL president. At the 1895 UMWA convention, the president of the Ohio miners, A. A. Adams, charged McBride and the leaders of the UMWA with selling out the miners during the previous year's coal miners' strike. Adams charged that McBride had exceeded his authority when he concluded the deal with the mine operators that ended the strike. To these charges were added rumors of bribery and accusations that McBride had been too cozy with Ohio mine operators. The miners appointed a committee to investigate Adams's charges. After a three-day investigation, the committee concluded that McBride had not acted improperly when ending the strike and there was no evidence to substantiate the bribery charges. But during the investigation, Mark Wild, an organizer for the ARU and president of the Columbus Trades and Labor Assembly, levied new charges against McBride, accusing McBride of paying him six hundred dollars to settle the Hocking Valley Railway strike in the summer of 1894. Wild charged that McBride and the Hocking Valley mine operators wanted to end the strike so that the mines could resume operations and the miners could go back to work.

McBride admitted to the convention that he had given Wild the money, but that it had been collected after the strike had been settled. The money, about a year's salary, had come from the Hocking Valley coal operators, who knew that Wild was destitute yet had settled the strike with the knowledge that he would be blacklisted. The operators felt that McBride, a fellow labor leader and active strike supporter, would be the proper conduit for the money. The UMWA investigation committee concluded that there was no evidence McBride had bribed Wild but did not exonerate the AFL president. McBride was not pleased. Calling the decision a "Scotch verdict"—guilty but not proved—McBride demanded that the committee continue its investigation so as to remove any suspicion of wrongdoing. The miners agreed and determined that McBride had done nothing improper.[48]

After the UMWA convention vindicated McBride, Wild asked the CTLA to investigate the charges. Wild insisted that the UMWA had in effect labeled him a bribe taker, and he wanted to be exonerated. After much debate, the CTLA opened an investigation. News of the charges circulated, and McBride's opponents within the AFL saw an opportunity to damage him. The AFL's executive council sent McGuire to Columbus to work with the local investigating committee. McBride would not be cleared of the charges until December, when McGuire announced he had found no evidence "that John McBride had betrayed the interests of organized labor, or been guilty of corrupt practices as alleged by Mark Wild or others."[49]

Not only did the charges cast a shadow over McBride's presidency and undermine his efforts to affect an AFL–Populist alliance, they also revealed divisions within Ohio Populism. All three principals—McBride, Adams, and Wild—were active in the Populist party. Adams and Wild had both run for office on the People's party ticket in 1894 and had attended McBride's labor party convention. Wild had even stood alongside McBride in the summer of 1894 when he announced his intention to create a labor party and merge it with the Populists. Nonetheless, all three men supported the People's party during the gubernatorial election of 1895.[50]

After the UMWA's convention, McBride's health deteriorated. In October 1894 he had been stricken with nicotine poisoning, which had kept him off the campaign trail that fall and from attending the AFL's convention. Although he recovered in time to take office, McBride suffered a relapse in the middle of February. Doctors ordered him to take a six-week cure at the thermal spas in Hot Springs, Arkansas. In his absence McBride delegated his authority to James Duncan, the AFL's second vice president. Bypassing the federation's first vice president McGuire, a close associate of Gompers and the man dispatched to investigate the Wild charges, McBride's action provoked controversy. Executive council member John Lennon charged that McBride had exceeded his authority by appointing a replacement "without the consent of the proper authority of the union."[51] The growing antagonism between McBride and the federation's executive council largely isolated McBride, making it more difficult for him to steer the federation's political course.

After McBride had recovered from his illness, he found that the AFL's finances were in trouble. In the first three months of 1895, the federation spent $5,490.66 while taking in only $2,406.44. Most of the $3,084.22 deficit was the result of "extra expenses" approved at the previous convention—lobbying for the Seamen's Bill, moving the federation's offices from New York to Indianapolis, a contribution to the Debs defense fund, and publication of the debate over the political program. August McCraith, the federation's secretary, concluded, "we have no money for special appropriations or anything of a costly nature." The AFL's financial straits kept McBride in Indianapolis, depriving him of the opportunity to use the presidency as a platform to spread his brand of unionism.[52]

Nonetheless, McBride began agitating for many of the reforms demanded by the labor-Populists. In the August 1895 *American Federationist*, McBride's editorial called for the restructuring of the American financial system. He told the readers, "The remonetization of silver . . . would, under existing conditions, only act as a palliative and reduce rather than remove the defects in our system of finance from which labor suffers the most." Demanding the issuance of greenbacks and the abolition of the nation's private banking system, he concluded, "We must take from speculators, bankers and brokers the power to control our medium of exchange before interest can be reduced to a minimum, usury be wiped out, and business done upon a cash rather than a credit basis."[53]

In the *American Federationist*'s October issue, McBride attacked the rising economic inequality. Using census figures, he argued that in 1850 American workers owned 62.5 percent of the nation's wealth, while the nonproducers controlled only 37.5 percent of the wealth. By 1890 workers controlled only 17 percent of the nation's wealth, while nonproducers controlled 83 percent. He blamed the change on "governmental favoritism to capital and the indifference and neglect of wage workers to the system of robbery." McBride then documented the increase of criminal activity between 1850 and 1890, concluding, "Capitalism, pauperism and crime go hand in hand, and the history of the world evidences the fact that wherever the former increases the two latter spread and flourish." Quoting Noah Webster, McBride insisted, "An equal distribution of property is the foundation of the republic," and he continued, "It is time the foundation was commenced." As a first step, he recommended the nationalization of railroads, telegraphs, telephones, and mines, and the municipal ownership of streetcars and gas, water, and electric plants. This was to be followed by the "collective ownership, by the people, of all such means of production . . . as [they] may from time to time elect to operate."[54]

By fall the AFL's improved financial situation allowed McBride to launch a speaking tour of the industrial Northeast and New England to champion the federation's entry into partisan politics. In every speech, according to the *Cleveland Citizen*, McBride "spoke in favor of independent political action along the lines of Populism." In Pittsburgh, he declared, "Corporate power must be dethroned and the people become the owners of all public necessities." The way to achieve this was clear: "If you want to restrict the privileges and abuses of capital you must pursue a different course in your trade unions, and I say to you it has come when labor must shake off partisan shackles and be free men. Be patriots, not partisans. . . . If I had my way there would be a labor party that would sweep all evils from the land." He concluded, "You can't strike a blow by strike or shot—you can't repeal a law by a boycott, but you can rout corporate power by intelligent use of the ballot."[55]

The AFL's political stance for the 1896 presidential election would be decided at the 1895 convention. It would be, the *Chicago Tribune* wrote, a "fight to the finish" between the radical McBride and the conservative Gompers. "[U]pon the outcome of the struggle will depend largely the future of organized labor in this country," the paper predicted. Commentators expected a close race. While McBride had the advantage of incumbency, Gompers had grounds to hope he could recover the federation's top office. McBride had alienated a couple of unions that had supported him the year before. McBride described the head of the Brewery Workers as having a "distorted brain." He had written the head of the International Machinists' Union that he had manifested "ignorance as an official" and had evidenced "boorishness as a man." Meanwhile, Gompers had spent much of 1895 traveling the nation on behalf of the garment workers, giving hundreds of speeches, while illness and the federation's financial straits had kept McBride from doing the same.[56]

Before the convention, the coalition of midwestern Populists and east coast Socialists that had put McBride into office showed signs of coming apart. Self-described Socialists such as J. Mahlon Barnes of the cigarmakers and John Tobin of the shoemakers were disappointed with McBride. His year in office had not produced the anticipated results. Not only was McBride's administration beset by scandal, financial difficulties, and health problems, it was constrained by the fragility of the federation and the 1894 convention's defeat of the preamble calling for the creation of a labor party. The Socialists talked of nominating Tobin to run against McBride, but on the eve of the convention decided to back McBride.[57]

Hoping to attract undecided delegates, McBride moderated his rhetoric at the convention. He continued to argue that only political action could alleviate labor's problems. "The self evident truth confronts us that wage workers cannot hope to be free in the shops, mines and factories while trudging in party slavery to the polls," he declared. Yet he retreated from his call for the creation of a labor party, realizing that AFL members did "not agree as to the scope of the political work needed" or "the methods employed in political reform work." Therefore he conceded, "At this time it is not independent party, but independent voting that will accomplish beneficial and speedy results."[58]

Despite McBride's retreat, on the afternoon of the convention's fourth day, Barnes introduced a resolution stating, "[t]hat it is as clearly the duty of union workingmen to organize and maintain a political party devoted exclusively to their own interests as to organize in trade and labor unions." As it did with all of the resolutions, the convention sent Barnes's motion to the Resolutions Committee. Delegates would not vote on the resolution until the convention's eighth day.[59] Although Barnes's exact intention remains unknown, the passage of the resolution would have clearly given McBride the authority to move the federation into partisan politics if he was elected to a second term. Barnes's original resolution can best be understood as the second step in a process to provide McBride the constitutional justification to steer the AFL into partisan politics through an alliance with the People's party. The first step was the reelection of McBride.

The presidential election took place in the afternoon of the convention's sixth day. Gompers eked out a victory, 1,041–1,023. Press reports confirmed that those favoring independent political action voted for McBride, while the dyed-in-the-wool trade unionists supported Gompers. The vote was so close that the result turned on a number of small issues. The brewery workers had supported McBride in 1894 and still favored independent political action. Yet they cast sixty votes for Gompers in 1895 largely because of other disagreements with McBride. James Gelson, delegate of the printing pressmen's union, had planned to cast his twenty-five votes for McBride, but he became ill on the morning of the election and did not vote.[60] Gompers's narrow election thwarted the ambitions of those who wanted to transform the federation into a partisan organization. Gompers remained opposed to any sort of partisan political activity. As president, he could effectively block the movement of the AFL into the political arena even if Barnes's resolution passed.

Two days after McBride's defeat, the convention considered Barnes's resolution. But with Gompers's election the issue had become meaningless. Opponents of partisan politics rose and offered a substitute declaring "party politics whether they be democratic, republican, socialistic, populistic, prohibition or any other, should have no place in the conventions of the AFL." The Populists and their allies put up almost no fight. Only Tobin voiced opposition to the substitute, accusing the traditional parties of "perpetuating the wage system." In the end the resolution passed by a lopsided margin, 1,460 to 158. Delegates representing close to 500 votes did not bother to cast ballots. Some delegates who had vocally supported political action, like UMWA delegates Phil Penna and Patrick McBryde, voted for the resolution, perhaps out of a desire for unity or out of fear of empowering Gompers to steer the federation's political course. Other supporters of political action, like Tobin and William Mahon, simply did not vote.[61]

Historians have pointed to the lopsided passage of the resolution as evidence of the federation's unanimous hostility toward partisan action by 1895.[62] But such assertions take the vote out of context. The real test of the strength of those wanting to transform the AFL into a partisan organization was the McBride-Gompers contest. Gompers alluded to this fact after the convention. In an editorial in the *American Federationist*, he agreed with those who considered "my election . . . as squelching and annihilating a certain school of thought in the American Federation of Labor." In a private letter he suggested his election had been a referendum "upon the issue that party politics should have no place in our Federation." Gompers made no reference to the subsequent vote prohibiting partisan activity within the AFL. Clearly, in Gompers's mind, his contest with McBride was the decisive vote in the defeat of those wanting to transform the federation into a partisan organization.[63] If the test of the strength of those in favor of a labor party at the 1895 convention was the McBride-Gompers contest, then those wanting to transform the federation were stronger than historians have argued. Only the illness of the printing pressmen's delegate secured victory for Gompers. Those wanting to take the federation into an alliance with the Populists were hardly annihilated or squelched, at least not in the short term. That would not come until the Populists' nomination of William Jennings Bryan fragmented those trade unionists who had coalesced around the People's party.

BY LATE 1895 OHIO'S LABOR-POPULISTS were frustrated—Coxey's gubernatorial bid had been a disappointment, McBride had been unable to hang onto the presidency of the AFL, and the People's party's national leadership had worked hard to undermine the movement of trade unionists into the party. Ohio trade unionists, though, continued to work with the People's party. As the *Cincinnati Chronicle* reminded its readers, "[the CLC has] always advocated the People's party, believing it better for the workers than the other two parties, and shall continue to advocate that which it considers to be the best for organized labor. . . . Our advice to our fellow workers is—Vote the People's party ticket."[64] While Populists around the nation turned their attention to the presidential election of 1896, Ohio trade unionists confronted yet another problem—a national leadership determined to transform the party into a silver party. Ohio trade unionists worked hard to ensure that the party would nominate a middle-of-the-road candidate and avoid fusion with one of the major parties. When these efforts failed, Ohio's labor–Populist alliance collapsed.

In late 1895 and early 1896 the People's party's national leadership, led by Taubeneck and Weaver, continued its efforts to unite all supporters of silver under the Populist banner. Fearful of both the influence of trade unionists—the so-called Socialists—and the formation of an independent silver party, these leaders insisted that only by concentrating on the free coinage of silver could the party ever attract enough supporters to challenge the traditional parties. Perhaps most important, the leaders expressed confidence that neither of the traditional parties would endorse the free and unlimited coinage of silver at a ratio of sixteen to one. Although silver Republicans dominated that party west of Mississippi, they were not nearly strong enough to challenge the eastern "sound money" men. Likewise, the Populist leaders assumed that Grover Cleveland would use his influence and prerogatives as president to ensure that the Democrats would not endorse the issue in 1896 or nominate a silverite. After all, they reasoned, if Cleveland mobilized federal officeholders beholden to him through patronage, he could control the one-third of the delegates needed to exercise an effective veto over the convention's platform and presidential nomination. If the People's party concentrated on the silver issues and eliminated "radical" planks from the platform, the party's leaders reasoned, then disgruntled silver Republicans and Democrats would naturally turn to the People's party.

While the Populist leadership was planning a campaign based on silver, they were in close contact with prominent free silver Democrats and Republicans who were intent on freeing their parties from the control of Wall Street bankers and "goldbugs." Led by former Nebraska congressman William Jennings Bryan and Missouri congressman Richard Bland, the free silver Democrats hoped to capitalize not only on the popularity of free silver but also the western and southern animosity toward Cleveland. Many of these leaders, especially Bryan, threatened to leave the Democratic party for a Populist-led silver party if the Democrats failed to endorse the free coinage of silver. Bryan was in contact with most of the People's party's western leaders, helping to convince them to hold a late convention. Bryan reasoned that if both parties opposed the free and unlimited coinage of silver at sixteen to one, bolting silverites would flock to the People's party, transforming it into a united silver party. If, by some remote chance, either of the two major parties endorsed silver, the People's party could unite with them on a free silver ticket.

Free silver Republicans, led by Colorado senator Henry Teller, were less optimistic of their chances of changing GOP's monetary policies but remained in the party in hopes of converting as many Republicans as possible to the free silver cause. The Populist leaders generally assumed that Teller and most western Republicans would bolt the party after the expected nomination of McKinley. Taubeneck, in fact, championed Teller for both the Democratic and the People's party nomination. If the Democrats did endorse the free coinage of silver and wanted the support of the Populists, he reasoned that the nomination of a former Republican like Teller would allow the People's party to retain its identity. If the Democrats refused to endorse the free coinage of silver, Teller would be both prominent and moderate enough to attract free silver Democrats and Republicans to the Populist party.[65]

Ohio trade union leaders opposed any attempt to trim the People's party platform or to fuse with either of the major parties on a silver ticket. Still, among the leaders, there was a fair degree of disagreement about the efficacy of the free and unlimited coinage of silver. At one extreme were those associated with Cleveland's CLU, especially *Citizen* editor Max Hayes. According to Hayes, the movement for the free and unlimited coinage of silver was being pushed hardest by those who had the most to gain by it—the owners of silver mines. Hayes, well versed in the single tax and the labor theory of value, maintained:

> Since most silver mine owners did not mix their labor with the land, their claims of ownership are illegitimate and ill-gotten. In fact, Silver barons have nothing in common with organized labor; they are exploiters—nothing more, nothing less. They are unequivocally in conflict with that divine, masterly declaration in the Omaha platform which plainly says, "Wealth belongs to him who creates it, and every dollar taken from industry without an equivalent is robbery. 'If any shall not work neither shall he eat.'"[66]

Those associated with Cincinnati's Central Labor Council sat on the other extreme. Cincinnati labor leaders expressed skepticism about the direct economic benefits of the free and unlimited coinage of silver, insisting that it "is not going to benefit the man who has nothing but his labor to sell." But they also began to invest in the issue a set of meanings that were at times far removed from the actual workings of bimetallism. Those opposed to free silver, the *Chronicle* asserted, represented the forces of corruption, wealth, and privilege, and supporters of the free silver fight were fighting for the uncorrupted, the masses, and the poor. Cincinnati labor leaders would have surely agreed with Bryan when he declared that the fight for free silver was "as holy as the cause of liberty—the cause of humanity."[67]

Most Ohio labor leaders fell somewhere between these two extremes, arguing that the free coinage of silver would improve the lives of workers but that it failed to address the primary cause of workers' distress. Cleveland's CLU president Peter Witt saw it as a necessary "step" in the march toward a cooperative commonwealth. ARU general secretary Sylvester Keliher told the CTLA's Independence Day picnic that the free coinage of silver would promote "justice" by ending the deflation that robbed indebted farmers and workers and enriched "the privileged and moneyed classes" but, he continued, "I am more concerned in that greater and more important battle . . . to reassert and maintain the liberties and freedom bought by the blood of our forefathers in 1776."[68]

While there was a diversity of opinion concerning silver, all of the state's labor unionists supported middle-of-the-road candidates for the party's nomination. The *Ohio Populist*, edited by two Columbus trade unionists, called for the nomination of Kansas's middle-of-the-road William Peffer for president and Debs for vice president. The *Cleveland Citizen* wanted the order reversed, with Debs heading the ticket. The *Cincinnati Chronicle* agreed, "With Debs at the head of the ticket, the party would stand a very good show of winning in the present campaign." Charles Martin, the national secretary of the UMWA-dominated International Order of the Knights of Labor and the Populists' 1894 nominee for Ohio secretary of state, explained that Debs "will do more to unite the labor vote than any man on earth. I believe that he can get 75 percent of the organized labor vote of the two old parties. He has the magnetism of Abraham Lincoln, and is certainly his equal as a speaker. If Debs gets into the St. Louis convention and makes a speech he will be the Populist candidate for president. Nothing on earth can stop him. He can stampede any audience in the country in his favor."[69]

In the summer of 1896, Ohio's Populists remained almost unanimous in their opposition to fusion and in their support for the Omaha platform. Toledo's Populists insisted it was "unwise to sacrifice the principles of the Omaha platform for a single issue" and maintained that "government ownership of all monopolies is the only natural solution of the industrial problem." Akron's Populists declared their opposition to fusion and their support for "the principles enunciated in the Omaha platform." Dayton's Populists argued that silverites were not true Populists and that only those who "stand by the Omaha platform" should be allowed to attend the party's national convention. Hugo Preyer, the chairman of the Ohio People's party's executive committee, insisted that the party should concentrate "on more important issues" than the free coinage of silver.[70]

Hocking Valley Populists, dominated by the UMWA, declared, "We fully endorse the Omaha platform." In Cleveland, the local People's party instructed its delegates to the national convention "to oppose by vote and voice, first, last, and all the time any and all attempts to abridge the Omaha platform by leaving out any plank, or any arrangement of words that would have the effect of nullifying the purpose of the Omaha platform as at present construed." As the *Citizen* insisted "no straddling, jumping-jack, eleventh hour, one idea, old-party politician will be acceptable to the Populists of this state."[71]

While Ohio's Populists were opposing those seeking to trim the Omaha platform, the state's free silver Democrats were seizing control of the Ohio Democratic party. Led by Allen W. Thurman, A. J. Warner, and John McLean, Ohio's free silver Democrats routed the party's bourbons at the state's Democratic convention. By a vote of 524 to 138, the convention ratified a platform declaring that "the money question is the vital and paramount question now before the people" and demanding "the restoration by the government, independent of other nations, of the unrestricted coinage of both gold and silver into standard money at the ratio of 16 to 1." Warner, the convention's chairman and one of the nation's foremost silverites, predicted that the party's national convention would endorse free silver and called for the state's Populists to join with the Democrats for the coming election. "As there is no room for but one party on the gold platform," he insisted, "so there will be room but for one platform on free silver. There must be no division of the silver forces on the eve of such a contest as we now enter."[72]

Warner's prediction proved correct. At their national convention in Chicago, the Democrats endorsed the free and unlimited coinage of silver at sixteen to one "without waiting for the aid or consent of any other nation." Moreover, the party passed a number of other planks pleasing to the Populists, including a condemnation of Cleveland's bond program, a constitutional amendment to allow Congress to pass an income tax, a denunciation of the military's intervention in the Pullman strike, and the abolition of "government by injunction." The passage of such a platform meant that the party would not be renominating Cleveland or anyone from his faction of the party.

Largely in response to his "Cross of Gold" speech, the Democrats nominated William Jennings Bryan, who had worked closely with the Populist leadership. The surprising nomination of Bryan placed the People's party in a bind. As Henry Demarest Lloyd explained, "If we fuse, we are sunk. If we don't fuse, all the silver men will leave us for the more powerful Democrats." Almost immediately prominent Populists lined up behind the nomination of Bryan. Kansas congressman Jerry Simpson suggested, "If this party should refuse to endorse Bryan the Populist party would not contain a corporal's guard in November."[73]

Although Ohio's Populists conceded that Bryan would probably receive the Populist nomination, they were not happy and looked for ways to avoid any sort of fusion with the Democrats. Columbus's P. J. Fishback suggested that the state's People's party would find few allies in their opposition to Bryan's nomination, but that they would nonetheless make the fight. Coxey, who admitted he would do almost anything to defeat McKinley, even proposed a plan whereby the People's party could retain its own identity if it nominated Bryan. As the *Citizen* cynically observed, Tom Watson, James Weaver, Herman Taubeneck, and other party leaders "will undoubtedly be found in the Democratic party before the chilly days of November arrive."[74]

Ohio's delegation to the 1896 People's party convention insisted that it would fight Bryan's nomination on principle. At an organizational meeting on the eve of the convention, the delegation announced its intention to support the nomination of Debs for president, the candidacy of middle-of-the-roader Ignatius Donnelly for convention chair, and the ratification of the entire Omaha platform. According to the *Columbus Press*, no more than five of the state's forty-nine delegates supported the nomination of Bryan or an alliance with the Democrats. To symbolize their opposition to fusion, the Ohioans designed badges with a picture of scissors and the inscription "No trimming at St. Louis" and procured a "middle of the road" gavel to be given to the convention chairman.[75]

Throughout the convention the Ohio delegation voted with the middle-of-the-roaders at every turn. The election of a convention chairman was the first test of the relative strength of Bryanites and middle-of-the-roaders. Bryanites supported Nebraska senator William V. Allen, while the middle-of-the-roaders sought the election of Maine's James Campion. When Campion's name was placed in nomination, the Ohioans joined the delegations from Texas, Alabama, Tennessee, and Mississippi in a procession around the convention floor. But it did little good, as Campion lost to Allen. In the second test of the middle-of-the-roaders' strength, the Ohio delegates voted forty-eight to one to nominate the vice presidential candidate before the presidential candidate. In this vote, the Ohioans were on the winning side.[76]

Although Bryan's nomination was considered assured, when the Nebraskan's name was placed in nomination the Ohioans joined the delegations from Texas and Missouri in refusing to allow their standards to be used in a celebratory parade. When the votes were counted, only twenty-one of the state's delegates voted for Bryan. The other twenty-eight split their votes between four middle-of-the-roaders. The main middle-of-the-road candidate, S. F. Norton, received seventeen votes, Debs garnered eight, Donnelly collected two, and one delegate voted for Coxey.[77]

After the convention, the People's party began crumbling. A significant number of Ohio labor-Populists, especially those in Cleveland, turned to the Socialist Labor party, but most of them reluctantly embraced some sort of fusion with the Democrats. Bryan and the Democrats had stolen the Populists' popular silver plank and much of their party's platform. Fusion with the Democrats offered some benefits—financial stability, a party apparatus with a proven track record, and, most important, improved chances of actually electing Populists to office—but the state's Democratic party still contained a sizable faction loyal to the policies of Grover Cleveland. Fusion was a bitter pill to swallow. In the end, most Ohio labor-Populists reluctantly joined the Democratic party, seeing in Bryan a dynamic national figure who could unite monetary reformers, defeat McKinley, and help elect candidates who held Populist ideals. As Coxey's *Sound Money* explained, "M stands for McKinley, Monopoly, and Misery," while "B stands for Bryan, Business, and Bread."[78]

While Ohio's People's party reluctantly moved toward fusion, the state's Democrats, especially the silver wing of the party, generally welcomed the Populists into the party. Not only did free silver Democrats such as Allan W. Thurman support many Populist ideals, they saw fusion as a way to defeat both the Grover Cleveland wing of the party and the Republican gold bugs. The Democrats, who had not controlled the governor's office or the general assembly since the election of 1891, felt that if they could win the 6–7 percent of the vote won by Ohio Populists in 1894 and 1895, this would be enough to secure victory in general elections. The city governments of Cincinnati and Cleveland were controlled by the Republicans, but the combined Populist and Democratic vote in both cities exceeded the Republican total. Fusion also promised inroads into traditional Republican strongholds such as the coalfields of southeastern Ohio, the Akron-Canton area, and the

Western Reserve, where the People's party had done surprisingly well. The promise of victory over the Republicans was so attractive that even bourbon Democrats such as Calvin Brice, who had opposed the nomination of Bryan and most of the party's 1896 platform, reluctantly supported fusion.

Ohio Populists took their first step toward fusion in August 1896 when party chairman Hugo Preyer called for all local People's parties to work with their Democratic counterparts to secure places for Populists on the Democratic slates. In nearly every county, most Populists agreed to work with the Democratic party and were able to secure nominations for Populists on Democratic tickets. Preyer and Coxey met with the state's Democratic leaders and worked out an arrangement in which the People's party would select five of the party's twenty-three presidential electors and fill two slots on the Democrats' state ticket. At its convention in late August, the People's party voted by a narrow margin to endorse this arrangement and support Bryan. The delegates selected perennial judicial candidate E. D. Stark to run for the Supreme Court and T. J. Craeger, a Springfield labor leader, to be the candidate for food and dairy commissioner on the Democratic ticket. The Populists also agreed not to run a separate slate of presidential electors.[79]

In an effort to assert its independence and maintain a distinct identity, the Ohio People's party in its 1896 convention ratified a separate platform calling for the adoption of Coxey's monetary plans, the initiative and referendum, and public ownership of all municipal monopolies. But after the election of 1896 and the defeat of Bryan, what was left of the Ohio People's party slowly crumbled. Efforts to cooperate but not merge with the Democratic party proved unworkable, and by the end of 1897 the Ohio People's party had vanished.[80]

AFTER LOSING HIS REELECTION bid in December 1895 to Samuel Gompers, John McBride returned to Columbus, bought a weekly newspaper, and immersed himself in UMWA affairs.[81] McBride and the UMWA leadership had tied their fates to the Populist party, and they could hardly abandon it. UMWA's Populists tried to redeem their strategy by going to work for Bryan and calling on the nation's coal miners to rally to the cause of silver. Both McBride and UMWA president Phil Penna stumped for Bryan and the Democratic party. McBride even set up a labor bureau in Chicago during the campaign, to distribute literature and coordinate Bryan's efforts among the nation's trade unionists. His newspaper insisted that the free coinage of silver would free the American people from the domination of the "British gold kings of London, and their auxiliaries in Wall street." McBride was so active on Bryan's behalf among the state's trade unionists that the *Cleveland*

Citizen accused him of being Bryan's biggest backer in Ohio. Penna, who was originally from Indiana, traveled with his old friend Eugene Debs to the coal towns of the Hocking Valley to campaign for Bryan, reminding miners of the actions of McKinley during the coal strike.[82]

The *United Mine Workers Journal* joined the fight. It warned miners "not to pay any attention to the efforts that will be made by the gold monarchy to divide them" and suggested that those refusing to get behind Bryan were doing the bidding of the Republican party. While not endorsing Bryan by name, the paper repeatedly ran the UMWA's declaration in favor of "the free coinage of silver at the ratio of sixteen to one independent of action of any other country, and the issue of legal tender paper money by the government only" in the place most papers reserved for the printing of their party's slate and insisted that the currency issue was the only issue of the campaign.[83]

After Bryan's defeat, McBride and Penna realized their political strategies had failed and that they would be of no use to the UMWA or the nation's miners. Each man announced that he would not be seeking any union office—Penna would not be running for reelection and McBride would not challenge Gompers for leadership of the AFL. They had hitched their horses to the Populist party and later to Bryan and were willing to accept the consequences for their failed strategy.

When the UMWA met in January 1897 for its annual convention, the delegates replaced the union's entire leadership with a more conservative group. Gone were those who had championed the union's alliance with the Populists, and in were men associated with the traditional parties. The new president was Michael Ratchford, a longtime Republican activist from Ohio's Tuscawarus Valley who was especially close to Marcus Hanna. During the previous fall's campaign, Ratchford had campaigned for McKinley.[84]

The election of Michael Ratchford and the new leadership represented a shift back to the strategy and orientation the UMWA had employed before the strike of 1894. Ratchford, sounding much like McBride in the 1880s and early 1890s, insisted that the problems facing the nation's miners were rooted not in the political arena but in market forces—the abundance of coal in the nation, the oversupply of miners and mines, and the slack demand because of the lingering effects of the Panic of 1893. The new leaders thought that the primary way to improve the lives of the nation's miners rested in the reestablishment of an industry-wide operator-labor agreement that would insulate miners' wages from the pernicious effects of the market. To raise the market price of coal to the level that would allow the creation of such an agreement, Ratchford and the UMWA launched a nationwide coal strike on July 4, 1897. Much to the surprise of all observers,

Ratchford's gambit worked. The strike led to the creation of the Central Cooperative Field—an area stretching from Western Pennsylvania to Iowa in which wage scales and differentials were set at the negotiating table and operators looked to the UMWA to provide stability to the chaotic industry. Ratchford would resign shortly after the strike, taking a job in the McKinley administration and engineering the election of his protégé John Mitchell as the new president of the UMWA.[85]

The AFL met for its annual convention in December 1896, less than two months following the defeat of Bryan. On the convention's third day a remarkable thing happened. After Samuel Gompers was nominated for president, John McBride asked that the convention's rules be suspended and that "the secretary be instructed to cast the entire vote of the convention for Delegate Gompers." McBride's motion carried, moving Gompers to tears. The man who had defeated him in 1894 and who had come so close to being reelected in 1895 conceded defeat. This simple act marked the triumph of Gompers and his brand of unionism over its last and most significant challenge. Although Max Hayes would mobilize the AFL's Socialists against Gompers at the end of the first decade of the twentieth century, never again would Gompers face a serious challenge for control of the AFL.[86]

While McBride never explained why he called for the convention to elect Gompers by acclamation, it is easy to speculate. His efforts to transform the federation into a partisan organization had been shattered by the fusion of 1896. Trade unionists who had worked with the People's party were now divided and fragmented. Most of them embraced the Bryan-led Democratic party, but significant numbers flocked to the Socialist Labor party. Still others found themselves out of office for their failed strategy. Those who opposed Gompers's nonpartisan strategy had neither a party nor a platform on which they could agree. Thus the final triumph of Gompers within the AFL reflected not so much an evolution in the thinking of the nation's trade unionists as it did the difficulties in creating a producer-based party within the American political system.

The triumph of Gompers and pure and simple unionism occurred on the eve of an extended period of national prosperity, which brought a period of tremendous growth to the AFL. In 1897 the AFL's membership stood at slightly more than 250,000 members. Seven years later membership had reached over 1,650,000. As the federation grew stronger so did Gompers's hold on the organization. Although there were numerous challengers to both Gompers and pure and simple unionism, none of these were able to come as close as McBride and the Populists did between 1894 and early 1896.[87]

8
Progressivism
That which Populism Never Dared to Dream

IN 1913 A REPORT in the *American Political Science Review* highlighted recent political developments in Ohio: "A radical constitution to which to conform, a radical legislature, and a radical governor . . . all have conspired to give the Buckeye State, according to conservative minds, a taste of that which populism, in its wildest vagaries, never dared to dream." Conservatives were not alone in noting that Ohio's state government, almost wholly remade with the ratification of thirty-four constitutional amendments in 1912, now embraced much of the Populist program. Cleveland socialist and labor leader Max Hayes traced the lineage of these reforms to the "grand old pioneer trade unionists, Knights of Labor, Populists, [and] Socialists." For Hayes, Ohio's new government provided the means through which the state's workers could "completely emancipate themselves from the thralldom of exploitation."[1]

In the wake of the fusion of 1896 and the breakup of Ohio's People's party, the state's labor leaders seeking to use the state to transform labor relations changed tactics not goals. With most of the former labor-Populists divided between Bryan's Democratic party and the Socialists, labor did not enjoy the unity that was needed to engage in partisan political action. After a few years figuring out how to organize themselves for reform, laborites seized upon one item of the Populist platform around which they could unite and which promised to provide the means through which they could enact the rest of their agenda: the initiative, referendum, and recall. The fight for direct legislation put trade unionists—Democrats as well as Socialists—at the center of the state's Progressive movement, which would culminate with the constitutional amendments of 1912.

Direct legislation's appeal to trade unionists was clear. As an Ohio Federation of Labor lobbyist declared, it offered the best chance of defeating the "corporations and political bosses" and purifying the state's political system. The initiative would afford trade unionists the opportunity to bypass what they saw as a corrupt general assembly, one that was dominated by business interests and the needs of the major parties, to have its agenda ratified by the people. In doing so, the initiative promised to eliminate the need for political parties altogether. Trade unionists from a multitude of political parties could unite behind an initiated piece of legislation or a referendum and work for its passage outside of partisan boundaries. The fact that trade unionists were divided among the political parties would make little difference. Direct legislation would also allow trade unionists to make alliances with farm groups, religious organizations, civic groups, even business organizations on an ad hoc basis, thereby avoiding long-term entanglements with groups that did not have labor's interest foremost on their agendas. Moreover, the referendum and recall promised to cleanse the body politic. Since they could be recalled by popular vote, politicians would be less likely to accept bribes or other illicit inducements. Trade unionists reasoned that business interests would not waste their money corrupting the legislature if their efforts could be undone at the ballot box.[2]

Although direct legislation was an important component of the state's Populist platform, Ohio trade unionist support for the initiative, referendum, and recall actually predated its support for the People's party. At its formation in 1887, Cleveland's Central Labor Union called for "Direct legislation through the initiative and referendum." Cincinnati's Central Labor Council formed the Direct Legislation League in 1893, about a year before it officially threw in with the Populists.[3] The Ohio State Trades and Labor Assembly began agitating for direct legislation at least a year before it entered into its de facto alliance with the People's party.[4] It made little sense for trade unionists to abandon this reform or their agenda after the collapse of the People's party, and Ohio trade unionists would be the most vocal supporters of direct legislation and the reforms associated with Progressivism.

While the Ohio Socialist party endorsed direct legislation almost immediately after the fusion of 1896, the Democrats did not get behind it until 1902. The collapse of the People's party in Ohio led to changes within Democratic coalitions in the state's urban areas. Most labor-Populists migrated to the Democratic party where they combined with Bryan supporters to battle more conservative elements for control of the party. These same battles raged at the state level. Self-described Progressives—Tom Johnson and his "young men," Frederic Howe, Peter Witt, and Newton Baker in Cleveland, Brand Whitlock in Toledo, and Herbert Bigelow in Cincinnati—and their trade unionist allies fought those in the party's more conservative wing led by Cincinnati's Judson Harmon and John R. McLean.

The alliance within the Ohio Democratic party between trade unionists and the Progressives centered on support of the initiative and referendum but included other issues that were central to the Populist agenda. Home rule for cities would allow municipalities to own their own streetcar lines, water and sewer systems, and other utilities, thereby removing the largest sources of corruption in urban affairs. Home rule would also allow cities to require those receiving city contracts to observe the eight-hour day. Both groups also supported efforts to regulate the hours and working conditions of children and women, increase employer liability for workplace injuries, create a nonpartisan judiciary, reform the tax code so that the wealthy could not shield their assets from collectors, extend suffrage to women, allow for the direct election of U.S. senators, and limit the use of injunctions during labor disputes.[5]

But while Democrats could win elections in cities, the party failed in every statewide election in the decade following the fusion of 1896. The Republican party dominated the state, despite its division into two factions. Marcus Hanna led one faction, while Senator Joseph Benson Foraker led the other. Although their rivalry was intense, the two men were pragmatists who could put personal differences aside when it suited their political ends. So firm was their control over the state that one state legislator would later observe, "Ohio at that time was managed like a private estate by Senators Hanna and Foraker." Neither man cared much for the agenda of Ohio trade unionists and their Progressive allies. Senator Foraker denounced their "populistic, communistic, and anarchistic creeds." Senator Hanna, who was sympathetic to those types of reforms that helped rationalize the economy to the benefit of corporations, accused the state's Progressives of standing on a "Populistic, Socialistic, and Anarchistic platform."[6]

The decade of Republican rule following the fusion of 1896 proved difficult for Ohio labor. Soon after the fusion, the OSTLA reorganized and changed its name to the Ohio Federation of Labor (Ohio State Federation of Labor after 1910), kicking out the remaining trade unions associated with the Knights of Labor and committing itself to the nonpartisan lobbying of the general assembly.[7] Despite these efforts, the state legislature failed to pass any significant legislation demanded by trade unionists. Tellingly, when the Ohio State Federation of Labor would later publish pamphlets boasting of its legislative accomplishments, the analysis would always begin in 1907.[8]

By that time Socialists had emerged as the most influential leaders in the state labor federation. These Socialists—Max Hayes, Robert Bandlow, and the federation's secretary treasurer Harry Thomas—had all been Populists and were affiliated with Cleveland's CLU. Socialist control of the Ohio Federation of Labor was so strong that in 1909 the AFL found a pretext—a jurisdictional dispute among electrical workers—to revoke the state federation's charter and set up a rival body. The split did not last long, as the two bodies soon united under Socialist leadership in order to prepare for the 1912 constitutional convention.[9] Despite their commitment to the Socialist party, the leaders of the Ohio Federation of Labor worked closely with Tom Johnson's men and other Bryan Democrats to enact direct legislation.

Starting around 1905, Ohio's political climate began to change, giving labor and its allies hope that reform might be possible. The Republican party was in turmoil. Marcus Hanna's death in 1904 left Joseph Foraker the undisputed leader of the party. But Foraker's close ties to Cincinnati's George "Boss" Cox proved costly. The year 1905 saw the publication of exposés by Henry Wright and Lincoln Steffens depicting Cox-dominated Cincinnati as the most corrupt city in the nation.[10] As historian Hoyt Landon Warner argues, these exposés created a reform impulse that "spread from city to city, from urban to rural districts until it became the central theme in the politics of the state." Whereas Hanna and his faction could have at least claimed the mantle of Progressivism (support for the National Civic Federation and the Erdman Act, for example), the Foraker faction could not, nor would it even try. As his biographer argues, Foraker was a "staunch believer in American laissez faire" who insisted that any attempt to curtail or regulate the activities of business was "in conflict with the teachings of political economy."[11] The Republican party, ignoring the growing sentiment for reform, renominated Myron Herrick for governor and ran on its record. After fifteen years of controlling the general assembly and the governor's office, the Republicans could hardly do otherwise. Herrick's reelection chances were also endangered because he had angered temperance advocates, an important Republican constituency, by signing a local option bill that opened the way for several counties to go wet.[12]

The Democrats, on the other hand, embraced the cause of reform. By

1905 the party was clearly in the hands of Progressives. John R. McLean, the party's most conservative force, had essentially bowed out of state party affairs, resigning his position on the Democratic National Committee and moving permanently to Washington to tend to his family's new purchase, the *Washington Post*.[13] Although the most radical of the Progressives, men such as Tom Johnson and Brand Whitlock, had considerable clout within the party, they by no means controlled it. In the words of one observer, it was a party "without bosses." At the 1905 convention, Johnson authored the platform, but the rest of the party refused to go along with his choice of gubernatorial nomination, Toledo mayor Brand Whitlock. Instead, delegates chose John M. Pattison. A former congressman from Cincinnati, Pattison had solid Progressive credentials, and the fact that he was considered a "dry" increased his appeal among those unhappy with Herrick's support of local option legislation. In his acceptance speech, Pattison attacked bossism and Cincinnati's George Cox, praised William Jennings Bryan, and committed himself to a platform that included the initiative and referendum, home rule for cities, direct election of U.S. senators, municipal ownership of utilities, and other planks that organized labor had endorsed for years.[14]

A month before the election, the Ohio Federation of Labor turned its annual convention into a pep rally for the initiative and referendum. At the request of Thomas Donnelly, the Cincinnati labor leader who ran for Congress on the Populist slate in 1894 and the Democratic-Populist fusion ticket in 1896, federation leaders invited Herbert Bigelow to address the convention. Bigelow, a Congregationalist minister from Cincinnati who was a single-taxer and a close ally of Tom Johnson, had been the Democrats' nominee for secretary of state in 1902. By 1905 he had become the state's leading proponent of direct legislation, heading up the Ohio Direct Legislation League. Bigelow's speech moved the convention to pass a resolution demanding that the general assembly submit a constitutional amendment providing for direct legislation to the voters of the state. For the rest of the convention, all other labor questions—workplace safety, convict and child labor, regulation of hours and conditions, and so on—took a backseat. When the federation's executive committee screened legislative candidates, the only question they considered was whether the candidate would support efforts to submit a constitutional amendment embodying the initiative and referendum to voters.[15]

Pattison won, making him the first Democrat to win the governor's office since 1889. The Democrats also took control of the Ohio Senate—for the first time since 1891. Labor organizations and their political allies were ecstatic, except for those in Cincinnati who saw the dry Pattison as a threat to the city's brewery workers and doubted his commitment to direct legislation. As Frederic Howe, who was elected to the state Senate that year, remembered, "We had a progressive governor, a progressive majority in the Senate, and the best Lower House that had been elected in years." At the start of the 1906 session, Howe and other Progressives took the lead in organizing the Senate, securing control of powerful committees and giving "reactionary members unimportant assignments."[16]

Sensing the opportunity to further its agenda, the Ohio Federation of Labor, for the first time in its history, organized a special legislative conference to pressure the legislature. Trade unionists from around the state gathered in Columbus to meet with legislators, coordinate letter-writing campaigns, and stir up enthusiasm for reform. Although the forty-some delegates went on record endorsing a number of reforms—abolition of child and convict labor, home rule for cities—they gave special attention to direct legislation, sending a letter to each legislator calling for the enactment of the initiative and referendum. The conference also decided that the time had come to employ a lobbyist in Columbus while the general assembly was in session, appointing James Robinson and soliciting contributions to defray the cost. William D. Mahon, the former Populist serving as president of the Amalgamated Association of Street Railway Drivers, chipped in the first hundred dollars.[17]

Things did not go well for labor and the Progressives, though. Not only did Pattison die about six months after taking office, but a few conservative lawmakers were able to stymie most of the Progressive agenda. Republican lieutenant governor Andrew Harris filled the rest of Pattison's term, which, due to a constitutional amendment switching gubernatorial and legislative elections from odd-numbered years to even-numbered years, ran through 1908. Although Harris supported many of the reforms advocated by labor and its Progressive allies, he did not share Pattison's commitment to the initiative and referendum.[18]

Labor and its Progressive allies were unable to convince the general assembly to submit a constitutional amendment providing the initiative and referendum to voters. Unlike regular legislation, constitutional amendments required passage by majorities of three-fifths in both the house and the Senate. The Senate passed the measure (Senate Joint Resolution 9), with five Republicans joining all but one of the Democrats in voting yes, but the measure got bogged down in the house judiciary committee. Four of the nine committee members supported the measure, but a fifth vote was needed to get the amendment to the house floor. The Ohio Federation of Labor's legislative committee quickly identified Representative George A. Bassett of Lucas County (Toledo) as the judiciary committee member most likely to switch from nay to yea and, in the words of the federation's chief lobbyist, "immediately proceeded to build fires to smoke him out." Federation officials solicited the aid of the Toledo Central Labor Union, which "made life so miserable for Mr. Bassett" that he agreed to vote to send the measure to the floor. Just when it looked as though house members would have the opportunity to vote on the direct legislation amendment, house leaders rearranged the schedule in such a way as to make it unlikely that the measure would be considered before the close of the session. Ohio Federation of Labor officials huddled with Howe and the leaders of the Direct Legislation League to plot their next move. Reluctantly they concluded, "the best thing to be done under the circumstances was to let it lay in committee until the next session rather than run the risk of losing what we had already accomplished."[19]

Other items on the Progressive agenda did not fare well. Although a bill ending contract convict labor became law (largely through the intervention of Howe on the Ohio Federation of Labor's behalf), legislation prohibiting children from working more than nine hours a day and past 10:00 P.M., regulating the conditions in coal mines, requiring safety equipment for railroad workers, plumbers, and streetcar operators, allowing counties to hire labor for public works projects, and increasing employer liability for workplace accidents, all languished in committees, essentially killed by the opposition of one or two legislators. As Howe remembered, "Our bills never came to a vote; they were blocked at some stage of the proceedings."[20]

The frustration of seeing one or two legislators repeatedly tie up labor legislation convinced J. A. Robinson, the Ohio Federation of Labor's first vice president and the head of its legislation committee, that the Ohio General Assembly would never pass significant legislation in the interest of labor. The only solution, he believed, was for labor to focus all of its energy and influence on the fight "for the immediate adoption of the Initiative and Referendum." Once that happened, labor would have little trouble enacting the rest of its agenda.[21]

Robinson set about doing just that. Following the adjournment of the 1906 session of the general assembly, Bigelow asked the Ohio Federation of Labor to allow Robinson to devote his full energies to work on behalf of direct legislation. The Direct Legislation League offered to pick up half of Robinson's salary, if the federation would kick in the rest. The federation could not come up with its share of Robinson's salary, but the Direct Legislation League agreed to pay the whole amount, and Robinson began traveling the state. Robinson and the Direct Legislation League worked to build support to bring the initiative and referendum measure (which had passed the Senate but never made it onto the house calendar) up for a vote when the general assembly reconvened. Speaking to civic, farm, and labor groups and whipping up public support for direct legislation, Robinson and other Direct Legislation League supporters succeeded in pressuring ninety-two legislators to sign a pledge to support the stalled measure once the legislature reconvened.[22]

When the general assembly reconvened in early 1908, the Direct Legislation League and the Ohio Federation of Labor continued working hand in hand. Bigelow, George King (who was assisting Robinson's efforts on behalf of the federation), and John Miller (the president of the Cincinnati CLC) visited Joseph Foraker. The delegation did not ask the Republican leader to support direct legislation—they had little hope of that—but, rather, they wanted him to support putting the issue before the people. Foraker, perhaps wanting to head off challenges within the Republican party, gave the delegation a letter to that effect.[23]

With the Democratic platform supporting direct legislation, the Republican leader in favor of putting the issue before the people, and over ninety legislators pledged to support the initiative and referendum, labor and its Progressive allies had high hopes. The Senate again passed the measure to place a constitutional amendment providing for direct legislation before the voters. In the house, however, opponents of direct legislation offered several amendments aimed at crippling it. In the end, the house passed a version of the measure that required that initiated legislation be approved by a majority of voters casting ballots in an election rather than a majority of those who cast votes on the issue. Ohio Federation of Labor officials met with Direct Legislation League leaders and decided to oppose the house version. They reasoned that the state's political climate was improving, and that it would be better to wait for a good bill than settle for a flawed one. After attempts to reconcile the house and senate versions failed, the measure died.[24]

Despite the setback concerning direct legislation, the 1908 session was a boon for the rest of labor's agenda. The general assembly passed the Reynolds Child Labor Bill. Named after its sponsor, Representative James Reynolds, an official in the Machinists' Union and ally of Tom Johnson, the law prohibited males under sixteen years of age and females under eighteen from working more than eight hours a day or forty-eight hours a week. Robinson would call the measure "the best child-labor law in the United States and probably in the world." The legislature also passed a measure increasing employer liability for workplace accidents by doing away with the doctrine of assumed risk and modifying the doctrine of contributory negligence and several other pieces of legislation demanded by labor.[25]

The Ohio Democratic party nearly came apart in 1908 as tensions between the Progressive and conservative wings intensified. The dispute centered on the party's platform and its choice for the gubernatorial nomination. The Progressives wanted the party to nominate Ohio tax commissioner and former Canton city attorney Atlee Pomerene, while conservatives and many moderates lined up behind former U.S. attorney general Judson Harmon, who opposed direct legislation. Progressives and trade unionists loathed Harmon, who as a member of Grover Cleveland's cabinet had refused to support Bryan in 1896 and had celebrated his defeat. But Harmon had won over many of the party's moderates by his performance investigating the Atchison, Topeka, and Santa Fe Railroad. In 1905 President Roosevelt had appointed Harmon, along with another attorney, to investigate charges that the railroad had violated a federal injunction by continuing to pay rebates to the John D. Rockefeller–controlled Colorado Fuel and Iron Company. Harmon and his fellow investigator found ample evidence to substantiate the charges and called on the administration to prosecute not only the corporations but also the individual corporate officers. When Roosevelt refused to charge the corporate officers, Harmon and the other investigator resigned, becoming unlikely martyrs in the fight against monopoly.[26]

The party forged a compromise of sorts. Harmon received the nomination, but the Progressives wrote the platform and got their way with the rest of the ticket. The platform embodied nearly all of the ideas of the Populist party—direct legislation, government ownership of all utilities, home rule for cities, wage and hour regulations, employer liability for workplace accidents, end of labor injunctions, and judicial and tax reform.[27] Although the Progressives got to write the platform and name most of the ticket, a few former labor-Populists had trouble standing behind Grover Cleveland's attorney general. For instance, Peter Witt complained that Harmon was "an agent of booze, the product of bosses, [and] the representative of predatory wealth" who had "knifed Bryan" in 1896. Harmon's nomination, according to Witt, was causing those "who [had] joined the Democratic party in 1896" to reassess those decisions. Witt, who had gone to work for Tom Johnson's administration by this time, tried to recruit Toledo's Brand Whitlock to launch a Sam Jones–style independent bid for governor.[28] Nothing came of Witt's attempts to nominate a third candidate, and Harmon's vow to work for the Democratic platform convinced the party's Progressive wing to stand behind him. As Tom Johnson said, "I make my fights before nominations, not afterwards."[29]

The year 1908 marked a turning point for the state's Republican party as well. William Howard Taft, Teddy Roosevelt's hand-picked successor, unseated his family's longtime rival in Cincinnati politics, Joseph Benson Foraker, as the leader of the party. The party nominated incumbent Andrew Harris and ran on a platform tinged with Roosevelt-style reform. Breaking with the past, the party called for the abolition of child labor, control of public utilities, primary elections, employer liability for workplace accidents, tax reform, referendum on franchises, and a series of good government proposals, nominating scores of reformers to run for the general assembly. The platform did not include, though, support for the initiative, referendum on general legislation, or the recall.[30]

Harmon defeated Harris, but other Democrats, especially those from the Progressive wing, did not fare well. Taft's long coattails helped elect Republicans to every statewide office except governor and treasurer and to a majority in both houses of the general assembly, where partisan lines began breaking down as conservatives from both parties combined to take on Republican and Democratic reformers. In the house, reformers took control, but in the Senate conservatives held sway.[31]

Conservative control of the state Senate and Harmon's lack of enthusiasm made it difficult for Ohio labor and the Direct Legislation League to make any headway on the initiative and referendum. A version of the bill acceptable to labor passed the house, but, in the words of the Ohio State Federation of Labor's legislative agent, "it was amended to death in the senate and was finally killed."[32] The failure to secure passage of the initiative and referendum in 1909 and 1910 convinced the leaders of the Direct Legislation League and the Ohio Federation of Labor to change tactics. Rather than working through the general assembly, they would mobilize for a possible constitutional convention.

The state's 1851 constitution had required that voters be asked every twenty years if they want another constitutional convention. In 1871 Ohioans chose to hold a convention, but three years later voters refused to ratify the proposed constitution. In 1891 the people refused to call a convention, but by 1910 a number of important groups in addition to the labor movement supported the call for a new constitutional convention. Business groups, led by the Ohio State Board of Commerce, hoped that a convention would allow them to reform the state's antebellum tax code, which taxed all property at a uniform rate. Both the "wets" and the "drys" wanted to use the convention to frame the state's liquor laws. Advocates of women's rights saw it as an opportunity to extend the franchise. Most important, trade unions and their Progressive allies hoped to enact direct legislation and a number of other structural changes that they thought would make the state's governments more responsive to the people.[33]

Sentiment in favor of the convention was so strong that both the Democratic and Republican parties prepared their ballots so that those who voted the straight party ticket would be counted in favor of holding a convention. This required those opposing the call for the convention to scratch "yes" off their ballot and write in "no." Such procedures all but guaranteed that voters would approve the call for the convention. When votes were tallied the call was approved by 693,263 votes to 67,718. Even the most enthusiastic reformers admitted that most voters had little idea of what they were voting for.[34]

After Ohio voters decided to hold the convention, Senate president William Green, a former UMWA official from Coshocton County and the future president of the AFL, introduced Senate Bill 15, requiring the nonpartisan election of delegates to the convention. Although opponents kept the bill bottled up in committee for over three months, Green used his position to bring it to the floor, and it passed in both houses by wide margins. The Cleveland Federation of Labor (the renamed CLU) insisted that a nonpartisan election would give "workers the opportunity to unite on good men . . . who will guard the interest of workers in making a new Constitution" and hold delegates responsible to their constituents rather than to party bosses. The federation's hopes proved to be correct. In the period before the election of delegates, Ohio labor and its progressive allies outworked business groups, basically securing control of the convention before the opening gavel. Writing fifteen years later, Ohio State Federation of Labor executive director Thomas Donnelly insisted that passage of the bill requiring the nonpartisan election of delegates was Ohio's labor's greatest accomplishment.[35]

The prospects of the constitutional convention excited Ohio's labor leaders. As Ohio State Federation of Labor president John Voll declared, "it means the opportunity to gain for the people the liberty which is due them. . . . It means, particularly for the toilers of our state, organized and unorganized, an opportunity to frame a constitution that cannot be used as an instrument (like the present one is used) to prevent humane legislation, or have it nullified through the state Supreme Court declaring it unconstitutional upon the merest technicality."[36]

Most labor leaders agreed with the Ohio State Federation of Labor's executive board that direct legislation was the most important reform needed. They argued that it held the promise of allowing labor and its allies to secure all of the other reforms needed. Direct legislation, they believed, would also cleanse the Ohio General Assembly. Labor leaders reasoned that business would not bother to corrupt the political process if their laws could be simply overturned through referendum.[37]

By January 1911 Ohio State Federation of Labor officers were meeting with Herbert Bigelow and others in the Direct Legislation League to discuss ways to ensure that the upcoming constitutional convention would support the initiative and referendum. These discussions came to fruition on June 1, 1911, when the Ohio State Federation of Labor, the Ohio State Grange, the Direct Legislation League, and like-minded civic groups organized the Progressive Constitutional League (PCL). Although Toledo mayor Brand Whitlock served as the league's president, Bigelow did most of the work. The PCL endorsed three specific reforms: initiative and referendum, home rule for cities (which would make municipal ownership of utilities possible), and recall of elected officials.[38] The new league worked to secure pledges in support of these reforms from those seeking election as delegates to the constitutional convention. Bigelow and PCL officials also worked to put together slates of sympathetic candidates in the state's largest counties.[39]

Labor, the PCL, and other civic groups organized quickly in Cincinnati to put together a slate of candidates pledged to support the initiative and referendum, home rule for cities, and the recall. Calling itself the United Constitutional Committee (UCC), the organization represented business groups, neighborhood associations, welfare organizations, and trade unions, including the CLC. The United Constitutional Committee allotted labor three of the nine positions on the slate, and the CLC chose William Halenkamp (printing pressman), John Hoffman (brewery worker), and Henry Cordes (Carpenters). Some in the UCC thought that labor had too many representatives and tried to have one replaced with Herbert Bigelow. Bigelow, though, refused to allow this. He was later added to the slate, replacing a local judge.[40]

The Columbus Federation of Labor and scores of local unions worked with an affiliate of the PCL, also called the United Constitutional Committee (UCC), in the nomination of Franklin County's delegates to the constitutional convention. Before selecting a slate, the UCC put forth a platform that included much of the progressive agenda—initiative and referendum, home rule, and judicial reform. The UCC, though, refused to endorse the recall, which prompted the Columbus Federation of Labor to threaten to withdraw its support. In the end the labor federation remained part of the UCC, largely because of the committee's support of direct legislation and home rule. At Bigelow's suggestion, the UCC allotted one of the three spots on the slate to a union member, who was to be selected by the Columbus Federation of Labor. The other two slots were to be filled by a farmer (chosen by the local grange) and a businessman or professional.

Some difficulty arose around the Columbus Federation of Labor's selection of a delegate. The federation originally elected iron molder J. W. Harberger, but some of the body's Socialists objected to both him and the method of selection. After much wrangling, Harberger withdrew his name, and the federation held another election, which Harberger won.[41] The difficulties over Harberger's election did not indicate a dispute within the Columbus Federation of Labor over labor's goals for the constitutional convention—both the Socialists and non-Socialists agreed on the primacy of direct legislation—but were the result of tensions over other matters.

During the summer of 1911, Cleveland laborites struggled over their approach to the election of delegates to the upcoming constitutional convention. In July the Cleveland Federation of Labor (CFL) considered an offer from the nonpartisan Municipal Association allowing CFL to name three labor leaders to its slate of ten delegates. The Municipal Association, organized in 1896 to campaign against corruption in city affairs and to agitate for home rule for cities, championed many of the structural reforms sought by labor—initiative and referendum, home rule, and women's suffrage. But by 1911 membership included a number of organizations that the Cleveland federation had come to distrust, such as the Builders' Association, the Employers' Association, and the local bar association. Accordingly, the CFL refused to work with the Municipal Association, one official insisting that the federation would not allow itself to be the tail of a "plutocratic kite." The Municipal Association, though, refused to take no for an answer and included Harry Thomas, a prominent Socialist and the Ohio State Federation of Labor's secretary treasurer, and other trade unionists on its slate of delegates.[42]

Shortly thereafter, one of the city's oldest and most powerful unions, Local 11 of the United Brother of Carpenters and Joiners, called for the city's trade unionists to sever their ties to the traditional parties and join the new Referendum party, which endorsed much of the Populist agenda. The carpenters told workers that "monopolies owe their wealth to special privileges given to them by the LAW, including judge-made laws, and under our present system of representative government there is no possible chance to secure laws of vital importance to the masses." In order to restore democratic values, "we, the many, must secure control and conduct of the affairs of government in all of its divisions, and we can only do this by first getting the PROPER TOOLS to work with—THE INITIATIVE, REFERENDUM, and RECALL." The party called for a labor convention to nominate a slate of delegates for the constitutional convention and to choose candidates for the upcoming city council election, but support for a new party was lukewarm and the carpenters concluded that they had to work for direct legislation in other ways.[43]

Instead, the CFL worked with the Cuyahoga County branch of the Progressive Constitutional League. The city's PCL sent letters to the city's labor, religious, civic, and business groups, asking that those willing to participate in the nomination of a slate of delegates pledged to the initiative and referendum send representatives to an organizational meeting. The CFL, committed as it was to direct legislation, sent representatives, who worked out an agreement that would allow the federation to name three of the slate's ten nominees in exchange for an explicit endorsement. Two weeks later, the Cleveland Federation of Labor named William Davio (lather), Thomas Farrell (waiter), and Stephen Stilwell (painters) to its three slots and gave the whole slate its official endorsement. The federation would later donate money to the PCL's campaign fund.[44]

Some of the CFL's Socialists criticized the federation's participation in the Progressive Constitutional League. In a front-page editorial in the *Citizen*, Max Hayes denounced the "nonpartisan" approach to the selection of delegates. "The contest for delegates to the Constitutional Convention will narrow itself down to a struggle for mastery between HUMAN RIGHTS versus PROPERTY RIGHTS," he said. For Hayes, those who were not workers and those who controlled property—like many on the PCL slate—simply should not be trusted; they would protect property rights before human rights. Despite the "nonpartisan" nature of the election, the Cleveland's Socialist party nominated a slate of delegates that included Harry Thomas, Max Hayes, and a number of other trade unionists. These delegates pledged to support the Socialist party's program for the constitutional convention, at the top of which was the initiative and referendum: "The majority of the people shall always have the right and the means to freely amend, alter, or abrogate all laws."[45]

While Cleveland laborites differed over how best to participate in the selection of delegates to the constitutional convention, there was little disagreement as to their priority. The carpenters who wanted to form the Referendum party, those who led the CFL into an alliance with the Progressive Constitutional League, the Socialists who denounced the CFL's approach, and even the few labor voices who spoke in favor of working with the Municipal Association all agreed that the initiative and referendum were the most important reforms needed. Direct legislation promised labor the means of enacting the rest of its agenda.

Shortly before the fall's election of delegates, the Ohio State Federation of Labor (OSFL) met in Cleveland for its annual convention. The convocation became a big pep rally for the initiative and referendum. According to the *Cleveland Citizen*, "The principal question before the convention was that of securing the adoption of the initiative, referendum, and recall at the coming Constitutional Convention, all other matters paling into insignificance." According to the convention's official platform, direct legislation was the only means by which workers could "drive from the thrones of power those who have so repeatedly and shamefully proven recreant to [the people's] trust." Officials reserved the most prominent speaking slot for Herbert Bigelow, who detailed the activities of the Progressive Constitutional League and reminded organized labor of the work that still needed to be done. Almost as an afterthought, the federation augmented its call for direct legislation with a broad-based set of demands that resembled those of the state's Populist party: home rule for cities, eight-hour days on public works, regulation of injunctions, prohibition of contract prison labor, child and female labor regulation, income and inheritance taxes, nonpartisan judicial elections, direct election of U.S. senators, workmen's compensation, and women's suffrage.[46]

The pre-election efforts of organized labor and its allies paid off. When the polls closed, voters had selected a majority of delegates pledged to support the PCL agenda. As Max Hayes pointed out in a *Citizen* editorial, "The fact that at least two-thirds [of the delegates] are classified as progressives assures the incorporation of labor's platform in the Constitution." OSFL official Thomas Donnelly would later boast that the labor's pre-election activities had allowed it and its allies to "secure control of the convention." The Ohio State Board of Commerce agreed with Hayes's and Donnelly's assessments, lamenting that "radicals, socialists, and members of labor unions voted their full strength, while conservatives neglected to vote."[47]

Labor was especially successful in the large cities. In Cleveland's Cuyahoga County, voters selected nine of the ten candidates on the PCL slate, including the three labor candidates (Davio, Farrell, and Stilwell), Robert Crosser, a disciple of the late Tom Johnson with whom labor had worked to secure the initiative and referendum for cities, and Thomas Fitzsimmons, an old ally of Cleveland's labor movement who had twice run for mayor on the Populist slate. The only non-PCL candidate selected was Harry Thomas, the OSFL secretary treasurer who had been endorsed by the Municipal Association but ran on the Socialist party slate.[48] In Cincinnati's Hamilton County and Columbus's Franklin County, UCC slates prevailed, sending trade unionists Halenkamp, Hoffman, Cordes, and Harberger to the convention. In all, 15 of the 119 delegates to the constitutional convention were trade unionists.[49]

The OSFL and trade unionists throughout the state adopted a two-pronged strategy to influence convention proceedings. First, the fifteen labor delegates formed a caucus to coordinate labor's voice at the convention. Under the leadership of Harry Thomas, the caucus—commonly called the "labor boys"—met on Monday afternoons, often with OSFL officials and other labor leaders.[50] Second, trade union leaders coordinated a campaign to lobby delegates. OSFL officials, working with representatives of the railroad brotherhoods and the UMWA, sent letters to all delegates outlining labor's program for the convention, met with individual delegates, and perhaps most important, kept local unions informed of the proceedings, urging them to deluge their delegates with letters, phone calls, and telegrams.[51]

The constitutional convention opened in Columbus on January 9, 1912. The first test of the progressives' strength involved the election of the convention president. The progressives, including all but one of the labor delegates, rallied behind Herbert Bigelow. The only labor delegate who did not vote for Bigelow was Harry Thomas, who for the first ten ballots followed his party's instructions and refused to vote for a non-Socialist candidate. Those opposed to Bigelow divided their support between three candidates: Caleb Norris, the choice of conservatives; D. F. Anderson, a labor-friendly candidate backed by the Anti-Saloon League; and Henry Elson, the "moderate" candidate. On the first ballot, Bigelow fell six votes shy of the sixty needed. Bigelow's support remained stable over the next nine ballots, while Anderson slowly picked up votes at the expense of Norris and Elson. Anderson's growing support prompted Thomas to break his pledge to the Socialist party. His vote along with those of several "wets" gave Bigelow enough to win on the eleventh ballot.[52]

The convention, with the support of labor and the leaders of the Progressive Constitutional League, decided that rather than rewriting the constitution from top to bottom it would propose a series of amendments to the existing constitution, which had been created in 1851. Each of these amendments would be submitted to the voters of Ohio, and those ratified by a majority vote would become part of the state's constitution. The leaders of the Progressive Constitutional League believed that such a tactic, giving the people an up or down vote on each issue, would ensure that direct legislation would not become entangled with other controversial issues like women's suffrage and prohibition. They feared that a proposed constitution loaded with many controversial issues might cause some voters to be sympathetic to the initiative and referendum to nonetheless vote in the negative. The convention's leaders were also mindful that in 1873 voters had turned down a new constitution, in part because of the length and complexity of the document.[53]

Bigelow's election led to immediate benefits for organized labor. He named eight trade unionists and half a dozen sympathizers to the labor committee, effectively giving the labor caucus the ability to write the employment amendments to be debated by the convention. Stephen Stilwell chaired the committee, which formulated amendments giving the general assembly explicit authority to write regulations requiring eight-hour days for public workers, prohibiting prison contract labor, making the workmen's compensation program compulsory, banning the use of coal screens, providing for mechanics' and builders' liens, and most important, regulating hours, wages, and working conditions of all workers. If such amendments were ratified, they would undercut the basis for nearly all of the Ohio Supreme Court decisions nullifying labor legislation.[54]

The only labor measure to meet serious opposition on the floor was one allowing the general assembly to prohibit prison contract labor. Rural delegates argued that such a measure would force prisons to put inmates to work growing their own food, a move that would deprive farmers of the opportunity to sell their produce to the prisons. In the end labor and its allies overcame this opposition, and the prison labor amendment joined the rest of the committee proposals on the ballot.[55]

The labor caucus spent most of its energy on the direct legislation proposal. Bigelow relied on Crosser, chairman of the convention's initiative and referendum committee, to shape the particulars of the proposal and guide it through the convention. Despite pledges from a majority of delegates to support direct legislation, Crosser's tasks were not easy. As he quickly found out, "While there are many who avow themselves to be believers in the initiative and referendum, there are not so many who are enthusiastic about it." Knowing that some type of direct legislation proposal would make its way out of the convention, opponents turned their attention to making the proposal as weak as possible.[56]

Opponents made little headway with the initiative and referendum committee, which Bigelow had stacked with supporters of direct legislation. The committee's proposal would require petitions signed by eighty thousand electors to place a constitutional amendment on the ballot, sixty thousand electors for regular law, and fifty thousand to have a referendum on a legislative act. Supporters and detractors alike called the plan "radical." No other state in the union had enacted a law giving so much power to the people.[57]

On the floor of the convention, opponents offered amendments to the proposal to limit the types of legislation subject to initiative and referendum, ensure that initiatives would go to the general assembly before going to the people, forbid the recall of judges, require a geographic distribution of petitioners, and increase the number of signatures required on petitions.[58] Opponents even circulated fake petitions among trade unionists. As the *Toledo*

Union Leader complained, "The scheme is an old one—to circulate petitions approving of such high percentages for the I&R to make it unworkable."[59]

After the proposal's second reading on the convention's floor, delegates watered it down, increasing the number of petitions that needed to be signed to send an issue before voters. Trade union officials promptly sprang into action. The OSFL, working with the railroad brotherhoods and the UMWA, quickly put out a thirteen-by-twenty-two-inch broadside that emphasized the broad support direct legislation and the PCL had received during the election of delegates. More important, the broadside questioned the motives and tactics used by those watering down the proposal and called the changes ill conceived. The broadside noted that the committee had spent six weeks studying and formulating the original proposal but that opponents had "introduced and passed [a new version] within an hour."[60] State federation leaders also worked with local labor bodies to apply pressure to delegates. The Columbus Federation of Labor, for instance, passed a resolution calling on Franklin County delegates to support an initiative and referendum with low petition requirements and few restrictions on the ability of the people to formulate their own legislation.[61]

In the end, delegates forged a compromise that made labor happy. If 3 percent of the number of voters in the previous gubernatorial election signed a petition proposing a law, that proposal should be considered by the general assembly. If the general assembly did not act or passed a different version of the bill, supporters of the original proposal could place it directly before the voters by submitting petitions of an additional 3 percent of the voters. Constitutional amendments could be placed directly before the voters by obtaining signatures from 10 percent of the voters, and electors could force a referendum on a regular bill by gathering the signatures of 6 percent of the voters. The final compromise also forbade the use of the initiative to introduce a single tax. Support for the single tax ran high in Ohio's labor movement, and the labor caucus worked against the ban, but in the end labor acceded to its inclusion, insisting that it could be eliminated later through an initiative amending the initiative and referendum procedures.[62]

The rest of the convention went labor's way, with amendments fulfilling much of the Populist agenda—limits on judicial review and labor injunctions, women's suffrage, municipal home rule. In many ways, labor considered these reforms to be just as important as those that came out of the labor committee. Limiting judicial review would make it more difficult for the state supreme court to declare labor legislation unconstitutional. Women's suffrage would increase the number of wage workers with the right to vote. Home rule would allow for municipal ownership of utilities and cities to require eight-hour days on public works. Curtailing labor injunctions would strip employers of a powerful weapon used against strikers and their leaders.

In all, the convention produced forty-two amendments to be submitted to the voters, and labor sung the praises of the convention's efforts. The *Toledo Union Leader* declared, "The Constitution . . . contains practically every demand made by the Ohio Federation of Labor" and had "provisions within itself [the initiative and referendum] to remedy all defects—the power is placed in the hands of the people."[63]

Soon after the convention adjourned, the OSFL convened a meeting of seventy-five of the state's most influential labor leaders to meet with Bigelow to plot strategy for the ratification campaign. The federation appointed one person in every county to coordinate labor's activities and work with other progressive groups. This person was to form a committee that would schedule speakers, distribute literature to trade unionists, work with other progressive groups, and convince ministers and priests to use the Sunday before the election to educate their parishioners. The federation also created a special campaign committee—headed by Thomas Donnelly, the former Populist candidate for Congress—that arranged for the printing of literature to be distributed to trade unionists, organized a speaking tour for Harry Thomas, Stephen Stilwell, and other labor delegates to the convention, and helped local unions stage campaign rallies.[64] Harry Thomas wrote a series of articles for union newspapers explaining, in layman's terms, each of the amendments supported by labor.[65]

The OSFL's campaign plan relied mostly on the work of local organizations. In Columbus, for instance, the Columbus Federation of Labor took the lead, forming a local campaign committee and distributing PCL literature to "every home in every precinct" in the city. The literature was designed to be informational, explaining the amendments in layman's language without comment or persuasive effort. Labor reasoned that the necessity of the amendments would be readily apparent to informed voters. The campaign committee also secured speakers to put into the field, worked with like-minded community groups, lobbied religious leaders to use their pulpits in support of the campaign, and organized voter informational activities for the annual Labor Day celebration.[66]

During the campaign, trade unionists emphasized the initiative and referendum more than any other issue. An editorial in the *Toledo Union Leader* declared, "For years we have protested against court usurpation, judicial tyranny and the failure of legislatures to hearken to workers' pleas. If the new constitution is adopted, we will place weapons in our hands that will remedy these ills." In an *American Federationist* editorial devoted to the upcoming ratification vote, Samuel Gompers mentioned the initiative and referendum proposal first and last. For him, direct legislation would provide the means for the people to "freely register their will and hold their legislative, administrative, and judicial agents responsible." Harry Thomas wrote, "Real representative government can only be restored by the Initiative and Referendum, which compels our legislatures to represent the wishes and interests of all people, instead of those of the privileged class."[67]

The OSFL, in cooperation with the railroad brotherhoods and the UMWA, printed over 250,000 pieces of literature and sent over 5,000 circular letters to local unions. The most circulated pieces of literature were three-by-five-inch cards with "The New Emancipation" written in large bright red block letters at the top. The message on the rest of the card varied. Some cards emphasized the initiative and referendum, and others the labor amendments. But every card concluded by calling on workers to vote for all forty-two amendments.[68] The federation spent so much money during the campaign that it had to levy a special assessment on locals.[69]

Laborites were not the only ones campaigning for the ratification of the amendments. Bigelow organized a speakers' bureau that coordinated the engagements of many prominent supporters and convention delegates so that they were sure to cover the whole state. Bigelow's speakers each spent three or four weeks on the road giving three or four talks a day. Cleveland mayor Newton Baker, for instance, was so busy working for ratification of the amendments that he delayed hitting the presidential campaign trail on behalf of his close friend and mentor Woodrow Wilson.[70]

Business groups launched a massive campaign to defeat all of the amendments, but especially the initiative and referendum and labor amendments. As one observer noted, "Every ruse and trick known to Big Business politicians was employed to frighten the people of Ohio from adopting the I&R. The whole corporate power of the state backed by Wall Street money and influence was thrown into the fight."[71] Leading this fight was Allen Ripley Foote, president of the Ohio State Board of Commerce. According to historian Hoyt Landon Warner, Foote first tried to "deluge the rural press with boiler plate crassly attacking the work of the convention," but editors refused to print much of the material because it was patently false. The Ohio State Board of Commerce then distributed pamphlets and circulars financed largely by utility interests.[72] Foote called the amendment to allow the general assembly to regulate hours, wages, and working conditions "a radical and arbitrary attempt to lay a foundation for a socialistic system of government." Most of Foote's bile, though, was reserved for the initiative and referendum, which he said would ruin representative government, threaten the sanctity of all private property including the home and hearth, and destroy the state's industrial prosperity. Ohio State Board of Commerce pamphlets even attacked the women's suffrage amendment: "Those in sympathy with or interested in the propaganda of the labor unions, socialists, and other radicals are supporting [women's suffrage] . . . so that the votes of women may be used for legislating by initiative and referendum."[73]

Despite the campaign of Foote and the Ohio State Board of Commerce, the OSFL was confident of success and began planning for political life under the new constitution. In August 1912, a full three weeks before the ratification election, the federation issued a call for a special labor convention to meet in October: "Ohio will have adopted a progressive constitution by the time that the convention meets, the IR goes into effect October 1 [and] home rule for cities in November." At the top of labor's post-ratification agenda was the need to elect a sympathetic governor and legislature who would enact laws conforming to the new constitution— minimum wage and hours laws, a compulsory workmen's compensation, eight-hour day for public works, and so on.[74]

The convention selected the Tuesday after Labor Day as the date for the special election to ratify the amendments. Convention secretary C. B. Galbreath insisted that the selection of that date was "not accidental." Convention managers were sure that workers would overwhelmingly support the convention's efforts, and that date "afforded the opportunity . . . to make a final appeal to the working men and their friends not to fail to come forth and vote on behalf of their cause."[75] Labor did not disappoint progressives like Galbreath. The OSFL asked local bodies to make the campaign the centerpiece of Labor Day celebrations.[76] In Toledo, the CLU invited Congressman James B. Cox, the Democratic gubernatorial nominee and vocal supporter of the proposed amendments, to speak at its annual picnic.[77] The Cleveland Federation of Labor hosted Simeon Fess, the constitutional convention's vice president.[78] Samuel Gompers spoke at Columbus's Labor Day festivities, telling the crowd of three thousand that the proposed labor amendments, the initiative and referendum, and women's suffrage provided the greatest opportunity for improvement that workers had ever had. He ended his talk by repeating the mantra of the state's progressives, "When in doubt, vote yes."[79]

When the votes were finally counted, labor had won a stunning victory. Thirty-four of the forty-two amendments were ratified. The amendments limiting injunctions and providing for women's suffrage were the only two deemed crucial to labor that went down to defeat. The OSFL executive board boasted that Ohio now had "the most progressive constitution among the states of the union."[80] The reform effort started during the Populist era was now complete.

Labor's success in the 1912 special election called to ratify the constitutional amendments carried over to the general election two months later. Voters elected the most pro-labor general assembly in the state's history and sent James Cox into the governor's office by a landslide. Twenty-three trade unionists served in the general assembly where they helped pass twenty-two bills endorsed by labor, including ones forbidding coal screens, establishing a nine-hour day for women, and reforming prison labor. The most important of these measures provided for compulsory workers' compensation and the creation of the Ohio Industrial Commission (OIC). Although the OIC's primary function was to oversee the compensation system (setting rates based on the danger of the occupation, adjudicating disputes, and keeping the books), it was also charged with establishing workplace safety rules, providing arbitration and conciliation services, setting up state employment agencies, and investigating unemployment issues.[81]

Since many of the new laws were in areas in which the new constitutional amendments had explicitly given the general assembly the power to legislate, there was little chance that the Ohio Supreme Court would invoke the doctrine of liberty of contract, which it had previously declared was implicit within the state's organic law, to overturn them. Besides, one of the new amendments had greatly restricted the ability of the court to declare such laws unconstitutional, in most cases requiring a super majority of justices to overturn legislative acts.

Trade unionists considered these reforms to be just the beginning. The referendum promised to remove corruption from the general assembly, and the initiative had placed within their hands the means to go directly to the people for needed legislation. Convinced that voters would reflexively recognize that labor's demands would promote the common good, trade unionists never doubted that direct legislation would serve as a counterweight to corporate power nor could they envision that businesses with deep pockets might avail themselves of direct legislation.

Additionally, the state's cities were now free from the general assembly's control. Passage of the municipal home rule amendment allowed cities to determine their own forms of government. Most important, home rule opened the way for government ownership of street railways, gas and electric companies, and other public utilities and allowed cities to pass ordinances regulating industrial relations—one of the key demands that pushed urban labor federations into an alliance with the People's party. In city after city, labor took prominent roles in the drafting of new municipal charters, ones that freed the cities to pursue the type of gas and sewer socialism that had been so important during the Populist campaigns.[82]

Conclusion

IN SEPTEMBER 1894, Jacob Coxey stood on the steps of the Ohio Statehouse in Columbus to celebrate the consummation of the state's labor–Populist alliance. He reminded the eight thousand to twelve thousand people gathered of the troubles afflicting the nation in the wake of the Panic of 1893: "There is an army of between 4,000,000 and 5,000,000 unemployed. Twenty million [the unemployed plus their families] have stopped eating the wheat raised by the farmer, and the farmer wants to know the reason that he cannot sell wheat. The laborer is thrown out of work because his employer has no money to pay him, and the latter cannot buy the farmer's wheat because he has not money with which to purchase it." Coxey declared that his non-interest-bearing-bond plan could help solve these troubles. The national government would issue bonds to states, counties, or cities to be used to pay for road construction and other internal improvements. Not only would the bonds circulate as greenbacks, increasing the money supply, the plan would also put people back to work. "Give employment to the people," Coxey concluded, "and they will consume the products and raise the prices," putting the nation on the path to prosperity.[1]

Although in 1894 the leaders of both major parties dismissed Coxey as a crank and his plan as heretical, forty years later, in the midst of an even worse economic downturn, his ideas would not seem so far-fetched or unorthodox. Franklin Roosevelt's New Deal provided large amounts of money to state and local governments to build roads, libraries, schools, courthouses,

and other public facilities. The purpose was not only to provide work to
the unemployed but also to inject much needed cash into the economy.
Those given work would consume, spending their wages on food, clothing,
automobiles, and other consumer goods. This increased demand, in turn,
would put others back to work, increasing further both demand and wages
and reversing the vicious cycle of economic depression.[2] Although Coxey
never uttered phrases like "counter-cyclical spending" or insisted that the
national government assume the responsibility for promoting mass con-
sumption, those ideas were a part of what he and Ohio's labor-Populists
were trying to accomplish. Ohio trade unionists rejected the laissez faire
orthodoxy of the late nineteenth century and called for an expansion of
government activity: regulation or public ownership of monopolies, elimination of the private banking system and the expansion of the money supply, public works with preference for union labor, the eight-hour day and
enforcement of health and safety regulations, and municipal ownership of
public utilities. They also called for reforms to cleanse the nation's political
system, most importantly direct legislation and women's suffrage.

Although there were a few exceptions, especially government ownership
of railroads, telephones, telegraphs, and mines, nearly all of the things on
the agenda of Ohio's labor-Populists were won during the Progressive and
New Deal eras. Rather than holding anti-modern ideals or hoping to re-
create a simpler economic time, Ohio's labor-Populists sought to reconcile
their needs with modern industry and production methods and helped foster the reforms that are associated with modern America. The trade unionists had faith in progress and urban life but wanted to make these things
work to their benefit.[3]

This book—when it gets right down to it—is about the centrality of the
labor movement to the American reform tradition. Urban trade unionists
did not—as much of the current historiography suggests—ignore the Populist movement, the last serious producerist challenge to the emergence of
corporate capitalism, or sit passively by as corporate elites or agrarians remade the government during the Progressive era. After the events of 1894,
urban and state labor federations throughout the nation, but especially in
Ohio and the Industrial Midwest, turned to the People's party for salvation. Trade union leaders saw within the People's party's Omaha platform
the type of reforms that they thought would revitalize the nation. But the
leaders of the People's party, fearing that labor's presence would taint the
party with radicalism and push it further from the American mainstream,
took steps to drive the trade unionists out of the party. These steps, including the emphasis on the free coinage of silver and the abandonment of the

Omaha platform, helped make the fusion of 1896 possible, contributing to the collapse of the party.

The end of the People's party did not transform the thinking of the state's trade unionists. Pure and simple unionism—with an emphasis on "more," an unwillingness to contest the legitimacy of corporations, and the privileging of economic tools over political ones in confrontations with capital—never took hold in Ohio. Nor did the state's urban trade unionists adopt the type of liberalism associated with the National Civic Federation, remaining deeply suspicious of business leaders like Mark Hanna, who the Cleveland Central Labor Union crowned the "King of Labor Crushers."[4] Ohio trade unionists remained wedded to producerist and republican ideals, even though they could not agree as to which political party best embodied those values. The labor federations in Cleveland and Columbus embraced the Socialist party, and the one in Cincinnati found itself in a local, class-based coalition with George "Boss" Cox's Republican machine. Those members of the middle class who the labor movement did work with— men such as Tom L. Johnson, Herbert Bigelow, and Samuel "Golden Rule" Jones—came out of producerist and anti-monopoly traditions, especially the single-tax and Bellamy nationalist movements.

Although the state's trade unionists could not agree on a party around which to coalesce after 1896, they did join together in the fight to enact the initiative, referendum, and recall. Direct legislation appealed to trade union leaders because it did not require members to give up their partisan allegiances and provided the labor movement with the means of fulfilling its agenda and ending the corruption undermining republican institutions. The campaign to enact direct legislation formed the core of the state's Progressive movement, bringing the Socialist-led Ohio State Federation of Labor into an alliance with the Bryan wing of the Democratic party. This alliance paid off at the constitutional convention of 1912, where the labor movement and its allies rewrote the Ohio Constitution along Populist lines, giving the state what Max Hayes called, "the greatest triumph that was ever secured by the laboring class in any state on the American continent, or perhaps, any country in the whole world."[5]

Notes

Introduction

1. *United Mine Workers Journal* (Columbus), August 9, 1894. Also see *Ohio State Journal* (Columbus), August 3, 4, 1894.

2. *United Mine Workers Journal*, August 9 (quotation), *Ohio State Journal*, August 3, 4, *Columbus Post-Press*, August 2, 3, *Columbus Dispatch*, August 3, 1894.

3. *Cleveland Citizen*, August 25, 1894.

4. Ibid. See also *Ohio State Journal*, August 15–17, *Columbus Dispatch*, August 16, 17, *Ohio State Journal*, August 16, 17, *United Mine Workers Journal*, August 23, 1894.

5. Martin J. Klotsche, "The 'United Front' Populists," *Wisconsin Magazine of History* 20 (1937): 375–89; Roger E. Wyman, "Agrarian or Working-class Radicalism? The Electoral Basis of Populism in Wisconsin," *Political Science Quarterly* 89 (Winter 1974–1975): 825–47; Chester McArthur Destler, "Consummation of a Labor-Populist Alliance in Illinois," in *American Radicalism, 1865–1901* (Reprint, Chicago: Quadrangle Books, 1966), 162–74; Chester McArthur Destler, "The Labor-Populist Alliance of Illinois in the Election of 1894," in *American Radicalism*, 175–211; Chester McArthur Destler, "Free Silver vs. Collectivism: Disintegration of the Labor-Populist Alliance in Illinois," in *American Radicalism*, 222–54; Nick Salvatore, *Eugene V. Debs: Citizen and Socialist* (Urbana: University of Illinois Press, 1982), 147–60; Irwin Marcus, Jennie Bullard, and Rob Moore, "Change and Continuity: Steel Workers in Homestead, Pennsylvania, 1889–1895," *Pennsylvania Magazine of History and Biography* 111 (Spring 1987): 61–75; John Brophy, *A Miner's Life: An Autobiography* (Madison: University of Wisconsin Press, 1964), 25–26; Michael Nash, *Conflict and Accommodation: Coal Miners, Steel Workers, and Socialism, 1890–1920* (Westport, CT: Greenwood Press, 1982); Richard Jules Oestreicher, *Solidarity and Fragmentation: Working People and Class Consciousness in Detroit, 1875–1900* (Urbana: University of Illinois Press, 1986), 242.

6. *National Labor Tribune* (Pittsburgh, PA), January 10 (first quotation), October 31 (last quotation), *Cleveland Citizen*, November 16, 1895. Also see *New York Times*, January 2, 1895. The term "independent political action" was in wide circulation among trade unionists in the 1890s, but it never had a precise meaning. For some, like McBride and the editors of the *Cleveland Citizen*, it entailed partisan action independent of the two traditional parties and became synonymous with Populism, but for others it simply meant nonpartisan political action.

7. Steven Ross, *Workers on the Edge: Work, Leisure, and Politics in Industrializing Cincinnati, 1788–1890* (New York: Columbia University Press, 1985); Zane L. Miller,

Boss Cox's Cincinnati: Urban Politics in the Progressive Era (New York: Oxford University Press, 1968), 14; Carol Poh Miller and Robert A. Wheeler, *Cleveland: A Concise History, 1796–1996* (Bloomington: Indiana University Press, 1997), 77–99; Henry L. Hunker, *Industrial Evolution of Columbus, Ohio* (Columbus: Bureau of Business Research, College of Commerce and Administration, Ohio State University, 1958).

8. On labor republicanism, see Sean Wilentz, *Chants Democratic: New York City and the Rise of the American Working Class, 1788–1850* (New York: Oxford University Press, 1984), 237–48.

9. John McBride, "Producers vs. Non-Producers," *American Federationist* 2 (October 1895): 145. McBride's 1895 editorial was a condensed version of a speech that he gave on quite a few occasions. For the full speech, see *United Mine Workers Journal*, September 10, 1891.

10. "A Manifesto to the Citizens of Hamilton County in General, and the Labor and Reform Organizations in Particular," broadside taped into Cincinnati Central Labor Council minute books, August 22, 1894, Special Collections Division, University of Cincinnati Library (hereafter cited as CLC minute books); "The Omaha Platform," in *A Populist Reader: Selections from the Works of American Populist Leaders*, ed. George Brown Tindall (New York: Harper and Row, 1966), 90–96.

11. For more on the ways that Populists recognized the benefits of industrialization and adapted their ideas accordingly, see Charles Postel, *The Populist Vision* (New York: Oxford University Press, 2007).

12. The Ohio People's party platform is reprinted in *United Mine Workers Journal*, August 23, *Columbus Post-Press*, August 16, *Columbus Dispatch*, August 16, *Ohio State Journal*, August 16, 1894.

13. *Cleveland Citizen*, August 25, 1894.

14. Ibid., October 27, 1894.

15. John D. Hicks, *The Populist Revolt: A History of the Farmers' Alliance and the People's Party* (Minneapolis: University of Minnesota Press, 1931, 1946; reprint, Lincoln: University of Nebraska Press, 1961), 115; Samuel Gompers, "Organized Labor in the Campaign," *North American Review* 155 (July 1892): 93. See also Richard Hofstadter, *The Age of Reform: From Bryan to FDR* (New York: Alfred A. Knopf, 1955), 99. Ironically, Gompers voted for both men that the People's party nominated for president—James Weaver in 1892 and William Jennings Bryan four years later; Samuel Gompers and Florence Calvert Thorne, *Seventy Years of Life and Labor: An Autobiography*, 2 vols. (New York: Dutton, 1925), 1:25. Destler, in *American Radicalism*, is the only prominent historian of Populism who has insisted that there was significant labor support for the People's party.

16. Lawrence Goodwyn, *The Democratic Promise: The Populist Moment in America* (New York: Oxford University Press, 1976), 141, 308; Norman Pollack, *The Populist Response to Industrial America: Midwestern Populist Thought* (1962; reprint, New York: W. W. Norton, 1966), 64–65.

17. Jeffrey Ostler, *Prairie Populism: The Fate of Agrarian Radicalism in Kansas, Nebraska, and Iowa, 1880–1892* (Lawrence: University Press of Kansas, 1993).

18. Klotsche, "'United Front' Populists"; Wyman, "Agrarian or Working-class Radicalism?"; Destler, *American Radicalism*, 162–211, 222–54. There was also significant labor support for the People's party in those areas traditionally associated with the Populist movement. See, for example, Matthew Hild, *Greenbackers, Knights of Labor & Populists: Farmer-Labor Insurgency in the Late-Nineteenth-Century South* (Athens: University of Georgia Press, 2008); Thomas A. Clinch, *Urban Populism and Free Silver in Montana* (Missoula: University of Montana Press, 1970); James Edward Wright, *The Politics of Populism: Dissent in Colorado* (New Haven, CT: Yale University Press, 1974); Alicia Ester Rodriquez, "Urban Populism: Challenges to Democratic Party Control in Dallas, Texas,

1887–1900" (PhD diss., University of California at Santa Barbara, 1999); Michael Kazin, *Barons of Labor: The San Francisco Building Trades and Union Power in the Progressive Era* (Urbana: University of Illinois Press, 1987), 16; William Issell and Robert W. Cherney, *San Francisco, 1865–1932: Politics, Power, and Urban Development* (Berkeley and Los Angeles: University of California Press, 1986), 135; Eli Goldschmidt, "Labor and Populism: New York City, 1891–1896," *Labor History* 13 (Fall 1972): 520–32.

19. Phillip Taft, *The American Federation of Labor in the Time of Gompers* (New York: Harper and Brothers, 1957); *Chicago Tribune*, December 9, 1895. See also Stuart B. Kaufman, *Samuel Gompers and the Origins of the American Federation of Labor, 1848–1896* (Westport, CT: Greenwood Press, 1973); Bruce Laurie, *Artisans into Workers: Labor in Nineteenth-Century America* (1989; reprint, Urbana: University of Illinois Press, 1997), 176–92.

20. Samuel Gompers, *The Samuel Gompers Papers*, ed. Stuart B. Kaufman, Peter J. Albert, and Grace Palladino, vol. 4, *A National Labor Movement Takes Shape, 1895–1898* (Urbana: University of Illinois Press, 1991), 7. Not knowing how to deal with McBride, many historians just ignore his year in office and act as if it carries no significance. For instance, Rosanne Currarino cites an October 1895 speech by Samuel Gompers as evidence that "the AFL leadership did not call for an end to wage labor." Currarino, "The Politics of 'More': The Labor Question and the Idea of Economic Liberty in Industrial America," *Journal of American History* 93 (June 2006): 17. But the same month that Gompers's speech appeared, AFL president McBride used the pages of the *American Federationist* to call for the "collective ownership by the people of all such means of production" as they may elect to operate. McBride, "Producers vs. Non-Producers," 145.

21. Currarino, "Politics of 'More,'" 17.

22. The two competing factions and their visions are best described in Victoria C. Hattam, *Labor Visions and State Power: The Origins of Business Unionism in the United States* (Princeton, NJ: Princeton University Press, 1993). Also see Laurie, *Artisans into Workers*, 176–210; Kaufman, *Samuel Gompers and the Origins of the AFL*, 147–222.

23. Hattam, *Labor Visions and State Power*; William Forbath, *Law and the Shaping of the American Labor Movement* (Cambridge, MA: Harvard University Press, 1991); Kim Voss, *The Making of American Exceptionalism: The Knights of Labor and Class Formation in the Nineteenth Century* (Cornell: Cornell University Press, 1993), 12.

24. *Proceedings of the Annual Convention of the American Federation of Labor* (hereafter *AFL Proceedings*), 1896.

25. Leon Fink, *Workingman's Democracy: The Knights of Labor and American Politics* (Urbana: University of Illinois Press, 1983); Goodwyn, *The Democratic Promise;* Gabriel Kolko, *The Triumph of Conservatism, 1900–1916* (Glencoe, IL: Free Press, 1963); James Weinstein, *The Corporate Ideal and the Liberal State, 1900–1918* (Boston, MA: Beacon Press, 1968); J. Morgan Kousser, *The Shaping of Southern Politics: Suffrage Reform and the Establishment of the One-Party South* (New Haven, CT: Yale University Press, 1974).

26. Elizabeth Sanders, *Roots of Reform: Farmers, Workers, and the American State, 1877–1917* (Chicago: University of Chicago Press, 1999); Robert D. Johnston, *The Radical Middle Class: Populist Democracy and the Question of Capitalism in Progressive Era Portland* (Princeton, NJ: Princeton University Press, 2003); Robert D. Johnston, "Re-democratizing the Progressive Era: The Politics of Progressive Era Historiography," *Journal of the Gilded Age and Progressive Era* 1 (January 2002): 68–92.

27. Julie Greene, *Pure and Simple Politics: The American Federation of Labor and Political Activism, 1881–1917* (Cambridge, UK: Cambridge University Press, 1998); Richard Schneirov, *Labor and Urban Politics: Class Conflict and the Origins of Modern Liberalism in Chicago, 1864–1897* (Urbana: University of Illinois Press, 1998); Richard Schneirov, "Labor and the New Liberalism in the Wake of the Pullman Strike," in Richard Schneirov, Shelton Stromquist, and Nick Salvatore, eds., *The Pullman Strike and the Crisis of the*

1890s: Essays on Labor and Politics (Urbana: University of Illinois Press, 1999), 204–32. Greene's work informs much of the interpretation here. She contends that pure and simple unionism triumphed not because it reflected the thinking of the nation's workers but because it was the only philosophy that could take into account the diversity of political opinion among the nation's trade unionists. On the labor movement's role in Progressive era reforms, also see Shelton Stromquist, "The Crisis of the 1890s and the Legacies of Producerism," in Schneirov, Stromquist, and Salvatore, *Crisis of the 1890s*, 179–203; Stromquist, "The Crucible of Class: Cleveland Politics and the Origins of Municipal Reform in the Progressive Era," *Journal of Urban History* 23 (January 1997): 192–220; Currarino, "Politics of 'More.'"

28. Tom L. Johnson, *My Story* (New York: B. W. Huebsch, 1911), 201. Of Ohio trade unionists only those in the UMWA embraced NCF-style reform. UMWA president Michael Ratchford and his protégé John Mitchell were especially close to Hanna, and the union benefited from its association with the NCF; Craig Phelan, *Divided Loyalties: The Public and Private Life of Labor Leader John Mitchell* (Albany: State University of New York Press, 1994).

29. C. L. Martzolff, "Recent Ohio Legislation Conforming to the Demands of the New Constitution," *American Political Science Review* 7 (November 1913): 639.

1—Organized Labor in Ohio Politics

1. *Columbus Dispatch*, July 23 (quotation), *Ohio State Journal* (Columbus), July 23, 1877; *Annual Report of the Ohio Bureau of Labor Statistics, 1877*, 289, 297. The unfolding of the 1877 railroad strike in Columbus—and in Ohio more generally—is briefly summarized in Robert V. Bruce, *1877: Year of Violence* (Indianapolis, IN: Bobbs-Merrill, 1959), 206–7; Jeremy Brecher, *Strike!* (1972; reprint, Boston, MA: South End Press, 1977), 14–16; J. A. Dacus, *Annals of the Great Strikes in the United States* (Chicago: L. T. Palmer & Co., 1877), 272–88.

2. *Columbus Dispatch*, July 23, *Ohio State Journal* (Columbus), July 23, 1877. A similar mass protest broke out some fifty miles east of Columbus in Zanesville on the same day. In Zanesville, though, the crowd targeted all manufacturing establishments rather than just the largest; Bruce, *1877*, 206; Dacus, *Annals of the Great Strikes*, 277.

3. David Montgomery, *Fall of the House of Labor: The Workplace, the State, and American Labor Activism, 1865–1925* (New York: Cambridge University Press, 1987), 9–13.

4. John Jarrett, "The Story of the Iron Workers," in *The Labor Movement: The Problem of To-Day*, ed. George E. McNeill (Boston, MA: A. M. Bridgeman and Company, 1887), 273; Lodge No. 11, Rollers, Roughers, Catchers and Hookers Union minute book, July 20, 1874, in the William Martin Papers, Darlington Memorial Library, University of Pittsburgh, PA. The ironworkers at the Columbus Rolling Mill had been at the forefront of the formation of the Amalgamated Association of Iron and Steel Workers. In the early 1870s, the nation's ironworkers were organized into four distinct craft unions (Roll Hands' Union, Heaters Association, Boilers' Union, and Sons of Vulcan), but in the fall of 1873 the three unions operating at the Columbus mill joined forces and began acting as one under the leadership of Plant. Soon thereafter, Plant, in his capacity as national president of the Roll Hands' Union, opened talks with the other three national unions that led to the formation of the Amalgamated Association of Iron and Steel Workers in August 1876. Plant would serve on the board of the new union, and Martin, who had been secretary of the Iron and Steel Roll Hands' Union, would later serve as secretary of the new union and first vice president of the AFL. "A Brief History of the Amalgamated Association of Iron and Steel Workers of the United States," in *Souvenir of the Eleventh Annual Reunion of the Amalgamated Association of the Iron and Steel Workers, Saturday June*

7th, 1890 (Pittsburgh, PA: Amalgamated Association of Iron and Steel Workers, 1890), 6–10; John Fitch, *The Steel Workers* (New York: Russell Sage Foundation, 1911), 84–87.

5. *Columbus Dispatch*, July 24, *Ohio State Journal*, July 25, 1877.

6. Gompers with Thorne, *Seventy Years of Life and Labor*, 48.

7. *Annual Report of the Ohio Bureau of Labor Statistics, 1877*, 12, 32.

8. Herbert Gutman, "The Labor Policies of the Large Corporation in the Gilded Age: The Case of the Standard Oil Company," in *Power and Culture: Essays on the American Working Class*, ed. Ira Berlin (New York: New Press, 1987), 213–54.

9. For municipal services and utilities, see, for example, Johnson, *My Story*, 114; Herbert Croly, *Marcus Alonzo Hanna: His Life and Work* (New York: Macmillan, 1923), 80–81; Miller, *Boss Cox's Cincinnati*, 57–110. For contractors, see, for example, Allen O. Myers, *Bosses and Boodle in Ohio Politics: Some Plain Truths for Honest People* (Cincinnati: Lyceum Publishing Co., 1895). For businesses, see, for example, Allan Nevins, *Study in Power: John D. Rockefeller, Industrialist and Philanthropist*, 2 vols. (New York: Charles Scribner's, 1953), 2:467–76; John Patterson Green, *Fact Stranger than Fiction: Seventy-five Years of a Busy Life with Reminiscences of Many Great and Good Men and Women* (Cleveland: Riehl, 1920), 196–97.

10. The episode is recounted in Henry Demarest Lloyd, *Wealth against Commonwealth* (1894; reprint, Englewood Cliffs, NJ: Prentice Hall, 1963), 129–36; Ida M. Tarbell, *The History of the Standard Oil Company*, 2 vols. (New York: Macmillan, 1925), 2:111–19. For an interpretation that absolves Standard Oil and John D. Rockefeller of any connection with Oliver Payne's scheme, see Nevins, *Study in Power*, 2:331–33, 469.

11. Ross, *Workers on the Edge*, 221.

12. Eugene H. Roseboom, *The Civil War Era, 1850–1873* (Columbus: Ohio State Archaeological and Historical Society, 1944), 24–26; Jon C. Teaford, *Cities in the Heartland: The Rise and Fall of the Industrial Midwest* (Bloomington: University of Indiana Press, 1993), 52.

13. Gutman, "Labor Policies of the Large Corporation," 214–17.

14. *Cleveland Leader*, October 10, 1873; Ross, *Workers on the Edge*, 16.

15. Derived from U.S. Bureau of the Census data. Historic Census Browser, University of Virginia Library, http://fisher.lib.virginia.edu/collections/stats/histcensus/ (accessed January 8, 2006).

16. Ross, *Workers on the Edge*, 221; M. A. Foran, *The Other Side: A Social Study Based on Fact* (Washington, DC: Gray & Clarkson, 1886), viii.

17. *Columbus Dispatch*, December 11, 1886.

18. Michael Pierce, "Martin Foran and the Creation of Cleveland's Labor Movement," in Warren Van Tine and Michael Pierce, eds., *Builders of Ohio: A Biographical History* (Columbus: Ohio State University Press, 2003), 173–75.

19. Peter Witt, "History of the Labor Movement in Cleveland," *Cleveland Recorder*, September 5, 1897, 11.

20. *Ohio State Journal*, April 14, June 26, 1884.

21. Ibid.; *Proceedings of the Ohio State Federation of Labor, 1928*, 14–15; *Columbus Dispatch*, June 25, 26, 1884.

22. John McBride, "The Democratic Party, the Party of the Workingman" (n.p., 1885). Also see, John McBride, "The Best of All Yet!" (n.p., 1884).

23. Paul Kleppner, *The Cross of Culture: A Social Analysis of Midwestern Politics* (New York: Free Press, 1970); McBride, "Democratic Party"; *Stark County Democrat* (Canton, Ohio), October 28, 1886; Ross, *Workers on the Edge*, 274 (Haley Bill); Lindley D. Clark, "Labor Laws that Have Been Declared Unconstitutional," *Bulletin of the United States Bureau of Labor Statistics* 321 (1922), 51.

24. *Wheeling and Terminal Railway Company v. Gilmore*, 8 Ohio C.C. 658 (1894); *Cincinnati Chronicle*, December 1892, May 1893; *L.W. Davis v. The State of Ohio* 30 Ohio

Weekly Law Bulletin 342; *National Labor Tribune*, June 21, 1894; *Arnold v. Yanders* 56 Ohio St. 417 (1897).

25. Cincinnati trade unionists, though, led by the Knights of Labor, formed a local branch of the United Labor party in the wake of the 1886 eight-hour-day strikes and increasing class tensions in the city. The party came close to capturing the municipal government but did not expand much beyond the southwestern part of the state. By 1888 Cincinnati trade unionists had recommitted themselves to nonpartisan political action. Ross, *Workers on the Edge.*

26. Witt, "Labor Movement in Cleveland," 10; Jean Y. Tussey, *An Introduction to the History of the Cleveland Labor Movement, 1865–1929* (Cleveland: United Labor Agency, AFL-CIO, 1996), 6; *Columbus Dispatch*, July 24, September 14, *Ohio State Journal*, July 25, 1877.

27. Ross, *Workers on the Edge*, 248–51.

28. Reginald Charles McGrane, "Ohio and the Greenback Movement," *Mississippi Valley Historical Review* 11 (March 1925): 526–42; Reginald Charles McGrane, *William Allen: A Study in Western Democracy* (Columbus: Ohio State Archaeological and Historical Society, 1925), 259–63; *Annual Report of the Secretary of State, 1878* (Columbus: Nevins and Myers, 1879), 207–21.

29. McGrane, "Greenback Movement," 537–40.

30. Ibid., 538–42; Destler, *American Radicalism*, 1–49; David Montgomery, *Beyond Equality: Labor and Radical Republicans, 1862–1872* (1961; reprint, Urbana: University of Illinois Press, 1981), 394, 406, 407.

2—Agrarian Radicalism and the Ohio People's Party

1. *Cleveland Plain Dealer*, July 31, *Warren Western Reserve Democrat*, August 7, *New Nation* (Boston, MA), September 12, 1891; Peter Argersinger, *Populism and Politics: William Alfred Peffer and the People's Party* (Lexington: University Press of Kentucky, 1974), 99.

2. Argersinger, *Populism and Politics*, 99; *New Nation*, June 20, July 4, *Ohio State Journal* (Columbus), August 28, September 3, 9, 12, 1891.

3. Hicks, *Populist Revolt*; Hofstadter, *Age of Reform*, 99; R. Douglas Hurt, "The Farmers' Alliance and the People's Party in Ohio," *Old Northwest* 10 (Winter 1984–1985): 439–62; John Sherman, *John Sherman's Recollections of Forty Years in the House, Senate, and Cabinet: An Autobiography* (Chicago: Werner, 1895), 2:1130.

4. Kleppner, *Cross of Culture*, 35–91; Richard J. Jensen, *The Winning of the Midwest: Social and Political Conflict, 1888–1896* (Chicago: University of Chicago Press, 1971), 58–88.

5. Ostler, *Prairie Populism*, 10.

6. *Ohio Farmer* (Cleveland), June 6, 1891; *Akron Beacon*, September 1, 1890; *Sandusky Daily Register*, August 17, 1891; *Cleveland Plain Dealer*, August 4, 1895.

7. *Ohio Farmer*, August 23, 30, 1890. Although both the National Farmers' Alliance (Northern Alliance) and the Farmers' Alliance and Industrial Union (Southern Alliance) were active in Ohio, the National Farmers' Alliance was the more popular of the two. The Southern Alliance would not have its first statewide organizational meeting until the spring of 1891. Unless otherwise noted, the term "Farmers' Alliance" will refer to the Ohio branch of the National Farmers' Alliance.

8. *Ohio Farmer*, August 23, 30 (Brigham); *American Grange Bulletin* (Cincinnati), August 14, 1890; Kleppner, *Cross of Culture*, 5–24.

9. *Ohio Farmer*, August 23, 30, *Columbus Post-Press*, August 14 (quotation), 15, *Ohio State Journal*, August 14, 15, 1890.

10. *Ohio Farmer*, August 16, October 4 (quotation), November 1, 8, *Plow and Hammer* (Tiffin), October 29, 1890.

11. *Ohio Farmer*, October 4, 18, 1890.

12. Ibid., October 4, 11, *Ohio State Journal*, August 29, *Columbus Post-Press*, August 29, 1890; Joseph P. Smith, *History of the Republican Party in Ohio*, 2 vols. (Chicago: Lewis Publishing, 1898), 1:590.

13. *Ohio State Journal*, August 15 (first quotation), 21 (Wilson), *Cleveland Leader*, November 2, 1890 (McKinley).

14. *Ohio Farmer*, September 13, 1890.

15. *Plow and Hammer*, October 15; *Ohio Farmer*, September 13, 1890 (quotations).

16. *Ohio Farmer*, October 11 (first quotation), 18 (second quotation), November 15, *American Grange Bulletin*, December 11, 1890.

17. *Ohio Farmer*, October 11, 25, November 1, 1890.

18. *Plow and Hammer*, October 15 (Likins), 22, 1890.

19. William Oxford Thompson, "Taxation" (Oxford, OH: n.p., 1894) (first quotation); *Akron Beacon*, September 1, 1890 (second quotation); also see Hoyt Landon Warner, *Progressivism in Ohio, 1897–1917* (Columbus: Ohio State University Press for the Ohio Historical Society, 1964), 7–10; Peter Witt, *Cleveland before St. Peter: A Handful of Hot Stuff*, 2nd ed. (Cleveland: C. Lezuis, 1899).

20. *Report of the Secretary of State, 1890*, 246–51.

21. *Proceedings of the Annual Convention of the Ohio State Grange* (hereafter *Ohio Grange Proceedings*), *1890*, 11 (Talcott), 19–20 (Swingle), 29 (third quotation).

22. *Ohio Grange Proceedings, 1890*, 11; *Ohio Farmer*, February 7, 1890.

23. *Ohio Grange Proceedings, 1890*; *American Grange Bulletin*, December 18, 25, 1890, January 8, 1891; *Ohio Farmer*, February 7, 1891.

24. Hicks, *Populist Revolt*, 205–9.

25. *Ohio State Journal*, January 21, 1891. See also *Ohio Farmer*, January 24, 1891; *Ohio Grange Proceedings, 1890*; *American Grange Bulletin*, March 12, 1890. The thirty-six farmers in the General Assembly included twenty-eight representatives and eight senators. Seven of the senators and sixteen of the representatives were Republicans, the rest Democrats.

26. *Ohio Farmer*, February 28; *American Grange Bulletin*, April 2, 1891.

27. *Ohio Farmer*, April 18, 25 (quotation), May 2, 9, *Cincinnati Enquirer*, July 16, 1891.

28. *Ohio Farmer*, May 16, *American Grange Bulletin*, May 14, 1891.

29. *Ohio State Journal*, May 28, 1891 (quotation); Hicks, *Populist Revolt*, 209–15; William F. Zornow, "Bellamy Nationalism in Ohio, 1891 to 1896," *Ohio State Archaeological and Historical Quarterly* 58 (April 1949): 152–70; Larry G. Osnes, "The Birth of a Party: The Cincinnati Populist Convention of 1891," *Great Plains Journal* 10 (Fall 1970): 11–24; Ernest I. Miller, "The Farmers' Party," *Bulletin of the Historical and Philosophical Society of Ohio* 15 (January 1957): 49–65.

30. *Ohio Farmer*, April 18, 1891.

31. Ibid., May 28, 1891.

32. The proceedings of the Ohio Farmers' Union convention were reprinted in *Ohio State Journal*, May 28, *Columbus Dispatch*, May 27, *Columbus Post-Press*, May 28, *Ohio Farmer*, June 6, 13, 20, 1891.

33. *Cincinnati Enquirer*, August 4, *Springfield Republic-Times*, August 6, *Dayton Journal*, August 7, 1891.

34. The proceedings of the Ohio People's party convention were reprinted in *Cincinnati Enquirer*, August 6, *Springfield Republic-Times*, August 5, 6, *Ohio Farmer*, August 25, 1891. Also see Jack S. Blocker Jr., *Retreat from Reform: The Prohibition Movement in the United States, 1890–1913* (Westport, CT: Greenwood Press, 1976), 52.

35. "Farmers and Working Men of Ohio Read and Consider: A Few Facts that Speak for Themselves" (n.d., n.p.); *Ohio State Journal*, August 7 (quotation), 28, *Athens Messenger*, September 19, 1891.

36. *Cincinnati Enquirer,* August 15, 1891; Jeffrey Ostler, "The Rhetoric of Conspiracy and the Formation of Kansas Populism," *Agricultural History* 69 (Winter 1995): 1–27; Sherman, *John Sherman's Recollections,* 2:1119–26; Charles L. Kurtz to H. S. Bundy, July 21, 1891, folder 6, Joseph Benson Foraker to Kurtz, August 5, 1891, folder 7, both in box 45, and C. E. Prior to Kurtz, September 22, 1891, folder 2, box 46, all in Charles L. Kurtz Papers, Ohio Historical Society, Columbus (hereafter cited as Kurtz Papers); Foraker to A. V. Dockery, June 22, Foraker to Murat Halstead, August 5, Foraker to J. Q. A. Campbell, August 16 (quotations), 1891, folder 4, box 27, Joseph B. Foraker Papers, Cincinnati Historical Society, Cincinnati, Ohio (hereafter Foraker Papers).

37. Sherman, *John Sherman's Recollections,* 2:1134.

38. *Columbus Dispatch,* June 12, July 5, August 15, *New Nation,* August 29, *Youngstown Vindicator,* September 12, 1891 (quotation). In 11 of the state's 107 Ohio House districts and 5 of the 26 Senate races, the People's party endorsed the Democratic nominee. These districts were located in heavily Republican areas in which neither the Democratic candidate nor the People's party's nominee had much hope of upsetting the incumbent. In one race, the People's party endorsed the Republican nominee. *Report of the Secretary of State, 1891,* 271–90.

39. *Warren Western Reserve Democrat,* September 18, *Sandusky Daily Register,* July 31 (Crawford), August 17 (Ellis), *Ohio Farmer,* October 17, 31, 1891.

40. H. Wayne Morgan, *William McKinley and His America* (Syracuse, NY: Syracuse University Press, 1963), 154–57; William McKinley, *Speeches and Addresses of William McKinley: From His Election to Congress to the Present Time* (New York: D. Appleton and Company, 1893); Sherman, *John Sherman's Recollections,* 1:1130–35; Joseph Benson Foraker, *Speeches of J. B. Foraker,* 2 vols. (n.p., n.d.), 2:22–53; *Cincinnati Commercial Gazette,* October 9, 1891.

41. *Cleveland Plain Dealer,* July 16, 1891; Smith, *Republican Party in Ohio,* 1:603 (quotation); Morgan, *McKinley and His America,* 154–57.

42. *Columbus Dispatch,* September 7 (first two quotations), *Cleveland Plain Dealer,* July 16 (third quotation), 1891. For an overview of the McKinley-Campbell contest's role in defining national politics, see Jensen, *Winning of the Midwest,* 154–65.

43. *Columbus Dispatch,* September 7 (Farmer), *Ohio State Journal,* June 29 (Barnes), *Springfield Republic-Times,* August 7, *Cleveland Plain Dealer,* July 31 (Peffer), *National Labor Tribune* (Pittsburgh, PA), October 24, 31, 1891.

44. *Marion (Ohio) Star,* November 20, 1891; Croly, *Marcus Alonzo Hanna,* 158–63; Morgan, *McKinley and His America,* 155. On the role of money in Ohio politics, see Myers, *Bosses and Boodle.*

45. Croly, *Marcus Alonzo Hanna,* 161–63; Sherman, *John Sherman's Recollections,* 2:1155–57; Smith, *Republican Party in Ohio,* 1:630, 644, 655.

46. *Report of the Secretary of State, 1891,* 298–357.

47. *Ohio Farmer,* January 30 (first quotation), March 19 (second quotation), 1892; *Ohio Grange Proceedings, 1891,* 26 (Grange).

48. *Ohio Farmer,* March 12, 19, 26, 1892.

49. The proceedings of the Ohio People's party convention were reprinted in *Akron Beacon,* August 17, 18, *Toledo Blade,* August 17, 18, 1892.

50. *Akron Beacon,* August 17, 18, *Columbus Dispatch,* August 18 (quotation), 1892. Most of the state's major newspapers held the People's party in such low regard they did not even bother to run coverage of the convention.

51. *Ohio Farmer,* February 23, 1893.

52. Ibid., February 9, 16, 1893.

53. Ibid., January 26, February 9, 23 (quotation), April 6, 27, May 11, 1893; Everett Walters, *Joseph Benson Foraker: An Uncompromising Republican* (Columbus: Ohio History Press, 1948), 124–25; Warner, *Progressivism in Ohio,* 7–10; Morgan, *McKinley and His America,* 159–60.

54. *Ohio Farmer*, April 27, 1893. See also *Ohio Grange Proceedings, 1892*, 39.
55. *Ohio Farmer*, May 4, June 8, 1893.
56. *Plow and Hammer*, January 4, 11, 1893.
57. Ibid., May 3, 1893.

3—Gas and Sewer Populism

1. *Cleveland Citizen*, May 14, 25, *Cleveland Plain Dealer*, April 16, 1892; Witt, "Labor Movement in Cleveland."
2. *Cleveland Plain Dealer*, June 26, *Cleveland Leader*, June 25, *Cleveland Citizen*, May 28, 1892; Witt, "Labor Movement in Cleveland," 11.
3. *Cleveland Leader*, June 25, 26 (quotation), *Cleveland Plain Dealer*, June 26, *Cleveland Citizen*, July 2, 1892; Witt, "Labor Movement in Cleveland," 11.
4. *Report of the Ohio Secretary of State, 1890*, 89–90, 285; *Cleveland Citizen*, February 20 (quotation), March 13, 27; *New Nation* (Boston, MA), February 28, 1891; Witt, "Labor Movement in Cleveland," 11; *Twenty-Year History of District Assembly 47, Knights of Labor* (Cleveland: District Assembly 47, 1902), 12.
5. *Cleveland Plain Dealer*, March 2, 1891; *Twenty-Year History of District Assembly 47*, 12; Max S. Hayes, *A History of Cleveland Labor* (1937; reprint, Cleveland: Greater Cleveland Labor History Society, 1987), 4. In one of the few articles discussing the Ohio People's party, William F. Zornow argues that the party was plagued by a rivalry between trade unionists and Bellamy nationalists. This argument ignores both the fact that most of the Nationalists he discusses were trade unionists and the harmonious relationship between the Franklin Club and the CLU. Zornow, "Bellamy Nationalism in Ohio."
6. *Cleveland Plain Dealer*, March 2 (quotations), *Cleveland Leader*, March 2, *Cleveland Citizen*, March 13, 1891.
7. *Cleveland Plain Dealer*, March 16, 23, *Cleveland Leader*, March 23, 1891.
8. *Cleveland Citizen*, February 20, 1891.
9. *Cleveland Citizen*, February 27 (quotation), March 6, 13, 20, 1891.
10. Gutman, "Labor Policies of the Large Corporation"; Witt, "Labor Movement in Cleveland," 11; Frederic C. Howe, *The Confessions of a Reformer* (1925; reprint, Chicago: Quadrangle Books, 1967), 85.
11. *Cleveland Plain Dealer*, April 6, 1891.
12. *Ohio State Journal*, May 28, 1891; Hicks, *Populist Revolt*, 209–15; Zornow, "Bellamy Nationalism in Ohio"; Osnes, "Birth of a Party"; Miller, "Farmers' Party."
13. *Cleveland Citizen*, April 3, 1891. On the importance of the Buell and Hazard circulars on Populist thought, see Ostler, "Rhetoric of Conspiracy."
14. *Cleveland Citizen*, February 20, September 19, 1891, March 16, 1892.
15. Ibid., February 20 (first quotation), August 1, September 19 (second quotation), 1891.
16. Ibid., March 13 (quotation), August 15, 1891.
17. Croly, *Marcus Alonzo Hanna*, 80–81; Johnson, *My Story*, 114.
18. *Cleveland Leader*, May 15, 16, June 21, 1892; Witt, "Labor Movement in Cleveland," 11; Leslie S. Hough, *The Turbulent Spirit: Cleveland, Ohio, and Its Workers, 1877–1899* (New York: Garland, 1990), 182–83.
19. *Cleveland Citizen*, June 11 (quotation), 17, *Cleveland Leader*, June 21, *Cleveland Plain Dealer*, June 21, 1892.
20. *Cleveland Plain Dealer*, June 21, 22, *Cleveland Leader*, June 21 (quotation), 22, 1892.
21. *Cleveland Plain Dealer*, June 24, 25, *Cleveland Leader*, June 24, 25, 1892; Hough, *Turbulent Spirit*, 188 (quotation); Witt, "Labor Movement in Cleveland," 11.

22. *Cleveland Citizen*, July 2, 1892. See also *Cleveland Leader*, June 26, 1892.

23. *Cleveland Citizen*, July 2, *Cleveland Plain Dealer*, June 26 (quotation), 1892.

24. *Cleveland Leader*, June 26 (quotation), *Cleveland Citizen*, June 26, July 2, 7, 1892.

25. *Cleveland Plain Dealer*, June 29, 1892; Witt, "Labor Movement in Cleveland," 11.

26. *Cleveland Citizen*, July 2, 7, 1892; Witt, "Labor Movement in Cleveland," 11; Hough, *Turbulent Spirit*, 188.

27. *Cleveland Citizen*, September 3, 1892.

28. *Cleveland Plain Dealer*, February 26, 1893. See also *Cleveland Citizen*, March 4, 1893.

29. *Cleveland Plain Dealer*, February 26, *Cleveland Citizen*, March 4, 18, 1893; Witt, "Labor Movement in Cleveland," 12.

30. *Cleveland Citizen*, March 11, 25, 1893.

31. *Cleveland Plain Dealer*, March 19, 26, 31, *Cleveland Leader*, March 26, 27, 1893.

32. *Cleveland Plain Dealer*, March 6, 31, April 2 (quotation), 6, *Cleveland Citizen*, April 1, 8, 1893.

33. *Cleveland Plain Dealer*, April 4, 1893. In 1892 Democratic presidential candidate Grover Cleveland carried the wards of the West Side with 65 percent of the votes (6,306 to 3,298), but in 1893 only 4,208 (52.5%) of these voters cast their ballots for the Democrat Blee, while 1,404 (17.5%) voted for Meyer and 2,399 (29.9%) voted for the Republican candidate.

34. *Cleveland Citizen*, April 8, 1893. See also Witt, "Labor Movement in Cleveland," 10.

35. *Plow and Hammer* (Tiffin), April 12; *Cleveland Citizen*, April 8, 1893.

36. The platform is reprinted in Smith, *Republican Party in Ohio*, 1:642.

37. Ibid., 637-642; Morgan, *William McKinley and His America*, 174–75; McKinley, *Speeches and Addresses*, 633–39; Sherman, *John Sherman's Recollections*, 2:1199; *Ohio State Journal*, June 8 (quotation), 9, 1893.

38. Thomas E. Powell, *The Democratic Party of the State of Ohio: A Comprehensive History of Democracy in Ohio from 1803 to 1912*, 2 vols. (Columbus: Ohio Publishing, 1913), 1:233–34; Smith, *Republican Party in Ohio*, 1:644; *Columbus Press-Post*, August 10 (quotations), 1893.

39. *Columbus Press-Post*, August 10–12, *Cleveland Plain Dealer*, August 11, 12, 1893.

40. The platform is reprinted in *Ohio Farmer*, July 13, 1893.

41. *Columbus Dispatch*, July 4, *Columbus Press-Post*, July 5, *Ohio Farmer*, July 13, 1893.

42. *Report of the Ohio Secretary of State, 1894*, 278–460.

43. Howe, *Confessions of a Reformer*, 189. See also Johnson, *My Story*, 83–85; Louis Post, notes for a Peter Witt biography, Peter Witt Papers, Western Reserve Historical Society, Cleveland; Carl Wittke, "Peter Witt, Tribune of the People," *Ohio Archaeological and Historical Quarterly* 58 (October 1949): 361–77; Arthur E. DeMatteo, "Death Knell for Progressive Leadership in Cleveland: Peter Witt and the Mayoral Election of 1915," *Ohio History* 111 (Winter–Spring 2002): 7–24.

44. Eric J. Karolak, "Hayes, Max Sebastian," *American National Biography Online*, http://www.anb.org/articles/15/15–00317.html (accessed May 21, 2009).

45. *Cleveland Citizen*, December 8, 15 (first quotation), 22 (Thomas), 1894.

46. Witt, "Labor Movement in Cleveland," 12; *Cleveland Citizen*, December 8, 15, 22, 1894.

47. *Cleveland Leader*, March 16, 17, 23, 25, 29, 31, 1895.

48. *Cleveland Citizen*, December 8 (quotation), 15, 22, 1894.

49. Ibid., December 8, 1894, January 19, February 16, 1895.

50. Ibid., February 23 (quotation), March 2, *Cleveland Plain Dealer*, February 21, 1895. By participating in the convention, the Cleveland section violated the Socialist Labor party's policy forbidding compromise with other political parties. For this, the SLP's executive committee suspended the Cleveland section. At the party's next national meeting, though, delegates lifted the suspension, much to the disgust of party leader Daniel DeLeon. Howard Quint, *The Forging of American Socialism: Origins of the Modern Movement* (Indianapolis, IN: Bobbs-Merrill, 1953), 171; *Proceedings of the Ninth Annual Convention of the Socialist Labor Party*, 19–21.

51. *Cleveland Citizen*, February 23, March 2, *Cleveland Plain Dealer*, February 21 (quotations), 1895; *Ninth Annual Convention of the Socialist Labor Party*, 19–21.

52. *Cleveland Citizen*, March 2, 1895.

53. Ibid., March 2, *Cleveland Plain Dealer*, February 23, 1895.

54. *Cleveland Plain Dealer*, March 22 (quotation), April 2, 1895.

55. *Cleveland Leader*, March 21, 1895.

56. Ibid., March 16, 17, 23, 25, 29, 31, *Cleveland Plain Dealer*, April 2, 1895.

57. *Cleveland Leader*, March 22, 26, 27, 1895; Thomas F. Campbell, "Mounting Crisis and Reform: Cleveland's Political Development," in *The Birth of Modern Cleveland, 1865–1930*, ed. Thomas F. Campbell and Edward M. Miggins (Cleveland: Western Reserve Historical Society, 1988), 301–4.

58. Ronald Weiner, *Lake Effects: A History of Urban Policy Making in Cleveland, 1825–1929* (Columbus: Ohio State University Press, 2005), 66.

59. *Cleveland Citizen*, April 10, 1895.

60. Ibid., March 21, June 13, November 23, 1895, March 21, 28, May 16, 1896.

61. Ibid., July 8, 1896.

62. Ibid., September 19, 1896.

63. Ibid., July 18, September 19, 26 (quotation), October 24, 1896, April 17, 1897; *Cleveland Plain Dealer*, July 11, September 20, 1896.

64. *Cleveland Plain Dealer*, July 11, 27 (quotations), September 27–29, October 2, 1896; *Cleveland Citizen*, May 6, 1897.

65. *Cleveland Citizen*, May 15, 1897.

66. Ibid., January 9, April 10, 1897.

67. Ibid., March 13, 1897.

68. Ibid., April 10, 1897. See also *Cleveland Plain Dealer*, April 6, 1897.

69. *Cleveland Citizen*, August 14 (quotation), September 11, 25, October 23, 1897.

70. Ibid., August 14, October 2 (quotations), 1897.

71. Ibid., January 8, 1897.

72. Croly, *Marcus Alonzo Hanna*, 251–59, 294; Howe, *Confessions of a Reformer*, 83–86.

73. Stromquist, "Crucible of Class."

74. *Cleveland Press*, April 1, *Cleveland Plain Dealer*, June 6, 8, 9, 1899; Johnson, *My Story*, 86–88.

75. *Labor Day Souvenir, 1901* (Cleveland: Cleveland Citizen, 1901), 23; *Cleveland Plain Dealer*, June 3, 1899 (quotation).

76. *Cleveland Plain Dealer*, June 11–13, 15, 25, *Cleveland Leader*, June 10–12, 14, 15, 24–26, 1899.

77. *Cleveland Plain Dealer*, June 25, July 6, 1899.

78. Ibid., July 18–28, *Cleveland Leader*, July 18–28, 1899; George P. Edwards, "Cleveland Strikes," *Harper's Weekly* 43 (August 5, 1899): 780–81; *London Spectator*, cited in "The Cleveland Strike," *Harper's Weekly* 43 (August 19, 1899): 808.

79. *Cleveland Plain Dealer*, July 18–28, 1899; George P. Edwards, "The Boycott in Cleveland," *Harper's Weekly* 43 (August 12, 1899): 804 (quotation); *Cleveland Citizen*, September 9, 30, 1899.

80. "Cleveland Strike," 808.

81. *Cleveland Citizen*, August 12 (first quotation), 19, September 2 (Debs), 1899.

82. Destler, *American Radicalism*, ix, 134, 160. Destler also included Tom L. Johnson in the list of those trying to bring Populist ideals to municipal government.

83. *Cleveland Citizen*, January 14, 21, August 26 (quotations), 1899.

84. Samuel Jones to Robert Bandlow, August 1, 1899, in Samuel Milton Jones Papers, Toledo-Lucas County Public Library, microfilm edition (hereafter Jones Papers), reel 3.

85. *Cleveland Citizen*, November 4, 1899.

86. Ibid., August 15 (first quotation), September 16 (second quotation), November 11, 1899.

87. Stromquist, "Crucible of Class," 209–15.

88. Ibid.; Warner, *Progressivism in Ohio*, 56; Johnson, *My Story*, 108–20; Kenneth Finegold, *Experts and Politicians: Reform Challenges to Machine Politics in New York, Cleveland, and Chicago* (Princeton, NJ: Princeton University Press, 1995), 82–100.

89. Oscar Ameringer, *If You Don't Weaken: The Autobiography of Oscar Ameringer* (New York: Henry Holt, 1940), 181–82. See also Johnson, *My Story*.

90. Montgomery, *Fall of the House of Labor*, 288. See also *Cleveland Citizen*, August 3, 1901; Quint, *American Socialism*, 350–79; Morris Hillquit, *History of Socialism in the United States*, 5th ed. (New York: Funk and Wagnalls, 1910), 276–78, 305–14; Salvatore, *Eugene V. Debs*, 183–206.

4—Government by Injunction and Labor Populism in Cincinnati

1. *Thomas v. Cincinnati, New Orleans & Texas Pacific Railway Company*, In re Phelan C.C.S.D. Ohio, W.D.62 F. 803 (1894).

2. See, for example, David Henry Burton, *Taft, Holmes, and the 1920s Court: An Appraisal* (Madison, NJ: Fairleigh Dickinson University Press, 1998), 46–47.

3. For an overview of these rulings, see Michael Pierce, "Organized Labor and the Law in Ohio," in Michael Les Benedict and John F. Winkler, eds., *The History of Ohio Law* (Athens: Ohio University Press, 2004), 883–910.

4. Ross, *Workers on the Edge*, 270–325; *Cincinnati Chronicle*, December 1892, May 1893, April 1894, June 1894; *L. W. David v. State of Ohio*, 30 *Ohio Weekly Law Bulletin*, 342–44 (1893); *Moores and Co., v Bricklayers Union*, 13 *Ohio Weekly Law Bulletin*, 48, 50 (1890); *Toledo, Ann Arbor, and Northern Michigan Railway v. Pennsylvania Co.*, 54 F 730, 739 (C.C.N.D. Ohio 1893).

5. "A Manifesto to the Citizens of Hamilton County in General, and the Labor and Reform Organizations in Particular," broadside taped into CLC minute books, August 22, 1894. William Forbath and Victoria Hattam both argue that trade unions responded to judicial hostility by embracing a form of anti-statism that insisted government should not interfere with the relations between labor and capital. This study suggests that Cincinnati trade unionists and their counterparts in the rest of Ohio responded to this hostility by joining with the Populists. Forbath, *Shaping of the American Labor Movement*; Hattam, *Labor Visions and State Power*.

6. Ross, *Workers on the Edge*, 202–3, 250–51, 294–325.

7. The proceedings are reprinted in *Cincinnati Commercial Gazette*, March 22, *Cincinnati Times-Star*, March 23, 1891. Also see *Cincinnati Commercial Gazette*, March 25, 1891.

8. *Cincinnati Chronicle*, February 1892; CLC minute books, March 4, 1891. On the origins of the Cincinnati CLC, see Ross, *Workers on the Edge*, 324.

9. Declaration of principles published in *Cincinnati Chronicle*, February 1892.

10. CLC minute books, June 6, October 3, 1889, December 17, 1890.

11. *Cincinnati Commercial Gazette*, May 31, August 7, *Cincinnati Times Star*, August 6, 1891; Osnes, "Birth of a Party"; Hicks, *Populist Revolt*, 209–15.

12. *Cincinnati Commercial Gazette*, August 5, 7, *Cincinnati Times-Star*, August 5, 6, 1891.

13. *New Nation* (Boston, MA), August 1, *Cincinnati Times-Star*, August 6, *Cincinnati Commercial Gazette*, August 5, 7 (quotation), 1891; Ross, *Workers on the Edge*, 312.

14. Foraker to Kurtz, September 7, 1891, folder 1, box 45, Kurtz Papers. Also see Foraker to Asa Bushnell, September 7, 1891, folder 4, box 27, Foraker Papers.

15. *Report of the Secretary of State, 1892*, 277.

16. James Matthew Morris, "The Road to Trade Unionism: Organized Labor in Cincinnati to 1893" (PhD diss., University of Cincinnati, 1969), 352–58.

17. CLC minute books, October 17, November 7, December 5, 1893; *Cincinnati Chronicle*, March, April, October, December 1893. The leaders of the merger movement were also the leaders of the Cincinnati People's party. The merger was proposed by a committee composed of William Brown and J. H. Heberle (both of whom were Populist candidates for the Ohio General Assembly in 1893), R. H. Wheeler (a member of the executive board of the Hamilton County People's party and master workman of Knights of Labor District Assembly 48), Frank Rist, and A. A. Varelman.

18. *Cincinnati Chronicle*, October 1893.

19. Miller, *Boss Cox's Cincinnati*, 59–110 (71); Walters, *Joseph Benson Foraker*, 124.

20. *Cincinnati Chronicle*, April (first quotation), July (third and fourth quotations), December 1892, February, March (second quotation), May 1893; CLC minute books, March 17, 1893.

21. *Cincinnati Chronicle*, December 1892, May, December 1893, December 1894 (quotation); CLC minute books, November 21, 1893, October 16, 1894.

22. *L.W. Davis v The State of Ohio* 30 *Ohio Weekly Law Bulletin* 342; *Cincinnati Chronicle*, December 1892, January, May 1893 (quotation).

23. *Cincinnati Chronicle*, February 1893.

24. *Cincinnati Chronicle*, February 1893; CLC minute books, January 5, March 1, 1892; *New Nation*, March 5, 1892; Howe, *Confessions of a Reformer*, 157–58 (quotation); *Ohio Farmer*, January 26, February 9, 23, April 6, 27, May 11, 1893; Walters, *Joseph Benson Foraker*, 124–25; Warner, *Progressivism in Ohio*, 7–10; Morgan, *William McKinley and His America*, 159–60.

25. "Direct Legislation League," broadside taped into CLC minute book, June 3, 1893; *Cincinnati Chronicle*, June 1893. On corruption in the Ohio General Assembly, see Myers, *Bosses and Boodle*; Green, *Fact Stranger than Fiction*, 193–209; James N. Giglio, *H. M. Daugherty and the Politics of Expediency* (Kent, OH: Kent State University Press, 1978), 8–13.

26. "Direct Legislation League," broadside taped into CLC minute book, June 3, 1893; *Cincinnati Chronicle*, June 1893.

27. Raymond Boryczka and Lorin Lee Cary, *No Strength without Union: An Illustrated History of Ohio Workers, 1803–1980* (Columbus: Ohio Historical Society, 1982), 148; *Cincinnati Chronicle*, August 1893.

28. *Cincinnati Chronicle*, August 1893.

29. Ibid., October 1893.

30. CLC minute books, February 6, 20, 1894; Miller, *Boss Cox's Cincinnati*, 88 (quotation).

31. *Cincinnati Enquirer*, March 8, *Cincinnati Tribune*, January 27, March 8, 1894. The Horstmann faction had the support of six of the seven members of the Hamilton County People's party's executive committee, and five of these six were active in the CLC—Thomas Butterworth, Frank Rist, John Crofton, Louis Benjamin, and John Jacobs.

32. Miller, *Boss Cox's Cincinnati*, 89; *Cincinnati Tribune*, March 16–19, 1894.

33. CLC minute books, March 20, 1894. See also *Cincinnati Chronicle*, February, March, *Cincinnati Commercial Gazette*, March 21, *Cincinnati Enquirer*, March 21, *Cincinnati Tribune*, March 24, 1894.

34. Miller, *Box Cox's Cincinnati*, 88. See also *Cincinnati Commercial Gazette*, March 21, 25, *Cincinnati Tribune*, March 24, 30, 1894.

35. *Cincinnati Chronicle*, March 1894.

36. *Cincinnati Enquirer*, April 3, 1894.

37. For a fuller discussion of the Pullman strike and boycott, see Almont Lindsey, *The Pullman Strike: A Story of a Unique Experiment and of a Great Labor Upheaval* (Chicago: University of Chicago Press, 1942); Salvatore, *Eugene V. Debs*, 114–46.

38. *Cincinnati Tribune*, June 27, 28 (quotation), 30, 1894; *Thomas v. Cincinnati, New Orleans & Texas Pacific Railway Company,* In re Phelan, S.D. Ohio, W.D. 62 F. (1894) 803.

39. *Cincinnati Tribune*, June 29, 1894.

40. Ibid., July 1, 2 (quotation), 3, 1894.

41. Ibid., July 3, 4, 1894.

42. *Cincinnati Tribune*, July 5 (quotation), *Cincinnati Commercial Gazette*, July 5, *Cincinnati Enquirer*, July 5, 1894.

43. CLC minutes book, July 5, 1894 (quotations); *Cincinnati Tribune*, July 6–9, 1894.

44. William McKinley to John A. Caldwell, July 5, 1894, William McKinley Letter-books, Ohio Historical Society, Columbus; *Cincinnati Commercial Gazette*, July 10, 1894.

45. *Cincinnati Tribune*, July 9, 10, 1894.

46. Ibid., July 17, 1894.

47. "A Manifesto to the Citizens of Hamilton County in General, and the Labor and Reform Organizations in Particular," broadside taped into CLC minute books, August 22, 1894; *Cincinnati Chronicle*, August 1894.

48. Phelan letter reprinted in both *Cincinnati Commercial Gazette* and *Cincinnati Enquirer*, September 9, 1894.

49. *Cincinnati Commercial Gazette*, September 9, *Cincinnati Enquirer*, September 9, *Cincinnati Chronicle*, October (quotation) 1894.

50. For a ward map of the city and a description of the composition of voters in each ward, see Miller, *Box Cox's Cincinnati*, 44.

51. *Cincinnati Chronicle*, November 15, 29, 1895.

52. Ross, *Workers on the Edge;* Miller, *Boss Cox's Cincinnati*, 14; Miller and Wheeler, *Cleveland*, 77–99; Hunker, *Industrial Evolution of Columbus*.

53. Ostler, *Prairie Populism*; H. E. Taubeneck, "The Philosophy of Political Parties: The Conditions and Elements Required for the Success of a New Party" (Chicago: Schulte Publishing, 1896), 5.

54. *Cincinnati Chronicle*, November 15, 1895.

55. William Peffer, *Populism: Its Rise and Fall* (Lawrence: University Press of Kansas, 1992), 109–14; *National Watchman* (Washington, DC), February 22, 1895, reprinted in Frank L. McVey, "The Populist Movement," *Economic Studies* 1 (August 1896): 200–201; "Populist Manifesto—February 22, 1895," reprinted in ibid., 201–2.

56. *Cincinnati Chronicle*, April 5, 19, May 31, June 7 (first quotation), September 13, October 4, 1895, June 5 (third quotation), July 17 (second quotation), 1896; *Cincinnati Enquirer*, July 26, September 8, 1895; *Sound Money* (Massillon), September 12, 1895.

57. *Cincinnati Chronicle*, July 17, August 21, 1896.

58. *Cincinnati Enquirer*, September 20, 23, *Cincinnati Chronicle*, October 22, 29, 1896.

59. *Cincinnati Chronicle*, August 21, October 16 (first quotation), 23, 30 (Debs and fourth quotations), *Cincinnati Enquirer*, October 3, 10 (Bryan), 27, 1896.

60. *Cincinnati Chronicle*, November 6, 1896.

61. Ibid., April 2 (Marx), June 25 (second quotation), 1897, June 2, 1899.

62. Ibid., March 26, April 2, 1897. See also Miller, *Boss Cox's Cincinnati*, 163–74.

63. *Cincinnati Enquirer*, March 12 (quotation), *Cincinnati Commercial Tribune*, March 7, 9, 12, 1897.

64. *Cleveland Citizen*, January 8, 1898; *Cincinnati Chronicle*, September 3 (quotation), October 12, 1897.

65. *Cincinnati Chronicle*, September 3, June 9, 1899.

66. Ibid., June 2, 1899 (first and second quotations), March 23, 1900; Miller, *Boss Cox's Cincinnati*, 174 (third quotation).

67. *Cincinnati Times Star*, March 26, 1903; Miller, *Boss Cox's Cincinnati*, 178.

68. *Twenty-fifth Annual Report of the Bureau of Labor Statistics to the Seventy-fifth General Assembly of the State of Ohio for the Year 1901* (Columbus: Fred J. Heer, 1902), 814–15.

69. *Cincinnati Chronicle*, February 21, 1903. See also Barbara L. Musselman, "The Quest for Collective Improvement: Cincinnati Workers, 1893–1920" (PhD diss., University of Cincinnati, 1975), 156; *Cincinnati Chronicle*, February 2, August 3, 1900, March 17, 1901.

70. Lincoln Steffens, *The Struggle for Self-Government: Being an Attempt to Trace American Political Corruption to Its Sources in Six States of the United States* (New York: McClure, Phillips, 1906), 161.

71. Miller, *Boss Cox's Cincinnati*, 178–80; *Cincinnati Times-Star*, April 2 (first quotation), *Cincinnati Enquirer*, March 18, 1903 (Ingalls); William Jennings Bryan, *The First Battle: A Story of the Campaign of 1896* (Chicago: W. B. Conkey, 1897), 571.

72. *Cincinnati Times Star*, March 4, 16, 26 (second quotation), April 1 (first quotation), 1903.

73. *Cincinnati Chronicle*, March 14, 21, 28 (first two quotations), April 4 (third quotation), *Cincinnati Times Star*, April 4, 1903.

74. *Cincinnati Chronicle*, March 28, April 4, 1903.

75. Miller, *Boss Cox's Cincinnati*, 175–85.

76. *Chronicle*, May 26, June 9, *Columbus Post-Press*, March 14, 28, June 1–3, *New York Times*, May 19, 1899; Martzolff, "Recent Ohio Legislation," 639; Thomas J. Donnelly, "Methods and Accomplishments in Ohio," *American Federationist* 33 (May 1926): 554.

5—Middle-class Reform and Labor's Embrace of Populism in Columbus

1. Washington Gladden, *The Cosmopolis City Club* (New York: Century Publishing, 1893), 45–46. The novel was originally serialized in *Century Magazine* 45 (1893).

2. In his memoirs Gladden suggested that his novel had served as inspiration for those forming the Chicago Civic Federation, out of which came the National Civic Federation. Washington Gladden, *Recollections* (Boston, MA: Houghton Mifflin, 1909), 330. Columbus's municipal reform movement of the early 1890s made the labor movement suspicious of these types of cross-class movements.

3. *Columbus Dispatch*, September 7, December 29 (quotation), 1891.

4. Ibid., September 7 (Thurman), 1891; Allen Nevins, *Grover Cleveland: A Study in Courage* (New York: Dodd, Mead, 1962), 171; *Cleveland Citizen*, March 4, 1893; McGrane, "Greenback Era"; *New York Times*, May 19, 1880.

5. *Columbus Dispatch*, September 1, 1890, September 7, 1891 (Karb).

6. *Cincinnati Commercial Gazette*, June 12, *Ohio State Journal* (Columbus), June 5 (Murphy), 6, 8, 10, *Columbus Dispatch*, June 5–10, *New York Times*, June 7, 1890.

7. *Ohio State Journal*, June 10, *Columbus Dispatch*, June 10, 1890.

8. *Ohio State Journal*, June 6–10, *Columbus Dispatch*, June 9–11, *New York Times*, June 9, 14, 1890.

9. *Columbus Dispatch*, June 12, 30, July 30, *New Nation*, July 18, 1891.

10. *Columbus Dispatch*, August 15, *Ohio State Journal*, August 15, *New Nation*, August 29, 1891.

11. *Ohio State Journal*, June 7, 13, 1891.

12. Jacob Dorn, *Washington Gladden: Prophet of the Social Gospel* (Columbus: Ohio State University Press, 1966), 308–14; *Ohio State Journal*, June 7, 1891, *Cincinnati Commercial Gazette*, June 12, 1890. For a detailed look at reform efforts, see Michael Pierce, "Washington Gladden's Columbus: The Politics of Municipal Reform in Columbus, Ohio, 1885–1915" (master's thesis, Ohio State University, 1993).

13. *Columbus Dispatch*, January 13, 21, 22, February 3, 10, *Ohio State Journal*, January 6, December 2, 7, 1892; Dorn, *Washington Gladden*, 313–14.

14. *New York Times*, November 9, *Ohio State Journal*, November 9, *Columbus Dispatch*, December 8, 1892.

15. *Columbus Dispatch*, November 7, *Ohio State Journal*, November 7, 11, 1892.

16. *Ohio State Journal*, November 11, 13, *Columbus Dispatch*, November 9, 10 (quotations), 11, 15, December 12, 1892, January 16, 1893; *Columbus Post-Press*, November 9, 10, 11, 1892.

17. *Columbus Dispatch*, December 13, 1892, January 3, 24, 1893.

18. *Columbus Dispatch*, March 14, 1893.

19. *Ohio State Journal*, March 19, 23 (quotations), 24, *Plow and Hammer*, March 29, *Columbus Dispatch*, March 9, *Cleveland Citizen*, April 1, 1893.

20. Washington Gladden, "The Anti-Catholic Crusade," *Century Magazine* 47 (March 1894): 789–95; *Columbus Dispatch*, November 7, *Ohio State Journal*, November 8, 1892, *Columbus Record*, March 23 (quotation), 30, 1893.

21. *Ohio State Journal*, November 7, 8, 12, *New York Times*, November 18, *Columbus Catholic Columbian*, November 26, 1892; *Columbus Dispatch*, March 20, 27, April 18, 1893; Gladden, "Anti-Catholic Crusade."

22. Gladden, *Cosmopolis City Club*. Though he never acknowledged the religious assumptions in his novel, Gladden emerged as one of the sharpest critics of the APA's campaign in Columbus; Gladden, "Anti-Catholic Crusade." The APA episode marked a turning point in Gladden's thought concerning municipal reform and government as he started distancing himself from the government he had helped to create. In 1895 Gladden, who had advocated the elevation of the business class just two years earlier, would join the CTLA in endorsing a Populist candidate for mayor. He would also support Samuel Jones when he ran for governor on what was essentially a Populist platform. Washington Gladden, "Mayor Jones of Toledo," *Outlook* 62 (May 6, 1899): 17–18. Gladden never joined the People's party, but he would become a fellow traveler.

23. *Columbus Dispatch*, March 22, 23, 27, April 1, 5, *Columbus Record*, March 23, 30, 1893.

24. *Columbus Dispatch*, August 1, 1893.

25. *Ohio Bureau of Labor Statistics Annual Report, 1894*, 217–25.

26. *Columbus Dispatch*, August 15, September 5, 1893.

27. Ibid., September 2, 12 (second quotation), 19 (first quotation), October 10, 1893.

28. Ibid., October 24–26, *Ohio State Journal*, October 24–26, 1893.

29. *Columbus Post-Press*, June 30 (quotation), July 1–3, *Ohio State Journal*, July 4, *Columbus Dispatch*, April 17, July 18, 1894.

30. *Columbus Post-Press*, July 1–3, 5, *New York Times*, July 4, 1894.

31. *Columbus Post-Press*, July 1, 10, 14, *New York Times*, July 13, 1894.

32. *Columbus Post-Press*, July 7, 8 (first two quotations) 9, *Columbus Dispatch*, August 14 (third quotation), 1894.

33. *Columbus Post-Press*, July 1, 2 (quotation), 9, 10, 1894.
34. Ibid., July 6 (first quotation), 7, 10 (McBride), 1894.
35. Ibid., July 15, 17–19, 28, 29, *Columbus Dispatch*, July 10, 1894.
36. *United Mine Workers Journal*, August 9, 1894.
37. *Columbus Post-Press*, August 3, 4 (quotation), 14, *Columbus Dispatch*, August 3, 4, 8, 9, 13, 14 (Wild), 1894.
38. *Columbus Dispatch*, August 20, 28 (second quotation), *Columbus Post-Press*, October 8 (Mahon), *Cleveland Citizen*, October 20, 1894. Mahon would leave the city soon after the election and move to Detroit. As national president of the Amalgamated Association of Street Railway Employees, he could not continue to work out of a city without an active local.
39. *Columbus Dispatch*, November 7, 13, 1894.
40. *Columbus Post-Press*, March 3, *Columbus Dispatch*, March 4, 1895.
41. *Columbus Dispatch*, March 12, 24, *Columbus Post-Press*, March 12, 1895.
42. *Columbus Dispatch*, March 13, 25, 26, 1895.
43. *Columbus Post-Press*, March 11, 14, *Columbus Dispatch*, March 12–19, 1895.
44. *Columbus Post-Press*, March 25, *Columbus Dispatch*, March 25, 1895.
45. *Columbus Dispatch*, March 26, 27, *Columbus Post-Press*, March 26, 27, 1895.
46. *Ohio State Journal*, September 3, (first quotation) *Columbus Press-Post*, September 2 (second quotation), *Columbus Dispatch*, September 2 (third quotation), *Sound Money*, October 17, 1895.
47. Election results in *Columbus Dispatch*, November 8, 1896.
48. *Sound Money*, March 21, 1896; "Prospectus of *The Ohio Populist*" (Columbus: Ohio Populist, 1894). No copies of the *Ohio Populist* are known to exist, but it was quoted in the *Southern Mercury*, January 30, July 2, 1896, then cited in Argersinger, *Populism and Politics*, 243.
49. *Sound Money*, July 16, *Columbus Press*, July 19 (quotation), 1896.
50. *Columbus Post-Press*, August 22–24, 1896; Paolo Coletta, *William Jennings Bryan*, 3 vols. (Lincoln: University of Nebraska Press, 1964), 1:169.
51. Bryan, *First Battle*, 359; Coletta, *William Jennings Bryan*, 1:168; J. Anthony Lukas, *Big Trouble: A Murder in a Small Western Town Sets Off a Struggle for the Soul of America* (New York: Simon and Schuster, 1997), 152–53; *New York Times*, May 11, 1900; John J. Lentz to Oscar Ameringer, August 10, 1929, folder 5, box 1, Oscar and Freda Ameringer Papers, Oklahoma State Historical Society, Oklahoma City.
52. *Ohio State Journal*, February 7, 12, 17–19, 1897; *Columbus Press*, June 26, 1896.
53. *Ohio State Journal*, March 10, 17–19, 28, 1897.
54. Ibid., April 6, 1897.
55. Ibid., July 2, 1897.
56. Ibid., June 16, 29, July 3, 1897.
57. Ibid., February 24, March 9, 1897.
58. Ibid., June 1, July 11, *Columbus Post-Press*, July 10 (quotations), 1897; *Historical Directory of the Ohio House of Representatives* (Columbus: Ohio House of Representatives, 1966), 126.
59. *Twentieth-Century Official Illustrated History of the Columbus Trades and Labor Assembly and Its Affiliated Organizations* (Columbus: CTLA, 1901), 271–72.
60. Marnie Jones, *Holy Toledo: Religion and Politics in the Life of "Golden Rule" Jones* (Lexington: University Press of Kentucky, 1998), 159–62.
61. *Columbus Post-Press*, March 14, 28, June 1–3 (quotations), 1899; Jones to Robert Bandlow, August 1, 1899, Jones Papers, reel 3.
62. Jones to James Cannon, August 1, 8, 11, September 9, 18, October 16, 1899, Jones Papers, reel 3; *Ohio State Journal*, September 4, 5, 1899; *History of the Columbus Trades and Labor Assembly*, 413–15; *The Trade Unions of Columbus, Their History, and Bio-*

graphical Sketches of Prominent Union Officers and Friends of Labor (Columbus: Columbus Trades and Labor Assembly, 1895), 42.

63. *Columbus Post-Press*, October 3 (quotation), 1903; *History of the Columbus Trades and Labor Assembly*, 271, 347–51.

64. *Ohio State Journal,* January 22, 1900 (quotation), January 7, February 18, 1901.

65. Ameringer, *If You Don't Weaken*, 153–57, 181–82 (quotation).

66. Warren R. Van Tine, "A History of Labor in Columbus, Ohio, 1812–1992," *Ohio State University Center for Labor Research Working Papers Series* 10 (1993): 33–34; Eric John Karolak, "The Socialist Party in a Midwestern Community: The Case of Columbus, Ohio" (master's thesis, Ohio State University, 1988), 207–32; *Ohio State Journal*, November 11, 1906, January 2, 6, 7, 9, 13, 15, 1907; Frank Morrison to the Executive Council of the AFL, December 31, 1906, in *The Samuel Gompers Papers*, vol. 7, *The American Federation of Labor under Siege, 1906–9*, 152–53. On the AFL's efforts to silence socialists who led urban labor federations, see Greene, *Pure and Simple Politics*, 133–36.

6—The United Mine Workers and the Making of Ohio's Labor–Populist Alliance

1. *United Mine Workers Journal*, August 9 (quotation), *Columbus Dispatch*, August 14, 1894.

2. *United Mine Workers Journal*, August 23 (quotation), *Columbus Dispatch*, August 16, 1894; Paul W. Glad, *McKinley, Bryan, and the People* (Philadelphia: Lippincott, 1964), 148–49.

3. *Columbus Post-Press*, August 17, *Ohio State Journal*, August 17, *Columbus Dispatch*, August 17, 1894; Carlos Schwantes, *Coxey's Army: An American Odyssey* (1985; reprint, Moscow: University of Idaho Press, 1994), 32.

4. *National Labor Tribune* (Pittsburgh, PA), January 10 (quotation), *New York Times*, January 2, 1895.

5. *National Labor Tribune*, February 1, 8, 1890. Until the establishment of the *United Mine Workers Journal* in 1891, the *National Labor Tribune* served as the UMWA's official organ.

6. John McBride with T. T. O'Malley, "Coal Miners," in McNeill, *The Labor Movement*, 254, 267 (quotation). See also Andrew Roy, *The Practical Miners' Companion; or Papers on Geology and Mining in the Ohio Coal Field* (Columbus: Westbote Printing Co., 1885), 91; Andrew Roy, *A History of Coal Miners of the United States*, 3rd ed. (Columbus: J. L. Trauger, 1907), 178–85.

7. David Brody, "Market Unionism in America: The Case of Coal," in *In Labor's Cause: Main Themes in the History of the American Worker* (New York: Oxford University Press, 1993), 131–74; *Miners' Independent* (Massillon), July 18, 1889, March 6, 1890; Roy, *Coal Miners*, 227–42.

8. *United Mine Workers Journal*, July 28, 1892; Edward W. Bemis, "The Coal Miners' Strike," *Outlook* 49 (May 12, 1894): 822–23. Richard Jensen suggests that the earnings of miners were higher than the Ohio Bureau of Labor Statistics estimated. He argues that the miners of Ohio and Illinois averaged $406 in 1890; Jensen, *Winning of the Midwest*, 240.

9. S. M. Jelly, *The Voice of Labor* (Philadelphia: H. J. Smith & Co., 1888), 351–52 (quotation); Croly, *Marcus Alonzo Hanna*, 1923), 89–92; Roy, *Coal Miners*, 242–61.

10. Partisan papers tended to exaggerate the influence of the mine vote. The *Ohio State Journal*, August 19, 1890, for instance, insisted that in 1890 the miners' union controlled ten thousand votes in Perry County alone. Given that there were twenty

thousand miners in the whole state, this number is clearly wrong. Also see *Columbus Press-Post*, September 12, 17, 1890, for the importance that the political parties attached to the miners' vote.

11. *Ohio State Journal* (Columbus), August 16, 19, September 14, 1890; *New York Times*, December 23, 1894; *Columbus Post-Press*, September 12, 1890; *Cleveland Citizen*, February 18, 1893.

12. Chris Evans, *History of the United Mine Workers of America*, 2 vols. (Indianapolis, IN: UMWA, 1918–1920), 1:3–29; Frank Julian Warne, *The Coal-Mine Workers: A Study in Labor Organizations* (New York: Longman, Green, 1905), 205–9.

13. *National Labor Tribune*, July 26, 1890; Roy, *Coal Miners*, 262–66.

14. Roy, *Coal Miners*, 262–66; Evans, *United Mine Workers*, 2:107 (quotation).

15. Roy, *Coal Miners*, 262–66; Evans, *United Mine Workers*, 2:102, 105–8, 114–16.

16. *United Mine Workers Journal* (Columbus), April 23, 30, May 7, 14, 1891; Evans, *United Mine Workers*, 2:128–30.

17. Evans, *United Mine Workers*, 2:105–8, 128–30; Roy, *Coal Miners*, 262–66 (quotation); *United Mine Workers Journal*, May 14, 1891.

18. *United Mine Workers Journal*, May 7, 1891; Jensen, *Winning of the Midwest*, 240.

19. *United Mine Workers Journal*, July 9, 1891; Green, *Fact Stranger than Fiction*, 197.

20. *United Mine Workers Journal*, July 9 (Jones), September 10 (McBride), 1891.

21. Ibid., December 24, 1891 (quotation), January 28, March 10, 1892; Evans, *United Mine Workers*, 2:159; Officers' expense book, box 23, District 6 Collection, United Mine Workers of America, Mahn Center for Archives and Special Collections, Ohio University, Athens.

22. *United Mine Workers Journal*, February 11, 19, 1892, March 9, 1893; Roy, *Coal Miners*, 300; *New York Times*, December 23, 1894; Evans, *United Mine Workers*, 2:188.

23. Evans, *United Mine Workers*, 2:194–95, 199, 203–4, 206–7; Roy, *Coal Miners*, 300.

24. *National Labor Tribune*, April 14, 1893.

25. *Cincinnati Enquirer*, November 3, 1892; *Columbus Dispatch*, April 6, 1893; Robert P. Skinner, "The New President of the American Federation of Labor," *Harper's Weekly* 39 (January 5, 1895): 4; *United Mine Workers Journal*, October 20, 1892.

26. Jensen, *Winning of the Midwest*, 240; *United Mine Workers Journal*, March 9, April 6 (Nugent), *National Labor Tribune* (Pittsburgh, PA), April 14, *Columbus Dispatch*, April 6, 12, 1893; Roy, *Coal Miners*, 302.

27. *United Mine Workers Journal*, January 5, 12, February 2, 23 (manifesto), March 30 (Davis), April 6, 1893.

28. Ibid., July 6, August 17, 24, 1893.

29. Ibid., September 5, 1893.

30. Ibid., December 28, 1893, January 4, 1894.

31. *Columbus Dispatch*, August 9, 24, September 19, *United Mine Workers Journal*, August 10 (quotation), 24, September 21, 1893.

32. *Columbus Dispatch*, October 3, *United Mine Workers Journal*, October 12, 1893.

33. *United Mine Workers Journal*, February 8, 1894; Evans, *United Mine Workers*, 2:303–4 (quotations); Roy, *Coal Miners*, 302–3; *Columbus Dispatch*, August 9, October 24, 1893, February 6, 1894.

34. *United Mine Workers Journal*, February 8, April 26, 1894.

35. *New York Times*, April 22, *United Mine Workers Journal*, March 15, 1894.

36. Destler, *American Radicalism*, 169–70.

37. *United Mine Workers Journal*, April 5, 12, 1894. On Davis and the People's party, see *Ohio State Journal*, June 29, 1891. On Davis more generally, see Herbert G. Gutman, "The Negro and the United Mine Workers of America: The Career and Letters of Richard L. Davis and Something of Their Meaning," in his *Work, Culture, and Society in Industrializing America: Essays in American Working-class and Social History* (New York:

Vintage Books, 1977), 121–208; Herbert Hill, "Myth-Making as Labor History: Herbert Gutman and the United Mine Workers of America," *International Journal of Politics, Culture, and Society* 2 (Winter 1988): 132–200.

38. *United Mine Workers Journal*, April 12 (McBride), 19, *Cleveland Citizen*, May 19, 1894. Chris Evans's *United Mine Workers*—basically a compilation of speeches, convention proceedings, and scale agreements—has omitted the resolution endorsing the political program as well as other documents suggesting support for Populism. Evans, who was serving as AFL secretary in 1894, opposed the political program. See Evans, *United Mine Workers*, 2:317–33.

39. Roy, *Coal Miners*, 303–4; Evans, *United Mine Workers*, 2:328–29; *United Mine Workers Journal*, April 12 (quotation), 19, May 10, 1894.

40. *Annual Report of the Ohio Bureau of Labor Statistics, 1894*, 125; *New York Times*, April 18, 22, 1894.

41. *Columbus Dispatch*, May 21, 22, *Columbus Post-Press*, May 21, *Cleveland Citizen*, May 26, *United Mine Workers Journal*, May 24, 1894.

42. *New Lexington Tribune*, April 25, *Pomeroy Weekly Tribune Telegraph*, May 23 (quotation), 30, 1894.

43. *Columbus Post-Press*, May 16 (quotation), *United Mine Workers Journal*, May 24, 1894.

44. Evans, *United Mine Workers*, 2:349–50. See also Roy, *Coal Miners*, 306–7; *Columbus Post-Press*, May 17, 1894; *Ohio Bureau of Labor Statistics Annual Report, 1894*, 126; *United Mine Workers Journal*, May 24, 1894.

45. Jeremy Brecher, *Strike!* (Boston, MA: South End Press, 1972), 69–78; *New York Times*, May 5, 1894; Roy, *Coal Miners*, 307–8; William McKinley to Asa Bushnell, July 5, 1894, McKinley to George Garretson, June 29, 1894, McKinley Letterbooks, Ohio Historical Society.

46. *Columbus Dispatch*, May 30, June 2, 1894; McKinley to James C. Howe, June 15, 1894, McKinley Letterbooks.

47. *United Mine Workers Journal*, June 14 (first quotation), 21 (second and third quotations), *Ohio State Journal*, June 10, 1894.

48. Evans, *United Mine Workers*, 2:350–57; Roy, *Coal Miners*, 308–10; *United Mine Workers Journal*, June 14, 21, 28, 1894.

49. Salvatore, *Eugene Debs*, 114–77; Ray Ginger, *The Bending Cross: A Biography of Eugene Victor Debs* (New Brunswick, NJ: Rutgers University Press, 1949), 85–84; Lindsey, *Pullman Strike*; Schneirov, Stromquist, and Salvatore, *Crisis of the 1890s*.

50. Ginger, *Bending Cross*, 121; Lindsey, *Pullman Strike*, 135; *United Mine Workers Journal*, June 19, *Columbus Post-Press*, July 6, 7 (quotation), 10, *Cincinnati Tribune*, June 26, 1894.

51. *United Mine Workers Journal*, August 9, *Columbus Dispatch*, August 8, 14, 1894.

52. Emery Bernard Howson, "Jacob Sechler Coxey: A Biography of a Monetary Reformer, 1854–1951" (PhD diss., Ohio State University, 1973); Russell B. Nye, "Jacob Coxey," in *A Baker's Dozen: Thirteen Unusual Americans* (East Lansing: Michigan State University Press, 1956), 209–32.

53. Schwantes, *Coxey's Army*, 23–33.

54. Ray Stannard Baker, *American Chronicle: The Autobiography of Ray Stannard Baker* (New York: Charles Scribner's Sons, 1945), 7; Schwantes, *Coxey's Army*, 46.

55. "Where Responsibility Lies," *Leslie's Weekly*, May 10, 1894; Howson, "Jacob Sechler Coxey," 141; Nye, *Baker's Dozen*, 216, 220–21; Thomas Byrnes, "The Menace of Coxeyism: The Character and Methods of the Men," *North American Review* 158 (June 1894): 700.

56. Gompers and Thorne, *Seventy Years of Life and Labor*, 2:11–12; *Public Opinion*, April 12, 1894, 43, April 19, 1894, 69, April 26, 1894, 94; Howson, "Jacob Sechler Coxey," 146 (quotation); Hicks, *Populist Revolt*, 322–23.

57. *Washington News* editorial reprinted in *Public Opinion*, April 5, 1894, 24; Howson, "Jacob Sechler Coxey," 146–47; Nye, *Baker's Dozen*, 224.

58. Martin Ridge, *Ignatius Donnelly: Portrait of a Politician* (Chicago: University of Chicago Press, 1962), 329–30; Gompers and Thorne, *Seventy Years of Life and Labor*, 2:1–12; *Public Opinion*, April 19, 1894, 70. The speech Coxey planned to give on the Capitol steps can be found in Howson, "Jacob Sechler Coxey," 429.

59. Howson, "Jacob Sechler Coxey," 171–75.

60. *Columbus Dispatch*, August 15, *Columbus Press-Post*, August 15, *Ohio State Journal*, August 16, 1894.

61. The proceedings of the convention are reprinted in *United Mine Workers Journal*, August 23, *Columbus Post-Press*, August 16, *Columbus Dispatch*, August 16, *Ohio State Journal*, August 16, 1894.

62. *New York Times*, August 20, 1894.

63. *Columbus Post-Press*, August 18, *Ohio State Journal*, August 18, *Topeka Advocate*, August 29, 1894.

64. *Columbus Dispatch*, August 28, 1894.

65. *Columbus Post-Press*, August 3, 4, 1894; Smith, *Republican Party in Ohio*, 1:655–56.

66. *Annual Report of the Ohio Secretary of State, 1894*, 261.

67. *Chicago Tribune*, December 9, 1895.

68. *AFL Proceedings, 1894*, 14.

69. *A Verbatum [sic] Report of the Discussion on the Political Programme, at the Denver Convention of the American Federation of Labor, December 14, 15, 1894* (New York: Freytag Press), 4.

70. *AFL Proceedings, 1894*, 14.

71. *Verbatum Report*, 40, 44, 50–51.

72. All five delegates who argued for passage of the preamble voted for McBride. Only one of the seven delegates who spoke against the preamble voted for McBride. Of the eight delegates who spoke in favor of plank 10, seven voted for McBride. Only three of the sixteen delegates who spoke in opposition to plank 10 voted for McBride. Of the twenty-three delegates who voted for both the passage of the preamble and the retention of the original plank 10, nineteen were for McBride. Nine of those nineteen delegates represented unions that voted for Gompers in 1893. *Verbatum Report*.

73. *National Labor Tribune*, January 10, 1895.

7—Labor Populism in Ohio and the Nation

1. *Cleveland Citizen*, January 5, 12, 1895.

2. *Cleveland Plain Dealer*, January 20, 1895.

3. Philip Foner, *History of the Labor Movement in the United States*, vol. 2, *From the Founding of the American Federation of Labor to the Emergence of American Imperialism* (New York: International Publishers, 1947), 325–26. See also *Report of the Ohio Secretary of State, 1894* (Columbus, 1895); Nash, *Conflict and Accommodation*, 54–55.

4. *Chicago Tribune*, December 9, 1895. See also Salvatore, *Eugene V. Debs*, 156–61; Foner, *History of the Labor Movement*, 2:287–326; Glad, *McKinley, Bryan, and the People*, 148–50; Destler, *American Radicalism*, 162–211; Klotsche, "'United Front' Populists"; Wyman, "Agrarian or Working-class Radicalism?"

5. Hicks, *Populist Revolt*, 333; Ridge, *Ignatius Donnelly*, 240 (quotation).

6. *Cleveland Citizen*, December 8, 1894; "The American Bimetallic Party: A New Political Organization: Statement of the Issue and an Address to the People" (Washington, DC: American Bimetallic League, 1895).

7. Destler, *American Radicalism*, 170 (quotation); Howson, "Jacob Sechler Coxey," 178–37; Ridge, *Ignatius Donnelly*, 240; Glad, *McKinley, Bryan, and the People*, 148–50.

8. *American Non-Conformist* (Indianapolis, IN), January 3, 10, 1895; *Cleveland Citizen*, December 8 (quotation), 22, 29, 1894, January 5, 12, 1895.

9. *Cleveland Citizen*, February 16, 1895. See also John McBride, "The Kind of Money Needed," *American Federationist* 2 (August 1895): 106–7.

10. "Judge Trumbull Writes a Populist Platform," *Public Opinion* 18 (1895), 30; Destler, *American Radicalism*, 229 (Lloyd). See also *American Non-Conformist*, January 3, 1895; *Chicago Tribune*, December 28–30, 1894; Chester McArthur Destler, *Henry Demarest Lloyd and the Empire of Reform* (Philadelphia: University of Pennsylvania Press, 1963), 279–80; Caro Lloyd, *Henry Demarest Lloyd, 1847–1903: A Biography* (New York: Putnam, 1912), 257.

11. *National Watchman* (Washington, DC), February 22, 1895, reprinted in McVey, "Populist Movement," 200–202. See also *American Non-Conformist*, February 21, *Cleveland Citizen*, February 16, 1895; Peffer, *Populism*, 109–14.

12. *National Watchman*, February 22, 1895. See also Destler, *American Radicalism*, 170, 228–29.

13. "American Bimetallic Party"; Peffer, *Populism*, 115–17; *Cleveland Citizen*, January 26, 1895.

14. Peffer, *Populism*, 117–19.

15. *People's Party Paper*, July 20, 1894. See also ibid., July 27, 1894; Barton Shaw, *The Wool-Hat Boys: Georgia's Populist Party* (Baton Rouge: Louisiana State University Press, 1984), 167–70; C. Vann Woodward, *Tom Watson: Agrarian Rebel* (1938; reprint, New York: Oxford University Press, 1966), 278–301.

16. *People's Party Paper*, November 15, 1895.

17. Ibid., November 29, 1895.

18. Ibid., December 27, 1895; *Sound Money*, December 24, 1895, January 7, 10, 1896.

19. *People's Party Paper*, January 17, 1896. Other historians note Watson's confrontation with Coxey and his pronouncements on socialism, but they place them in different contexts. See Robert M. Saunders, "The Transformation of Tom Watson, 1894–1895," *Georgia Historical Quarterly* 56 (Fall 1970): 343–47; Shaw, *Wool-Hat Boys*, 171–73; Bruce Palmer, *"Man over Money": The Southern Populist Critique of American Capitalism* (Chapel Hill: University of North Carolina Press, 1980), 169–82.

20. *People's Party Paper*, December 27, 1895. The plank in question was the land plank, which called for the end of landholding for speculative purposes.

21. Thomas E. Watson to Marion Butler, December 23, 28, 1895, Marion Butler Papers, Southern Historical Collection, Wilson Library, University of North Carolina, Chapel Hill, microfilm edition, reel 1.

22. *New York Times*, May 16, August 20, November 8, *Cleveland Plain Dealer*, November 7, 8, 1894.

23. *Cleveland Plain Dealer*, January 20, 1895; Howson, "Jacob Sechler Coxey," 224, 258 (quotation).

24. *Sound Money*, July 25, 1895.

25. Croly, *Marcus Alonzo Hanna*, 176–77; Smith, *Republican Party in Ohio*, 1:659–64.

26. Smith, *Republican Party in Ohio*, 1:663–64 (platform); *New York Times*, May 29, 1895 (Sherman); Powell, *Democratic Party of the State of Ohio*, 338.

27. *Columbus Dispatch*, August 1, 2, *Columbus Post-Press*, August 1, 2, 1895.

28. *Columbus Post-Press*, August 2, 1895.

29. *Columbus Post-Press*, August 2, *Columbus Dispatch*, August 2, *Sound Money*, August 8, 1895.

30. *Cleveland Citizen*, August 8, 1895.

31. *Sound Money*, August 8, October 3, 1895.

32. *Columbus Dispatch*, August 1 (quotation), 2, *Sound Money*, October 3, 1895. Stark did receive the party's nomination for Supreme Court judge, but this was mostly because tradition dictated that the party nominate a lawyer, and as the trade unionists were proud to point out, there were no lawyers among those pushing for broad-gauge reform.

33. *Columbus Post-Press*, August 18–21, *Cleveland Plain Dealer*, August 17–21, 1895; Powell, *Democratic Party of the State of Ohio*, 1:338–40.

34. *Columbus Post-Press*, August 21, *Sound Money*, August 22, 1895.

35. *Cleveland Plain Dealer*, August 21–22, *Cincinnati Enquirer*, August 21–22, *New York Times*, August 21, 1895.

36. *Sound Money*, July 11, August 22 (second quotation), 29 (third quotation), September 5, 12 (first and fourth quotations), 1895.

37. *Sound Money*, September 12, 26, 1895.

38. The schedules of Coxey and these speakers appeared in *Sound Money* throughout the fall.

39. *Sound Money*, July 11, 1895.

40. *Cleveland Citizen*, August 10, 1895. See also *Cleveland Plain Dealer*, September 3, *Columbus Press-Post*, September 2, *Columbus Dispatch*, September 2, *Ohio State Journal*, September 3, *Sound Money*, October 17, 1895.

41. *Jackson Standard Journal*, September 4, *Sound Money*, September 4, 12, October 10, 24, *Cleveland Citizen*, November 15, 1895.

42. *Cincinnati Enquirer*, September 8, *Cincinnati Tribune*, September 8, *Cincinnati Chronicle*, September 13, October 25, November 1, 1895.

43. *Cincinnati Chronicle*, September 13, October 25, November 1 (quotation), 1895.

44. *Cincinnati Chronicle*, November 15, 1895.

45. *American Nonconformist*, January 17, 1895.

46. McBride, "Our Official Policy," *American Federationist* 1 (February 1895): 282. See also *National Labor Tribune*, December 27, 1894; *Columbus Dispatch*, January 29, 1895; "Socialism (Limited)," *Nation* 60 (January 3, 1895): 4.

47. *American Non-Conformist*, January 3, 17 (quotation), 1895; P. J. McGuire to August McCraith, February 18, 1895, cited in Taft, *The AFL in the Time of Gompers*, 127; *Verbatum Report*; *Cleveland Citizen*, January 5, 1895.

48. *Columbus Dispatch*, February 14, 15, March 12, May 10, *National Labor Tribune*, February 21, *Columbus Press*, February 13–16, 1895; Evans, *United Mine Workers*, 2:365–66, 368–71.

49. AFL executive council minutes, April 24, December 9, 1895, *The American Federation of Labor Records: The Samuel Gompers Era* (Microfilming Corporation of America, 1979), reel 2.

50. *United Mine Workers Journal*, August 9, *Columbus Dispatch*, August 14, 1894.

51. *American Federationist* (March 1895); John Lennon to August McCraith, February 27, Lennon to McBride, February 27, 1895, *American Federation of Labor Records*, reel 59.

52. AFL executive council minutes, April 22–24, 1894, *American Federation of Labor Records*, reel 2; *AFL Proceedings, 1895*, 12.

53. McBride, "Kind of Money Needed."

54. McBride, "Producers vs. Non-Producers."

55. *Cleveland Citizen*, November 16, *National Labor Tribune*, October 31, 1895.

56. *Chicago Tribune*, undated clipping found in *American Federation of Labor Records*, reel 24. *New York Press*, July 21, 1895; *Cleveland Citizen*, November 9, 1895; Taft, *AFL in the Time of Gompers*, 127.

57. *New York Times*, December 10–12, 1995; *Chicago Tribune*, undated clipping.

58. *AFL Proceedings, 1895*, 15–16.

59. Ibid., 53, 77.

60. *New York Herald*, December 15, 1895.

61. *AFL Proceedings, 1895*, 79–80.

62. See, for example, Sanders, *Roots of Reform*, 85; John R. Commons et al., *History of Labor in the United States*, 4 vols. (1918; reprint, New York: Augustus M. Kelley, 1966), 2:514.

63. *American Federationist* 2 (February 1896): 224–25; Gompers to W. H. Milburn, September 23, 1896, *American Federation of Labor Records*, reel 59.

64. *Cincinnati Chronicle*, November 15, 1895.

65. The best account of the maneuvering within the People's party in early 1896 is Robert F. Durden, *The Climax of Populism: The Election of 1896* (Lexington: University of Kentucky Press, 1965). Also see Glad, *McKinley, Bryan, and the People*, 151–55; Hicks, *Populist Revolt*, 340–79.

66. *Cleveland Citizen*, January 5, 12, February 16 (quotation), 1895.

67. *Cincinnati Chronicle*, August 1893, April 5, 19, May 31, September 13, October 4, 1895, June 5, July 17 (first quotation), 1896; William Jennings Bryan, "Cross of Gold Speech," at *History Matters*, http://historymatters.gmu.edu/d/5354/ (accessed June 17, 2009); Michael Kazin, *A Godly Hero: The Life of William Jennings Bryan* (New York: Alfred A. Knopf, 2007), 59–61 (second quotation).

68. *Columbus Post-Press*, July 6, 1896; Witt, "Labor Movement in Cleveland," 10–11.

69. *Cincinnati Chronicle*, June 5 (first quotation), *Cleveland Citizen*, March 21 (Martin), June 13, November 23, 1895; *Columbus Press*, July 19, *Sound Money*, July 16, 1896; Argersinger, *Populism and Politics*, 243. In the winter of 1895, the UMWA, which had been affiliated with both the Knights of Labor and the AFL, ended a long-running dispute with the leadership of the Knights of Labor by forming the rival International Order of the Knights of Labor. Hoping to attract those Knights who had been alienated by Daniel DeLeon and James Sovereign, the miners selected Charles Martin to run the new order.

70. *Sound Money*, May 22, June 5, 16, 1896. It is uncertain as to whether the central labor bodies of Dayton, Toledo, and Akron formed formal alliances with the People's party, but in each city the local Populist party enjoyed significant labor support. Central body officials openly identified themselves with the People's party and ran for office as Populists. Additionally, in each city the People's party polled best in the working-class wards and neighborhoods.

71. *Sound Money*, March 20, 24, April 21, *Cleveland Citizen*, March 21 (quotation), 28, May 16, 1896.

72. *Columbus Post-Press*, June 24, 1896.

73. Lloyd, *Henry Demarest Lloyd*, 259; Durden, *Climax of Populism*, 25.

74. *Cleveland Citizen*, May 30, 1896. See also *Sound Money*, July 10, 16, 1896.

75. *Columbus Post-Press*, July 20, 23, *Cincinnati Enquirer*, July 21, 22, 1896.

76. *Columbus Post-Press*, July 24, *Cleveland Plain Dealer*, July 24, 1896.

77. *Columbus Post-Press*, July 24, *Cleveland Plain Dealer*, July 24, 1896.

78. *Sound Money*, July 30 (quotation), September 3, November 5, 1896.

79. *Sound Money*, August 27, September 3, 10, *Cleveland Citizen*, August 29, *Columbus Press*, August 26, 27, 1896.

80. *Sound Money*, August 27, *Columbus Press*, August 26, 27, 1896.

81. McBride bought the *Columbus Record*, which had been an American Protective Association organ and close to the city's Republican party, and transformed it into a labor newspaper. It is unclear why McBride, nominally a Roman Catholic and hostile to the Republicans, retained the paper's name. No copies of the paper from McBride's era are known to exist, but it was often quoted in the *United Mine Workers Journal*.

82. *United Mine Workers Journal*, August 27 (quotation), September 23, 30, *Sound Money*, October 29, 1896; *Cleveland Citizen*, July 10, 1897; Coletta, *William Jennings Bryan*, 1:169.

83. *United Mine Workers Journal*, July 30 (quotation), September 10, 17, 23, 1896.

84. Evans, *United Mine Workers*, 2:435–56; Roy, *Coal Miners*, 321, 323; *Ohio State Journal*, January 17, 1897.

85. Roy, *Coal Miners*, 327–38. K. Austin Kerr, "Labor-Management Cooperation: An 1897 Case," *Pennsylvania Magazine of History and Biography* 99 (January 1975): 45–71; Phelan, *Divided Loyalties*, 26–46.

86. *AFL Proceedings, 1896.*

87. American Federation of Labor, *History, Encyclopedia Reference Book* (Washington, DC: American Federation of Labor, 1919), 63.

8—Progressivism

1. Martzolff, "Recent Ohio Legislation," 639; *Cleveland Citizen*, September 7 (Hayes), 1912.

2. See for example, *Columbus Post Press*, March 8, 1908; Herbert Bigelow, "Address," *Proceedings of the Ohio State Federation of Labor, 1911*, 68–76; J. A. Robinson, "Report of the Secretary of the Legislative Committee," *Proceedings of the Ohio State Federation of Labor, 1906*, 21.

3. Hayes, *Cleveland Labor*, 4–5 (quotation); "Direct Legislation League," broadside taped into CLC minute books, June 3, 1893; *Cincinnati Chronicle*, June 1893.

4. *Proceedings of the Annual Convention of the Ohio State Trades and Labor Assembly, 1894*, 13.

5. See, for example, Johnson, *My Story*, 156–205; Warner, *Progressivism in Ohio*.

6. Howe, *Confessions of a Reformer*, 157–58; Johnson, *My Story*, 201 (Hanna); *Cincinnati Enquirer*, October 17, 1903, cited in Walters, *Joseph Benson Foraker*, 205 (Foraker).

7. *Proceedings of the Ohio State Federation of Labor, 1897*. Between 1897 and 1909, state trade unionists used the names Ohio Federation of Labor and Ohio State Federation of Labor interchangeably.

8. See for example, Ike S. Byrum, "What a Real Constructive State Federation Has Done with the Aid of Sister Organizations in the Past Five Years in Giving to the Working Men, Women and Children of Ohio, Some of the Best Labor Legislation in the World: Report of Legislative Agent, Ike S. Byrum and Executive Board of the Ohio State Federation of Labor, the 70th General Assembly of Ohio 1911 and Record of Labor Laws Enacted since 1907" (Cleveland: Ohio State Federation of Labor, 1911); Ohio State Federation of Labor, "Achievements of the Ohio State Federation of Labor, State Branch, American Federation of Labor, 1907–1944: A Brief Resume of What Has Been Accomplished by Labor of Ohio upon the Legislative Field by Unity of Action" (Columbus: Ohio State Federation of Labor, 1944).

9. Patricia Terpak Rose, "Design and Expediency: The Ohio Federation of Labor as a Legislative Lobby, 1883–1935" (PhD diss., Ohio State University, 1975), 70–72, 76–77; *Cleveland Citizen*, October 16, 23, 30, 1909; "Excerpts from Accounts of the 1909 Convention of the American Federation of Labor in Toronto," in *The Samuel Gompers Papers*, vol. 8, *Progress and Reaction in the Age of Reform, 1909–1913*, ed. Peter J. Albert and Grace Palladino (Urbana: University of Illinois Press, 2001), 16–17. On the efforts of Gompers and the AFL leadership to purge Socialists, see Greene, *Pure and Simple Politics*, 133–36.

10. Henry C. Wright, *Bossism in Cincinnati* (Cincinnati: Self-published, 1905); Lincoln Steffens, "Ohio: A Tale of Two Cities," *McClure's Magazine* 25 (July 1905): 293–311.

11. Warner, *Progressivism in Ohio*, 160–61; Walters, *Joseph Benson Foraker*, 2.

12. Warner, *Progressivism in Ohio*, 160–61; Russell H. Anderson, "Myron T. Herrick, 1904–1906," in *The Governors of Ohio*, 2nd ed. (Columbus: Ohio Historical Society, 1969), 140–43; Walters, *Joseph Benson Foraker*, 210.

13. John R. McLean was so conservative that his *Washington Post* spoke positively of a possible Foraker presidential campaign in 1908; Walters, *Joseph Benson Foraker*, 209.

14. Warner, *Progressivism in Ohio*, 161–62 (quotation); Howe, *Confessions of a Reformer*, 159-60; Ophia D. Smith, "John M. Pattison, 1906," in *Governors of Ohio*, 144–47.

15. *Proceedings of the Ohio State Federation of Labor, 1905*, 4, 6; Frank Parker Stockbridge, "Ohio Wide Awake," *Everybody's Magazine* 27 (November 1912): 696–707.

16. *Cincinnati Chronicle*, January 20, 1906; Howe, *Confessions of a Reformer*, 160–62 (quotations); Brand Whitlock to Norman Hapgood, April 8, 1908, in *The Letters and Journals of Brand Whitlock*, ed. Allan Nevins, 2 vols. (New York: D. Appleton-Century, 1936), 1:91–92. See also undated clippings, scrapbook 1, box 7, Herbert Seely Bigelow Papers, Cincinnati Historical Society.

17. *Cleveland Citizen*, February 3, March 3, *Cincinnati Chronicle*, February 10, 24, 1906.

18. Dwight L. Smith, "Andrew L. Harris," in *Governors of Ohio*, 148–50; Warner, *Progressivism in Ohio*, 191, 193–96.

19. J. A. Robinson, "Report of the Legislative Committee," *Proceedings of the Ohio State Federation of Labor, 1906*, 18–21.

20. Ibid., 18–20; Howe, *Confessions of a Reformer*, 162–63 (quotation).

21. Robinson, "Report of the Legislative Committee," 21.

22. J. A. Robinson, "Report of First Vice President," in *Proceedings of the Ohio State Federation of Labor, 1907*, 10–11; Llewelyn Lewis, "President's Report," ibid., *1908*, 17; Whitlock to William Allen White, April 8, 1908, in *Letters and Journals of Brand Whitlock*, 90–91; *Cleveland Citizen*, January 4, 11, 1908.

23. *Cleveland Citizen*, January 4, 11, 1908. Foraker's opposition to direct legislation remained strong. In his autobiography he denounced "the Initiative, the Referendum, and all other Socialistic ideas." Joseph Benson Foraker, *Notes on a Busy Life* (Cincinnati: Stewart and Kidd, 1916), 205, also 531–54.

24. Warner, *Progressivism in Ohio*, 194–96; *Toledo Union Leader*, March 27, April 10, 17, 1908.

25. *Cincinnati Chronicle*, May 23, 1908.

26. Warner, *Progressivism in Ohio*, 211–16; Elizabeth J. Hauser, "Introduction," in Johnson, *My Story*, xvi; E. B. Whitney, "Judson Harmon," *North American Review* 187 (June 1908): 835–36; Wittke, "Peter Witt," 366. Bryan and his Ohio allies would have their revenge against Harmon by derailing his 1912 presidential bid. Bryan's denunciation of Harmon as a "reactionary" and a Wall Street favorite ended the Ohioan's hope for the Democratic nomination. James M. Cox, *Journey through My Years* (New York: Simon and Schuster, 1946), 133; *New York Times*, January 3, 1912; Arthur C. Cole, "Judson Harmon," in *Dictionary of American Biography*, ed. Dumas Malone, 21 vols. (New York: Scribner's, 1943), 18:277–78.

27. Warner, *Progressivism in Ohio*, 215–16; Robert M. Crunden, *A Hero in Spite of Himself: Brand Whitlock in Art, Politics, and War* (New York: Alfred A. Knopf, 1969), 197; Powell, *Democratic Party in Ohio*, 1:419; Judson Harmon to M. B. Chase, May 16, 1908, unnumbered folder, box 1, Judson Harmon Papers, Cincinnati Historical Society. The platform was printed in the *Columbus Press-Post*, May 6, 1908.

28. Peter Witt to Brand Whitlock, May 7, to Simon Hickler, May 14, to Judson Harmon, June 8, 1908, folder 1, box 1, Peter Witt Papers, Western Reserve Historical Society, Cleveland, OH; also Wittke, "Peter Witt," 366.

29. Elizabeth J. Hauser, "Introduction," in Johnson, *My Story*, xvi. Also see Newton D. Baker to Daniel Kiefer, June 17, 1908, folder 17, box 3, Newton Baker Papers, Western Reserve Historical Society. The Progressive wing supported Harmon's reelec-

tion bid, insisting he was an "honest administrator of state affairs" and much better than his Republican opponent, Warren G. Harding. See Whitlock to Lincoln Steffens, October 31, 1910, in *Letters and Journal of Brand Whitlock*, 139.

30. Warner, *Progressivism in Ohio*, 219–22. Some of the intrigues of the Foraker-Taft rivalry are detailed in the Foraker Papers; see especially, boxes 75–94, which contain the senator's correspondence for 1908. On Taft's opposition to direct legislation, see William Howard Taft, "The Initiative and the Recall," in *The Collected Works of William Howard Taft*, ed. David Burton, 8 vols. (Athens: Ohio University Press, 2001–2004), 5:56–68.

31. Warner, *Progressivism in Ohio*, 222–23.

32. Albert Pitt, "Report of the Legislative Agent," in *Proceedings of the Ohio State Federation of Labor, 1909*, 61–62 (quotation); Thomas Rumsey, "Report of the Executive Board," ibid., 55–58; Llewellyn Lewis, "President's Report," ibid., 52–54; Peter Witt to Judson Harmon, January 11, 1913, Witt Papers.

33. Barbara A. Terzian, "Ohio's Constitutional Conventions and Constitutions," in Benedict and Winkler, *History of Ohio Law*, 40–87.

34. Charles B. Galbreath, "The Constitutional Convention of Ohio and Its Work and a History of Previous Conventions," *Columbus Sunday Dispatch Centennial Library Edition*, August 25, 1912, 35.

35. Donnelly, "Methods and Accomplishments in Ohio," 554. See also *The Labor Day Yearbook 1911, and Souvenir Program of the Ohio State Federation of Labor Convention* (Cleveland: Ohio State Federation of Labor, 1911), 26; "What a Real Constructive State Federation Has Done with the Aid of Sister Organizations in the Past Five Years in Giving the Working Men, Women, and Children of Ohio Some of the Best Legislation in the World: Report of the Legislative Agent Ike S. Byrum and Executive Board of the Ohio State Federation of Labor" (Cleveland: Ohio State Federation of Labor, 1911), 4–5; Craig Phelan, *William Green: Biography of a Labor Leader* (Albany: State University of New York Press, 1989): 20–21.

36. John Voll, "President's Report," *Proceedings of the Ohio State Federation of Labor, 1911*, 17.

37. "What a Real Constructive State Federation Has Done," 4–5. See also *Toledo Union Leader*, June 30, 1911.

38. *Toledo Union Leader*, January 13, 1911; "Executive Board Report," *Proceedings of the Ohio State Federation of Labor, 1911*, 21.

39. Warner, *Progressivism in Ohio*, 297; Robert Bigelow, "Address," *Proceedings of the Ohio State Federation of Labor, 1911*, 68–76; Stockbridge, "Ohio Wide Awake," 707.

40. Lloyd Sponholtz, "The 1912 Constitutional Convention in Ohio: The Call-Up and Nonpartisan Selection of Delegates," *Ohio History* 79 (Summer/Autumn 1970): 213–14; Warner, *Progressivism in Ohio*, 299.

41. *Ohio State Journal*, July 23, September 2, 9, 13, 16, 1911; Sponholtz, "The 1912 Constitutional Convention," 214–15; Warner, *Progressivism in Ohio*, 298–99.

42. *Cleveland Citizen*, July 22, August 19, *Cleveland Plain Dealer*, July 8, 1911; Sponholtz, "The 1912 Constitutional Convention," 216–17; Warner, *Progressivism in Ohio*, 330; *Cleveland Citizen*, August 19, 1911; Stephen Stilwell, "In Memoriam: Harry D. Thomas," *Proceedings of the Ohio State Federation of Labor, 1913*, 37.

43. *Cleveland Citizen*, August 5 (quotation), 1911, January 20, 1912. On the local's role in Cleveland's labor movement, see Hayes, *Cleveland Labor*, 7.

44. *Cleveland Citizen*, August 19, September 2, 9, 1911. At that time, $25 was enough money to print about thirty thousand pieces of campaign literature; see Harry D. Thomas, "Secretary-Treasurer's Report," *Proceedings of the Ohio State Federation of Labor, 1912*, 20.

45. *Cleveland Citizen*, August 26, September 9, 23, 30, 1911.

46. Ibid., October 21, 1911. See also Herbert Bigelow's "Address," and "Program for Constitutional Convention," in *Proceedings of the Ohio State Federation of Labor, 1911*, 68–76, 96–97; *Labor Day Yearbook 1911, and Souvenir Program*, 4.

47. *Cleveland Citizen*, November 11, 1911; Donnelly, "Methods and Accomplishments in Ohio," 554; Ohio State Board of Commerce, "Constitutional Convention Proposals" (Columbus: Journal of Commerce, 1912), 24. Also see Robert Crosser, "The Initiative and Referendum Amendments in the Proposed Ohio Constitution," *Annals of the American Academy of Political and Social Science* 42 (September 1912): 191; Stockbridge, "Ohio Wide Awake," 707.

48. Crosser was so close to the labor movement that Harry Thomas would address him as "brother" in official OSFL correspondence, despite the fact that he was an attorney and law professor. See, for example, Thomas to Crosser, March 17, 1911, folder 5, box 1, ser. 1, Robert Crosser Papers, Ohio Historical Society, Columbus.

49. *Toledo Union Leader*, January 26, 1912; *Cleveland Citizen*, December 23, 1911, June 1, 1912.

50. *Toledo Union Leader*, January 26, *Cleveland Citizen*, April 12, 1912; Donnelly, "Methods and Accomplishments in Ohio," 554; Samuel Gompers, "The Ohio Constitutional Amendments" (Cleveland: Ohio State Federation of Labor, 1912), 1; "Executive Board Report," *Proceedings of the Ohio State Federation of Labor, 1912*, 22–23. There is some debate as to the number of trade unionists at the convention. Ernest I. Antrim, a delegate from Van Wert County, wrote that there were twenty-one union members among the delegates, while historian Hoyt Landon Warner places the number at ten. Ernest I. Antrim, "The Ohio Constitutional Convention," *Independent* 72 (June 1912): 1423–26; Warner, *Progressivism in Ohio*, 312–13. The number used here is the one used by the trade unionists themselves.

51. *Cleveland Citizen*, December 2, 1911, January 20, February 10, 1912. For samples of letters sent by local unions to delegates, see folder 12, box 1, ser. 1, Crosser Papers. For samples of OSFL circulars to local unions, see International Brotherhood of Electrical Workers Local 54 Papers, Ohio Historical Society (hereafter IBEW Papers).

52. Warner, *Progressivism in Ohio*, 314; Galbreath, "Constitutional Convention of Ohio and Its Work and a History of Previous Conventions," 35–36; Stilwell, "In Memoriam: Harry D. Thomas," 37; *Journal of the Constitutional Convention of the State of Ohio* (Columbus: F. J. Freer Printing, 1912), 7–15.

53. Warner, *Progressivism in Ohio*, 317–18. On the 1873 constitutional convention, see Terzian, "Ohio's Constitutional Conventions and Constitutions," 60–63.

54. *Toledo Union Leader*, May 3, 1912; Warner, *Progressivism in Ohio*, 334–37.

55. Warner, *Progressivism in Ohio*, 336–37; Henry Elson, "Making a New Constitution for Ohio," *Review of Reviews* 46 (July 1912): 85; Galbreath, "Constitutional Convention of Ohio and Its Work," 37.

56. Crosser, "Initiative and Referendum Amendments," 191.

57. *Ohio State Journal*, March 22–28, 1912; Crosser, "Initiative and Referendum Amendments," 191–202; Warner, *Progressivism in Ohio*, 320–24. A comparison of state initiative and referendum procedures can be found in Charles B. Galbreath, "Provisions for State-wide Initiative and Referendum," *Annals of the American Academy of Political and Social Science* 43 (September 1912): 81–109.

58. *Ohio State Journal*, March 22–28, 1912; Crosser, "Initiative and Referendum Amendments," 191–202; Warner, *Progressivism in Ohio*, 320–24. Also see various letters, folder 13, box 1, ser. 1, Crosser Papers.

59. *Toledo Union Leader*, March 1, 1912. See also *Cleveland Citizen*, March 2, 1912.

60. Copy of the broadside can be found in folder 13, box 1, ser. 1, Crosser Papers. The changes introduced at the second reading are too complicated to be rehearsed here, but they are detailed in Crosser, "Initiative and Referendum Amendments," 191–202; Warner, *Progressivism in Ohio*, 320–24.

61. *Ohio State Journal*, March 26, 1912.

62. Crosser, "Initiative and Referendum Amendments," 198–202; Warner, *Progressivism in Ohio*, 322–23.

63. *Toledo Union Leader*, May 24, 1912.
64. "Executive Board Report," *Proceedings of the Ohio State Federation of Labor, 1912*, 23; OSFL circular to trade and labor unions and central bodies of Ohio, June 26, 1912, IBEW Papers; *Toledo Union Leader*, May 24, 1912.
65. Both the *Toledo Union Leader* and the *Cleveland Citizen* carried the articles in the summer of 1912.
66. *Ohio State Journal*, July 15, 1912; OSFL circular, June 26, 1912, IBEW Papers.
67. *Toledo Union Leader*, June 14, 1912; *American Federationist* editorial reprinted in Gompers, "Ohio Constitution Amendments," 1; Thomas from *Toledo Union Leader*, June 28, 1912.
68. Harry Thomas, "Secretary-Treasurer's Report," *Proceedings of the Ohio State Federation of Labor, 1912*, 20. Samples of these cards can be found in IBEW Papers.
69. John Voll and H. D. Thomas to Trade and Labor Unions of Ohio, June 26, 1912, IBEW Papers.
70. Newton D. Baker to A. Mitchell Palmer, August 31, 1912, folder 9, box 5, Baker Papers; Baker to G. B. Martin, August 20, 1912, folder 8, ibid.
71. Cited in David D. Schmidt, *Citizen Lawmakers: The Ballot Initiative Revolution* (Philadelphia: Temple University Press, 1989), 258.
72. Warner, *Progressivism in Ohio*, 339–40. See also Sponholtz, "The 1912 Constitutional Convention," 212–13.
73. Ohio State Board of Commerce, *Proposed Amendments to the Ohio Constitution to be Adopted or Rejected* (Columbus: Stoneman, 1912), 39, 69.
74. *Cleveland Citizen*, August 17, 1912.
75. Charles B. Galbreath, "The Vote on the Ohio Constitution," *Independent* 73 (December 19, 1912): 1407–10.
76. OSFL circular, June 26, 1912, IBEW Papers; *Toledo Union Leader*, May 24, 1912.
77. *Toledo Union Leader*, August 30, 1912.
78. Harry D. Thomas to Simeon Fess, July 10, 1912, folder 4, box 5, Simeon Fess Papers, Ohio Historical Society.
79. *Ohio State Journal*, September 3, 1911.
80. "Executive Board Report," *Proceedings of the Ohio State Federation of Labor, 1912*, 21.
81. George F. Burba, "The Ohio Law for Workmen's Compensation," *Review of Reviews* 48 (July 1913): 90–93; Phelan, *William Green*, 20–21; Boryczka and Cary, *No Strength without Union*, 149; *Proceedings of the Ohio State Federation of Labor, 1913*; John Moore to William Green, January 7, 1913, William Green Papers, folder 2, box 1, Ohio Historical Society.
82. *Cleveland Citizen*, June 14, 1913.

Conclusion

1. *Columbus Post-Press*, August 17, *Ohio State Journal*, August 17, *Columbus Dispatch*, August 17, 1894.
2. On the linkages between Coxey's plan and the New Deal, see Schwantes, *Coxey's Army*. On the New Deal more generally, see Ellis Hawley, *The New Deal and the Problem of Monopoly: A Study in Economic Ambivalence* (Princeton, NJ: Princeton University Press, 1966); Robert McElvaine, *The Great Depression: America, 1929–1941* (1983; reprint, New York: Three Rivers Press, 1993).
3. For a fuller discussion of these themes, see Postel, *Populist Vision*.
4. Witt, *Cleveland before St. Peter*, 25.
5. *Cleveland Citizen*, September 7, 1912.

Bibliography

Primary Materials

Archival

American Federation of Labor (AFL) Records. The Samuel Gompers Era, 1866–1924, microfilm edition.

Oscar and Freda Ameringer Papers. Oklahoma State Historical Society, Oklahoma City.

Newton Baker Papers. Western Reserve Historical Society, Cleveland.

Herbert Seely Bigelow Papers. Cincinnati Historical Society, Cincinnati.

Marion Butler Papers. Southern Historical Collection, Wilson Library, University of North Carolina, Chapel Hill, microfilm edition.

Cincinnati Central Labor Council Collection. Special Collections Division, University of Cincinnati Library, Cincinnati.

Jacob S. Coxey Papers. Ohio Historical Society, Columbus, microfilm edition.

Robert Crosser Papers. Ohio Historical Society, Columbus.

Simeon Fess Papers. Ohio Historical Society, Columbus.

Joseph B. Foraker Papers. Cincinnati Historical Society, Cincinnati.

William Green Papers. Ohio Historical Society, Columbus.

Judson Harmon Papers. Cincinnati Historical Society, Cincinnati.

Max S. Hayes Papers. Ohio Historical Society, Columbus.

International Brotherhood of Electrical Workers (IBEW) Local 54 Papers. Ohio Historical Society, Columbus.

Samuel L. Jones Papers. Toledo Public Library, Toledo, microfilm edition.

Charles L. Kurtz Papers. Ohio Historical Society, Columbus.

William Martin Papers. Darlington Memorial Library, University of Pittsburgh, Pittsburgh.

William McKinley Gubernatorial Letter Books. Ohio Historical Society, Columbus.

United Mine Workers of America (UMWA), District 6 Collection. Mahn Center for Archives and Special Collections, Ohio University, Athens.

Peter Witt Papers. Western Reserve Historical Society, Cleveland.

Newspapers and Periodicals

Akron Beacon
American Federationist (Indianapolis, and Washington, DC)
American Grange Bulletin (Cincinnati)
American Non-Conformist (Indianapolis)
Athens Messenger
Chicago Tribune
Cincinnati Chronicle
Cincinnati Commercial Gazette
Cincinnati Enquirer
Cincinnati Times-Star
Cleveland Citizen
Cleveland Leader
Cleveland Plain Dealer
Cleveland Recorder
Columbus Catholic Columbian
Columbus Dispatch
Columbus Post-Press
Columbus Press
Columbus Press-Post
Columbus Record
Dayton Journal
Harper's Weekly
Jackson Standard Journal
Leslie's Weekly
Marion Star
McClure's Magazine
Miners' Independent (Massillon)
National Labor Tribune (Pittsburgh)
National Watchman (Washington, DC)
New Lexington Tribune
New Nation (Boston)
New York Herald
New York Times
Ohio Farmer (Cleveland)
Ohio State Journal (Columbus)
Outlook
People's Party Paper (Atlanta)
Plow and Hammer (Tiffin)
Pomeroy Weekly Tribune Telegraph
Public Opinion
Sandusky Daily Register
Sound Money (Massillon)
Southern Mercury (Dallas)
Springfield Republic-Times
Stark County Democrat
Toledo Blade
Toledo Union Leader
Topeka Advocate (Kansas)
United Mine Workers Journal (Columbus)
Warren Western Reserve Democrat

Washington News
Youngstown Vindicator

Convention Proceedings and Reports

Annual Report of the Ohio Bureau of Labor Statistics, 1877–1900.
Annual Report of the Ohio Secretary of State, 1884–1900.
Proceedings of the Annual Convention of the American Federation of Labor, 1894–1897.
Proceedings of the Annual Convention of the Ohio State Grange, 1890–1893.
Proceedings of the Annual Convention of the Ohio State Trades and Labor Assembly, 1893–1896.
Proceedings of the Ninth Annual Convention of the Socialist Labor Party.
Proceedings of the Ohio State Federation of Labor, 1897–1913, 1928.
A Verbatum [sic] Report of the Discussion on the Political Programme, at the Denver Convention of the American Federation of Labor, December 14, 15, 1894. New York: Freytag Press, 1895.

Legal Cases

Arnold v. Yanders, 56 Ohio St. 417 (1897).
L. W. David v. State of Ohio, Ohio Weekly Law Bulletin, 342, 344 (1893).
Moores and Co., v. Bricklayers Union, 13, *Ohio Weekly Law Bulletin* 48, 50 (1890).
Thomas v. Cincinnati, N.O. & T.P. RY. Co.; In re Phelan Circut Court, S.D. Ohio, W.D. 62 F. (1894).
Toledo, Ann Arbor, and Northern Michigan Railway v. Pennsylvania Co., 54 F 730, 739 (C.C.N.D. Ohio 1893).
Wheeling and Terminal Railway Company v. Gilmore, 8 Ohio C.C. 658 (1894).

Published

"Achievements of the Ohio State Federation of Labor, State Branch, American Federation of Labor, 1907–1944: A Brief Resume of What Has Been Accomplished by Labor of Ohio upon the Legislative Field by Unity of Action." Columbus: Ohio State Federation of Labor, 1944.

Amalgamated Association of Iron, Steel, and Tin Workers of North America. *Souvenir of the Eleventh Annual Reunion of the Amalgamated Association of the Iron and Steel Workers, Saturday June 7th, 1890.* Pittsburgh, PA: Amalgamated Association of Iron and Steel Workers, 1890.

"The American Bimetallic Party: A New Political Organization: Statement of the Issue and an Address to the People." Washington, DC: American Bimetallic League, 1895.

Ameringer, Oscar. *If You Don't Weaken: The Autobiography of Oscar Ameringer.* New York: Henry Holt, 1940.

Antrim, Ernest I. "The Ohio Constitutional Convention." *Independent* 72 (June 1912): 1423–26.

Baker, Ray Stannard. *American Chronicle: The Autobiography of Ray Stannard Baker.* New York: Charles Scribner's Sons, 1945.

Brophy, John. *A Miner's Life: An Autobiography.* Madison: University of Wisconsin Press, 1964.

Bryan, William Jennings. *The First Battle: A Story of the Campaign of 1896.* Chicago: W.

B. Conkey, 1897.

Burba, George F. "The Ohio Law for Workmen's Compensation." *Review of Reviews* 48 (July 1913): 90–93.

Byrnes, Thomas. "The Menace of Coxeyism: The Character and Methods of the Men." *North American Review* 158 (June 1894): 697–701.

Central Labor Union (Cleveland, Ohio). *Labor Day Souvenir, 1901.* Cleveland: Cleveland Citizen, 1901.

Clark, Lindley D. "Labor Laws that Have Been Declared Unconstitutional." *Bulletin of the United States Bureau of Labor Statistics* 321 (1922).

"The Cleveland Strike." *Harper's Weekly* 43 (August 19, 1899): 808.

Cox, James M. *Journey through My Years.* New York: Simon and Schuster, 1946.

Crosser, Robert. "The Initiative and Referendum Amendments in the Proposed Ohio Constitution." *Annals of the American Academy of Political and Social Science* 42 (September 1912): 191–202.

Dacus, J. A. *Annals of the Great Strikes in the United States.* Chicago: L. T. Palmer & Co., 1877.

Donnelly, Thomas J. "Methods and Accomplishments in Ohio." *American Federationist* 33 (May 1926): 550–55.

Edwards, George P. "Cleveland Strikes." *Harper's Weekly* 43 (August 5, 1899): 780–81.

Elson, Henry. "Making a New Constitution for Ohio." *Review of Reviews* 46 (July 1912): 83–86.

Evans, Chris. *History of the United Mine Workers of America.* 2 vols. Indianapolis, IN: United Mine Workers of America, 1918–1920.

"Farmers and Working Men of Ohio Read and Consider: A Few Facts that Speak for Themselves." n.p., n.d.

Fitch, John. *The Steel Workers.* New York: Arno Press, 1911.

Foraker, Joseph Benson. *Notes on a Busy Life.* Cincinnati: Stewart and Kidd, 1916.

———. *Speeches of J. B. Foraker.* n.p., n.d.

Foran, M. A. *The Other Side: A Social Study Based on Fact.* Washington: Gray & Clarkson, 1886.

Galbreath, Charles B. "The Constitutional Convention of Ohio and Its Work and a History of Previous Conventions." *Columbus Sunday Dispatch Centennial Library Edition*, August 25, 1912.

———. "Provisions for State-Wide Initiative and Referendum." *Annals of the American Academy of Political and Social Science* 43 (September 1912): 81–109.

———. "The Vote on the Ohio Constitution." *Independent* 73 (December 1912): 1407–10.

Gladden, Washington. "The Anti-Catholic Crusade." *Century Magazine* 47 (March 1894): 789–95.

———. *The Cosmopolis City Club.* New York: Century Publishing, 1893.

———. "Mayor Jones of Toledo." *Outlook* 62 (May 1899): 17–21.

———. *Recollections.* Boston, MA: Houghton Mifflin, 1909.

Gompers, Samuel. "The Ohio Constitutional Amendments." Cleveland: Ohio State Federation of Labor, 1912.

———. "Organized Labor in the Campaign." *North American Review* 155 (July 1892): 91–96.

———. *The Samuel Gompers Papers.* Edited by Stuart B. Kaufman, Peter J. Albert, and Grace Palladino. 11 vols. Urbana: University of Illinois Press, 1986–2009.

Gompers, Samuel, and Florence Calvert Thorne. *Seventy Years of Life and Labor: An Autobiography.* 2 vols. New York: Dutton, 1925.

Green, John Patterson. *Fact Stranger than Fiction: Seventy-five Years of a Busy Life with Reminiscences of Many Great and Good Men and Women.* Cleveland: Riehl, 1920.

Hayes, Max S. *A History of Cleveland Labor.* 1937. Reprint, Cleveland: Greater Cleveland Labor History Society, 1987.

Hillquit, Morris. *History of Socialism in the United States.* 5th ed. New York: Funk and Wagnalls, 1910.

Howe, Frederic C. *The Confessions of a Reformer.* New York: Scribner's, 1925. Reprint, Chicago: Quadrangle Books, 1967.

Jarrett, John. "The Story of the Iron Workers." In McNeill, *The Labor Movement,* 268–311.

Jelly, S. M. *The Voice of Labor.* Philadelphia: H. J. Smith & Co., 1888.

Johnson, Tom L. *My Story.* New York: B. W. Huebsch, 1911.

Labor Day Souvenir, 1901. Cleveland: Cleveland Citizen, 1901.

The Labor Day Yearbook 1911, and Souvenir Program of the Ohio State Federation of Labor Convention. Cleveland: Ohio State Federation of Labor, 1911.

Lloyd, Caro. *Henry Demarest Lloyd, 1847–1903: A Biography.* New York: Putnam, 1912.

Lloyd, Henry Demarest. *Wealth against Commonwealth.* 1894. Reprint, Englewood Cliffs, NJ: Prentice Hall, 1963.

Martzolff, C. L. "Recent Ohio Legislation Conforming to the Demands of the New Constitution." *American Political Science Review* 7 (November 1913): 639–47.

McBride, John. "The Best of All Yet!" n.p., 1884.

———. "The Democratic Party, the Party of the Workingman." n.p., 1885.

———. "The Kind of Money Needed." *American Federationist* 2 (August 1895): 106–7.

———. "Our Official Policy." *American Federationist* 1 (1895): 282.

———. "Producers vs. Non-Producers." *American Federationist* 2 (October 1895): 144–45.

McBride, John, and T. T. O'Malley. "Coal Miners." In McNeill, *The Labor Movement,* 241–67.

McKinley, William. *Speeches and Addresses of William McKinley: From His Election to Congress to the Present Time.* New York: D. Appleton and Company, 1893.

McNeill, George E., ed. *The Labor Movement: The Problem of To-Day.* Boston, MA: A. M. Bridgeman and Company, 1887.

McVey, Frank L. "The Populist Movement." *Economic Studies* 1 (August 1896): 131–209.

Myers, Allen O. *Bosses and Boodle in Ohio Politics: Some Plain Truths for Honest People.* Cincinnati: Lyceum Publishing Co., 1895.

Ohio State Board of Commerce. "Constitutional Convention Proposals." Columbus: Journal of Commerce, 1912.

———. "Proposed Amendments to the Ohio Constitution to Be Adopted or Rejected." Columbus: Stoneman, 1912.

Peffer, William A. *Populism: Its Rise and Fall.* Edited by Peter Argersinger. Lawrence: University Press of Kansas, 1992.

Powell, Thomas E. *The Democratic Party of the State of Ohio: A Comprehensive History of Democracy in Ohio from 1803 to 1912.* 2 vols. Columbus: Ohio Publishing, 1913.

"Prospectus of *The Ohio Populist.*" Columbus: Ohio Populist, 1894.

Roy, Andrew. *A History of Coal Miners of the United States.* 3rd ed. Columbus: J. L. Trauger, 1907.

———. *The Practical Miners' Companion; or Papers on Geology and Mining in the Ohio Coal Field.* Columbus: Westbote Printing Co., 1885.

Sherman, John. *John Sherman's Recollections of Forty Years in the House, Senate, and Cabinet: An Autobiography.* Chicago: Werner, 1895.

Skinner, Robert P. "The New President of the American Federation of Labor." *Harper's Weekly* 39 (January 1895): 4.

Smith, Joseph P. *History of the Republican Party in Ohio.* 2 vols. Chicago: Lewis Publishing, 1898.

"Socialism (Limited)." *Nation* 60 (January 3, 1895): 4.

Steffens, Lincoln. "Ohio: A Tale of Two Cities." *McClure's Magazine* 25 (July 1905): 293–311.

———. *The Struggle for Self-Government: Being an Attempt to Trace American Political*

Corruption to Its Sources in Six States of the United States. New York: McClure, Phillips, 1906.

Stockbridge, Frank Parker. "Ohio Wide Awake." *Everybody's Magazine* 27 (November 1912): 696–707.

Taft, William H. *The Collected Works of William Howard Taft*. Edited by David Burton. 8 vols. Athens: Ohio University Press, 2001–2004.

Taubeneck, H. E. "The Philosophy of Political Parties: The Conditions and Elements Required for the Success of a New Party." Chicago: Schulte Publishing, 1896.

Thomas, H. D. *Labor Amendments to the Constitution of the State of Ohio*. Cleveland: Ohio State Federation of Labor, 1912.

Thompson, William Oxford. "Taxation." Oxford, OH: n.p., 1894.

The Trade Unions of Columbus, Their History, and Biographical Sketches of Prominent Union Officers and Friends of Labor. Columbus: Columbus Trades and Labor Assembly, 1895.

Twentieth-Century Official Illustrated History of the Columbus Trades and Labor Assembly and Its Affiliated Organizations. Columbus: Columbus Trades and Labor Assembly, 1901.

Twenty-Year History of District Assembly 47, Knights of Labor. Reprint, Cleveland: Greater Cleveland Labor History Society, 1987.

Warne, Frank Julian. *The Coal-Mine Workers: A Study in Labor Organizations*. New York: Longmans, Green, 1905.

"What a Real Constructive State Federation Has Done with the Aid of Sister Organizations in the Past Five Years in Giving the Working Men, Women, and Children of Ohio Some of the Best Legislation in the World: Report of the Legislative Agent Ike S. Byrum and Executive Board of the Ohio State Federation of Labor." Cleveland: Ohio State Federation of Labor, 1911.

Whitlock, Brand. *The Letters and Journals of Brand Whitlock*. Edited by Allen Nevins. 2 vols. New York: D. Appleton-Century, 1936.

Whitney, E. B. "Judson Harmon." *North American Review* 187 (June 1908): 831–37.

Witt, Peter. *Cleveland before St. Peter: A Handful of Hot Stuff*. 2nd ed. Cleveland: C. Lezuis, 1899.

———. "History of the Labor Movement in Cleveland." *Cleveland Recorder*, September 5, 1897, 9–11.

Wright, Henry C. *Bossism in Cincinnati*. Cincinnati: n.p., 1905.

Secondary Sources

Published

American Federation of Labor: History, Encyclopedia Reference Book. Washington, DC: American Federation of Labor, 1919.

Argersinger, Peter. *Populism and Politics: William Alfred Peffer and the People's Party*. Lexington: University Press of Kentucky, 1974.

Benedict, Michael Les, and John Winkler, eds. *The History of Ohio Law*. Athens: Ohio University Press, 2004.

Blocker, Jack S. Jr. *Retreat from Reform: The Prohibition Movement in the United States, 1890–1913*. Westport, CT: Greenwood Press, 1976.

Boryczka, Raymond, and Lorin Lee Cary. *No Strength without Union: An Illustrated History of Ohio Workers, 1803–1980*. Columbus: Ohio Historical Society, 1982.

Brecher, Jeremy. *Strike!* 1972. Reprint, Boston, MA: South End Press, 1977.

Brody, David. "Market Unionism in America: The Case of Coal." In *In Labor's Cause: Main Themes in the History of the American Worker*, 131–74. New York: Oxford

University Press, 1993.

Bruce, Robert V. *1877: Year of Violence*. Indianapolis, IN: Bobbs-Merrill, 1959.

Burton, David Henry. *Taft, Holmes, and the 1920s Court: An Appraisal*. Madison, NJ: Fairleigh Dickinson University Press, 1988.

Campbell, Thomas F. "Mounting Crisis and Reform: Cleveland's Political Development." In *The Birth of Modern Cleveland, 1865–1930*, ed. Thomas F. Campbell and Edward M. Miggins. Cleveland: Western Reserve Historical Society, 1988.

Campbell, Thomas F., and Edward M. Miggins, eds. *The Birth of Modern Cleveland, 1865–1930*. Cleveland: Western Reserve Historical Society, 1988.

Clinch, Thomas A. *Urban Populism and Free Silver in Montana*. Missoula: University of Montana Press, 1970.

Coletta, Paolo. *William Jennings Bryan*. Vol. 1, *Political Evangelist, 1860–1908*. Lincoln: University of Nebraska Press, 1964.

Commons, John R., et al. *History of Labor in the United States*. 4 vols. 1918. Reprint, New York: Augustus M. Kelley, 1966.

Croly, Herbert D. *Marcus Alonzo Hanna: His Life and Work*. New York: Macmillan, 1923.

Crunden, Robert M. *A Hero in Spite of Himself: Brand Whitlock in Art, Politics, and War*. New York: Alfred A. Knopf, 1969.

Currarino, Rosanne. "The Politics of 'More': The Labor Question and the Idea of Economic Liberty in Industrial America." *Journal of American History* 93 (June 2006): 17.

DeMatteo, Arthur E. "Death Knell for Progressive Leadership in Cleveland: Peter Witt and the Mayoral Election of 1915." *Ohio History* 111 (Winter–Spring 2002): 7–24.

Destler, Chester McArthur. *American Radicalism, 1865–1901*. Reprint, Chicago: Quadrangle Books, 1966.

———. *Henry Demarest Lloyd and the Empire of Reform*. Philadelphia: University of Pennsylvania Press, 1963.

Dorn, Jacob. *Washington Gladden: Prophet of the Social Gospel*. Columbus: Ohio State University Press, 1966.

Durden, Robert F. *The Climax of Populism: The Election of 1896*. Lexington: University of Kentucky Press, 1965.

Finegold, Kenneth. *Experts and Politicians: Reform Challenges to Machine Politics in New York, Cleveland, and Chicago*. Princeton, NJ: Princeton University Press, 1995.

Fink, Leon. *Workingman's Democracy: The Knights of Labor and American Politics*. Urbana: University of Illinois Press, 1983.

Foner, Philip S. *History of the Labor Movement in the United States*. 5 vols. New York: International Publishers, 1947–1978.

Forbath, William. *Law and the Shaping of the American Labor Movement*. Cambridge, MA: Harvard University Press, 1991.

Giglio, James N. *H. M. Daugherty and the Politics of Expediency*. Kent, OH: Kent State University Press, 1978.

Ginger, Ray. *The Bending Cross: A Biography of Eugene Victor Debs*. New Brunswick, NJ: Rutgers University Press, 1949.

Glad, Paul W. *McKinley, Bryan, and the People*. Philadelphia: Lippincott, 1964.

Goldschmidt, Eli. "Labor and Populism: New York City, 1891–1896." *Labor History* 13 (Fall 1972): 520–32.

Goodwyn, Lawrence. *The Democratic Promise: The Populist Moment in America*. New York: Oxford University Press, 1976.

The Governors of Ohio. 2nd ed. Columbus: Ohio Historical Society, 1969.

Greene, Julie. *Pure and Simple Politics: The American Federation of Labor and Political Activism, 1881–1917*. Cambridge, UK: Cambridge University Press, 1998.

Gutman, Herbert. "The Labor Policies of the Large Corporation in the Gilded Age: The

Case of the Standard Oil Company." In *Power and Culture: [Gutman's] Essays on the American Working Class,* ed. Ira Berlin, 213–54. New York: New Press, 1987.

———. "The Negro and the United Mine Workers of America: The Career and Letters of Richard L. Davis and Something of Their Meaning." In his *Work, Culture, and Society in Industrializing America: Essays in American Working-class and Social History,* 121–208. New York: Vintage Books, 1977.

Hattam, Victoria C. *Labor Visions and State Power: The Origins of Business Unionism in the United States.* Princeton, NJ: Princeton University Press, 1993.

Hawley, Ellis. *The New Deal and the Problem of Monopoly: A Study in Economic Ambivalence.* Princeton, NJ: Princeton University Press, 1966.

Hicks, John D. *The Populist Revolt: A History of the Farmers' Alliance and the People's Party.* Minneapolis: University of Minnesota Press, 1931, 1946. Reprint, Lincoln: University of Nebraska Press, 1961.

Hild, Matthew. *Greenbackers, Knights of Labor & Populists: Farmer-Labor Insurgency in the Late-Nineteenth-Century South.* Athens: University of Georgia Press, 2008.

Hill, Herbert. "Myth-Making as Labor History: Herbert Gutman and the United Mine Workers of America." *International Journal of Politics, Culture, and Society* 2 (Winter 1988): 132–200.

Historical Directory of the Ohio House of Representatives, 1803–1965/66. Columbus: Columbus Blank Book Co., 1966.

Hofstadter, Richard. *The Age of Reform: From Bryan to FDR.* New York: Alfred A. Knopf, 1955.

Hough, Leslie S. *The Turbulent Spirit: Cleveland, Ohio, and Its Workers, 1877–1899.* New York: Garland, 1990.

Hunker, Henry L. *Industrial Evolution of Columbus, Ohio.* Columbus: Bureau of Business Research, College of Commerce and Administration, Ohio State University, 1958.

Hurt, R. Douglas. "The Farmers' Alliance and the People's Party in Ohio." *Old Northwest* 10 (Winter 1984–1985): 439–62.

Issell, William, and Robert W. Cherney. *San Francisco, 1865–1932: Politics, Power, and Urban Development.* Berkeley and Los Angeles: University of California Press, 1986.

Jensen, Richard J. *The Winning of the Midwest: Social and Political Conflict, 1888–1896.* Chicago: University of Chicago Press, 1971.

Johnston, Robert D. *The Radical Middle Class: Populist Democracy and the Question of Capitalism in Progressive Era Portland.* Princeton, NJ: Princeton University Press, 2003.

———. "Re-democratizing the Progressive Era: The Politics of Progressive Era Historiography." *Journal of the Gilded Age and Progressive Era* 1 (January 2002): 68–92.

Jones, Marnie. *Holy Toledo: Religion and Politics in the Life of "Golden Rule" Jones.* Lexington: University Press of Kentucky, 1998.

Kaufman, Stuart B. *Samuel Gompers and the Origins of the American Federation of Labor, 1848–1896.* Westport, CT: Greenwood Press, 1973.

Kazin, Michael. *Barons of Labor: The San Francisco Building Trades and Union Power in the Progressive Era.* Urbana: University of Illinois Press, 1987.

———. *A Godly Hero: The Life of William Jennings Bryan.* New York: Alfred A. Knopf, 2007.

Kerr, K. Austin. "Labor-Management Cooperation: An 1897 Case." *Pennsylvania Magazine of History and Biography* 99 (January 1975): 45–71.

Kleppner, Paul. *The Cross of Culture: A Social Analysis of Midwestern Politics, 1850–1900.* New York: Free Press, 1970.

Klotsche, Martin J. "The 'United Front' Populists." *Wisconsin Magazine of History* 20 (June 1937): 375–89.

Kolko, Gabriel. *The Triumph of Conservativism, 1900–1916.* Glencoe, IL: Free Press, 1963.

Kousser, J. Morgan. *The Shaping of Southern Politics: Suffrage Reform and the Establishment of the One-Party South.* New Haven, CT: Yale University Press, 1974.

Laurie, Bruce. *Artisans into Workers: Labor in Nineteenth-Century America.* 1989. Reprint, Urbana: University of Illinois Press, 1997.

Lindsey, Almont. *The Pullman Strike: A Story of a Unique Experiment and of a Great Labor Upheaval.* Chicago: University of Chicago Press, 1942.

Lukas, J. Anthony. *Big Trouble: A Murder in a Small Western Town Sets Off a Struggle for the Soul of America.* New York: Simon and Schuster, 1997.

Malone, Dumas. *Dictionary of American Biography.* 21 vols. New York: Scribner's, 1943.

Marcus, Irwin, Jennie Bullard, and Rob Moore. "Change and Continuity: Steel Workers in Homestead, Pennsylvania, 1889–1895." *Pennsylvania Magazine of History and Biography* 111 (Spring 1987): 61–75.

McElvaine, Robert. *The Great Depression: America, 1929–1941.* 1983. Reprint, New York: Three Rivers Press, 1993.

McGrane, Reginald Charles. "Ohio and the Greenback Movement." *Mississippi Valley Historical Review* 11 (March 1925): 526–42.

———. *William Allen: A Study in Western Democracy.* Columbus: Ohio State Archaeological and Historical Society, 1925.

Miller, Carol Poh, and Robert A. Wheeler. *Cleveland: A Concise History, 1796–1996.* Bloomington: Indiana University Press, 1997.

Miller, Ernest I. "The Farmers' Party." *Bulletin of the Historical and Philosophical Society of Ohio* 15 (January 1957): 49–65.

Miller, Zane L. *Boss Cox's Cincinnati: Urban Politics in the Progressive Era.* New York: Oxford University Press, 1968.

Montgomery, David. *Beyond Equality: Labor and Radical Republicans, 1862–1872.* 1961. Reprint, Urbana: University of Illinois Press, 1981.

———. *Fall of the House of Labor: The Workplace, the State, and American Labor Activism, 1865–1925.* New York: Cambridge University Press, 1987.

Morgan, H. Wayne. *William McKinley and His America.* Syracuse, NY: Syracuse University Press, 1963.

Nash, Michael. *Conflict and Accommodation: Coal Miners, Steel Workers, and Socialism, 1890–1920.* Westport, CT: Greenwood Press, 1982.

Nevins, Allan. *Grover Cleveland: A Study in Courage.* New York: Dodd, Mead, 1962.

———. *Study in Power: John D. Rockefeller, Industrialist and Philanthropist.* 2 vols. New York: Charles Scribner's, 1953.

Nye, Russell B. *A Baker's Dozen: Thirteen Unusual Americans.* East Lansing: Michigan State University Press, 1956. Oestreicher, Richard Jules. *Solidarity and Fragmentation: Working People and Class Consciousness in Detroit, 1875–1900.* Urbana: University of Illinois Press, 1986.

Osnes, Larry G. "The Birth of a Party: The Cincinnati Populist Convention of 1891." *Great Plains Journal* 10 (Fall 1970): 11–24.

Ostler, Jeffrey. *Prairie Populism: The Fate of Agrarian Radicalism in Kansas, Nebraska, and Iowa, 1880–1892.* Lawrence: University Press of Kansas, 1993.

———. "The Rhetoric of Conspiracy and the Formation of Kansas Populism." *Agricultural History* 69 (Winter 1995): 1–27.

Palmer, Bruce. *"Man over Money": The Southern Populist Critique of American Capitalism.* Chapel Hill: University of North Carolina Press, 1980.

Phelan, Craig. *Divided Loyalties: The Public and Private Life of Labor Leader John Mitchell.* Albany: State University of New York Press, 1994.

———. *William Green: Biography of a Labor Leader.* Albany: State University of New York Press, 1989.

Pierce, Michael. "Martin Foran and the Creation of Cleveland's Labor Movement." In *Builders of Ohio: A Biographical History*, ed. Warren Van Tine and Michael Pierce, 164–77. Columbus: Ohio State University Press, 2003.

———. "Organized Labor and the Law in Ohio." In Benedict and Winkler, *History of Ohio Law*, 883–910.

Pollack, Norman. *The Populist Response to Industrial America: Midwestern Populist Thought.* 1962. Reprint, New York: W. W. Norton, 1966.

Postel, Charles. *The Populist Vision.* New York: Oxford University Press, 2007.

Quint, Howard H. *The Forging of American Socialism: Origins of the Modern Movement.* Indianapolis, IN: Bobbs-Merrill, 1953.

Ridge, Martin. *Ignatius Donnelly: Portrait of a Politician.* Chicago: University of Chicago Press, 1962.

Roseboom, Eugene H. *The Civil War Era, 1850–1873.* Columbus: Ohio State Archaeological and Historical Society, 1944.

Ross, Steven J. *Workers on the Edge: Work, Leisure, and Politics in Industrializing Cincinnati, 1788–1890.* New York: Columbia University Press, 1985.

Salvatore, Nick. *Eugene V. Debs: Citizen and Socialist.* Urbana: University of Illinois Press, 1982.

Sanders, Elizabeth. *Roots of Reform: Farmers, Workers, and the American State, 1877–1917.* Chicago: University of Chicago Press, 1999.

Saunders, Robert M. "The Transformation of Tom Watson, 1894–1895." *Georgia Historical Quarterly* 56 (Fall 1970): 339–56.

Schmidt, David D. *Citizen Lawmakers: The Ballot Initiative Revolution.* Philadelphia: Temple University Press, 1989.

Schneirov, Richard. "Labor and the New Liberalism in the Wake of the Pullman Strike." In Schneirov, Stromquist, and Salvatore, *Crisis of the 1890s*, 204–32.

———. *Labor and Urban Politics: Class Conflict and the Origins of Modern Liberalism in Chicago, 1864–1897.* Urbana: University of Illinois Press, 1998.

Schneirov, Richard, Shelton Stromquist, and Nick Salvatore, eds. *The Pullman Strike and the Crisis of the 1890s: Essays on Labor and Politics.* Urbana: University of Illinois Press, 1999.

Schwantes, Carlos. *Coxey's Army: An American Odyssey.* 1985. Reprint, Moscow: University of Idaho Press, 1994.

Shaw, Barton. *The Wool-Hat Boys: Georgia's Populist Party.* Baton Rouge: Louisiana State University Press, 1984.

Sponholtz, Lloyd. "The 1912 Constitutional Convention in Ohio: The Call-Up and Nonpartisan Selection of Delegates." *Ohio History* 79 (Summer/Autumn 1970): 209–18.

Stromquist, Shelton. "The Crisis of the 1890s and the Legacies of Producerism." In Schneirov, Stromquist, and Salvatore, *Crisis of the 1890s*, 179–203.

———. "The Crucible of Class: Cleveland Politics and the Origins of Municipal Reform in the Progressive Era." *Journal of Urban History* 23 (January 1997): 192–220.

Taft, Philip. *The American Federation of Labor in the Time of Gompers.* New York: Harper and Brothers, 1957.

Tarbell, Ida M. *The History of the Standard Oil Company.* 2 vols. New York: Macmillan, 1925.

Teaford, Jon C. *Cities in the Heartland: The Rise and Fall of the Industrial Midwest.* Bloomington: University of Indiana Press, 1993.

Terzian, Barbara A. "Ohio's Constitutional Conventions and Constitutions." In Benedict and Winkler, *History of Ohio Law*, 40–87.

Tindall, George Brown, ed. *A Populist Reader: Selections from the Works of American Populist Leaders.* New York: Harper and Row, 1966.

Tussey, Jean Y. *An Introduction to the History of the Cleveland Labor Movement, 1865–1929.* Cleveland: United Labor Agency, AFL-CIO, 1996.

Van Tine, Warren R. "A History of Labor in Columbus, Ohio, 1812–1992." *Ohio State University Center for Labor Research Working Papers Series* 10 (1993).

Van Tine, Warren R., and Michael Pierce, eds. *Builders of Ohio: A Biographical History.* Columbus: Ohio State University Press, 2003.

Van Tine, Warren R., C. J. Slanicka, Sandy Jordan, and Michael Pierce. *In the Workers' Interest: A History of the Ohio AFL-CIO, 1958–1998.* Columbus: Center for Labor Research, 1998.

Voss, Kim. *The Making of American Exceptionalism: The Knights of Labor and Class Formation in the Nineteenth Century.* Cornell: Cornell University Press, 1993.

Walters, Everett. *Joseph Benson Foraker: An Uncompromising Republican.* Columbus: Ohio History Press, 1948.

Warner, Hoyt Landon. *Progressivism in Ohio, 1897–1917.* Columbus: Ohio State University Press for the Ohio Historical Society, 1964.

Weiner, Ronald R. *Lake Effects: A History of Urban Policy Making in Cleveland, 1825–1929.* Columbus: Ohio State University Press, 2005.

Weinstein, James. *The Corporate Ideal and the Liberal State, 1900–1918.* Boston, MA: Beacon Press, 1968.

Wilentz, Sean. *Chants Democratic: New York City & the Rise of the American Working Class, 1788–1850.* New York: Oxford University Press, 1984.

Wittke, Carl. "Peter Witt, Tribune of the People." *Ohio Archaeological and Historical Quarterly* 58 (October 1949): 361–77.

Woodward, C. Vann. *Tom Watson: Agrarian Rebel.* 1936. Reprint, New York: Oxford University Press, 1966.

Wright, James Edward. *The Politics of Populism: Dissent in Colorado.* New Haven, CT: Yale University Press, 1974.

Wyman, Roger E. "Agrarian or Working-class Radicalism? The Electoral Basis of Populism in Wisconsin." *Political Science Quarterly* 89 (Winter 1974–1975): 825–47.

Zornow, William F. "Bellamy Nationalism in Ohio, 1891 to 1896." *Ohio State Archaeological and Historical Quarterly* 58 (April 1949): 152–70.

Unpublished Dissertations and Theses

Howson, Emery Bernard. "Jacob Sechler Coxey: A Biography of a Monetary Reformer, 1854–1951." PhD diss., Ohio State University, 1973.

Karolak, Eric John. "The Socialist Party in a Midwestern Community: The Case of Columbus, Ohio." Master's thesis, Ohio State University, 1988.

Morris, James Matthew. "The Road to Trade Unionism: Organized Labor in Cincinnati to 1893." PhD diss., University of Cincinnati, 1969.

Musselman, Barbara L. "The Quest for Collective Improvement: Cincinnati Workers, 1893–1920." PhD diss., University of Cincinnati, 1975.

Pierce, Michael. "Washington Gladden's Columbus: The Politics of Municipal Reform in Columbus, Ohio, 1885–1915." Master's thesis, Ohio State University, 1993.

Rodriquez, Alicia Ester. "Urban Populism: Challenges to Democratic Party Control in Dallas, Texas, 1887–1900." PhD diss., University of California at Santa Barbara, 1999.

Rose, Patricia Terpak. "Design and Expediency: The Ohio Federation of Labor as a Legislative Lobby, 1883–1935." PhD diss., Ohio State University, 1975.

Index

Waite, Davis, 182, 194, 196
Warner, A. J., 46, 182, 192, 207
Warner, Hoyt, Landon, 232
Warren County, 34
Washington, DC, 165, 167, 217
Washington County, 46
Washington News, 167
Washington Post, 217
Watchorn, Robert, 150, 154
Watson, Tom, 11, 185–87, 208
Weaver, James, 11, 53–54, 68, 134, 138, 173, 182, 185, 187, 204, 208
Webster, Noah, 7, 200
Weiner, Ronald, 79
Weitzenecker, Max (Columbus), 135
Wellston, 195
Western Federation of Miners, 139
Wheeler, Robert (Cincinnati), 108, 251fn.17
Whitlock, Brand, 88, 215, 217, 221, 224
Wild, Mark, Hocking Valley Railroad strike, 131–33; and People's party in Columbus, 133–34, 135; bribery charges, 144, 198–99
Wilkins, M. L., 30

Williams, D. E. (Columbus), 135
Willits, John, 30
Wilson, Thomas, 35, 38
Wilson, Woodrow, 15
Wisconsin, 5, 181
Witt, Peter (Cleveland), 59, 61, 73–74, 206; and 1892 street railway strike, 58, 66–67; and local labor-Populist alliance, 68; opposition to SLP, 77, 83–84; support for Bryan, 80, 82–83; 1899–1900 street railway strike, 86; Jones 1899 gubernatorial campaign, 88; alliance with Johnson, 89, 91; Progressive movement, 215, 221; photo of, 90
Wolf, Harry C. (Cleveland), 60
Women's suffrage, 9, 10, 25, , 73, 113, 147, 170, 190, 215, 222, 225, 227–28, 230, 230, 236
Wood County, 36
Woodbridge, C. E. (Cleveland), 59, 66, 69
Workingman's party, 26–27

Zanesville, 168